Contents

6 Contents

Introduction to the Modern Britain Series

The main purpose of this series of readers is to introduce students to the study of their own society. We hope to do this by presenting material within a sociological frame of reference. Sociology is a word that has many overtones but in its broadest sense it refers to an attempt to study society in a disciplined and systematic way. There are many specific theories within the subject area of sociology, just as there are in any field of knowledge, even physics, chemistry or engineering; and of course, not all sociologists would agree with each and every theory which any other sociologist would put forward. But nevertheless we are now in a situation where an impressive amount of research and writing has been undertaken within British society especially since the last war. One of the results of this kind of work is that it becomes possible to examine many familiar aspects of our own society in new and unfamiliar ways. This is a characteristic consequence of studying sociology, in fact, that it provides a focus for studying events and suggests criteria of relevance which allow us to 'make sense' of at least part of the bewildering mosaic of social phenomena. Sociology provides a frame of reference, an approach, which allows us to make some sense of our society even where it would be impossible to consider more than a fraction of the mass of material which is being produced about it.

As everybody has an interest in being informed and in understanding how their own society works, this series of books is intended in a real sense for the general reader, but perhaps more particularly for those who are undertaking some relatively structured learning about Britain today.

An increasing number of people are taking courses on 'British society' which have a bearing on their training or reflect their concern to understand social processes and social functions. For many, given the reading available, this may reflect a heavy diet of factual material (the number of households, rate of divorce, circulation of newspapers and the like) which becomes largely concerned with what *is* rather than with *how* or *why*. It tends to lose out on sociological perspective and relevance. The result of an attempt to absorb an undifferentiated mass of unrelated statistics is twofold. In the first place we tend to suffer from a sort of mental indigestion – 'Did 14·375 per cent of red-haired Glaswegians vote Conservative in the 1964 General Election?... or did Pinza win the Derby in 1953?... Does it matter?'... – which may lead us to the even more disturbing conclusion that *all* statistics are equally meaningless. Such learning is possibly easily absorbed for examination purposes, but equally quickly forgotten afterwards if it cannot be assimilated to any more general framework of understanding.

For some others the first introduction to the work of the social sciences is at a more rarefied level and their intellectual diet may become excessively rich in the esoteric ramifications of some currently fashionable theories. This presents problems of a different kind, for this produces a tendency to rule out of consideration any 'facts', findings or insights that don't happen to fit the theory, and thus valuable learning possibilities may be lost.

It is our view that the two approaches mentioned are equally unsatisfactory for the student who is a beginner. But we need to distinguish different senses in which we use the term 'beginner'. It is true that a particular person may have previously had no intensive contact with the social sciences. So in that sense he is starting from scratch. But in another sense he is already something of an expert, for he has lived in this society, or one similar to it, all his life. This, then, must constitute the starting point of the process of learning. In the first place the teacher has to begin where the student happens to be, with a particular experience of life and a system of beliefs and attitudes which help him to explain that experience. He already has views about his society, although they may be misinformed or based on untenable assumptions about how things happen. In this situation, it seems to us he requires material which allows him to examine some of his preconceptions. As Walter Lippmann, the American writer, has said: 'For the most part we do not first see, and then define, we define first and then see. We are told about the world before we see it. We imagine most things before we experience them. And these preconceptions, unless education has made us acutely aware, govern deeply the whole process of perception.' Aneurin Bevan made a similar point when he wrote 'It is inherent in our intellectual activity that we seek to imprison reality in our description of it. Soon, long before we realize it, it is we who become the prisoners of the description. From that point on, our ideas degenerate into a kind of folklore which we pass to each other, fondly thinking we are still talking of the reality around us.' Of course, sociologists have their 'folklore' just as do any other group in society and we would not wish to claim any more for this series of books of readings than that they may stimulate the student to consider *alternative* perceptions and constructions of social reality to those which he brings to the study of his own society. With this basis, the enquiring student of whatever age or background, may go in one of several directions. He may perhaps undertake systematic study or reading about some other society or culture on the basis of the concepts and perceptions he has found useful in the study of his own, or he may begin to examine some specific aspect of society, say the extended family system, in more depth and detail.

Our decision to compile the first book in this series – *The Sociology of Modern Britain* – arose from our experience in teaching a wide range of students, many of whom were adults, in university extramural and on undergraduate and postgraduate courses, on professional courses of many kinds, and in several educational institutions. We recognized a number of factors which made the courses on this theme less satisfactory than they might have been. Our series is an attempt to remedy some of these deficiencies. In our experience of introductory courses, much original and relevant work never finds its way to the student body, even though it may be mentioned in the reading lists. University libraries may have only single copies of a journal containing an article recommended to many students. The problems are much worse in other educational settings. For the general reader, the public library may represent a treasurehouse of material and documentation, but it may also present a façade of baffling impenetrability to the reader who is interested in a particular topic – say the educational system – but doesn't quite know what he wants. Faced with a row of books all of which apparently contain information of some relevance to the topic, how is he to choose between them? One or two bad choices, a few wasted visits, and the initial enthusiasm may be dissipated in a puzzled frustration which may create a permanent antipathy to the subject. Often these problems may be compounded by teachers who are not themselves trained in the subject and who feel equally in need of a frame of reference. Systematic teaching demands this. Too often, perhaps, subjects may be introduced to students as a series of disconnected episodes of merely intrinsic interest.

It is clear that the audience we have aimed at covers a wide range. There are members of the general public whose interest in the nature of their society may have been stimulated by television programmes, colour supplements and the like. These may or may not move on to adult classes, or courses of study such as those provided by the Open University, Extramural Departments, the WEA, and by local authorities. Many students at Colleges of Education, Technical Colleges, and Colleges of Further Education, undertake general introductory courses in sociology, much of the content of which relates to Britain, and these are beginning to develop in the sixth forms of some schools. Professional or pre-professional courses of training, in-service and refresher courses for such groups as hospital administrators, managers and social workers, are more and more common. As the amount of this provision in the social sciences increases, the problems of teaching it and gaining access to relevant material become, if anything, greater than they have been before.

Each book in the series is intended as an *introductory* reader. An attempt has been made to introduce a range of topics and approaches with a balance between what is descriptive and what is analytical and conceptual. Had we been trying to meet the needs of university students near the end of their courses our selection would have been quite different in a number of respects.

Every chapter has an introductory section which is designed to pose some of the important questions which arise in the particular context of our readings without providing a detailed commentary on all the relevant sociological concepts and issues. These introductory sections attempt also to link certain pertinent themes, which are not dealt with in specific extracts, to further reading. Each book can be used profitably in conjunction with one of the textbooks in current use. The Textbook Reference section at the end contains detailed references to the most relevant themes that the courses for which we are catering will wish to cover.

The readings follow the introductory section in each chapter. Because of the audience it was felt unnecessary to reproduce the detailed footnotes and references many of them contained. As far as possible many of the most important references in the text to authors or books have been included in the Further Reading at the end of the relevant chapter. The common practice of numbering tables according to their place in the particular reading rather than their place in the work from which they are taken has been followed. Most of the readings are, of course, edited or abbreviated versions of the original texts, which inevitably repay fuller and more detailed study if time permits.

As far as further reading is concerned, we concentrate on books which are reasonably easy to obtain. Many are in paperback and using our source books it would be possible to obtain a wide range of material quite cheaply. Others will lead the student to utilize libraries. *Further Reading* suggestions at the end of each chapter contain, in the main, articles or books referred to in the readings. A more comprehensive guide to relevant reading on Social Welfare is to be found in the *Bibliography and Reader Reference* at the end of the book.

Several criteria have guided us in the course of our selection of readings. Readability is one of these, and although the extracts vary in difficulty it is hoped that the most difficult can be tackled successfully with the help of the references and discussion of major points in the chapter introductions. The variations in the level of the readings, and the different approaches to be found in them, are not fortuitous: they are designed to pose questions from which every student must start. Some are deliberately short, lending themselves to class discussion; others may be more properly studied independently. In some cases the readings deal with similar material from different points of view, and this is a deliberate policy to make links between themes which cut across the boundaries of chapters, and reinforce, for example, the sense of inter-relationships between social institutions and an awareness of the cumulative consequences of social change. We have chosen work which is not on the whole readily available to the student, often from journals and books to which he is unlikely to have access. We have tended to avoid choosing from paperbacks, though in one or two cases books have reappeared in paperback after our original selection was made.

There are many personal elements which arise in making a choice of readings and we have tried to be explicit about some of them, but our focus throughout has been upon the specific needs and requirements of taking introductory courses, largely in non-university settings, and of general readers outside of the major educational institutions.

It is hoped that this series of source books of readings will go some way to meeting some of the needs of students and teachers involved in the kinds of courses we have mentioned. We hope also that they will prove interesting in their own right to general readers and that they may lead into a more systematic examination of some of the issues we have attempted to raise here.

Their value will depend on the extent to which they are used. They are above all intended to assist interested readers in the process of initially learning about the nature of their own society. Though it is hoped to cover all or most of the major aspects of contemporary society in this series, of course, any one book stands on its own. They are not intended to promote any particular sectarian or theoretically purist position. In our experience of textbook and other one-sided approaches this is an unnecessary attempt to do the teacher's job for him and is anyway fairly rapidly seen through by students. We have been very much encouraged and helped by feedback from students and teachers about *The Sociology of Modern Britain* and *Social Problems of Modern Britain*, the first two books in the series. Above all, we welcome comments and criticisms from all those teaching and studying in this field, at whatever level.

Eric Butterworth
David Weir

Chapter One

Background to Social Welfare

This reader provides an introduction to the broad field of social welfare in Britain. It begins with some matters of definition and scope. Chapter 1 presents differing ideas about social policy, social administration and the complex of issues that come under the heading 'the Welfare State'. Chapters 2 and 3 consider some of the groups in need, problems of definition, and approaches to meeting needs. The complex nature of decision-making and the execution of policy in the field of social welfare is apparent, and in Chapter 4 further issues about aims and outcomes are pursued. Although intentions behind provision may be straightforward, what is made available will have unexpected as well as expected consequences. The question 'who benefits from the activities of an organization?' is a relevant one. In theory, the organization serves the interests of its clients or its constituency but its purposes may be affected and its priorities changed by the power of the administrators and professionals who work for it. Reorganization in order to rationalize procedures and bring resources to bear more effectively to assist clients was a consequence in England and Wales of a debate in the 1960s: reorganization provides the basic focus for Chapter 5. Because of it most of the social services and those staffing them were brought together in large departments. Although the presence of social workers and other professionals could be (and was by some) interpreted as a guarantee against an impersonal approach the fact was that these bodies faced the problems of all large-scale organizations where the rules and conventions devised to cope with the problems of size and effectiveness could be in conflict with the aim of providing the best possible service and support for clients in their family situations. This matter is not open to simple solution. Finally, in Chapters 6 and 7 the focus changes to examine, first, new and recent

approaches to social welfare provision which have been
devised, and then the range of strategies proposed to combat
the key problems in the field at the present time: the varieties
of social deprivation and inequality.

Social welfare is an omnibus term used to cover a wide range
of activities in society. These activities are concerned with the
maintenance or promotion of social well-being. Some
organizations or agencies operate almost exclusively in the field
of social welfare: the social services are a case in point. But
what goes on elsewhere can have a great effect on social well-
being. Economic changes, such as the decline of some
industries and the growth of others, pollution in consequence
of the rapid exploitation of natural resources, provide examples
which affect the quality of life of the individual. Social welfare
has to be seen against the social changes which are taking
place in society, the social, economic and political systems
which exist there, and the social problems which arise.
Moreover, the work of many agencies and organizations has
welfare aspects: provision for health and leisure for their
employees by certain industrial undertakings is just one case in
point.
 Initially the concept of social welfare was a relatively limited
one, being used to identify specific forms of provision,
particularly those which guaranteed a certain minimum
standard of social or economic assistance. The assumption
underlying the services geared to meet the needs of the
unfortunate or the indigent was that these should come into
play when, in the words of Wilensky and Lebeaux, 'the normal
structures of supply, the family, and the market break down'.
Often, stigma was attributed to those who were helped, or at
least some of them in the distinctions made between 'deserving'
and 'undeserving' poor. Essentially, this was a *residual* concept
of social welfare, perceiving those needing assistance as being
in discrete groups or categories: the old, the blind, the deaf,
the physically or mentally handicapped, and a number of others.
 Most current definitions of social welfare emphasize an
institutional concept, and this is the focus we adopt in the
reader. In the kind of society which exists in Britain and in
other advanced countries of the west there has been widespread

recognition of the need to provide some basic services as a right of citizenship. If we consider all those affected in any one week by the social services, as recipients of benefits or allowances, or as dependants of these people, the total will be over a quarter of the population of the country even if we exclude family allowances and any other allowances paid irrespective of income. Although a substantial number of recipients and their dependants may be the same from one week to the next, especially with those who are chronically sick, long-term unemployed or old age pensioners, a much higher proportion of the population is affected by the kinds of support and the levels of benefit which are provided over a period of time than is suggested by figures on a week-by-week basis. Whereas the *residual* view of social welfare implies that those in need are relatively discrete groups which require a concentration of resources upon them as the main priority of policy, the *institutional* view implies that most people are likely in their lives to need help to meet various crises and eventualities for which it is difficult to plan adequately and that responsibility for help rests with the state.

Social welfare is best seen, in the words of one definition of it, as a 'dynamic activity that has grown out of, and is constantly influenced by, evolving social, economic, political and cultural trends'. It can only achieve an established pattern by failing to adapt to changing situations. It consists of a pattern of organized activities. One part of those activities, say a certain agency or service, could focus on individuals, groups or categories, communities or neighbourhoods, or larger aggregates. What can be provided ranges from straight financial support (in a form such as income maintenance) to care of various kinds (in institutions and at home, for example), treatment (for conditions which have already developed), and prevention. Among the main characteristics of social welfare provision are that services are organized to meet a wide range of needs: these are complex and extensive at the smallest organizational level. Secondly, the services depend on specialization of functions: along with this goes differential status. Those who are concerned with 'clients' and provide 'therapy' for them enjoy the highest status. Whatever the movements towards broader-based organizations which attempt to integrate these specialized skills the implications of what exists and how it has been developed have to be faced for the consequences of the historical experience remain with us. Finally, the services are extensive. They play a big part in our society and in its economy.

The organizations active in the field of social welfare can be classified according to a number of criteria. Their *auspices* may be statutory or voluntary ones, or a combination of the two, as in cases where government money is used to finance agency services carried out by voluntary bodies. The statutory auspices may be from central or local government or from quasi-governmental sources. The combinations possible are extremely varied, as are the scope and purposes of many of the voluntary agencies involved in social welfare.

The *geographical area* covered is another criterion. The changes in local government structure from April, 1974, affect some services. The area may range from a small locality to a regional and national level. Some organizations will have international links which will have an influence on their policies and what they are prepared to undertake. Interestingly, Roland Warren, in his *The Community in America*, sees the vertical links between the central body and the local branch as restricting more and more the scope of planning by the latter kind of body; he sees, too, the greater importance of agencies with these vertical organizational systems.

The third criterion is the *functional field* in which the organization or agency operates. Reference has already been made to financial payments, care, treatment and prevention. A more comprehensive description would distinguish between fields on the basis of their purposes, the skills involved, and the clientele. The purposes, or programmes, would range from those providing employment, involved with housing, health, income, family welfare, to those providing recreational and sporting activities. Some organizations have a functional field determined by the *skills* which are shown by those employed. These could be specialized activities such as social work (case work, group work, or community work) and forms of vocational and other counselling. The *clientele* forms the organizing principle for some organizations: examples are the old, children, youth, and categories of people in similar situations (since frequently a condition or problem becomes the basis for developing a service).

The main features of social welfare provision in the advanced capitalist societies of the world are often referred to as 'The Welfare State'. There is a continuing debate, some of it being reflected in the pages that follow, about its antecedents and the extent to which it occurs in all industrialized societies irrespective of whether their political and social organization is capitalist or communist. The term came into existence about thirty years ago to indicate that the state had moral and spiritual responsibilities and functions for the promotion of human welfare. Since then it has become all things to all men. Its critics have seen it as a convenient cover for totalitarian government or socialism without being very successful in making objective analyses of it. It has been characterized as 'a major instrument of redistribution of wealth from rich to poor; as a means of impoverishing the professional and middle classes; as a denial of charity and cultural excellence; as the cause of social decadence among the working population; and as the responsible agent in undermining the virtues of thrift, individual effort, and family stability', according to Titmuss in his paper, 'The Welfare State: Images and Realities'. Those who support the Welfare State stress that it provides a measure of security for all and enhances equality of opportunity.

The essence of the Welfare State, according to Wilensky and Lebeaux, is: 'Government-protected minimum standards of income, nutrition, health, housing, and education for every citizen, assured to him as a political right, not as charity'. More specifically, Wedderburn writes that the Welfare State 'implies a State commitment of some degree which modifies the play of market forces in order to ensure a minimum real income for all. By implication, if not explicitly, this is done to protect individuals against the hazards of incapacity for work arising through sickness, old age and unemployment. There is also general agreement that the objectives of the Welfare State will include a guarantee of treatment and benefit for sickness and injury, and the provision of education'. She goes on to say there is less agreement about whether the essential goal includes maintaining full employment, economic growth, or ensuring that the best standards for social services are offered to all.

On the historical development Gunnar Myrdal states 'In the last half-century, the State, in all the rich countries in the Western World, has become a democratic "Welfare State", with fairly explicit commitments to the broad goals of economic development, full employment, equality of opportunity for the young, social security, and protected minimum standards as regards not only income, but institutions, housing, health and education, for people of all regions and social groups'. The views quoted illustrate a fairly general agreement on the major elements together with certain differences in emphasis: they extend the discussion outside the boundaries of social welfare proper into considerations of political rights, economic prosperity, and the management of the economy.

The State now 'intervenes, regulates, and directs' in Western societies much more than in the past. The trend appears to have gathered momentum irrespective of the ideological stance of the Governments concerned or their attitudes towards the Welfare State and expenditures on social welfare. For example, in Britain a rhetoric of private enterprise has gone along with a greater, though perhaps inadvertent, control over the lives of individuals in periods when Conservatives have been in power. This is indicated by the great growth of expenditure on social welfare in Britain during this century, both as a proportion of Government expenditure and as a proportion of the Gross National Product. Public spending around 1900 represented 10 to 12 per cent of the total expenditure, of which about one third went to social services. Now public spending represents over half the total expenditure and nearly a quarter of this goes to social services (including housing). At the earlier date the local authorities spent most of it and raised a lot of it, whereas at present most is raised as well as spent by central government. In general the more highly developed the society the more money and resources tend to be spent on social welfare. How far this is likely to continue depends on a number of factors. One of the arguments used by the *laissez faire* economists is that choice should take the place of public expenditure financed by heavy levels of taxation: thus the percentage of national income spent on welfare services would drop because less would be required to keep the majority of the population away from dependence on state provision.

With affluence the possibilities for people to make their own provision is so much greater. What may then arise is a situation where the 'residual poor' or as they have been called occasionally the 'clinical poor' remain and the bulk of provision is expended on them. Such issues are the subject of continual political and ideological debate.

From country to country the character of the services provided, the methods used in making them available, those who are eligible for them, and the means of financing them vary, and this may be true within one country not only from time to time but also from place to place.

There is a danger in regarding the Welfare State only in terms of material factors such as standards of living. If we assess it by those standards alone then we are in danger of ignoring the social costs that affluence has brought. There is the need to consider the provision of social welfare in relation to the structure of our society and the nature of the social problems with which it is concerned. The most economically developed countries, with the highest incomes per head, appear to exhibit the greatest concern over social problems. It has been argued recently by E. J. Mishan, an economist, that 'the continual pursuit of economic growth by Western societies is more likely on balance to reduce rather than increase social welfare'. Among the reasons he gives are that the machines and institutions associated with modern rates of growth make the modern city less habitable and life less satisfying.

Arguments about the 'quality of life' in relation to economic growth have implications for the allocation of resources in society. 'Welfare is a compound of material means and immaterial ends; it is located somewhere on the axis which runs between the poles of wealth and happiness', as Marshall has expressed it, and many of the choices to be made are difficult ones. They may concern our perceptions of the common good and our personal interest. In a stirring simile Lord Beveridge, thirty years ago, wrote:

We should regard Want, Disease, Ignorance and Squalor as common enemies of us all, not as enemies with whom each individual may seek a separate peace, escaping himself to personal prosperity, while leaving his fellows in their clutches. This is the meaning of social conscience; that one should refuse to make a separate peace with a social evil.

There are questions about the balance between public and private effort and the extent to which, within the public sector, choices of a social welfare kind are made. How much money for example should be spent on defence as opposed to improving the capacity of social and community workers to assist groups to achieve their objective? How much attention should be given to the provision of employment opportunities for the disabled or the mentally retarded or other handicapped groups as opposed to the expenditure of money on statutory benefits? How much, within the field of health, should be spent on developments in heart surgery or organ transplants as opposed to forms of prevention affecting far more people? How much should be spent on environmental improvements as opposed to the amount spent on drugs prescribed through the National Health Service? These alternatives are not absolute, of course, but choices have to be made in a situation where resources are always more limited than we hope.

It has been said that the core of social welfare is to be found in the ways in which the social services of a country are established and administered. It involves 'the development of collective action for social welfare – collective action on the part of the government, employers, philanthropic bodies and consumers to meet human needs'. The main social services in Britain are concerned with the groups which are socially disadvantaged and served by the agencies for social security, health and welfare.

The way in which the social services operate is the field of administration and of public administration. Policies are not only the product of decisions in the political arena but of the administrative procedures which are devised to carry them out. The kind of service obtained is not just the outcome of the law on the statute book but of the kinds of resources that are available in the area: there may be many differences between the services offered in rural as opposed to urban areas, and many inequalities between the finance available, too. Personnel come to their tasks with different priorities and perceptions: some are viewed as 'professionals', others as officials or custodians. Those who are involved in the operation of social welfare are drawn from a diversity of backgrounds. They may or may not be trained in a formal sense. As Donnison notes: 'Policy-making and administration are not separate activities. The "policies" of a social service are its functions – what it does – which may or may not coincide with its official aims. Its "administration" consists of the processes – going on at all levels, inside and outside the organization concerned – which determine those functions. Neither can be studied or understood in isolation from the other.'

The Readings in the first chapter illustrate conceptions of social welfare in a historical and contemporary context. In the first reading, from an address delivered at the British National Conference on Social Welfare in 1967, **Titmuss** considers the 'indefinable abstraction', the Welfare State, and some models of public welfare. One to which he gives much attention, the Public Burden model, sees public welfare expenditure, especially that which is redistributive in intent, as a burden and as hampering economic growth. Paradoxically, as the author points out, whereas increase in retirement pensions from public funds is seen as such a burden, an increase in occupational schemes, where the public sector subsidizes the private sector, is not seen in this way. In both, however, there are additions to consumption demand.

The focus of public comment within this country and internationally on the Welfare State as a concept draws attention to what seems to be the irresponsibility in subsidizing such a large-scale programme in a situation where economically the position of the country is poor. In a most interesting example Titmuss points to the way in which the advanced countries, notably the United States, have attracted professional expertise from other countries; doctors have been drawn from Britain to America and from Asia to Britain. Thus even arrangements for social welfare have all kinds of implications outside the country involved and bring about some consideration, not so much of a Welfare State as a 'Welfare World'.

The main part of the reading is taken up with a

consideration of universalist and selectivist approaches to provision. As Titmuss points out these raise questions about the stigmatization of particular groups, our social rights, and the question of preventing social problems rather than tackling them once they arise. To put it briefly, universalist services are those provided on the basis of right, irrespective of the situation of the clients or consumers, whereas selectivist services are provided on the basis of means tests and other ways which relate provision to the financial position of the recipients.

Titmuss also discusses the concept of disservices as opposed to services. He says that all the emphasis has been on the benefits of welfare whilst for many the services provide not benefits or increments to welfare at all, but 'partial compensations for disservices, for social costs and social insecurities which are the product of a rapidly changing industrial-urban society'. The balance of this consideration of major issues is towards looking at the individual and his needs against the background of the changing society in which he lives. It is pointed out that selective provision has almost invariably been of much poorer quality than universalist provision and finally the general conclusion provides a challenge to conventional thinking about the Welfare State, and conventional assumptions about it, in its view of positive discrimination, whereby those who are not properly provided for are given more resources in order to bring them up to standard. Titmuss therefore argues for a structure of universalism on which selective positive discrimination can be built. He sees social welfare essentially not as a burden which has to be borne but as an instrument of change and adaptation in our society.

Marshall believes that it is not possible to assume what will be the social policies of the rest of this century in Britain on the basis of what we have at the present time. He helps to put the changes which have taken place in the period since 1945 in their proper perspective, seeing the foundations of present social services provision in the Second World War and these views about the historical background, and the importance of developments, contrast in a number of ways with those put forward by Saville in a later reading. Marshall points to the changing view of the social services when he says that previously they were viewed as 'discreet arrangements for looking after the skeleton in the cupboard' and as a kind of first aid for social casualties, to a view of social services which became 'a centre-piece in the *tableau vivant* of the good society and a permanent, praiseworthy and admirable feature of twentieth century life'. Optimistic attitudes which arose from assumptions about the effect of provision on the basic social problems were dealt severe blows in the 1950s and 1960s when it was discovered that poverty was still very prevalent. Nor did the discovery of these social facts give comfort to the ideas of those who believed that 'the whole Welfare State apparatus must itself be regarded as a passing phase', and that by the exercise of individual judgement and care in making provision for oneself the basic state services could eventually be dismantled.

Marshall refers to 'diswelfare' and the considerations and priorities that have to be taken into account. For example, he would emphasize the importance of services and environmental improvements at the present rather than merely transfers of money income and he sets the working-class way of life firmly within the context of an insecurity which it is hard for middle class members of society to appreciate. Finally he raises questions about professional freedoms of the workers in the social services and the remarkable absence of consumer research into the provision which is made, which are considered in more detail in Chapters 4 and 5.

Lafitte, in the reading taken from his inaugural lecture, quotes Myrdal on social policy in its broadest sense, which includes 'the continuous growth in the volume of public, quasi-public and private interventions in social life', interventions which are 'no longer sporadic but more and more take the form of a continuing activity, steered to influence and control a social process in a certain direction'.

Social policy in Britain – easier to describe than define – is seen to be shaped by the specific context of 'the first great "underdeveloped" nation to embark on the unknown adventure of industrialism'. The implications of affluence, and citizenship in such a society, are explored against a background of themes involving choice and priorities: 'mastery of the physical apparatus and circumstances of life and work; protection of the economically, socially, physically or mentally weak; prevention of ill-health, enforced idleness, and interruption of income; determination of those general needs, provision for which ought not to be settled – or neglected – by market operations; regulative and redistributive measures, initially to secure the barest modicum of necessaries and opportunities for all, but now ranging more widely.'

Lafitte considers the free market as a means of providing goods and services and concludes that the less unequal the purchasing power of consumers the more satisfied we are with the market's services in a free society. He argues that a growing sector of services not commercially operated is required to keep disparities in purchasing power within bounds.

Saville, in a reading taken from a much longer article written in the late 1950s, presents a version of the historical development of the Welfare State and its relationship to socialism which has a continuing relevance. The view of the past that Saville challenges is one which sees in the Welfare State and the legislation of the Labour Government of 1945-51, for example, the cumulation and the fulfilment of socialist or pre-socialist policies. Saville questions the idea of a capitalism 'reformed almost out of recognition' and links the whole issue of Welfare State and social welfare with the wider purposes of society. All kinds of questions which it would be fruitful to pursue are raised. He also points to the inadequacy of a view of the Welfare State which focuses achievements entirely on the periods of Liberal and Labour rule.

Welfare State and Welfare Society
R. M. Titmuss

Reprinted with permission from *Commitment to Welfare*,
George Allen & Unwin, London, 1968, pp. 124-36

INTRODUCTION

I am no more enamoured today of the indefinable abstraction
'The Welfare State' than I was some twenty years ago when, with
the advent of the National Health, National Insurance and other
legislative promissories, the term acquired an international as
well as a national popularity.

The consequences have not all been intellectually stimulating.
Generalized slogans rarely induce concentration of thought; more
often they prevent us from asking significant questions about
reality. Morally satisfied and intellectually dulled, we sink back
into our presumptive cosy British world of welfare. Meanwhile,
outside these islands (as well as inside) there are critics – economic
and political critics – who are misled into confusing ends and
means, and who are discouraged from undertaking the painful
exercise of distinguishing between philosophical tomorrows and
the current truths of reality in a complex British power structure
of rationed resources, and great inequalities in incomes and
wealth, opportunities and freedom of choice.

From what little is known about the reading habits of international bankers and economists, I think it is reasonable to say
that they do not include much in the way of studies on welfare and
the condition of the poor. How then are their views shaped about
the British 'Welfare State'? This we do not know, but at least we
can say that if we mislead ourselves, we shall mislead them. But
the matter does not end there. Models of public welfare can
assume different forms and contain different assumptions about
means and ends. Concepts of welfare can imply very different
things to different people.

One particular model is the *Public Burden Model of Welfare*. In
general terms, this sees public welfare expenditure – and particularly expenditure which is redistributive in intent – as a burden;

an impediment to growth and economic development. Given this model of the British patient, the diagnosis seems simple. We are spending too much on 'The Welfare State'. Such explanations are, moreover, encouraged by the concept of private economic man embedded in the techniques of national income accounting. An increase in public retirement pensions is seen (as it was seen internationally during the balance of payments crisis in 1964) as an economic burden. A similar increase in spending power among occupational (publicly subsidized private) pensioners is not so seen. Yet both involve additions to consumption demand.

INTERNATIONAL ASPECTS OF WELFARE

If we insist, come what may, on the continued use or misuse and misapplication of the term 'The Welfare State' then we must accept the consequences of international misunderstanding. We cannot assume that observers abroad share, or will share, the social or moral criteria we may apply to welfare; to many of our creditors and currency colleagues in Western Germany, France and the United States, the 'Welfare State' is equated with national irresponsibility and decadence; an easy way of living off foreign loans. To the political scientist as well as the economist these opinions are relevant facts in the same way as (according to some sociologists) social class is what men think it is. These opinions do not, moreover, differ markedly from those expressed in the published statements on welfare during the past fifteen years by bankers, insurance directors, financiers and others in the City of London.

Many of these monetary experts abroad appear to place a different valuation on countries which depend heavily on 'borrowing' human capital as distinct from those which borrow financial capital. For such transactions, no payment is made to the lending country; there are no interest charges, and there is no intention of repaying the loan.

Since 1949 the United States has absorbed (and to some extent deliberately recruited) the import of 100,000 doctors, scientists and engineers from developed and developing countries. In about eighteen years the United States will have saved some $4,000 million by not having to educate and train, or train fully, this vast quantity of human capital. It has spent more on consumption goods; less on public services. It has taxed itself more lightly while imposing heavier taxation on poorer countries. Estimates have been made that this foreign aid to America is as great or greater than the total of American aid to countries abroad since 1949. Moreover, such estimates leave out of account the social and economic effects in Britain (and much more significantly in the poor countries of the world) of having to train more doctors, scientists and engineers, and of having to pay heavily inflated rewards to prevent American recruitment with all their harmful repercussions on incomes, prices and levels of taxation.

In medicine alone, foreign doctors now account for nearly 20 per cent of the annual additions to the American medical profession. The world now provides as much or more medical aid to the United States in terms of dollars as the total cost of all American medical aid, private and public, to foreign countries. A study I have made recently of the columns of the *British Medical Journal* and the *Lancet* from 1951 to 1966 shows that advertisements for British doctors (often accompanied by recruiting campaigns and sometimes actively encouraged by senior British doctors) rose from a yearly average of 134 in 1951 to over 4,000 in 1966. The total number of newly qualified doctors in Britain in 1966 was around 1,700; each of them cost about £10,000 to train, excluding expenditure on student maintenance.

The United States is not alone in attempting to develop its welfare systems (and Medicare) at the expense of poorer countries through the discovery that, today, it is much cheaper and less of a public burden to import doctors, scientists and other qualified workers than to educate and train them. Britain is also relying heavily on the skills of doctors from poorer countries – due in part to the belief less than five to ten years ago among Ministers and leaders of the medical profession that we were in danger of training too many doctors. And, we may add, the belief among liberal economists and sections of the medical profession that Britain was spending too much on the Health Service which was in danger of bankrupting the nation. Even as late as 1962, there were influential voices in the British Medical Association who were speaking of the profession's recent experience of a 'glut of doctors' and the need to avoid medical unemployment in the late 1960s. Guilty as we have been in our treatment of doctors from overseas, and in our failure in the past to train enough health workers for our own national needs, at least it cannot be said that we are deliberately organizing recruitment campaigns in economically poorer countries.

These introductory reflections on some of the international aspects of welfare point, I believe, to three general conclusions. First, they underline the dangers in the use of the term 'The Welfare State'. Second, they remind us that we can no longer consider welfare systems solely within the limited framework of the nation-state; what we do or fail to do in changing systems of welfare affects other countries besides ourselves. Third, to suggest one criterion for the definition of a 'Welfare Society'; namely, a society which openly accepts a policy responsibility for educating and training its own nationals to meet its own needs for doctors, nurses, social workers, scientists, engineers and others. Just as we have recognized the injustices and the waste in the unrestricted free international movement of goods, material and capital, so we must now recognize the need for the richer countries of the world to take action to protect the poorer countries from being denuded of skilled manpower.

To this end, a number of measures could be taken, some unilaterally, some by international agreement. Among the most important would be for the rich countries to decide to spend less on personal consumption goods and more on training young people for the social service professions; to decide to devote more of their resources for genuine international aid to the poorer countries; to decide to ban the deliberate recruitment overseas of skilled manpower; to decide to revise and broaden their immigration policies so that movement between countries is not restricted to the highly educated and trained; and to take other measures too complex to discuss in this paper.

For the rich countries of the world to take action in such ways would represent a few modest steps towards the notion of 'a Welfare World'. Those countries assuming leadership with policies of this nature might then with some justification regard themselves as 'Welfare Societies'.

This principle of community responsibility for the provision of adequate resources to implement the objectives of national legislation is particularly relevant to the whole field of welfare. The quantity, territorial distribution and quality of any country's social services – education, medical care, mental health, welfare, children's and other personal community services – depends enormously on the quantity and quality of staff; professional, technical, auxiliary and administrative. To enact legislation designed to create or develop services yet not to invest adequately in the training of doctors, nurses, social workers, teachers, and many other categories of skilled manpower and womanpower is a denial of this principle of community responsibility. To rely on the private market and autonomous professional bodies to fulfil these training needs is nothing less than a ridiculous illusion. The private national market has failed lamentably in this country and in the United States to produce enough doctors, teachers, social workers and nurses. To resort to the international market to remedy the deficiency of national social policies can only have tragic consequences for the poorer countries of the world.

In considering the international aspects of these welfare manpower issues there is one further observation I wish to make before turning to other Conference themes. It seems to me the height of collective immorality for the rich countries of the world to preach to the poorer countries about the economic benefits of family planning while, at the same time, making it more difficult for these countries to develop family planning programmes by drawing away the skilled manpower they need for the infra-structure of services required in which to provide birth control as well as death control services.

I want now to consider certain other questions of principle in systems of welfare.

UNIVERSALIST AND SELECTIVE SOCIAL SERVICES

In any discussion today of the future of (what is called) 'The Welfare State' much of the argument revolves round the principles and objectives of universalist social services and selective social services. Time does not seem to have eroded the importance of this issue.

I think it is unnecessary, therefore, to remind you in detail of the many complex questions of principles, goals, methods and assumptions involved in this debate. In regard to some of them – and particularly the question of freedom of choice – I have set out my views in a recently published lecture *Choice and 'The Welfare State'*.

Consider, first, the nature of the broad principles which helped to shape substantial sections of British welfare legislation in the past, and particularly the principle of universalism embodied in such post-war enactments as the National Health Service Act, the Education Act of 1944, the National Insurance Act and the Family Allowances Act.

One fundamental historical reason for the adoption of this principle was the aim of making services available and accessible to the whole population in such ways as would not involve users in any humiliating loss of status, dignity or self-respect. There should be no sense of inferiority, pauperism, shame or stigma in the use of a publicly provided service; no attribution that one was being or becoming a 'public burden'. Hence the emphasis on the social rights of all citizens to use or not to use as responsible people the services made available by the community in respect of certain needs which the private market and the family were unable or unwilling to provide universally. If these services were not provided for everybody by everybody they would either not be available at all, or only for those who could afford them, and for others on such terms as would involve the infliction of a sense of inferiority and stigma.

Avoidance of stigma was not, of course, the only reason for the development of the twin-concepts of social rights and universalism. Many other forces, social, political and psychological, during a century and more of turmoil, revolution, war and change, contributed to the clarification and acceptance of these notions. The novel idea of prevention – novel, at least, to many in the nineteenth century – was, for example, another powerful engine, driven by the Webbs and many other advocates of change, which reinforced the concepts of social rights and universalism. The idea of prevention – the prevention and breaking of the vicious descending spiral of poverty, disease, neglect, illiteracy and destitution – spelt to the protagonists (and still does so) the critical importance of early and easy access to and use of preventive, remedial and rehabilitative services. Slowly and painfully the lesson was learnt that if such services were to be utilized in time and were to be effective in action in a highly differentiated, unequal and class-saturated society, they had to be delivered through socially approved channels; that is to say, without loss of self-respect by the users and their families.

Prevention was not simply a child of biological and psychological theorists; at least one of the grandparents was a powerful economist with a strongly developed streak of nationalism. As Professor Bentley Gilbert has shown in his recent book, *The Evolution of National Insurance: The Origins of the Welfare State*, national efficiency and welfare were seen as complementary. The sin unforgivable was the waste of human resources; thus, welfare was summoned to prevent waste. Hence the beginnings of four of our present-day universalist social services: retirement pensions, the Health Service, unemployment insurance and the school meals service.

The insistent drumming of the national efficiency movement in those far-off days before the First World War is now largely forgotten. Let me then remind you that the whole welfare debate was a curious mixture of humanitarianism, egalitarianism, productivity (as we would call it today) and old-fashioned imperialism. The strident note of the latter is now, we may thank our stars, silenced. The Goddess of Growth has replaced the God of National Fitness. But can we say that the quest for the other objectives is no longer necessary?

Before discussing such a rhetorical question, we need to examine further the principle of universalism. The principle itself may sound simple but the practice – and by that I mean the present operational pattern of welfare in Britain today – is immensely complex. We can see something of this complexity if we analyse welfare (defined here as all publicly provided and subsidized services, statutory, occupational and fiscal) from a number of different standpoints.

AN ANALYTICAL FRAMEWORK

Whatever the nature of the service, activity or function, and whether it be a service in kind; a collective amenity, or a transfer payment in cash or by accountancy, we need to consider (and here I itemize in question-form for the sake of brevity) three central issues:

(1) What is the nature of entitlement to use? Is it legal, con-

tractual or contributory, financial, discretionary or professionally determined entitlement?

(2) Who is entitled and on what conditions? Is account taken
of individual characteristics, family characteristics, group
characteristics, territorial characteristics or social-biological
characteristics? What, in fact, are the rules of entitlement? Are
they specific and contractual – like a right based on age – or are
they variable, arbitrary or discretionary?

(3) What methods, financial and administrative, are employed
in the determination of access, utilization, allocation and
payment?

Next we have to reflect on the nature of the service or benefit.
What functions do benefits, in cash, amenity or in kind, aim to
fulfil? They may, for example, fulfil any of the following sets
of functions, singly or in combination:

(1) As partial compensation for identified disservices caused by
society (for example, unemployment, some categories of
industrial injuries benefits, war pensions, etc.). And, we may
add, the disservices caused by international society as exempli-
fied recently by the oil pollution resulting from the Torrey
Canyon disaster costing at least £2 million.

(2) As partial compensation for unidentifiable disservices
caused by society (for example, 'benefits' related to programmes
of slum clearance, urban blight, smoke pollution control,
hospital cross-infection and many other socially created
disservices).

(3) As partial compensation for unmerited handicap (for
example, language classes for immigrant children, services for
the deprived child, children handicapped from birth, etc.).

(4) As a form of protection for society (for example, the
probation service, some parts of the mental health services,
services for the control of infectious diseases, and so on).

(5) As an investment for a future personal or collective gain
(education – professional, technical and industrial – is an
obvious example here; so also are certain categories of tax
deductibles for self-improvement and certain types of subsidized
occupational benefits).

(6) As an immediate and/or deferred increment to personal
welfare or, in other words, benefits (utilities) which add to
personal command-over-resources either immediately and/or

in the future (for example, subsidies to owner-occupiers and council tenants, tax deductibles for interest charges, pensions, supplementary benefits, curative medical care, and so on).

(7) As an element in an integrative objective which is an essential characteristic distinguishing social policy from economic policy. As Kenneth Boulding has said, '. . . social policy is that which is centred in those institutions that create integration and discourage alienation.' It is thus profoundly concerned with questions of personal identity whereas economic policy centres round exchange or bilateral transfer.

This represents little more than an elementary and partial structural map which can assist in the understanding of the welfare complex today. Needless to say, a more sophisticated (inch to the mile) guide is essential for anything approaching a thorough analysis of the actual functioning of welfare benefit systems. I do not, however, propose to refine further this frame of study now, nor can I analyse by these classifications the several hundred distinctive and functionally separate services and benefits actually in operation in Britain today.

Further study would also have to take account of the pattern and operation of means-tested services. It has been estimated by Mr M. J. Reddin, my research assistant, that in England and Wales today local authorities are responsible for administering at least 3,000 means-tests, of which about 1,500 are different from each other. This estimate applies only to services falling within the responsibilities of education, child care, health, housing and welfare departments. It follows that in these fields alone there exist some 1,500 different definitions of poverty or financial hardship, ability to pay and rules for charges, which affect the individual and the family. There must be substantial numbers of poor families with multiple needs and multiple handicaps whose perception today of the realities of welfare is to see only a means-testing world. Who helps them, I wonder, to fill up all those forms?

I mention these social facts, by way of illustration, because they do form part of the operational complex of welfare in 1967. My main purpose, however, in presenting this analytical framework was twofold. First, to underline the difficulties of conceptualizing and categorizing needs, causes, entitlement or gatekeeper functions, utilization patterns, benefits and compensations. Second, to suggest that those students of welfare who are seeing the main problem today in terms of universalism versus selective services are presenting a naïve and oversimplified picture of policy choices.

Some of the reasons for this simple and superficial view are, I think, due to the fact that the approach is dominated by the concept or model of welfare as a 'burden'; as a waste of resources in the provision of benefits for those who, it is said, do not need them. The general solution is thus deceptively simple and romantically appealing; abolish all this welfare complexity and concentrate help on those whose needs are greatest.

Quite apart from the theoretical and practical immaturity of this solution, which would restrict the public services to a minority in the population leaving the majority to buy their own education, social security, medical care and other services in a supposedly free market, certain other important questions need to be considered.

As all selective services for this minority would have to apply some test of need – eligibility, on what bases would tests be applied and, even more crucial, where would the lines be drawn for benefits which function as compensation for identified disservices, compensation for unidentifiable disservices, compensation for unmerited handicap, as a form of social protection, as an investment, or as an increment to personal welfare? Can rules of entitlement and access be drawn on purely 'ability to pay' criteria without distinction of cause? And if the causal agents of need cannot be identified or are so diffuse as to defy the wit of law – as they so often are today – then is not the answer 'no compensation and no redress'? In other words, the case for concentrated selective services resolves itself into an argument for allowing the social costs or diswelfares of the economic system to lie where they fall.

The emphasis today on 'welfare' and the 'benefits of welfare' often tends to obscure the fundamental fact that for many consumers the services used are not essentially benefits or increments to welfare at all; they represent partial compensations for disservices, for social costs and social insecurities which are the product of a rapidly changing industrial-urban society. They are part of the price we pay to some people for bearing part of the costs of other people's progress; the obsolescence of skills, redundancies, premature retirements, accidents, many categories of disease and handicap, urban blight and slum clearance, smoke pollution, and a hundred-and-one other socially generated dis-services. They are the socially caused diswelfares; the losses involved in aggregate welfare gains.

What is also of major importance today is that modern society is finding it increasingly difficult to identify the causal agent or agencies, and thus to allocate the costs of disservices and charge those who are responsible. It is not just a question of benefit allocation – of whose 'Welfare State' – but also of loss allocation – whose 'Diswelfare State'.

If identification of the agents of diswelfare were possible – if we could legally name and blame the culprits – then, in theory at least, redress could be obtained through the courts by the method of monetary compensation for damages. But multiple causality and the diffusion of disservices – the modern choleras of change – make this solution impossible. We have, therefore, as societies to make other choices; either to provide social services, or to allow the social costs of the system to lie where they fall. The nineteenth century chose the latter – the *laissez faire* solution – because it had neither a germ theory of disease nor a social theory of causality; an answer which can hardly be entertained today by a richer society equipped with more knowledge about the dynamics of change. But knowledge in this context must not, of course, be equated with wisdom.

If this argument can be sustained, we are thus compelled to return to our analytical framework of the functional concepts of benefit and, within this context, to consider the role of universalist and selective social services. Non-discriminating universalist services are in part the consequence of unidentifiable causality. If disservices are wasteful (to use the economists' concept of 'waste') so welfare has to be 'wasteful'.

The next question that presents itself is this: can we and should we, in providing benefits and compensation (which in practice can rarely be differentially provided), distinguish between 'faults' in the individual (moral, psychological or social) and the 'faults of society'? If all services are provided – irrespective of whether they represent benefits, amenity, social protection or compensation – on a discriminatory, means-test basis, do we not foster both the sense of personal failure and the stigma of a public burden? The fundamental objective of all such tests of eligibility is to keep people out; not to let them in. They must, therefore, be treated as applicants or supplicants; not beneficiaries or consumers.

It is a regrettable but human fact that money (and the lack of it) is linked to personal and family self-respect. This is one element in what has been called the 'stigma of the means test'. Another element is the historical evidence we have that separate discriminatory services for poor people have always tended to be poor quality services; read the history of the panel system under National Health Insurance; read Beveridge on workmen's compensation; Newsom on secondary modern schools; Plowden on standards of primary schools in slum areas; Townsend on Part III accommodations in *The Last Refuge*, and so on.

In the past, poor quality selective services for poor people were the product of a society which saw 'welfare' as a residual; as a public burden. The primary purpose of the system and the method of discrimination was, therefore, deterrence (it was also an effective rationing device). To this end, the most effective instrument was to induce among recipients (children as well as adults) a sense of personal fault, of personal failure, even if the benefit was wholly or partially a compensation for disservices inflicted by society.

THE REAL CHALLENGE IN WELFARE

Today, with this heritage, we face the positive challenge of providing selective, high quality services for poor people over a large and complex range of welfare; of positively discriminating on a territorial, group or 'rights' basis in favour of the poor, the handicapped, the deprived, the coloured, the homeless, and the social casualties of our society. Universalism is not, by itself alone, enough: in medical care, in wage-related social security, and in education. This much we have learnt in the past two decades from the facts about inequalities in the distribution of incomes and wealth, and in our failure to close many gaps in differential access to and effective utilization of particular branches of our social services.

If I am right, I think that Britain is beginning to identify the dimensions of this challenge of positive, selective discrimination – in income maintenance, in education, in housing, in medical care and mental health, in child welfare, and in the tolerant integration of immigrants and citizens from overseas; of preventing especially the second generation from becoming (and of seeing themselves as) second-class citizens. We are seeking ways and means, values, methods and techniques, of positive discrimination without the infliction, actual or imagined, or a sense of personal failure and individual fault.

At this point, considering the nature of the search in all its ramifying complexities, I must now state my general conclusion. It is this. The challenge that faces us is not the choice between universalist and selective social services. The real challenge resides in the question: what particular infrastructure of universalist services is needed in order to provide a framework of values and opportunity bases within and around which can be developed socially acceptable selective services aiming to discriminate positively, with the minimum risk of stigma, in favour of those whose needs are greatest.

This, to me, is the fundamental challenge. In different ways and in particular areas it confronts the Supplementary Benefits Commission, the Seebohm Committee, the National Health Service, the Ministry of Housing and Local Government, the National Committee for Commonwealth Immigrants, the policy-making readers of the Newsom Report and the Plowden Report on educational priority areas, the Scottish Report, *Social Work and the Community*, and thousands of social workers and administrators all over the country wrestling with the problems of needs and priorities. In all the main spheres of need, some structure of universalism is an essential pre-requisite to selective positive discrimination; it provides a general system of values and a sense of community; socially approved agencies for clients, patients and consumers, and also for the recruitment, training and deployment of staff at all levels; it sees welfare, not as a burden, but as complementary and as an instrument of change and, finally, it allows positive discriminatory services to be provided as rights for categories of people and for classes of need in terms of priority social areas and other impersonal classifications.

Without this infrastructure of welfare resources and framework of values we should not, I conclude, be able to identify and discuss the next steps in progress towards a 'Welfare Society'.

The Role of the Social Services

T. H. Marshall

Reprinted with permission from 'The Role of the Social Services',
Political Quarterly, vol. 40, no. 1, Jan.-March 1969, pp. 1-11

There are occasions when forecasts of the future state of a changing social situation can lean heavily on the projection of trends
observable in the present and recent past. That is not the position
in the case of social policy today. Thirty or forty years ago it was
different. Evidence was then to hand on the basis of which it
might have been possible to predict the evolution of something
like the Welfare State of the 1940s. The events of the previous
thirty or forty years pointed in that direction. Three movements
had started towards the end of the nineteenth century, taken a
decisive step forward shortly before the First World War and
been reactivated soon after it; and it was pretty clear in the 1930s
that they had not yet arrived at their logical terminus. They were
the invention of social insurance, the break-up of the Poor Law,
and the pursuit of equal educational opportunity. Having
achieved universal, comprehensive social insurance plus family
allowances on the Beveridge model, an almost free national
medical service, secondary education for all, and a complex of
local, personal, social services available to all citizens and not
only to paupers, they could go no further without some change of
direction or adoption of new ideas or administrative devices. The
future could not be a simple projection of the past; it had become
problematical.

NEW DIRECTIONS

In the case of education the change of direction has already taken
place. First came growing dissatisfaction with the eleven plus,
followed by a definite swing away from the selective system of
1944 towards the comprehensive school. The future of the
independent schools is still in the White – or Blue or Green –
Paper stage. So is that of the social services, as generally defined.
We have just had, or are eagerly awaiting, reports and recom-

mendations on the reorganization, in some quite fundamental ways, of the medical services, the personal social services, the social security machinery and local government. It is a grand exercise in stock-taking and preparing for the start of a new phase of development.

The change of mood and outlook which took place between the mid-forties, when the previous trend reached its climax, and the mid-sixties, when reappraisal took positive shape, is more profound than it might appear to be if judged only by its surface manifestations. We must not forget that the foundations of the Welfare State were laid during the war, and that the British, having got social security written into the text of the Atlantic Charter, greeted the Beveridge Report as the blueprint of the new society for which they were fighting. After the war they believed that they had created a model which the rest of the world would follow. The basic principles enshrined in this model were mutual aid organized by and for the entire community, and equality of status and of opportunity for all. It marked also the full realization of a conception of the role of the social services which had been adumbrated by Lloyd George but had since then been sleeping. In place of the images, progressively discarded, of the social services as discreet arrangements for looking after the skeleton in the cupboard, as the provision of first-aid to patch the wounds of social casualties, as compensation for the damage caused by defects in the economic system, and in general as a burden to be kept as light as possible and retained for as short a time as possible, there was presented the vision of the social services as a centre-piece in the *tableau vivant* of the good society and a permanent, praiseworthy and admirable feature of twentieth-century life.

OPTIMISM AND ALARM

Signs that the mood was beginning to change appeared in the 1950s. In the first phase of this change was an element of optimism, but also a feeling of alarm. On the one hand people were saying that economic progress had solved the basic problem of poverty and that the residue of this problem could be handled by a much less elaborate machine than the one we had created. On the other hand there was anxiety about the expected increase in the number of pensioners and the cost this would involve, even with minimal pensions, and also about the increase in the absolute cost of the National Health Service in its attempt to fulfil its obligation to offer a service which was not minimal, but optimal. Both these lines of thought were such as to revive in some quarters what Professor Titmuss has called the 'Public Burden Model of Welfare'. It was hoped that, in time, the burden would be lifted, and the dimensions of our social problems drastically reduced, by the natural growth of productivity and affluence. Consequently, as a Liberal spokesman remarked, 'the whole Welfare State apparatus must itself be regarded as a passing phase'. This view and that of the architects of the new society of the 1940s are diametrically opposed to each other.

The second phase in the change of mood was marked by doubt and disillusion. Independent and official research revealed that basic poverty had not been abolished – far from it. The Welfare State machinery for health and welfare was not running smoothly, nor achieving the optimum standard at which it aimed. Vital problems of housing and rent control were the subject of controversy and experiment and still awaited an agreed solution. The defects in the services were due partly to inadequate finances and partly to ill-designed administration. In addition, the British Welfare State was no longer a model for the world to copy, and at several points it had been outstripped, both in efficiency and in the resources assigned to it, by other countries.

BEVERIDGE PRINCIPLES DISCARDED

Meanwhile opinion had been changing about some of the Beveridge principles. His principle that the sharp distinction between insurance and assistance should be emphasized was abandoned and, in fact, reversed. The statement on the blue page of the Pension Book that 'people over pension age have a right under the Ministry of Social Security Act 1966 to a guaranteed income', achieved, if necessary, with the help of a 'supplementary pension', is a direct denial of the view that there can be no right where there is a test of means. But changes of name and language may be found to conceal, rather than to solve, the problem. Secondly, the notion that social insurance should follow as closely as possible the rules that govern commercial insurance, since they are essentially the same kind of operation, gradually lost its force. It had never really been the basis of official policy (nor did Beveridge want it to be), but it had had an inhibiting effect on public and political opinion. It encouraged the 'public burden' view of the social services and the attitude which treated every increase in pension rates as a present to pensioners of income to which they were not entitled, because they had not paid for it. Thirdly, following common practice elsewhere, flat-rate insurance was supplemented by an earnings-related element, first for pensions and later for the other principal benefits. This breached the Beveridge principle that all additions to the uniform basic rate should be the result of free choice and private enterprise, and it raised the question whether it was right that public social security measures should become involved with, or reflect, the inequalities of income prevailing in the economic world at large.

UNANSWERED QUESTIONS

Thus at least three questions of fundamental importance were being asked, all of which still remain open. First, if there is a right to a guaranteed income, how is its magnitude to be determined, and how does it differ from the earlier concepts of the 'poverty line' and the 'subsistence level'? Secondly, if the entitlement to a pension is not closely connected with contributions, what is its real basis – is it past work, or present need, or, as the Pension Book suggests, simply age? Thirdly, does the grading of social insurance contributions and benefits by reference to earnings (1) violate the principle of equality so firmly entrenched in the concept of the Welfare State, and (2) hand over to the State an area of discrimination which ought to be left to free choice and private enterprise?

When it is said, as it was by some in the 1950s, that with the rise in the general standard of living poverty had become exceptional, this can mean one or both of two things. 'Exceptional' may have a quantitative reference, and the statement then means that the poor are a minority, and a small one. Or it may be given a structural reference, implying that real poverty is found only outside the normal structure of the economy and the social services. It has now been found that, though the poor are certainly a minority (but not quite as small a one as was once believed), poverty is not exceptional in the second sense. It exists within the economic structure, wherever full-time earnings are insufficient to keep an average family out of poverty, and it exists within the structure of the social services, wherever poverty exists, even when full use is being made of the help those services offer. In addition, poverty due to failure to draw benefits that are payable is also in a sense structural, in so far as it is caused by the lingering stigma attached to 'assistance'. Structural poverty can be remedied only by structural changes. It cannot be regarded as a hangover from a past period of scarcity which will dwindle to insignificant proportions, nor can it be treated by minor adjustments to the details of the existing economic and social service systems.

COMPENSATING 'DISWELFARE'

There are some who believe that the troubles with which the social services try to deal are deeply rooted in the economic system. Professor Titmuss, for example, has stressed the fact that for many consumers the services are not really benefits or increments to welfare at all; they are partial compensation for the 'socially generated disservices' and 'socially caused diswelfare' associated with a 'rapidly changing industrial-urban society'. 'They are part of the price we pay to some people for bearing part of the costs of other people's progress.' Since we cannot 'name and blame the culprits' and oblige them to make redress, we must either provide social services or 'allow the social costs of the system to lie where they fell'. This is a modern version of the casualty relief view of the role of the social services. It identifies the cause of the damage as structural – located in the economy – but does not suggest ways in which social policy itself might induce any remedial structural changes.

Others take a less gloomy view about the 'diswelfare' caused by industrial change. There are, of course, casualties to be cared for, due notably to low wages, industrial injury and unemployment, and there always have been. But on this view action can be taken within the ambit of social policy to make or induce industry to install, improve and standardize its own services on behalf of these casualties, and to plan the co-ordination of the efforts of the two parties, the public and the private. Obvious examples are the recognition of approved occupational pension schemes as sub-stitutes for the State graded pensions (though we may expect changes here), legislation about dismissals and redundancy pay-ments, and proposals that employers should take full responsi-bility for benefits during short-term sickness. Not only do the public social services become in this way linked with industry, but social policy, in the process of forging these links, can induce structural changes – even if minor ones – in the economic system. The rates and regulations of retirement pensions, and the provi-sion of day nurseries for pre-school children should reflect the considered views of social policy about the welfare of older men and women and young mothers; but they also directly affect the labour market for these classes of potential employees.

The most difficult point of interaction between the social services and industry is that of low earnings. The more generous the standards of benefit become, the more likely it is that they will be higher than the present market value of significant sections of the labour force. It has been a firm principle, ever since the reversal of Speenhamland policy, that relief, or benefits, should not be used to subsidize wages. But, if wages remain below the standard rate of benefit, then the unemployed will be better off than those who are working – hence the so-called 'wage-stop'. The traditional remedy was to push up the wages, and trust that industry would find ways of paying them or that the men would find other jobs. In the present state of the economy, with automa-tion threatening to reduce the demand for some classes of manual labour, this may not be easy. So the question arises whether, in the interests of equity and the smooth running of the social services, these low wages should be subsidized from public funds. The employed, like the retired, would then have a 'right' to a 'guaranteed income'.

IS SOCIAL EQUALITY THE ULTIMATE AIM?

A third level of thinking about the role of the social services can be represented by the statement of a French authority that 'the modification of the structure of society has been one of the ambitions of modern plans of social security'. This is a different matter from their impact on the economy in the ways just dis-cussed. It could be taken to mean that social security has not been content to aim simply at income maintenance, either at a flat rate or a graduated one, or at the elimination of poverty, but has deliberately been designed to promote the development of a more egalitarian society. It can hardly be said that British social security has done this, but there are those who believe that it should. And although the combined effects of social security and taxation towards the equalization of *money* incomes is almost certainly less than might appear on the surface, the social services proper – in health, welfare, education, housing, etc. – have undoubtedly had a profound effect on the distribution of *real* income. This has been their aim, and the policy directing them has always been influenced, and sometimes inspired, by ideas of equity and social equality. Here again, it is hard to say how much progress has been made by these means towards the goal of a more egalitarian society, but it will not be denied that it is a legitimate part of the role of the social services, as at present organized, to pursue this goal.

But there are certain ideas, much canvassed in recent years, which suggest a rather different role for the public social services. They stem from a belief in the overriding value of choice in matters of welfare, and propose that the door to this should be opened by having mixed systems of medical, educational and other services, part public and part private. Those wishing to buy private service would be able to withhold part of their compulsory contribution to the cost of the public services and transfer it to the service of their choice, while maximum use, it is assumed, would be made of voluntary insurance to spread the risks. What would the effect be on the role of the public services? At present this role is a dual one. There is first the responsibility for establishing and maintaining a structure through which resources, sufficient in quantity and variety, are made available when and where needed throughout the country, and for seeing that it works. Secondly, it is the duty of the authorities to ensure that nobody in need of a service is unable to obtain it for lack of ready money, and that the same quality of service is provided, whether it is paid for in full, or in part, or not at all by the consumer.

If the first of these two roles were retained (as in fact it must be), the public services would be left to carry out a complicated and expensive task with reduced resources, while the private enterprises would be made free of a burden which they could never really have carried, and given a great competitive advantage. If only the second role were retained, we should be back with a two-tier system, the lower sector of which must concentrate on catering for the poorer classes of society. It would surely take some time after the adoption of such a scheme for it to become clear what exactly the role of the public services was to be. This is a disturbing thought.

THE NEGATIVE INCOME TAX IDEA

So far we have been discussing the interaction between social policy and certain elements of the social and economic structure. The device known as 'negative income tax' would go further than this and, by amalgamating social security (or sections of it) with direct taxation, would deprive the social service entirely of its character as an independent entity. The scheme revolves round the focal point of an estimated 'break-even' income, such that the recipient of it may be reasonably considered to be neither liable to pay any income tax nor entitled to receive any subvention. The estimate would, of course, take account of the number of individuals dependent on the income and the various commitments for which tax rebates are normally allowed, and it is obvious that some difficult value judgements are involved. Incomes above the 'break-even' point would be taxed progressively in the usual way and incomes below that point would be given a subsidy to bring them as near to it as was considered compatible with the preservation of economic incentives. This very crude description must serve as a basis for considering the implications for the role of the social services.

First, the universality of the Beveridge plan is dropped, and the element of the social service role which is incorporated into the tax system is that of meeting proved needs; it functions selectively. One might say that its aim is to eliminate poverty, and that, if it could be perfectly administered, it would do so, in so far as poverty is a matter of income only. But it sets its sights higher than that; the aim of negative income tax is positive welfare. Secondly, it does not, because it cannot, fulfil the role of dealing selectively with individual needs without a test of means; but it uses the return of income in place of the 'means test'. Thirdly, because it is focused on needs, as estimated, it would, if applied to social security as a whole (which it need not be), sweep away those entitlements which, in the present system, constitute the right to particular kinds of benefit. The issue is clearest in the case of pensions. As was pointed out earlier, there have been several different conceptions of the basis of the right to a pension. The stress was once laid on contributions, then more simply on age (and retirement) with contributions determining eligibility rather than amount, and the recent trend has been towards the idea of superannuation. This means that all occupations should be pensionable in the same sense as the civil service and armed forces are today. The pensions would be related to average or terminal earnings and sufficient to support both a man and his wife, with provision (built-in or separately arranged) for his widow. They would thus reflect a section of the range of income differentials in the economic world and, since this range would exclude the extremes, the implied endorsement would be only of inequalities generally accepted as legitimate, and would not be incompatible with a general policy of equalization. Negative income tax, if applied to standard as well as to supplementary pensions, would wipe out these titles and substitute the relationship between total income and an approved standard of wellbeing. The implications for the role of social security are obvious. It would be confined to a selective treatment of 'need', leaving pensions in the true sense to be organized occupationally by employers, no doubt under public supervision but not necessarily with public subsidy.

The last point about negative income tax which is directly relevant to our theme is one which figures prominently in the fierce criticism levelled at it by Professor Titmuss. Selectivity, he says, based on gross money incomes and normal commitments is quite unfit to deal with poverty and deprivation. The circumstances are far too complex and quite beyond the reach of a mass, impersonal, computerized service. He is convinced that selective treatment of special needs is possible only on the basis of a generous, universal system of benefits. Selectivity, or positive discrimination, should then be exercised in terms of categories, not of income levels, but of types of need or situation, such as, perhaps, the handicapped, coloured immigrants, 'educational priority areas', and so forth. This would reduce to the minimum the necessity of selective treatment by 'means test' at the individual level.

The kind of integration to which these ideas point is quite different from that achieved by negative income tax, it is integration between the cash benefit system and the welfare services. In this country, according to Tony Lynes, there is very little of this. He maintains in a recent article that 'the British social security system is remarkable for the extent to which welfare visiting and the provision of benefits in kind and other services have been kept separate from the administration of cash benefits'. The step taken towards closer relationships by the Children and Young Persons Act of 1963 was a characteristically cautious one, allowing Children's Departments, if necessary, to give assistance in kind and, in exceptional circumstances, in cash. As for integration within the welfare services themselves, the movement in this direction has now culminated in the Seebohm Committee's plan for Social Service Departments, which carries important implications for the role of the personal welfare services.

THE RANGE AND DEPTH OF SERVICES

Of these, two are outstanding; they concern the range and depth of public responsibility for personal welfare, and the functions and qualifications of social workers. It is clear that the proposed integration is intended to lead to an increase in both the range and the depth of the services included. It is not so much a question of introducing new ideas as of underlining old ones. It has long been accepted that agencies should not wait passively for cases to come to them, but should be on the lookout for them; they should (discreetly) advertise their wares and strongly urge those who need them to ask for them. When they take up a case, they should aim, not only at relief, but at cure, and the Report rightly insists that there is something even better than cure, namely, prevention. It follows that in the diagnosis and treatment of every case the situation must be viewed as a whole. The responsibility is a formidable one, and the crucial question is with what kind of authority should the welfare agencies be invested to enable them to carry and to discharge it?

There are two kinds of authority. One is the authority attached to an office, which confers power to mobilize resources and to issue instructions, or even orders. In the case of welfare officers the power to mobilize resources, that is to say, to direct the flow of services and physical aids to the places where they are most needed, is of great importance. The power to give instructions or orders is limited, but exists in some cases, notably in the care of children. Hence the current controversy over the White Paper 'Children in Trouble'. Professor Handler of Wisconsin concluded an article on 'The Coercive Children's Officer' with the remark that social workers are now 'administrative officials exercising governmental powers'. Though not new, this is becoming an increasingly salient aspect of the role of the social services today, and will probably continue to do so in future. The other kind of authority is that of the expert, and it confers the power to influence the conduct of others by offering them the fruits of knowledge and experience. Much of the authority exercised by social case-workers – and without some authority they could have no influence – is of this kind. So it is important to know what sort of expertise they have.

THE AUTHORITY AND KNOWLEDGE OF SOCIAL WORKERS

Here we meet a dilemma. A welfare service which aims at being preventive, curative and comprehensive poses problems of diagnosis and prognosis of great difficulty and complexity. But the fact that investigation must study the situation as a whole means that no single specialism can cope with it. The choice lies between employing several specialists on one case, or trusting to the judgement of a single generalist. The Seebohm Committee advocates the latter course, because it believes that 'a family or individual in need of social care should, as far as possible, be served by a single social worker' (para. 516). The expertise would be available at a higher level. But it goes on to say it is expected that in the future 'as the service develops, specializations will cluster differently and new types of specialization emerge', but 'it would be unwise to attempt to define these now' (para. 524). Perhaps so, but it should be remembered that the role of a social service, especially a personal welfare service, must be tailored to the capacities of those who are to execute it.

In conclusion, the keynote seems to be integration – integration within the social security system and the welfare services and between them, and also between either or both of them and the economy at large, in some cases by setting up administrative units and in others by imposing a common pattern or plan. The future role of the social services will depend very much on how these integrative processes work out, and no assessment can be made of trends in social policy without bringing economic policy and educational policy into the picture.

Social Policy in a Free Society

F. Lafitte

Reprinted with permission from *Social Policy in a Free Society*, An Inaugural Lecture delivered in the University of Birmingham, 18 May 1962, pp. 8-14

Social policy, our unifying interest, is more easily described than defined. If economic policy is concerned with maximizing wealth and with the citizen-producer, one might say that social policy looks to the distribution of economic enjoyments and to the citizen-consumer. Yet the distinction is of limited validity, as Muirhead saw when he wrote: 'Beyond and inclusive of the economic structure of society there lay that of nation and State, with all that constituted a man's citizenship. With the advance of democracy this was calling more and more loudly for intelligent study.' For him social policy embraced not only the standard of living and distributive justice in economics but the economic structure itself, corrective justice, and the civic life. Again, one might say that social policy treats of the distribution of power and opportunities among citizens outside the political sphere: relations between rich and poor, masters and servants, trade-unionists and non-unionists, landlords and tenants, men and women, parents and children, courts and criminals, the normal and the abnormal in body or mind. On this view the whole quality of social life and human relations is of interest to social policy; and there is no point in stopping anywhere short of Professor Macbeath's comprehensive statement, in the Hobhouse tradition:

Social policies are concerned with the right ordering of the network of relationships between men and women who live together in societies, or with the principles which should govern the activities of individuals and groups so far as they affect the lives and interests of other people.

I cannot dissent from this view, yet I shrink from its broad sweep. Less ambitiously I would say that, in our kind of society, social policy is not *essentially* interested in economic relations but is very much concerned with the extent to which economic relations and aspirations should be allowed to dominate other aspects of life; more specifically that social policy addresses itself to a whole range of needs – material, cultural, emotional – outside the wide realm of satisfactions which can conveniently be left to the market. There is attraction too in Professor Myrdal's description of 'social policy in its broadest sense' simply as a convenient way of referring to 'the continuous growth in the volume of public, quasi-public and private interventions in social life' – interventions which are 'no longer sporadic but more and more take the form of a continuing activity, steered to influence and control a social process in a certain direction'.

Implied in all the foregoing accounts of social policy is the judgement that, if left alone by political authority, the state of society would rapidly become intolerable. Through collective action, in particular by imposing the State's directing power on the forces of the market, we seek to steer society, along paths it would not naturally follow, towards accepted goals unattainable without public organization – the great communal Super-Ego, as it were, striving to marshal the drives of the great social Id. Through social policy we assert the primacy of non-economic over economic values, our belief that the way of life matters more than the ways of getting a living. In this sense social policy is as old as mankind. Anthropologists and economic historians have surely taught us that most men at most times have lived in communities – advanced as well as primitive – whose economic systems were submerged in their social relationships. Regarded in this light, our initial response to our industrial revolution could be seen as a stupendous aberration from the normal courses of mankind. Social policy could be seen as our determination to return to the old norm in a world transformed by industrialism. The Victorian attempt to establish a competitive, self-regulating market economy founded on the motive of individual gain implied, as Karl Polanyi puts it, 'no less than the running of society as an adjunct to the market. Instead of economy being embedded in social relations, social relations are embedded in the economic system'. This was the supreme Victorian blasphemy: that society had no right to control its economic arrangements, no cause collectively to establish institutions for the civic good; but must allow all social arrangements to be determined by the forces of the market.

Protest against this blasphemy in the name of human values was one main strand in social policy. A second strand was the discovery that the social results of *laissez faire* were economically inefficient, a third that they were imperially and militarily inefficient. Moreover, economic liberalism was but one facet of an outlook which also comprised commitment in principle to a democratic way of life and optimism about the liberating and ameliorative end-results of industrialism. These hopes were not illusory. In itself industrialism makes neither for democracy nor for equality. But the early Victorian business class *did* set us on the road to a freer and less unequal society. From this road their successors, not without misgivings, did not turn back when the working man was eventually admitted to citizenship – and social policy wove in its fourth strand, turning increasingly to redistributive measures.

The fifth strand derives from the very nature of a way of life transformed in a few lifetimes by science and industry. For the common man this transformation has been the greatest liberation in history. He has gained release from grinding poverty and toil, from ignorance, from famine, plague and the social plague of mass unemployment. His opportunities and choices have been vastly enriched. But the mass of people could not have secured these advantages save through the building up of the State during the past two lifetimes as a major influence in the ordering of society. Without well-developed public services and State intervention at countless points, for how many months could we maintain our intricately interdependent, rapidly changing, urbanized mass society? This fifth strand is the one most commonly overlooked. Yet every nation committed or wanting to commit itself to urban-industrial life finds the same need for public organization of its social superstructure, for an extensive communal sector of services and amenities, for public direction of social change and a fostering of the sciences of social control and communication. And this need arises independently of political systems – in Japan, India, Turkey, Egypt as in Russia, Germany, Sweden and the United States – because it is inherent in the industrial civilization we share or aspire to share. Bismarck, Lenin, Lloyd George and Roosevelt are, for instance, all pioneers of social security. Trade-unionists in Russia and America are equally concerned to secure part of their wages in social services charged to industry. Farmer-labour alliances reach much the same conclusions about communal provision of medical-care in Saskatchewan today as in Denmark sixty years ago. Compulsory education, public or co-operative housing, town and community planning, social income for the dependent family – these are all shared recognitions of shared needs engendered by advancing industrialism.

British social policy has been shaped by its specific context – its emergence in the first great 'underdeveloped' nation to embark on the unknown adventure of industrialism, lacking then all the arts of controlling social change subsequently so painfully acquired. Industrialism added to the glaring inequalities of Old England new inequalities and social difficulties which made State intervention progressively more necessary; but it was promoted by a class of innovators who saw themselves building a free society in which State intervention would become progressively less necessary. The themes of social policy hitherto have been: mastery of the physical apparatus and circumstances of life and work; protection of the economically, socially, physically or mentally weak; prevention of ill health, enforced idleness, and interruption of income; determination of those general needs, provision for which ought not to be settled – or neglected – by market operations; regulative and redistributive measures, initially to secure the barest modicum of necessaries and opportunities for all, but now ranging more widely.

These themes need continual rescoring with improved harmony in a composition dedicated to the unfinished business of working out the implications of citizenship in a free society. The problem is to give those inseparable words, Responsibility, Freedom, Equality and Fellowship, a richer and less confused content in the kind of society we are moving toward. As the world goes, that society will be affluent – a car-owning if not a property-owning democracy. It will be fully employed, with a security of incomes not known beyond two decades past, but exposed to creeping monetary inflation. Large and impersonal industrial, financial and public organizations, more prone to bureaucracy than to fellowship, will increase their dominance. In the name of equal opportunities we shall move nearer to meritocracy, so concentrating more of society's failures at the most menial levels. With one voice we will press for equalization through communal services obliterating social distinctions, with another for unequal economic rewards to mark occupational differences and differentially sanctify our measurements of men's social worth.

A free society cannot deploy its citizen-workers by prescription or conscription. It must rely on the device of unequal rewards. Yet industrialism, with which democracy lives in uneasy symbiosis, would, unchecked, engender disparities of wealth which would affront its worker-citizens' democratic sentiments and jeopardize their liberties. Mr Douglas Jay is among the many Socialists who now believe that this would remain true even of an industrialism founded on common ownership. If therefore a free society cannot radically reduce disparity of *generated* incomes, it will turn increasingly to *redistribution*. Considered in this light, social services are not mere devices to equip citizens for intelligent competition as workers and consumers. Nor are they temporary crutches to help the working man on his upward climb from dependence to autonomy, to be thrown away at the door of the Affluent Society. On the contrary, a large sector of communal services, growing at least as fast as the economy itself, is an indispensable instrument for a society which wants to make its industrialism serve democratic ends. In addition we may expect further public action to abate inequalities resulting from accumulations of wealth. Fifty years ago we thought it indefensible that the upper tenth should own 90 per cent of personal wealth. Are we likely indefinitely to tolerate their present control of nearly 80 per cent?

Sixty-nine years ago Alfred Marshall argued against Booth's projected universal pensions – and by implication against most other social services – with these words:

They do not contain in themselves the seeds of their own

disappearance. I am afraid that, if started, they would tend to become perpetual. I regard all this problem of poverty as a mere passing evil in the progress of man upwards; and I should not like any institution started which did not contain in itself the causes which would make it shrivel up, as the causes of poverty itself shrivelled up.

The causes of poverty *are* at last shrivelling up. We are near to the point, anticipated even earlier by Marshall, when, 'by occupation at least, every man is a gentleman'. But we expect neither our social services nor the State itself to wither away. Though we have grown beyond Marshall's wisdom, yet our younger generation is the first in history with the capacity to shape its life by his Victorian ideal of a maturing into responsible citizenship through the discipline of self-reliance. That ideal is not so outmoded nor so peripheral to responsible freedom that it ought not to receive more weight in future social policy. Is it not time that we aimed quite firmly at de-proletarianizing the working-class way of life, by progressive removal from it of what remains of insecurity and hand-to-mouth living and all the habits that go with them? Given this aim of greater self-reliance, and if simultaneously the communal sector is to be enlarged (as I have argued), then we shall want to concentrate communal endeavour more on services and environmental improvements than on transfers of money income.

Transfers will have to be extended in any event, chiefly because we will not indefinitely tolerate the submerged status of our largest remaining impoverished class – the old. During the next generation 'property-owning democracy' will not mean much more for most people than the accumulation of wealth in the form of contractual rights to income in retirement. Even this process, and the self-reliance needed to sustain it, will not advance with requisite speed and order unless they are fostered by State action. We shall have to deny men the right to spend all they earn during their working years. Part of their earnings will have to be deferred and pooled to yield retirement pensions, which will be maintained in real value by reference to changes in prices and current earnings. This system, though State-organized, should not be State-monopolized. Variety of provision and habits of long-term budgeting and saving will be better secured by an orderly blending of private with State arrangements. With this must be coupled some public control, more effective than that of the Treasury, over the chaotically developing system of 'fringe benefits' (to which employment pensions belong), whereby employers are arrogating the power of redistributing men's earnings in order to finance private, and largely tax-free, social services.

With this main exception, I hope the emphasis in social policy will shift away from transfer payments. We are still only tinkering with the vast housing and planning problems forced on us by rising standards, demographic trends, and the survival of the squalid industrial districts we built in our Early Steam Age towns. For the first time since the industrial revolution we are so placed that we can build dwellings, not chiefly to enlarge our stock, but to scrap and replace the millions of outworn structures which disgrace our civilization. For the first time, too, the dwellings we do need to add to our stock are mainly required for the old and others without growing children. And for the first time the private landlord, denied through mistrust in the twentieth century a chance to prove the virtue he failed to display in the nineteenth, has at last been given his freedom. He is using it to give up landlordism for good. Within ten years we shall urgently need new forms of housing tenure combining the advantages, but not the drawbacks, of the owner-occupation and the council tenantry between which we are becoming increasingly divided. None of these problems, in particular that of urban renewal, will be solved in a civilized manner without wide extensions of public enterprise.

In education, medical care and the welfare services there are also great challenges. Is a 'classless' standard of social service possible in a 'class-divided' society? Social policy cherishes and strengthens the family and also enlarges personal freedom and responsible choice. Can it then deny increasingly affluent citizens the right to buy the education or medical care they think best for their children or themselves? If it respects their freedom of choosing and spending, on what terms can it expect that all classes will prefer to use the public social services? In theory we look to education to lay the foundations of citizenship through the mutual understanding derived from a shared culture. In practice we proclaim our belief that this aim is incompatible with that widening of opportunities for social promotion which every ambitious parent wants for his child. We prefer a system which demotes some as steadily as it promotes others, segregating children educationally by social class and sex, and by abilities and aptitudes uncertainly assessed before puberty. Will 'parity of esteem' ever be attainable if our educational system comes to be seen as foredooming large numbers of children to a sense of failure?

The free market is the finest engine yet devised for attuning the supply of goods and services to the wants of citizens. In a free society, the less unequal the purchasing power of consumers the more satisfied we are with the market's services. One of the conditions for keeping purchasing power disparities within bounds, however, is the maintenance of a growing sector of services not commercially operated. We do not want the operations of social services to be governed by the purchasing power of individual users. But we should be insisting very strongly on alternative ways of obliging these services to attend to users' wants, feelings and expectations. In part, we have been bemused by the belief that experts have some simple magic enabling them to know just what education or medical care are best suited to each child's or patient's needs. Even were such needs readily ascertainable by reference to ability, aptitude or clinical state, education is more than cultivation of abilities and aptitudes, medical care more than treatment of clinical states. In part, also, the widespread neglect of consumer research by the social services – research going beyond needs into preferences and attitudes – reflects the 'lower-class' traditions the services have not fully outgrown. In the case of medical care, the shift from the private to the public sector is so recent that we are only just initiating the study of medical economics. Yet we need more – a sociology and social psychology of medical care institutions, of relations between doctors and other health workers and between all of them and patients, and of the formation of patients' own attitudes to ill health and its management. And since, for technical, social and moral reasons, medicine will never move back into the private sector, we need also a sociology of the medical profession itself to establish (among much else) the essentials of professional freedom in an unprecedented situation.

The Welfare State: An Historical Approach

J. Saville

Reprinted with permission from 'The Welfare State: An Historical Approach', *New Reasoner*, 3, Winter 1957-8, pp. 5, 6, 11, 12-17, 20-24

This conviction that the Welfare State is, if not a halfway, then a part-way house to socialism, and that the same road will lead to socialism, is based upon three main premises:

(1) that the managerial revolution, among other things, has resulted in the owners of capital no longer having a decisive influence over business decisions, and in their political power being much weakened;

(2) that the techniques of full employment are of such a character, and are so well understood, that prolonged mass unemployment is not likcly to reappear; and the Labour movement is now so strong that in this, as in other matters, there is no likelihood of the clock being put back;

(3) that the growth of the Welfare State – and in particular the levelling up of incomes and the extension of social services have largely abolished primary poverty.

Given these circumstances, the Labour movement must continue to push hard for social reform and for further economic changes; and on past evidence there is no reason to believe that the political problems, against the background of a more mature and greatly strengthened working-class movement, will in any way prove insuperable.

The arguments developed in the present essay are concerned to deny certain of these propositions. The Welfare State, it will be suggested, has come about as a result of the interaction of three main factors: (1) the struggle of the working class against their exploitation; (2) the requirements of industrial capitalism (a convenient abstraction) for a more efficient environment in which to operate and in particular the need for a highly productive labour force; (3) recognition by the property owners of the price that has to be paid for political security. In the last analysis, as the Labour movement has always recognized, the pace and tempo of social reform have been determined by the struggle of working-class groups and organizations; but it would be historically incorrect and politically an error to underestimate the importance of either of the other factors in the situation. To do so would be to accept the illusion that the changes are of greater significance than in fact they are, as well as to misread the essential character of contemporary capitalism.

The political problems associated with social reform became immensely complicated with the rise of the modern Labour movement. The intelligent bourgeois – Mrs Webb's 'great employer' – was confronted with a complete programme of radical reform put forward in the name of those who were now the majority of the electorate. In the 1860s the demands of the politically articulate sections of the working class were largely those which the rare enlightened entrepreneur or the liberal humanitarian were already advocating but within two or three decades large parts of the working-class programme had become specifically socialist, and on paper at least went beyond the boundaries of existing society. The new political problem for the propertied classes was a two-fold one: on the one hand to accept those economic and social demands which made no serious inroad into property rights (an acceptance which always involved conflict with the simple-minded traditional conservatives who always fail to appreciate the new territory they are moving through) and on the other, to recognize those claims which, implicitly or explicitly, were concerned with fundamentals and which must either be side-stepped or smothered. As Cardinal Manning so nicely put the problem, in 1888, in a letter to his friend J. E. C. Bodley: 'If the Landlords, Householders and Capitalists will "engineer a slope" we may avert disastrous collisions. If they will not, I am afraid you will see a rough time.'

The question of timing was, and is, crucial; for what may be a major victory for the working class at one point in time and which may well lead to significant changes in the internal balance of political forces in the country, is not necessarily of the same importance when it has been long delayed. From the standpoint of property, delay must always be supported: for delay gives opportunity for the vested interests to mobilize themselves, and on the other side it has often a marked centrifugal effect upon the forces of reform, who can rarely agree about the relationship of short-term with long-term aims. Coal nationalization is an excellent case in point. The first serious demand for coal nationalization came in 1919, a year when the desire for change was immensely strong among large sections of the people. Of all the years in the twentieth century, not excluding 1926, 1919 had probably the greatest potential for radical reform. The 'passion of Labour' to remake the world was echoed by many outside the movement. The Labour Party's new programme 'Labour and the New Social Order', adopted in the middle of 1918, called for the common ownership of land, the railways, coal, electric power and among other industries 'the manufacture and retailing of alcoholic drink'. The opening months of 1919 were a time when a political explosion seemed inevitable. There were mutinies in the Army by soldiers who wanted quicker demobilization; Clydeside saw the 40-hour week strike (Jan. 27-Feb. 11); there was the threat of a national coal strike backed by the other members of the Triple Alliance (railway men and transport workers). Among large sections of the people there was not only an immense war weariness but a widespread rejection of the old order; and it was to be expected that politicians and publicists alike, following this mood, would go on record for change. So we find Winston Churchill, during his election campaign in Dundee in December 1918, advocating railway nationalization; and J. L. Garvin, editor of the *Observer*, noting that nationalization of coal, electricity and transport was 'inevitable'. But the situation never seriously got out of hand, for the leadership of the Labour Party and the trade unions were easily fooled, and in Lloyd George the ruling class had a politician of genius. Lloyd George played for time – the Sankey Coal Commission and the National Industrial Conference were his principal instruments, and by a judicious mixture of lies, half-truths, evasion and deceit Lloyd George saw the year through to tame conclusions. A combination of an extension of social insurance in 1919 with the beginning of mass unemployment in the spring of 1920 completed his efforts on behalf of the propertied classes. But had coal nationalization been achieved in 1919 the political consequences would have been immense, for among other things it would have meant that Lloyd George's major aim would have been defeated and the position of Labour would have been tremendously strengthened. In the event, coal nationalization, the pivot of the whole situation in the years immediately after 1918, was delayed for over two decades; and when it came it was a matter of the State taking over a bankrupt industry from the incompetent mine owners who could congratulate themselves only on the compensation they successfully extorted from the Labour Government. As a political act coal nationalization in 1945 was of minor significance.

The British political situation has always contained certain special and difficult features that have demanded much subtlety of manoeuvre on the part of the bourgeois politicians. Compared with America, Britain was a closed and less dynamic economy with vertical movement for the working class severely restricted and with emigration as the main avenue of escape; while compared with France, Britain was overwhelmingly proletarian. It was this fact of a predominantly working-class society that occasioned Lloyd George's famous comment, quoted by Lenin in *Left Wing Communism* (Lenin dedicating his pamphlet 'to the Right Honourable Mr Lloyd George as a token of my gratitude for his speech of March 18, 1920, which was almost Marxist and, in any case, exceedingly useful for Communists and Bolsheviks throughout the world'). The passage quoted by Lenin reads:

> If you go to the agricultural areas I agree that you have the old party divisions as strong as ever: they are far removed from the danger [of Socialism]. It does not walk in their lanes. But when they see it, they will be as strong as some of these industrial constituencies now are. Four-fifths of this country is industrial and commercial; hardly one-fifth is agricultural. It is one of the things I have constantly in mind when I think of the dangers of the future here. In France the population is agricultural, and you have a solid body of opinions which does not move very rapidly, and which is not very easily excited by revolutionary movements. That is not the case here. This country is more top heavy than any country in the world, and if it begins to rock, the crash here, for that reason, will be greater than in any land.

It was not numbers only – although the working-class majority in the nation certainly worried the Victorians – but political cohesiveness that presented the dangers. The working class had been kept outside the civic pale for two decades after 1848 – one of the payments made in return for the hysteria that Chartism generated. Despite the absence of political democracy after 1850 there took place the great development of skilled trade unionism and a growing political sense of unity and solidarity among the working people. It was these developments that produced the widespread anxiety over 'the leap in the dark' when the vote was given for the first time to sections of the urban workers in 1867. In many towns this made the working-class the majority of the voters, and the many correctives and brakes upon full democracy are an indication of the fears that were aroused. Universal suffrage was introduced only by stages, and it was not until 1884 that most of the miners and the agricultural labourers received the vote. Even then many workers remained outside the franchise. But delaying tactics of this kind (in addition to plural voting for property owners and the many tiresome difficulties put in the way of the working-class voter recording his vote) could work effectively only for a few decades; and in the long run, given the working-class majority among the electorate, both Tories and Liberals were forced to adapt themselves to the political demands of this new audience. Both parties made careful and sustained appeals; but while the Tories, with their record on factory legislation and their anti-bourgeois bias, were never without working-class support in the towns, and for different reasons in the countryside, most workers attached themselves to the Liberal Party and the politically conscious among them became part of its left wing. To lead the left wing in the 1870s and 1880s were a group of Radical leaders – Bradlaugh, Dilke and Chamberlain – whose historical role was to delay for several decades the emergence of an independent Labour Party representing the industrial workers. Given the facts of British society, an independent workers party was historically inevitable; but compared with similar situations elsewhere – Germany for example – the development of an independent working-class political force was extraordinarily slow; and among the reasons for the long period of gestation was the vigour and the liveliness, as well as the personal courage and ability, of the Radical leaders. The crux of the Radical position – and it states the central assumptions of the Welfare State of the twentieth century – was summed up in a famous phrase which Joseph Chamberlain used in 1885. His speech on this occasion marked the opening of the campaign for the Unauthorized programme, an early blue-print of the Welfare State of today. 'I ask', said Chamberlain, 'what ransom will property pay for the security which it enjoys?'

Now ransom, as Chamberlain's biographer sorrowfully noted, is an 'ugly' word. It went, explained Garvin, far beyond Chamberlain's real intention which was only that 'private property must pay to be tolerated'. Chamberlain himself immediately recognized his error, and anxious to correct what he appreciated was a serious mistake, substituted for ransom in all his later speeches, the less explosive word 'insurance'. This, said Garvin, was what he was henceforth to 'speak and think'. The programme that Chamberlain was explaining to his audiences, and which because of his use of such an ungentlemanly word as ransom was to appear much more radical than in fact it was, has provided the framework within which the modern Welfare State has been built. Chamberlain and his colleagues recognized that State intervention was developing at an accelerated rate, and it was further accepted that much of the intervention must be on behalf of labour against the predatory claims of capital. The division between classes was too great for the political health of society; and new positions must be built as a result of which confidence between employers and workers could grow. Not, of course, that Chamberlain in any way accepted the idea of displacing private enterprise; his concern was always, wrote Garvin, 'to supplement it [private enterprise] powerfully where it was no longer adequate for social justice and national needs'. As the last phrase shows, Chamberlain was fully aware of the relationship between welfare and economic efficiency, although his primary concern was with political stability.

Chamberlain pioneered within the old established parties and those who followed him did no more than enlarge upon the foundations he had laid. Among these the Fabians are by far the most important, and in many fields of social policy it was the Fabians, directed by the Webbs, who provided the detailed blue-prints for the legislation of the twentieth century. Believing in the inevitability of gradualness, the Fabians emphasized the ways in which collectivist practices and legislation had been increasing steadily throughout the second half of the nineteenth century; and how what we have come to call the Welfare State developed naturally and inevitably, despite intensive political opposition, out of the individualism of the early years of Victorian England. As Sidney Webb wrote in 1889:

> The 'practical man', oblivious or contemptuous of any theory of the Social Organism or general principles of social organization, has been forced by the necessities of the time, into an ever deepening collectivist channel. Socialism, of course, he still rejects and despises. The individualist Town Councillor will walk along the municipal pavement, lit by municipal gas and cleansed by municipal brooms with municipal water, and seeing by the municipal clock in the municipal market that he is too early to meet his children coming from the municipal school hard by the county lunatic asylum and municipal hospital, will use the national telegraph system to tell them not to walk through the municipal park but to come by the municipal tramway, to meet him in the municipal reading room by the municipal art gallery, museum and library, where he intends to consult some of the national publications in order to prepare his next speech in the municipal town hall, in favour of the nationalization of the canals and the increase of the government control over the railway system. 'Socialism, sir', he will say, 'don't waste the time of a practical man by your fantastic absurdities. Self-help sir, individual self-help, that's what's made our city what it is.'

Like the Benthamites, their predecessors, the Fabians were primarily concerned with efficiency and social justice; like Chamberlain, they sought to influence the traditional parties. In practical terms what they have done is vastly to enlarge the meaning of 'supplement' to private enterprise; and the twentieth century has witnessed a most striking growth of State intervention. It is this change in the role of the State that has confused so many as to the essential characteristics of contemporary society; but what has not changed is that State intervention still 'supplements' private enterprise, in Chamberlain's meaning of the terms. After more than half a century of overt socialist thought and agitation and majority Labour Governments the fundamental structure of society remains unaltered.

As the quotation from Sidney Webb indicated, the growth of municipal and State enterprise in social and economic affairs had already proceeded a long way by the end of the nineteenth century. Sidney Webb's list of collectivist measures is by no means complete; and among those omitted were factory legislation and the establishment of a factory inspectorate, the elementary beginnings of a housing policy, and the introduction of workmen's compensation. This last achievement began an important new stage in the relationships between capital and labour and represents one of the pillars of the Welfare State.

In the twentieth century the legislative structure of the Welfare State, erected upon Radical-Fabian foundations, was carried through in three main periods of social reform. These were:

(1) The Liberal Governments of 1906-1914; and among the major social reforms of the successive Liberal Governments may be noted the following:

1906 meals for necessitous school children

1907 medical inspection of school children

1908 the first Old Age Pensions

1909 the first Trade Boards Act and the establishment of a minimum wage in selected industries

1911 the beginnings of national health and unemployment insurance.

(2) The second main period of reform, not as spectacular or as concentrated in time as that of the Liberal Governments after 1906, was the years of the First World War and the inter-war years. The pace of change was uneven and slower, but the Conservative administrations – the minority Labour Governments, in this as in all other matters, making a poor showing – continued to extend social security benefits. Among the reforms of this second period, the most important were the 1918 Maternity and Child Welfare Act; the 1919 Housing and Town Planning Act (which introduced subsidies on a considerable scale and took the Government into the business of housing); the 1920 Unemployment Insurance Act, which brought nearly all workers earning below £250 a year into the scheme; the 1926 Hadow report on education and the slow improvement in educational structure and organization in the years which followed; the 1927 Widows, Orphans and Old Age Contributory Pensions Act; and the 1934 Unemployment Act.

(3) The Labour Government, 1945-1950. In general this short period after the Second World War may be compared with that of the Liberal Government after 1906, although in terms of

social policy the Labour Government showed much less originality and initiative and were more in the stream of tradition than were the Liberals before 1914. Hence the relative ease with which social legislation was passed after 1945, largely because the proposals represented a minimum which the Tories had already accepted in principle. The main contribution of these years was to make an extended range of social security benefits available to the whole population. Among these were the raising of the school leaving age, a comprehensive health service, retirement pensions and family allowances. It was a modest programme, and a couple of decades overdue by the standards of the previous half century and its achievement was followed by a partial retreat in 1950 with the imposition of charges for certain health services.

This growth in social security benefits in the twentieth century has involved an increase in expenditure per head of population of about twelve times between 1900 and 1950 (allowing for changes in the value of money). But the starting point was from a very low level, and for an economy as industrially advanced and as economically wealthy as that of Britain, the pace of change has been surprisingly slow. It is the success of the determined opposition to reform that merits attention – not the social legislation that has been achieved. The range and distribution of social security in Britain represents no more than elementary social justice for the mass of the people; and from the side of industry it can be reckoned as a sound economic investment. The struggle for any particular reform has always in this country aroused so much opposition that when it is achieved it is at least understandable that those who have spent half a lifetime on its behalf too easily believe that with its enactment a new period in social history is beginning. Members of Parliament in particular are cautious individuals (if not by temperament and training then certainly by adaptation to the Parliamentary scene) and they are especially liable to emphasize the difficulties of legislative change. When it comes, its results are usually exaggerated and its significance grossly over-estimated.

A main reason why public opinion in general, and the Labour movement in particular, have become confused as to the essentially bourgeois nature of the Welfare State is that both in the propaganda of the Labour Party and in the criticisms of its opponents, the legislation of the 1945 Labour Government was labelled 'socialist'. The melancholy business of making a collection of the idiotic and wildly unrealistic statements of Labour's intellectual leaders concerning the 'social revolution' of the postwar years must be left to others; but it must be noted that given the attribution of 'socialist' to the measures of nationalization and 'free' social security benefits, even the rank and file of the Labour movement began to believe this propaganda which came as much from those who purport to be its friends as from its enemies. With most of the Labour 'New Thinkers' the changes in the last twenty years have been elevated to a radical transformation in the character of society. Mr Crosland, one of the more articulate of the Labour Party's economists, has argued that with the legislative achievements of the 1945 Government we have all been involved in 'a major historical change'. This revolution, it is no less, Mr Crosland used to call 'statism' (although he has since discarded the term).

> With its arrival, the most characteristic features of capitalism have all disappeared: the absolute rule of private property, the subjection of the whole of economic life to market influences, the domination of the profit motive, the neutrality of government, the typical *laissez faire* division of income, the ideology of individual rights. This is no minor modification; it is a major historical change.

It should be remarked, first of all, that nowhere, except in the more remote parts of Scandinavia and among Labour publicists in Britain, is this sort of viewpoint seriously argued. As for the claim that the Welfare State is an early form of a socialist society, it must be emphasized that both in Western Europe and the United States social security schemes are placed firmly within the framework of a free enterprise economy and no one suggests that what is a natural development within a mature capitalist economy should be given new names. In Britain the socialists before 1914 did not make this mistake, and it is worthwhile to look again at the discussions in which they considered the relationship between social reform and socialism.

The general proposition that most socialists accepted before 1914 was that the State, from the proceeds of a progressive system of taxation, should pay for social reform. When, in 1911, Lloyd

George introduced the principle of compulsory contributions into the new insurance schemes, the left wing socialists Lansbury, Snowden, Keir Hardie and a few others went into vigorous opposition, with MacDonald and the majority of the Labour Party supporting Lloyd George. In the Commons George Lansbury and Snowden were the most vehement opponents of the new measures (Lloyd George much annoying the Tories by taunting them that 'Lansbury had taken the position of leader of the Opposition'). Their main arguments can be summed up as follows:

(1) that social reform must at all times be paid for by those best able to bear the burden and not by those whose economic and social condition the reform was intended to benefit;

(2) that the principle of compulsory contribution not only placed at least a part of the financial burden upon the poor but by avoiding the necessity of having to raise the whole financial amount by taxation it thereby side-stepped the political problem involved in a drastic redistribution of wealth;

(3) that it was a retrograde measure. As Snowden said in the House of Commons, 6 July, 1911; '. . . the principle of State financial responsibility is embodied in nearly all recent legislation – in the Workmen's Compensation Act, in Public Health Acts and even in the Old Age Pensions legislation.'

Fortunately for Mr Crossman these arguments have for the most part been forgotten by the Labour movement; and the latest Labour Party proposals are based firmly upon the contributory principle which Mr Crossman, following Beveridge, has elevated into a virtue. The increasing acceptance of the principle by successive Governments in the twentieth century has meant that the social services have developed in such a way that the financial burden upon the rich has been very largely cushioned. Even more striking however – and it is a matter on which there has been virtually no hostile comment from Labour theoreticians – is the growth of direct and indirect taxation upon working-class incomes to the point where much of the expenditure upon social services is no more than a transfer of income by taxation within the working class. Or, to put the matter more simply, to a very considerable extent the working class pay for their own social security benefits by compulsory contributions and a high level of indirect taxation.

One study of this problem was made by an American scholar,

Findley Weaver, in *The Review of Economics and Statistics* (August 1950). His main conclusions are given below, and they deserve to be widely known. His study relates to the years 1948 and 1949.

> The outstanding feature of the post-war growth in redistribution is not that of taking from the 'classes', and giving to the 'masses'. The main feature is that the benefits of redistribution cut across income groups and are largely related to consumption. As a general proposition, the working class pays enough additional in beer, tobacco, and purchase taxes, and other indirect levies to meet the increased cost of the food subsidies and health and education expenditures, while the increase in the direct taxes they pay covers the rise in their transfer money receipts.
> . . . Most of the post-war increase in personal taxes has been levied indirectly on consumption and has fallen on those who smoke and drink or consume non-utility clothing and household goods. The incidence of these regressive taxes is mainly on the working class who are also the chief recipients of the benefits of redistributive governmental expenditures. Generally, the low income group pays for its benefits, the redistribution being within the group based largely on considerations as to the most socially desirable forms of consumption.

All this has a good deal of bearing upon the much disputed matter of the levelling up of incomes in the years since 1940; and while this question must be left to another occasion for a detailed analysis, there are some points that can be made here. There is, in the first place, no doubt that there has been some levelling up of incomes in favour of the working class. The figures are widely known and have been used by Labour commentators such as Mr Strachey and Mr Crosland to indicate the magnitude of the social changes which they believe have taken place. There are three points to be made in this connection. The first is that at least part of the additional share of the national income accruing to the working class in the post-war years has been absorbed by higher indirect taxation to pay for the increased social services. Secondly, the major redistribution occurred during the war years; and since then, the official calculations show a slow but persistent trend towards greater inequality. This is, of course, what must always be expected of capitalism, for it continuously generates inequality. Thirdly, the official calculations of income distribution, the basis for many sweeping generalizations made by those who are convinced they have been living through major historical changes in Britain since 1945, omit three factors whose individual and collective effect is to increase sharply the inequality of incomes. These are (1) capital gains, (2) expense allowances, and (3) tax evasion; and only the politically innocent really believe that the official figures of taxable income for the upper income brackets represent the true position.

Concerning the distribution of property in the country there is no dispute. The Welfare State, with its higher death duties and its supposedly crippling and burdensome taxation upon the rich, has effected practically no change in the distribution of private capital.

The Welfare State is the twentieth-century version of the Victorian ideal of self-help; and since this involves, in addition to benefits, high taxation on alcohol and tobacco, it must be said that these aspects of the Welfare State, taken by themselves, cannot be objected to by socialists. The State now 'saves' for the working class and translates the savings into social services. As the *Economist* remarked in 1950 of the social services: 'It is still true that nobody – or practically nobody – gets anything for nothing.' Since the Welfare State in Britain developed within a mature capitalist society, with a ruling class long experienced and much skilled in the handling of public affairs, its growth and development has been slow and controlled; and the central interests of private property have never seriously been challenged. Britain remains a society in which the distribution of capital wealth is no more equal than it was half a century ago; and although income distribution has proved more amenable to political pressure from the Labour movement, there exists within any capitalist society strong and powerful tendencies offsetting egalitarian measures.

Further Reading:
Background to Social Welfare

W. D. BIRRELL, and others (Eds.), *Social Administration, Readings in Applied Social Science*, Penguin Books, 1973.

A. H. HALSEY (Ed.), *Trends in British Society since 1900*, Macmillan, 1972.

T. H. MARSHALL, *Social Policy*, Hutchinson, 3rd edition, 1969.

G. MYRDAL, *Beyond the Welfare State*, Duckworth, 1960.

D. WEDDERBURN, 'Facts and Theories of the Welfare State', in R. Miliband and J. Saville (Eds.), *The Socialist Register*, Merlin Press, 1965.

H. WILENSKY and C. LEBEAUX, *Industrial Society and Social Welfare*, The Free Press, 1965.

Chapter Two

The Deprived: Groups in Need

The word 'need' frequently occurs in social welfare. The *Seebohm Report* stated that the 'personal social services are large scale experiments in ways of helping those in need'. But what is meant by need? First, it is employed to indicate a basic requirement for physical survival. Thus any person *needs* a minimum amount of food, drink and shelter in order to live at all. Second, it describes the necessary minimums to attain certain standards or modes of life. A person may have enough food to prevent death but in our society it would be agreed that also he *needs* certain provisions of income, housing, education and health in order to reach the lowest levels considered essential for normal living. It follows that need is both social and relative. It is social in being defined, according to standards of communal life, relative in that its meaning will vary from age to age and from society to society.

In a broad way the State or organized society as a whole functions to meet needs. Its industries provide food, consumer goods and financial incomes for its members. Its education and health services may be regarded as existing not just for the poorest sections but as a means of developing the skilled and manual talents of all persons in order to meet the demand of industry for labour. None the less, some social services do apply only to minorities of the population. In this connection, Slack, in a book recommended at the end of this chapter, distinguishes between:

(1) services for needs related to dependencies arising from normal stages of human life common to everyone – childbirth, infancy, childhood, preparation for adulthood and old age: and
(2) those to help minorities who suffer the 'misfortune' of poverty, unemployment, homelessness, disability, etc.

This chapter is concerned mainly with (2), the needs of certain groups who can be distinguished from the population at large.

Who or what determines that some people have unmet needs of such importance that they should be categorized as a group requiring special help from the social services? After all, tropical fish enthusiasts are an identifiable entity with extra expenditures not met by most people. Why should their needs not be regarded as requiring extra help? The answer is that society does not consider the ownership of tropical fish as necessary to an acceptable mode of living. But what is 'society', who determines what is 'need'? Bradshaw has identified four ways through which need is defined and accepted.

(1) *Normative Need* Social scientists, government officials or other 'experts' frequently fix need within a particular definition and decide that anyone outside is 'in need'. An example of this normative process is found in the Housing Act (1957) which contained a formula for calculating numbers in overcrowded conditions (according to numbers of persons, habitable rooms and floor space). Many experts, however, have adopted a more simple calculation which reveals the numbers of persons per room. Those in households with an average of over $1\frac{1}{2}$ persons per room are classed as being in housing need.

(2) *Felt Need* Felt need concerns what people say they want when asked. For instance, surveys have asked the elderly if they want home helps or meals on wheels. Their replies may indicate a need for these services quite different from that as determined by outside officials.

(3) *Expressed Need* When a felt need is translated into a demand or active request it becomes an expressed need. Thus pressure group organizations of the elderly publicly demand that their needs for higher pensions be met.

(4) *Comparative Need* The resources available to certain groups or geographical areas can be assessed and compared. Those falling far behind the others can be deemed as in need by comparison.

The operation, either alone or in combination, of these

determinants of need, in interaction with the prevailing standards of living, leads to the recognition of certain groupings as being in need. Amongst those upon whom attention has been focused in recent years are the homeless, the physically handicapped, the poor, and single parent families. However, the mere recognition of their needs does not mean that action is taken to meet them. It can be argued that their continued existence serves particular functions in our society. The marking out of 'the poor' may be interpreted as a warning to others of their fate if they do not uphold the prevailing work ethic. Further, the identification of the poor may be necessary in order to emphasize the advantages of the privileged. Again, it may be deemed wise not to meet the financial needs of unmarried mothers on the premise that the availability of help would encourage others to have illegitimate children. Implicit in such arguments is the belief that those in need are responsible for their condition and hence undeserving of aid. But even the disappearance of these attitudes would not ensure that services were provided. Groups in need require scarce resources and hence must compete with the demands of others. Those representatives and officials involved in the political processes which allocate resources may be sympathetic yet decide that higher priority must go to the demands of road building, arms manufacture and industrial investment.

The categorization of persons into need groupings is, then, a two-edged sword. It can mean that they become the target for public condemnation, the very identification of their need setting them apart from other people. For this reason, some social scientists prefer to identify geographical areas of need rather than groups in need. On the other hand, it does enable social policy to be directed towards those groups so identified. Further, the very realization that there are others in like circumstances may encourage those in need to act together. Jordan, in a recommended book, claims that the receipt of Supplementary Benefit and Family Income Supplement creates a 'new claiming class' and predicts that their joint action will lead to social change.

Before focusing attention on particular groups, it is worth noting that the very term 'groups in need' is disliked by some commentators. The disapproval appears to spring from the belief that it implies that those in need are to be studied in isolation from the rest of society and that it conveys condemnation or blame. More recently the expression, 'the socially deprived' has gained popularity, with social deprivation being regarded as a condition causing hardship by comparison with the rest of the population so that sections of society are moved to alleviate it. The term is taken to mean that the poor, homeless, single-parent families, etc. are deprived by others and so are to be regarded as victims not initiators. No doubt, in time any term takes on connotations not originally intended and in this volume 'the deprived' and 'groups in need' will be used inter-changeably.

Groups in need are illustrated in this chapter by five readings. The poor and homeless are groupings whose plight has been discussed for years. The needs of motherless families and immigrants, on the other hand, although no doubt in existence for generations, are only now finding forceful expression. The final selection concerns socially deprived areas for need and encompasses geographical locations as well as groupings of similar types.

Each reading attempts to establish that a particular need is widespread and should be alleviated. In the light of the discussion of the determinants of need, it is of interest to note the approaches adopted in the readings. **Fairhall** and **Field** both initially use the lowest level of Supplementary Benefit as the poverty line. The basic weekly rates of Supplementary Benefit are subject to periodic reviews. In July 1974, they were £8·40 for a single householder and £13·65 for a married couple. Payments are also made for dependent children and a 'reasonable' amount for rent and rates. Anyone below it is considered in need of an adequate financial income. These authors are employing a normative definition of poverty, the one accepted by the Government and many social scientists. Using it, the numbers in need would appear surprisingly high. The Department of Health and Social Security reported that in November 1971 2,909,000 people were dependent upon Supplementary Benefit. However, these figures do not show the numbers receiving less than the Supplementary Benefit minimum. Nicholas Bosanquet, the economist, estimated in

1972 that two million persons were in that position. These included full-time workers with low earnings, persons who refused to claim Supplementary Benefit, and those in receipt of it but whose entitlement had been reduced below the basic rates (as happened, for instance, to claimants whose previous earnings were less than what they would have received from Social Security). The normative definition does make for an easy calculation of numbers in financial need. However, it is not necessarily a valid measure of poverty and it is noteworthy that in his contribution Frank Field, the Director of Child Poverty Action Group, proceeds to argue that an acceptable standard of life is not possible on the Supplementary Benefit scales, let alone below it. He explains that recipients are supposed to purchase normal clothing replacements from their weekly income. However, he then cites case studies which indicate that this amount does not allow the purchase of requirements which the Supplementary Benefits Commission itself lists as a general guide. Field's arguments have now been strengthened by Evason's study (recommended at the end of this chapter) in Belfast of three household types: those with incomes below Supplementary Benefit rates (official poverty): those on or just above it (called 100 per cent): and those 40 per cent above it. She found that not only did the official poor experience recurrent financial crises, debts and material and nutritional hardships, but similar problems were met by young families at the 100 per cent level. She concluded that 'if we want a poverty line above which there is freedom from the crudest choices in expenditure and the constant crises noted, then for a two-parent household with three or less young children, we should think in terms of a poverty line of 120 per cent. For larger households, the 140 per cent level appears just adequate to meet their needs'. If such a successful challenge was made to the normative definition then obviously the numbers in official poverty would be increased. To the two million below the minimum rate would be added Bosanquet's estimate of four million on it and another four million just above it – a total which constitutes nearly a fifth of the population.

Wherever the poverty line is set, a number of research studies do allow the poor to be categorized into two main sections – those dependent upon Supplementary Benefit, and low-wage earners. Particularly vulnerable to the former are the elderly, fatherless families, the long-term unemployed, and the physically handicapped. But it must be added that many outside of these groupings are in or near poverty. Indeed, the number of low-wage earners is such as to suggest a spread across many kinds of persons. *The Department of Employment Gazette* (November 1972) revealed that in April 1972, out of a work force of 16·1 million, 100,000 adult men and 1·3 million women were earning less than £15 per week. The numbers rose to 600,000 and 2·9 million at £20 per week.

Turning to homelessness, the reading by **Morton** draws heavily on the research of Greve and Glastonbury. She points out that the normative or official definition of homelessness is of persons without a roof over their heads who are received into local authority temporary accommodation. The Department of Health and Social Security enumerated 25,969 such persons in England at the end of 1971. This concept of measurement has been heavily criticized. It does not say how many people are given homes but just how many are given shelter. Morton explains that local authorities tend to assist homeless families not childless couples or single persons. Moreover, others are turned away either because the authorities lack accommodation or because they are not considered homeless within the meaning of the National Assistance Act (1948). Since Morton wrote, matters have worsened, for the Local Government Act (1972) – which is effective from 1974 – reduces the local authorities' duty to help under the 1948 Act to a permissive power. Hence the numbers of persons received into local authority accommodation may fall although the numbers without homes may rise.

The voluntary society, Shelter, has campaigned for the meaning of homelessness to be broadened to embrace all persons in grossly unsatisfactory housing. This definition would raise the numbers of the homeless to around three million. As such, it may be considered a form of expressed need. For although not voiced by those actually in housing need, it is expressed by an organization widely regarded as speaking on their behalf.

Motherless families differ from the need groups discussed so far. Their deprivation refers not to a single want – of finance or housing – but to a cluster of needs which may result from the absence of a mother. The Plowden Report of 1967, *Children and their Primary Schools*, indicated that about 40,000 children of primary school age in England and Wales were with their fathers only. The 1966 sample census estimated that 174,510 children were in motherless families but these figures would include homes where the father co-habited with a woman not his wife. The actual number of all age children cared for by a father alone is probably between these two figures and as such constitutes a sizeable group.

Not all motherless families would regard themselves as having special needs. But **Wilding's** research did establish that motherlessness created a vulnerability to certain deprivations and that many of the fathers were prepared to articulate their needs. Wilding (and his colleague, George) have published findings which show over two-thirds of the fathers admitting that their situation caused them loneliness or depression. Many declared that their greatest need was for help with the care of their children and home.

Felt needs such as these spring from subjective involvement but, as they convey the actual experience of being in need, they merit the careful attention of social workers, officials and policy makers.

Immigration is an emotive subject which has loomed large in British political life in the 1960s and 1970s. Some articulate politicians have been little worried about the needs of coloured immigrants and much more concerned to stereotype them as a threat to the British way of life. Much argument, therefore, has centred on the numbers entering the country and on the very definition of 'coloured' and 'immigrant'. The official figures of the Registrar-General estimated that in 1971 out of a population of 53¾ million about 1½ million people in Britain were either born in or were the children of parents born in the New Commonwealth (taken to be all Commonwealth countries excluding Australasia and Canada). Coloured immigrants, predominantly from the West Indies, Pakistan and India, are very much a minority in Britain but, it would seem, very much concentrated in a few urban areas. Concern that the social, economic and material needs of immigrants were not

being met, caused the Runnymede Trust to commission a
West Indian, **Gus John,** to investigate Handsworth in
Birmingham, an area known to contain many West Indians.
Extracts from his report make up a further reading. In it, he is
at pains to point out that he did not attempt a scientific
research project but rather to present an impressionistic
account of what it is to be black in Britain. Noticeably, Gus
John accepts local residents' own definition of their needs, in
other words he talks about felt needs and his report
concentrates on the subjects which they deemed important.
He establishes that being black means a vulnerability to
deprivations not experienced by most people.

The reading by **Holman** on areas of social deprivation
employs the comparative need approach. It suggests that
certain districts compare badly, on a large number of indices of
need, with the country as a whole. The indices include
measures of deprivation – such as overcrowding, ill-health and
unemployment – combined with a lack of adequate services in
terms of few social workers, old schools, insufficient day
nurseries and so on. So far, studies have been able to argue
that specific localities, for instance, Notting Hill in London,
Soho in Birmingham, St Ann's in Nottingham, are
characterized by multiple deprivation. But they have not been
able to establish the total number of such localities in Britain.
All that can be said is that applications to the urban
programme (see Chapter 6) for special grants for socially
deprived areas have numbered not hundreds but thousands.

Whatever the measure used, all the authors argue that needs
are not being met and recommend further statutory
intervention. However, not everyone would accept their
recommendations. In other words, value differences are
involved. Values can be defined as desirable standards or
objectives and, clearly, two kinds are employed in the
readings. First, there are social values which the contributors
assume are accepted by society at large and yet which their
studies reveal to be transgressed. Thus Wilding believes that
prevailing child care standards are sometimes threatened
because of the difficulties faced by motherless families. Morton
contrasts the refusal to help the homeless with the general
belief that everyone should have shelter. John, in claiming

that unless reforms come a dangerous situation will arise amongst black youth, is appealing to the general desire for a peaceful and non-violent society. Second, they assert their own values. Field believes that supplementary benefit rates *should* be more generous. Wilding claims that it *should* be a social objective to provide the motherless with more resources. In short they are arguing that present ideas of what people need are fixed too low and that society should be prepared to meet higher levels.

THE LIFE OF THE DEPRIVED

The case for extra help for those in need is sometimes strengthened by making public the kind of sufferings they endure. The readings show that the persons concerned did not have just the single need which put them in a particular group but that this deprivation was frequently associated with others. Many of the motherless families lost not only a mother but also some of their income. In turn, one-parent families and those with low incomes were particularly vulnerable, as Glastonbury's research establishes, to homelessness. Then the combination of poor housing conditions and an inability to afford food of a high nutritional value led to illness and disease. Faced with not one but numerous deprivations, many in need found themselves in 'twilight zones'. Their lack of purchasing power meant that they had to accept those areas deemed least desirable by the rest of society.

The multiplicity of deprivations can lead to a second-class mode of life. Statistics may show the numbers in need but the case studies in the readings vividly describe the humiliating minutiae of their lives. Many families were dependent for clothing on jumble sales or cast-offs. The rapid increases in the price of food meant that many went short of fruit, meat and milk. Those with low incomes could put nothing aside for luxuries or special occasions. A major bill for the electricity or a pair of shoes could mean a crisis with a choice between paying it or the rent. A substantial number of the fathers of motherless families had to accept a fall in their standard of living, a curtailment of their social and even occupational lives and, in some cases, had to take almost any form of substitute care for their children. The homeless, as Morton reveals, could be shunted from one agency to another like unwanted Stateless persons shuttlecocking between hostile countries. Perhaps above all, life was second rate in that it lacked a vital element of normal living – some degree of choice in everyday decisions.

The inferior life became worse when the deprived felt they were being blamed for their condition. A consistent refrain from these and other studies was the humiliation felt in having to ask for help from unfriendly officials. The rejecting behaviour of officials must not be exaggerated, indeed, a half of the fathers in Wilding's study spoke favourably about their treatment at Social Security offices. But the condemnatory attitudes of some officials combined with public hostility towards those in long-term receipt of benefits could have adverse effects on those in need. The nature of these effects will be explored in the next chapter.

Of all aspects of the life of the deprived, the implications for children are the most likely to touch the public conscience. The absence of a mother adversely affected the mental and physical health of over 20 per cent of Wilding's sample. Children reared in deprived areas are more susceptible to disease, illness and death. There is a well established correlation between poor housing conditions and under-attainment at school. The West Indian children appeared particularly liable to depriving conditions which hindered their educational progress. Children from low-income families may have to forgo school treats, feel humiliated by the receipt of free school meals, wear clothes inferior to others. In brief, they may be treated in ways similar to their parents and be destined for the same kind of life. The readings reveal not only that the children did suffer but that their parents, far from acting irresponsibly, strove to protect them. Some women sought night jobs so that their children would not want financially. Others took their children to the doctors but would not pay prescription charges for themselves. The men in motherless families bore the roles of both spouses in order that their children would miss nothing. The overall impression is of parents attempting vainly to shield their offspring from overwhelming odds. If society tolerates groups in need then it also tolerates children in need.

PROPOSALS FOR CHANGE

The readings are but a selection of many studies which, in the last decade, have demonstrated that groups in social need are still a feature of society. The reasons for their continuance are being widely debated and it is worth noting the opinions found in the readings. Morton draws attention to Glastonbury's view that personality inadequacies are a major cause of some individuals becoming homeless. The other contributors, on the other hand, tend to seek explanations in the deficiencies of social policies and social services. Consequently, most of the proposals for change call for reforms in the objectives, manner and delivery systems of government policies and agency services. The CPAG, whose views are represented by Field, consistently argues for less emphasis on means-tested benefits and more on universal supports such as family allowances. Wilding, too, would diminish reliance on Supplementary Benefit by the introduction of a compulsory State insurance scheme to cover the event of motherlessness. John, in his book, advocates extensive reforms in housing allocation policies, in curricula geared to black children, and in increased provision of pre-school facilities. Holman calls for more resources to be directed towards socially deprived areas. In addition to these broad policy changes, the contributors also urge reform at the agency level. Officials should treat clients with more understanding and respect. Local authority departments are encouraged to provide more day care facilities, domiciliary helps and temporary accommodation.

The discovery of social need as identified by the readings would appear to constitute a good argument for the implementation of the proposed reforms. However, their case is part of a classic dilemma. Social justice, as perceived by these writers, should have a bias towards equality of treatment to be attained, if necessary, by statutory intervention. Yet many of the resources of our society are distributed not according to social need but to individuals' economic or social power. The question is thus shown to be one of values which themselves have strong connotations. It is a political choice whether a society values most a social system which attempts to give its members what they need or that which rewards them according to notions of their economic worth or their political power.

Survival on the Breadline

John Fairhall

Reprinted with permission from 'Survival on the Breadline',
Guardian, 26 July 1971

There are few things more insulting than talking about how the
poor live without knowing what you are talking about. It is a
field where theories will not serve, and feelings can be grossly
misleading. Public spirited politicians can be as far from reality as
saloon bar pundits. Only the facts will do.

Such facts are in short supply. Nothing available to the
Government gives an up-to-date and accurate picture of just how
a poor family survives economically, what it spends its money on,
how consumption patterns and diet change as prices rise and
social security benefits alter. By the time the Government has its
statisticians' reports, a new situation has arrived.

It was to fill this gap – a critical gap in a time of rising unemployment, Common Market negotiations, and above all last
April's cutting back of free milk and school meals, and the
increase of prescription, dental and optical charges – that the
Guardian and the Child Poverty Action Group collaborated to
report facts gathered in pilot research carried out by the Group.

The families selected were chosen at random in one locality.
All have at least three children – four families have four and two
five children. All have a household income which after allowing
for tax and employment expenses is no more than supplementary
benefit level. This is worked out at under £26 a week gross where
the husband is working and at under £28 a week where both
husband and wife work.

The lowest income was £15 a week and the average near £21.
Seven families were receiving some form of social security
benefit, including supplementary benefit, unemployment or
sickness pay.

Five families were in arrears with their rent, by amounts
ranging from £3 to £104. Seven families had no savings at all and
only one had more than £10. Members of two families had
resorted to stealing. There was little continuity of employment:

11 families had had a change in their employment situation during the previous year.

The 14 families spent on average 41 per cent of their income on food and a further 22 per cent on housing (all were in rented accommodation). These proportions are well above national averages, as Table 1 shows.

Table 1. Households with two adults and three or more children

		£10-£25 income only (UK)	Households in London Survey
	%	%	%
Housing	11	12	22
Food	31	36	41
Clothing	9	7	5
Heat and light	7	8	5
Household sundries	10	8	7
Miscellaneous (e.g. fares, pocket money, entertainment)	32	29	20

(Figures in the first two columns are taken from the 1969 Family Expenditure Survey.)

To attempt to work out the averages for the 14 families of expenditure on specific items would be pointless as miscellaneous expenditure makes up such a large proportion of the total. Three family budgets, each for the same week, are given in Table 2.

Family A is a deserted wife and her four children aged 4-11, receiving supplementary benefit. Family B is a single woman working full-time, with three children aged 5-13. Family C is a husband working full-time, with the wife working part-time, with three children aged 3-10.

Total spending on food for the three families for the week is: Family A £6.75; B £4.79; and C £9.39. The wives generally shopped around for bargains but when money was particularly short fruit and meat were the first to go from the shopping list. More than half said they never bought new clothes but relied on jumble sales or secondhand shops. Of those in arrears with their rent, the most frequent cause was having to buy shoes.

Ten of the families said they could not afford to pay the increased prescription, dental and optical charges introduced in April. Three mentioned that they now looked in the market for home cures rather than go to the doctor. Two said that when they received a prescription with several items, they got from the

chemist only the item that looked most important. One house-
wife bought secondhand spectacles from a market stall. The
average time since the last visit to a dentist was four years.

The Government's campaign to publicize the availability of
Welfare benefits had obviously had only limited success. Of
seven families already receiving social security benefits, six knew
they could be entitled to free prescriptions, dental and optical
treatment. But of the seven families not on social security, four
did not realize that such benefits were available. Six of this seven
thought the income for a family with three children had to be
below £14 a week in order to claim. (On the figures given to the
researcher at least three families were clearly entitled.)

Table 2

Amount spent on	Family A £	B £	C £	Amount spent on	A £	B £	C £
Rent	5.77	2.32	5.46	Soup	–	0.06	0.13
Light and heat	0.70	0.30	2.00	Meals out	–	–	1.65
Bread	0.65	0.20	0.42	Dinner money	–	–	1.20
Cakes/biscuits	0.12	–	0.51	Dog food	0.75	–	–
Cereal	0.32	–	0.09	Beer	–	0.63	1.25
Meat	1.20	1.08	1.60	Cigarettes, tobacco	1.82	0.13	1.80
Fish	–	0.12	–	Household cleaners	0.40	0.10	0.22
Butter, Margarine and Lard	0.32	0.25	0.11	Newspaper	0.24	0.10	0.10
Milk	1.08	0.70	0.82	Fares	0.05	1.40	1.20
Cheese	–	0.20	–	Launderette and cleaners	0.50	0.85	0.45
Eggs	0.10	–	0.36	Provident clothing	2.60	–	–
Potatoes	0.64	0.20	0.47	Hairdresser	–	–	1.00
Other veg.	0.40	0.46	0.32	Doorlocks and key	–	1.25	–
Fruit	0.24	0.71	0.29	Gifts for sister	–	1.20	–
Sugar	0.16	0.08	0.20	Postage stamps	–	0.09	–
Sweet money	1.30	0.73	0.80	Church collection	–	0.05	–
Tea	0.20	–	0.42	Toys	–	0.90	–
				Total Expenditure	19.56	14.11	22.87
				Total Income	19.30	15.90	22.30

All the 14 families knew that free school meals could be
claimed and nine families were receiving them. Three other
families appeared to be eligible but had not claimed.

The price increase had not changed the pattern of school meals.

At least three mothers were continuing to give their older children money to buy lunch time snacks, usually pie and mash.

The loss of the cheap milk tokens (worth 35p a week per child) had caused one mother with five children to reduce the amount of milk bought from three pints to one pint a day. She had applied for free milk but after five weeks had had no reply to her application.

A conservative estimate is that each child under 16 requires a pint of milk a day and each adult half a pint. By these standards the 14 families were on average getting $1\frac{1}{2}$ pints a day too little at home. None of the families bought extra milk during the holidays or at weekends.

With incomes under great pressure, the dearer school meals, which affected five families, and the loss of cheap milk, affecting three families, had caused considerable hardship.

The extra expense had made one mother take a night job. Another now bought a pair of tights once a month instead of weekly; this was her only spending on clothing. Other economies mentioned were reducing the weekend shopping and 'cutting down biscuit money for the kids'.

Nine families knew of rent rebates but only two were receiving rebates although another three were evidently eligible. Only three families out of the 14 knew of the rate rebate system and none were receiving any benefit. Despite Government publicity only one family had heard of the Family Income Supplement scheme. Two of the seven families with a working head appeared to be eligible. None had applied.

Nine families were getting school clothing allowances but only one knew of school maintenance allowances and then did not understand how the system worked.

Virginia Bottomley, the research worker who carried out the survey, describes the district where the families lived as 'a dismal area blighted by redevelopment. The more wealthy and manageable families had moved out, leaving behind in disproportionate density the elderly, large families, unsupported mothers and the disabled.'

People there know at first hand what poverty means. It was summed up by an unemployed head of one of the 14 families – a man who had applied for 20 jobs the previous week. 'Poverty is having to save up to buy your food.'

Skinflint Society

Frank Field

Reprinted with permission from Skinflint Society,
Guardian, 5 November 1971

People out of work, and with slender resources, have a right to
draw supplementary benefits. Social and community workers
report that these families have considerable difficulties in
managing on their weekly payments, and that it is often impossible to meet the cost of clothing or to find the money for gas and
electricity bills.

As well as providing a minimum standard of living, the Supplementary Benefits Commission issues a guide to its officers in
deciding what extra help families should have in meeting their
clothing needs. How well does this procedure of allowing exceptional needs grants operate? Do families obtain the help they
require?

To test the Commission's policy of awarding to each according
to his needs, nine families were asked to report on how they
manage to clothe themselves. The replies of seven of them are
given here.

What are claimants expected to buy from their supplementary
benefit? Does a weekly allowance cover only the bare necessities
(whatever they are) or is there a margin for 'a little of what you
fancy'?

The Supplementary Benefits Commission (SBC) maintains that
the replacement of clothing and footwear is 'a re-occurring and
continuing living expense which is provided for in the Supplementary Benefit scale rate'. The Commission will therefore award
an exceptional needs grant only in circumstances where claimants
can show that the expenditure could not be met from the weekly
scale rate, or from any disregarded income.

The 'Supplementary Benefits Handbook' gives an example of a
likely case for a discretionary grant. It is of a patient leaving
hospital after a long period of time who had not been drawing the
full-rate scale while in hospital.

The Commission's policy is clear. Claimants are supposed to

cover the replacement of clothing and bedding from their weekly payments. What is important, therefore, is whether claimants *can* provide from this source of income. Is it possible, for example, to purchase the stocks of clothing which are listed in B/O 40?

This form is meant for internal use in the SBC, but a copy was sent to the Child Poverty Action Group's offices. The Commission claims that it is merely 'an aid' to officers when deciding how they should operate their discretionary powers. 'It is quite definitely not intended to be . . . a minimum (or maximum) standard of clothing and bedding.'

Leaving aside the question of whether it defines minimum or maximum requirements, can families living on supplementary benefits maintain themselves around this standard? If they can from where do they obtain their supplies? If they cannot, we need to bring into question either the adequacy of the scale rates, or the functioning of discretion within the Supplementary Benefits system.

The first nine families who came into contact with CPAG's Citizens Rights Office during one week were asked if they would help to answer these questions and seven of them gave detailed replies. We cannot judge whether the families are representative of the 1·9 million people below pensionable age dependent on SB. There is too little information on them to match their representativeness or otherwise. But at the very least they do tell us how the system of 'individualized justice' has worked for seven families.

Mrs Bradshaw is divorced, bringing up four children on her own. Since her husband left her she had been dependent on the Supplementary Benefits Commission for her income. On checking Mrs Bradshaw's allowance, we found that not only was she receiving less than her minimum entitlement, but that during the four years on benefit she had received grants totalling only £7.65 – or under £2 a year. Her request for extra help had been met with the suggestion 'why don't you get off assistance and earn your money?'

Needless to say, the only jobs available would pay less than her weekly allowance, as well as adding to the worry a mother bringing up children alone has during school holidays, or when one of the children becomes ill.

Another Supplementary Benefits officer warned her not to ask too often for grants: 'We'll take your book and cut off £2 to pay for them'. When Mrs Bradshaw asked why this should happen, she was told 'because you can't look after your money good enough, see'.

Matching her requirements against the number of items claimants should have, Mrs Bradshaw's position appears similar to the other six mothers. They either have no stockings – 'Can't afford them' – or only one pair. All except one mother possessed only the shoes they were wearing. The exception, Mrs Wicks, had three pairs, all of which had been bought at 5p a pair at a jumble sale.

One mother had been unable to afford even a single nightgown. Many of her clothes were bought from jumble sales or given to her by friends, 'but there are some things you like to have new, and if you can't well you go without'. One other mother had a single nightdress and the other four had two, the scale laid down by the SBC. All the mothers owned two bras, although one wore her daughter's 'cast-offs'. All the mothers possessed overcoats, but Mrs Wicks claimed hers had 'come to its last home'.

Both Mrs Bradshaw's and Mrs Wicks's children needed clothes. Mrs Bradshaw's boys, and there are three, had only one pair of trousers each. Neither of Mrs Wicks's two boys had an overcoat or a raincoat. Their anoraks had to play a double part of overcoats and jackets. They had only one pair of trousers each and were one pair of socks below what was laid down in the clothing scale. The boys had one pair of pyjamas each, but both sets were too small for either of them to wear.

The Wicks had received a grant towards their children's clothing 'but £11.50 doesn't go very far. I was supposed to buy Michael an overcoat, but instead I bought each an anorak, because the younger had no coat either.'

Mrs Wilson is separated from her husband. During her 18 months on benefit no one had ever told her that the SBC could make exceptional needs payments. During the summer holidays she had sent the children to stay with their father. The only clothes they possessed were the ones they stood up in 'so he had to buy some'. This he duly did but apart from the sweaters and shirts, both the boys were below the suggested scale rate. Neither of them had pyjamas and only one had an overcoat.

Mrs Bull found clothes 'a terrible problem'. She relied heavily on her daughter who 'was generous with her cast-offs'. But there was no similar source of supply for her children. She had been given a grant for a raincoat for her eldest son but 'how can you spend it on him when the other one's need is as great'? Mrs Bull solved this dilemma at some annoyance to the 'Education people', who had awarded her the grant, by buying a cheap duffel coat.

Both boys had a pair of shoes each, in addition to a pair of plimsolls. Likewise the eldest son had the statutory two pairs of trousers, the other, two pairs of jeans; 'and thank God he prefers them'. Similarly, the older boy had one pair of pyjamas while the younger brother wears 'various bits of cast offs'. Mrs Bull added: 'They just don't seem to have pyjamas in jumble sales around here.'

Mrs Meacher's two daughters have five years between them which 'makes for difficulties in handing down'. Both had the minimum clothes, barring one pair of shoes which Mandy was lacking. Their overcoats, jackets and one of their dresses had been either given or bought at local jumble sales.

Mrs Bull's daughter was now working 'so there's no problem here'. Mrs Starkey's daughter was the same age, and working too. But she 'never claimed a stitch of clothing in all the nine years her dad was unable to work'.

Only two of the families had the father living at home. Mr Starkey had more clothes than the guide lines in B/O 40 'because my son buys them for me. I have not worked for nine years because of multiple sclerosis, and the son sees I don't go without'. Mr Wicks, who works 'when it's available in these parts', had only one pair of trousers and only one of pyjamas. On all other counts he was at or above the scale rates and the SBC had provided a grant for one pair of shoes, but his jacket and shoes had 'come from the jumble sale'.

The Starkeys had an adequate supply of blankets. A grant from the SBC had enabled them to buy an extra pair 'to keep Mr Starkey warm'. However, there were only two sheets per bed which would have made for considerable difficulties even if Mr Starkey had not been slowly dying. Mrs Wicks's supply of bedding was above the scale, although all of it had been bought when her husband was at work.

The 18 months on assistance had seen Mrs Wilson's stocks

slowly depleted, and now no bed in the house had the amount of bedding advised in B/O 40. Mrs Bradshaw had adequate supplies from 'the good times' and Mrs Bull, while having an adequate number of blankets, had only one pair of sheets per bed and 'all of them are on their last legs'. Mrs Meacher was in the same position, while Mrs Hall, who had only been on benefit a few weeks, was, in comparison, sleeping a life of luxury.

The families relied heavily on jumble sales for their clothing. If the sales didn't have their requirements, like bedding, then they went without. Those families with grown-up sons and daughters benefited from their children's cast-offs. With one exception none of the parents had obtained clothing grants to meet their own needs.

The man who had recently been in work was quite well dressed compared with the advisory scales. However, with growing children, the advantages of recently being in work were quickly lost.

Some of the families had benefited from exceptional needs grants. Mrs Wicks had been able to buy a new dressing gown, not on the scale, before she returned to hospital for the birth of her third child. He died soon after birth, and the Wicks were presented with a £4 burial bill. This was only paid by the Commission after much pressure from the Citizens Rights Office.

Likewise with the electricity bill. They had been in darkness for six weeks and both sons had been ill with measles, and still the Commission refused an exceptional needs payment. 'Don't you realize they had a grant for clothing last year?' Again, after much persuasion from the CRO, the Newcastle office paid the bill. The Wicks, plus one other family, were the only ones to gain this form of help.

The lives of these families on supplementary benefit are dominated by an unrelieved dreariness of hand-to-mouth budgeting, and their clothes are largely cast-offs or bargains from jumble sales.

Individual officers had, in some cases, exercised their discretion in favour of the claimants. Such action meant that families were able to buy something new, but the impression gained was one of grossly overworked officers, forever battling against the rising tide of claimants.

If the SBC met the needs of only a few people, and not the

needs of nearly five million, then, possibly, a system of basic allowances and discretionary additions could work. If we judge it by reports from welfare rights organizations all over the country, the system does not and cannot work.

There is an urgent need, therefore, to lift people off SB and to increase the scale rates so that the remaining claimants are less dependent on the whim of officers for meeting individual needs. Families in contact with welfare rights workers do get extra help but what of all those millions of others who have no one to shout for them? How many jumble sales are they away from reaching a decent minimum standard of living?

Motherless Families

Paul Wilding

Reprinted with permission from 'Motherless Families',
New Society, vol. 21, no. 517, 24 August 1972, pp. 382-4

What exactly does it mean to a family to be left without a mother? This was the question that we set out to answer in a survey of families in the east midlands who had been left motherless by the mother's death, desertion or separation. It is a question which has been surprisingly little studied.

Altogether in our study we interviewed nearly 600 fathers who were referred to us mainly by local authority health, education and children's departments, by the family allowances section of the Department of Health and Social Security, and by the Supplementary Benefits Commission. It was a mixed income and social class group, with the higher income groups and social classes rather under-represented, almost certainly due to our sources of referral. Widowers made up just under half the sample.

To understand just what motherlessness does mean to a family, it is vital to consider what the situation means to the father. His feelings and attitudes are crucial to the way the new family unit functions. Unless these are taken into account, it is impossible to understand the social consequences of motherlessness.

To the vast majority of fathers in our sample, the death or departure of their wife meant shock and upset of varying degrees. In all, 86 per cent of the widowers described their feelings in these terms, and 66 per cent of the separated and divorced. For the widowers, the situation was stark and unrelieved. 'End of the world as far as I was concerned', said one. 'If someone had put me against a wall and wanted to shoot me, I wouldn't have cared'. It was all loss without any compensations except for the few who were glad for their wife's sake that her suffering was over. This meant that for the widowers everything was worse after the wife's death.

Feelings among the divorced and the separated were much more varied, ranging between the extremes of desperation and comparative indifference. Their immediate situation lacked the finality of the widowers'. For some, there was an element of relief or satisfaction. For many there was anger, which gave them a vital bitter energy and a determination to do their best by their children. The fathers themselves were often surprised by how they felt. 'I couldn't believe it when she went', one father explained. 'I was lost for a week. I was in a dream. And the funny thing was that I had told her to go if she couldn't change her ways'. Others made the painful discovery, as one put it, that 'however bad she is, it was still companionship'.

The effects of the loss of wife and mother are often long lasting, if not permanent. Our sample of families had, on average, been motherless for three to four years but, when interviewed, 38 per cent of the fathers said they still felt lonely or depressed sometimes or occasionally, and 30 per cent said they felt this way all the time.

Depression was the product of sadness for what had happened and regret for the pattern of life imposed by their situation – the domestic burdens, the problems of combining work and the care of the children, the loss of income, the responsibilities which could be shared with no one else, the never ending succession of days filled with work, and evenings and weekends filled with chores.

Loneliness was the result of a number of factors. It was partly the product of a high degree of isolation from other adults – particularly in the evenings and at weekends, when fathers had to be at home to do the chores and look after the children. 'I don't get much grown-up talk now', was how one father put it. Partly, too, it was the product of the loss of a particular person. It was also the result of the restrictive effect of the family situation on the father's social life. Half the fathers said they had been going out less since the family became motherless. The reasons they gave for this fell into two groups. There were the restrictions imposed by circumstances such as domestic duties, care of the children and lack of money. And, secondly, there were the restrictions imposed by feelings – loss of interest in meeting people, and the feeling that no one wanted a man on his own, and so on. 'People shun you when you are a widower', one father complained. 'Probably they think you are going to ask them to do something for you.' Most fathers felt that people behaved differently towards them because of their family situation and the attitudes they mentioned fell almost equally into those considered as more helpful and those considered less helpful and unsympathetic.

In his initial state of shock and upset the father has to wrestle with a number of crucial decisions. If he decides to try to care for the children on his own, he is then faced with the problems of combining this responsibility with his work. For some of the fathers this proves impossible. There may be children under school age and no nursery facilities. There may be no relatives, friends or neighbours who can make good the gaps in such provision. The children may all be at school but the father's hours of work may not fit round the school day. His job may involve shift work which cannot be reconciled with adequate care of the children before and after school, and there may be no other work available. Overall, nearly 30 per cent of our sample had drawn Supplementary Benefit at some stage to enable them to stay at home and look after the children and nearly 20 per cent were doing so at the time of interview.

Fathers drawing Supplementary Benefit tended to have larger families than fathers who managed to carry on at work. A larger family, of course, meant greater domestic burdens. It also meant more Supplementary Benefit. The loss of income for the larger low income family becoming dependent on Supplementary Benefit was, therefore, likely to be less than for the smaller family. So if a father with a large family continued to work, he often incurred greater stress for a marginal gain in income.

Most fathers drawing Supplementary Benefit didn't like doing so. 'A lot of people class it as a stigma and that's how I feel about it', said one. Fathers felt that they ought to be at work. Without a job they were less than men. More than half those who had drawn benefit to stay at home to look after their children spoke favourably of their contacts with the Supplementary Benefit officers and only a quarter described their contacts unfavourably. Nevertheless, fathers resented the means testing inherent in the system and the low level of benefit which they received for undertaking a task which saved society the expense of taking the children into care. Fathers were also bitter about the way in which they felt the community classed them with scroungers abusing the welfare state.

Those fathers who continued to work had to regard their work in a new light. No longer could they look at it solely from the point of view of its economic rewards, the satisfactions, if any, which it brought and the other criteria by which most people assess their job. For many, a new and overriding criterion asserted itself – the compatibility of work with the care of children. Because of this new concern, the absence of the mother does affect the father's earning capacity. Nearly a quarter of the fathers in our sample who were in full-time work at the time of interview had suffered a drop in earnings since the family became motherless – and this at a time of unprecedented general wage increases. Half the fathers reporting a fall in earnings had suffered a loss of £6 a week or more. Two reasons predominated – loss of overtime and change of job.

Of the whole sample – working and non-working – 44 per cent said their income had gone down since the family became motherless. The seriousness of this needs no emphasis, but, in fact, it is only half the story. What became quite clear was that motherlessness, while reducing income, also increases expenditure – though it is extremely difficult to set a precise figure on the extra costs involved. A man who loses his wife no longer has to support her but, on the other hand, he loses those services which are part of the role and function of a wife and mother to render – the ability and the time to make and mend clothes, to buy wisely and cheaply, and to improve the value of what she buys by her own labours. Of those fathers who had been managing on their own for a year or less – the group whose replies are perhaps the most reliable – 88 per cent said they spent more than before the family became motherless.

A less obvious cause of increased expense was 'compensating expenditure' – that is, expenditure on minor luxuries such as sweets and toys for the children, drinks and cigarettes for the father, in an attempt to compensate for the physical and emotional strains and stresses of the motherless state. 'I don't suppose I should', said one father, 'but I do give the children more to try to make up for their mother.'

What was clear, too, was that extra expenditure could mitigate many of the practical problems which motherlessness brought. Some of the more affluent fathers emphasized how they depended on their cars for the smooth functioning of domestic arrangements – to take children to day nurseries or to daily minders or to fetch daily helps – and that without a car the complicated pattern on which they depended would break down. An affluent minority of fathers, earning over £2,000 a year, mentioned the value of the telephone as a means of remote control of children in school holidays, or when the children had problems when alone at home. Such aids and solutions were only open to a minority. Very many more fathers lacked the initial resources to buy the services to enable them to remain at work, or in their existing jobs, and so to maintain their incomes.

Our study was not directly concerned with the effect of motherlessness on the children. We were limited to examining the fathers' view of the situation, which may well differ from what would be found by interviewing the children, talking to their teachers, and so on. Given the widespread belief in our society that the mother is vitally important to the young child, it is interesting that only 64 per cent of fathers claimed their children missed their mother when she left or died. As might be expected, widowers were more likely than other fathers to say this. As many as 40 per cent of those fathers who were separated and divorced claimed quite definitely that the children had not missed their mother.

When we asked more specific questions about the effect of the mother's loss, the majority of fathers felt that motherlessness had no immediate effects on the children. Just over 20 per cent described adverse effects on the children's mental and physical health and about the same proportion said they had been more difficult to handle. A majority of the fathers claimed that the family's motherlessness had brought them and the children closer together. Not only do the children have to rely on the father to a greater extent than in the normal two-parent family, but the father also becomes more dependent on the children for company, for co-operation and for comfort. The consciousness of their difference from other families, and the way in which their motherless situation was sharply brought home to them at times like Christmas, birthdays and holidays, could be a powerful force binding the family together.

Motherlessness inevitably means dependence. If a father gives up work he becomes dependent on the Social Security system for his income. If he combines full-time work and care of the children, then he becomes dependent on the help of relatives and friends or the social services to care for pre-school children during the working day; to keep a watching eye on older children at home by themselves after he has left for work in the morning and before his return in the evening; to care for children who are sick and so on. The difficulties of organizing such care over a period of, perhaps, several years and the stress and strain on the father in trying to make sure that all eventualities have been provided for, need little emphasis.

Fathers found their main source of support and help in their relatives, both immediately after the wife's death or departure and subsequently. 'Without the family I just couldn't have done it', said one father, the worst of whose troubles were over. Only a third of fathers received no help from relatives at all. Friends and neighbours helped nearly a third with the initial problems and even more helped over the whole period of motherlessness. Their great advantage was that they were close at hand and could provide help in the unanticipated domestic crisis as well as the regular occasional service. One father listed the many people who had helped him – his mother, his boss, his boss's wife, but he concluded: 'It's my neighbour that stands out. She has given us food many times. But it's not that. She looks after my son after school and on a few evenings when I am away. You see I need her help most. I *couldn't* do that myself'.

Overall, two kinds of help dwarfed all the rest in their importance to fathers – day care of children and domestic help. This was help which relatives, friends and neighbours could fairly easily provide, and it was help which could be crucial. It was also help which the social services were ill equipped to supply. The personal social services, in fact, failed in two ways. They failed to reach most of the fathers and, when they did, they generally failed to provide any very useful help. About half of the fathers received some help from the personal social services at the beginning but the number fell off very sharply as the situation stabilized itself. Help from relatives fell off, too, but nothing like so sharply as help from the social services. The basic reason for the very sharp fall-off in help from the social services was that they either could not supply what the father required (generally day nursery or nursery school places) or, if they could supply help (such as domestic help), they could not do so on a long-term basis.

When we asked fathers to say which source of help they found most useful at the time of interview, nearly half named their own relatives, with their parents being far and away the most important. Friends and neighbours came next, followed by the wife's relatives, the children, and eventually the personal social services (mentioned as the most useful source of help by 4 per cent of fathers).

The most striking finding of our study, however, was not the inevitable child-care problems which motherlessness brings, nor the relative insignificance of the preventive role of the social services in helping this particular group of families. It was that out of the many problems with which fathers were confronted, financial problems were the major continuing difficulty. In an affluent society, such a finding is encouraging. It means the major problem is soluble – if the will is there. The provision of an insurance benefit on similar lines to the widows' scheme could go a long way towards easing the situation.

Varieties of Homelessness

Jane Morton

Reprinted with permission from 'Varieties of Homelessness',
New Society, vol. 18, no. 461, 29 July 1971

'It's not *how* people become homeless that matters', says Peter O'Callaghan, who runs the emergency service at Shelter's Housing Aid Centre in west London. 'It's the fact that they *are* homeless and unable to do anything about it.' Sometimes, he adds, as he listens to a tale of woe, he is very tempted to say: 'Hard luck, mate – if you had thought of this a bit sooner, you wouldn't be in this mess now . . . People do such foolish things, you know.'

But it wouldn't do a bit of good. 'You've got to remember – and keep reminding yourself – that they're *all* victims of a situation that is ultimately out of their control.'

In September 1970 – the latest date for which figures were available to John Greve and his co-authors for use in their study, *Homelessness in London*, no fewer than 2,787 families were in temporary accommodation provided by the London boroughs. This was an increase of 77 per cent over the figure for September 1966.

These families are, moreover, only the tip of an iceberg, whose true dimensions can only be guessed at. For each family given temporary accommodation or rehoused directly by a London borough in the year ending with September 1970, a second made an unsuccessful application.

In all, about 10,000 families approached the boroughs in the course of that year, of whom about 3,000 were admitted to temporary accommodation (while about 1,400 moved on from temporary to permanent council accommodation and roughly as many again left to go elsewhere) and about 800 were directly rehoused. As Greve shows, too, those turned away, by and large, were the same kind of people as those admitted.

But if one regards all these as 'homeless' – although the unsuccessful applicants subsequently found some kind of roof to put over their heads – then it's hard to deny the title to those living in comparable discomfort who did not need to approach a welfare department. Greve, taking his cue from Shelter, would accept that any family is homeless who 'because of the physical housing conditions in which they are forced to live cannot have normal family life'. Which brings the count straight up to 50,000 families on doubling up alone, before one starts to look at standards of accommodation. And this is still drawing the line at families with young children.

Homelessness is not, of course, a phenomenon confined to London, as Bryan Glastonbury's parallel study of south Wales and the West Country, *Homeless near a Thousand Homes*, made clear. But it is rather more likely to occur in London – where there are more than twelve persons in temporary accommodation for every 10,000 in the population, compared with only two in England and Wales outside of London. It is in London, too, that the homeless family consists, on the whole, of very ordinary people – poorer, blacker and more prolific than the average, perhaps, but not characterized by personal inadequacy as the out-of-London homeless tend to be.

The reason for this, says Greve, is that London still suffers from genuine housing shortage – indeed, a worsening housing shortage, as the dwindling supply of privately rented accommodation is competed for by a growing number of households who either cannot or do not wish to buy and have little or no hope of a council tenancy.

His solution, broadly, is to recognize this type of homelessness as an integral part of London's housing problem – not as an isolated welfare problem, though the support of the social services will still sometimes be needed – and to deal with it through normal housing channels. More specifically, he would like housing policy to move forward on a broad front, as Professor Cullingworth has recommended and Lambeth is attempting to practise. The traditional council job of providing rented housing should be supplemented, he believes, by help with house purchase, help to move to a less congested area, help with tenancy problems and so on.

The first of these is beginning to happen already, as the growing numbers of homeless families moving directly or indirectly into regular council accommodation indicates. It's an unpleasant route to a council house, but a fairly sure one, especially if you are more than usually poor and prolific. The second can be expected to develop alongside the new housing subsidy policy, with its disregard of traditional sectors and stress upon the individual solution to the individual problem. Both are desirable.

But are they particularly relevant to the homelessness problem that exists now? Will they stop that second family which the system fails today – let alone the five or six more who count as homeless under Greve's definition – slipping through a hole in the net tomorrow as well? Is there not, perhaps, something else that should be done?

The vague outlines of this something else take shape when you start to meet some of the families who are slipping through the net now. Every single council runs a rationing system to keep demand for and supply of contemporary accommodation in balance. These systems vary fantastically, as Greve notes. One authority will only accept families made homeless by illegal eviction; a second will also accept the legally evicted, even where the eviction was for rent arrears, but will make the latter wait a good deal longer before rehousing them into permanent accommodation; a third will rehouse anyone directly into permanent accommodation.

What doesn't emerge nearly clearly enough from Greve, however, is the way in which the rationing system depends upon the politically acceptable amount of temporary accommodation in the area – and it's not really a politically acceptable commodity on either side of the political fence. To the left, it often seems a way by which incomers and layabouts jump the housing list: to the right, it seems to discourage a man from standing on his own two feet. Nobody plans for a certain amount of emergency accommodation in the light of the housing character of the area, though it's common knowledge that a lot of landlord's housing, and a big unskilled population, mean families at risk.

Most only provide it when the alternative is a scandal. Nobody is above sending a family off to reluctant relatives, and far too many will suggest taking the children into care, while the parents go on looking for accommodation, before trying to house the family as a unit.

But the tripwire which probably leads to more unsuccessful applications than any other is the stipulation that the family should be 'local'. For a start, most London administrative boundaries are unknown at ground level. Secondly, the problem of finding accommodation where they will accept children is such that the kind of family that ends up homeless will probably have made many moves in search of it. It is, thirdly, a bit rough on the newcomers who are inevitable in a city like London.

You can see the point of this restriction. No area wants to attract homeless families from all over London. Every borough is probably prepared to shoulder a fair share of the problem, but not unless every other borough does too. Rather like the counties and gypsy camp sites.

Three cases histories – which could have cropped up almost anywhere in the London area, so the councils in question should not feel they are being singled out – illustrate how easy it is to become very homeless indeed and yet receive no help. They also underline Peter O'Callaghan's point about the effort needed, sometimes, to suppress a moralizing attitude.

Graham Gadd and his family are living in a tent beside the Caterham by-pass. At first sight you might think it was an archetypal Surrey picnic party. The butter is on a plate and the four children, Nicholas (ten), Simon (eight), Sarah (five) and Katherine (20 months), have spotless white socks on. This will be their sixth week under canvas and Christine Gadd is nearly at breaking point.

The gap they fell through is probably best described as the what-a-pity-we-can't-help gap. The Gadds have long connections with the Croydon area, on both sides of the greater London boundary. Graham, a freelance photographer, has done work for local papers for close on 20 years. His livelihood requires, in fact, that he stay in the area.

They had been living with an uncle whose house went with his job until a year ago, when the uncle retired. They hadn't worried much about this, for their name, they thought, should by now be near the top of the local district council's housing list. But when they visited the housing manager, they found to their horror that their name wasn't on the list at all. It went on properly this time, but there wasn't a hope of an early house and they had to stay within the district, somehow, until one did come up.

Unfortunately, it's not the kind of area where privately rented housing abounds. They were prepared to pay £10 a week in rent: they could find nothing. And though Graham averages about £25 a week clear it comes in bursts, which doesn't exactly impress the building societies. He would prefer not to take on a mortgage, anyway, because of the effect it might have upon his work. His wife backs him in this.

No one is contesting that the Gadds have a valid claim upon Surrey county, which is the welfare authority. The council just doesn't happen to have any accommodation. Perhaps they would come back in September? The council would be buying up some houses in Caterham for a road project then. Taking the children into care was suggested to the Gadds, and indignantly rejected. So was camping at the somewhat rowdy local gypsy encampment. An official has been along to point out that it's strictly illegal to camp on the public highway. But they haven't attempted to move them. Christine Gadd doubts if they would dare. But she doesn't know if she can last out, either.

Patrick and Joan Valimaa are also playing chicken with their local authority, in this case the borough of Ealing. They're squatting in a tiny turn-of-the-century terrace house that was compulsorily purchased for demolition and may now be improved instead. The street is dotted with empty houses, which Ealing refuses to use as temporary accommodation. Meanwhile, it is reliably reported to be spending about £700 a week on bed-and-breakfast accommodation for about 30 families.

The Valimaas don't really have to squat. Patrick clears £35 in a poor week as a pipe-fitter; perhaps £42 in a good week. They only have two children, Yvette, who's nearly three, and one-year-old Michael. But by the time Joan discovered that they could probably manage a mortgage, she was so angry that she was determined that they should squat on principle and brought two more families into the street to squat with them.

You could call their gap the I'm-just-doing-my-job gap. They were legally evicted from furnished accommodation, but only because the landlady needed their rooms. They scoured the area for another place – uselessly. They should have been eligible for temporary accommodation. But they were told none was available. A bed-and-breakfast arrangement was offered, but no one told them that they would get help towards the cost, which was going to work out at about £30 a week, so they refused it. On going to check how their application for a regular council tenancy was getting on, Joan discovered that it had been put on the deferred list, since her husband's income was so high. Why didn't they try house purchase? But the loans department looked only at Patrick's basic wage, which is £21, not his actual earnings, which is what the housing department had been working on, and said the Valimaas could only afford a mortgage of £2,300. Even a modest family house in Ealing costs about £6,000. Then Patrick came across this street of empty houses and they decided to help themselves.

Part of the trouble may well have been Joan's own sharp tongue. But who feels like speaking soft when you find the people you relied on passing you on from hand to hand like a hot potato? The council knows where the Valimaas are. The surveyors who are working on the street have a cup of coffee with the squatters when invited. Their water rate payments have not been returned. They, too, are unlikely to be forcibly moved.

John and Elizabeth Shine are now in a short-life GLC property in Bromley-by-Bow, made available by Shelter against its principles because no one else would help.

You could call it the sorry-wrong-number gap. They are, in fact, a classic family at risk, of the kind that everybody's regular housing service, let alone their emergency services, was created to help. They came over from Ireland in the early 1960s, met and married in London and lived for six years in one room in the Brixton area which cost them £4.25 a week – all they could afford out of John's £12 a week basic (£16 with overtime) as a British Rail porter. Their name was on the housing list from the day they married, but Lambeth has one of the longest lists in London. By 1969, John had moved on to linesman's work and was clearing £29 a week, but Patrick, the eldest of their three children, was ill and their doctor urged them to take him back to Ireland.

So they voluntarily gave up their tenancy and went over to Mallow, near Cork. John tried for a year to get work, while they lived in a derelict house. Patrick's health, after an initial improvement, got worse again and the second child, William Martin, fell into poor health too. At John's insistence, they came back to London, to find that the house they'd lived in was full and their names had been removed from the housing list because they had been gone more than twelve months. Lambeth told them to go back to Ireland.

Instead, they went to the Shelter Housing Aid Centre, which sent them to the Simon Community Trust's central London hostel. When their money ran out, three days later, the hostel sent them down to the Ministry of Social Security emergency office at Great Guildford Street, which gave them travel warrants and sent them on the first boat to Dublin. In Dublin, they slept rough for two nights while John looked again for work. When a friendly priest heard their story, he gave them their fare back to London again.

This time they spent two weeks with the Simon Community, while they tried to find a place to stay. They even went down to Clacton to see if they could have a beach hut for the winter. The community finally passed them over to Westminster welfare department, which gave them yet another travel warrant and sent them, protesting, back to Ireland. It took John two days to raise their fares back. Four nights after leaving it, they were back at the hostel, and for the next six weeks, Elizabeth haunted the SHAC with her three children, begging Peter O'Callaghan to do something.

Now, on principle, Shelter does not take on cases where statutory authorities have a responsibility, and this was as clear a case as Peter had seen. So he 'sweet-talked' her, as he puts it – and Elizabeth started screaming her head off. She had, after all, crossed the Irish Sea five times in three months with three small children, two of them unwell, not knowing for two days running where they would spend the next night.

So they got their house and are grateful for it, although it's in worse condition than Joan Valimaa's and they're being charged £6.65 a week for it out of wage-stopped benefits of £16.65. John's not going back to work until their fourth child is born in two months' time. Elizabeth's still liable to get hysterical on her own.

What makes one most angry about a story like that is that there is not only no justification in law for this kind of buck-passing – as there is no justification for any of the rationing techniques in use or for providing no support at all when accommodation is full. There is, in this case, actually a prohibition against it. Part Three of the National Assistance Act, 1948, from which the homeless family services spring, specifically enjoins: 'Where a person in the area of a local authority is a person with no settled residence, or, not being ordinarily resident in the area of the local authority, is in urgent need of residential accommodation under this part of this act, *the authority shall have the like duty to provide residential accommodation for him as if he were ordinarily resident in their area*' (my italics).

Going back to the source revealed something else. In section 34 of Part Three, it emerges that the minister responsible for these services is entitled to ask local authorities to prepare a scheme for providing them and can substitute a scheme of his own if he is not satisfied with it. The Children and Young Persons Act, 1963, which gave children's departments a blank cheque to be spent in any way that would diminish the need to take children into care, contains something similar.

Granted, the new subsidy system – which is expected to thin out council waiting lists and increase vacancies – should make it much easier for councils to house those for whom there just isn't enough privately rented accommodation on the market. It might even make landlords slightly less reluctant to let to families.

But this is going to take time. So, even if it's only for a ten-year period, we must have planned provision of temporary accommodation and allocate it consistently. The only criterion that is relevant, in fact, is that outlined in the act – the family's inability to help itself. If the London boroughs cannot agree how much each should be providing, then the ministers responsible must be prepared to take the initiative.

Race in the Inner City

Augustine John

Reprinted with permission from A. John, *Race in the Inner City*, Runnymede Trust, 1972 (2nd edition), pp. 14-20, 25-8, 33-4

EDUCATION

Education, I discovered early on, is one of the areas in which the problems of a poor area, the stresses on an immigrant community (and in particular the increased sharpness with which the normal inter-generational conflicts are felt in such a community), and the problems of colour focus themselves most clearly.

Studies of educationally deprived areas, both here and in the United States, have shown that one key factor in the poor performance of children in such areas is the absence of adequate preparation for school, i.e., the absence of pre-school play facilities. Handsworth is certainly a deprived area in that respect.

The number of day-nurseries run by the city authorities cater, in my view, for an insignificant number of children of pre-school age as a result of which there is a flourishing trade in unofficial child-minding. I observed fifteen child-minding 'establishments' of this type, and it was clear to me that although they obviously fulfil a need (otherwise they would not have come into existence), nevertheless the circumstances in which they function make it impossible for them to do more than look after the children – and even that not too well.

In 12 of the 15 I observed, the children had little or no play facilities; even three-year-olds had no books or writing tablets, nor did they get enough attention from the child-minders, who were content to have the children following them around until they were put to sleep or were taken home by their mothers.

What kind of need drives mothers to entrust their children to such 'establishments'? The large majority of the mothers who used these unofficial services had at least one other child living with them, and some had the added burden of maintaining other children in the West Indies. They all stressed their need to work very long hours (frequently in poorly paid jobs) to be able to make ends meet.

Some claimed that the official day-nurseries or pre-school playgroups were too far from their homes and that they were not open early enough to enable them to get their children to them before going off to work. What is more, the official nurseries are seen as too distant and unfamiliar – this psychological distance between citizens and officialdom (however benevolent) is, of course, one of the principal features of life in a deprived area.

As one woman put it: 'My mind is more at rest when I know that my child is being cared for by Mrs X, whom I know and who has kept two other children for me, than by the people at the day nursery'. Another mother observed: 'These day nurseries were not meant for people like us. They were meant for people who could afford to stay at home and who simply take their children there to get them off their apron strings.' These were widely shared sentiments.

There are still many parents who believe that education only starts when the child enters school. In families where both father and mother go out to work – and this is true of English as well as West Indian families – the child's subsidiary education at home is likely to be minimal. Parents come home from work, children are fed, washed and put to bed, only to be woken up and taken out to the child-minder once more the next morning.

Moreover, in terms of socialization and emotional development, this arrangement causes conflict in children at a number of points, as when their parents impose one line of discipline and the child-minder another, so that what was permissible with the parents suddenly, and bewilderingly, becomes impermissible with the child-minder. But even if the child-minder is aided by the adults at home, there still remains the prospect of another divergent line of discipline, for when the child goes into school from such a background he has to come to terms once again with divergent, if not conflicting, notions of what is and is not permitted. The teacher soon complains of naughtiness, lack of co-operation, inattentiveness, bullying – a portrait of a 'problem child'.

To stand on Grove Lane or Rookery Road around 6.30 in the morning and to watch streams of West Indian mothers taking toddlers by the hand into child-minding establishments – dingy front-rooms in which anything from half-a-dozen to a dozen children will be herded for the rest of the day, a paraffin oil-heater in a corner in the winter – is to observe a very different world from the one inhabited by social scientists, teachers and officials. In view of the almost total absence of any formative education, it would hardly be surprising if these children did not become 'problems' during their first years at school. They will certainly require special attention, and if the teacher does not have the resources to provide special attention or fails to recognize the need for it, then these children might well start and finish in the bottom stream – today's 'problem child', tomorrow's drop-out or delinquent.

Is this too gloomy a forecast? In order to establish how children from such a background were actually faring at school, I spoke to roughly 200 children, the majority of whom were still at school and a smaller number who had left school during the last year (1969).

The progress of both groups seemed to depend on the sort of grounding in education they had had before entering school; the amount of room, time and quiet in which to work at home; the interest their parents took in their work; the attitudes of their teachers towards them.

The most interesting features of the perceptions of these children were the way in which they thought their teachers regarded them, and the view they took of the connection between school and the world of work.

Of the pupils I interviewed, 75 (roughly two out of five) said they had 'smashing teachers' who cared and were helpful. The others made comments like:

> If you don't push yourself and try to be one up on everybody else, you haven't got a hope in hell.
> Man, those teachers just don't care. School is a bind. Teachers not only think you stupid but the sort of things they teach you make you yourself believe that you're stupid. I think some of them are just born racialist.
> The teachers in my school need to be sitting in with the class and being taught. We seem to be landed with a load of teachers who have just got through their teacher training. Sometimes I wonder how some of them did. You talk to some of my mates over there. I am sure they would tell you the same thing. I think they deliberately send second-rate teachers into Handsworth; and then they turn round and say because there are so many black kids in the school the standard of education is being lowered.

The educational scene in Handsworth, up to school-leaving age, presents a depressing spectacle. Only a detailed study can reveal how much of the failure in achievement of these black children is a product of educational deprivation as such (and would therefore be found in all children in a similar situation), how much a product of the failure of teachers, frequently ill-prepared to teach in the kinds of schools in which they find themselves, who may be driven to justify their failure by describing the children as ineducable, or more summarily, 'black little horrors'. A study of this sort, rather than the currently fashion-able discussion of genetically inherited differences in ability, would clearly help in retrieving some of the wastage of human potential I observed in Handsworth. For myself, in the mean-while, I can only recall the question of the black girl whose remarks I quoted earlier. It was not so much a question, much more a statement, a reproach:

> Few black children get into grammar schools in Handsworth – I could only think of about three. Are black people so stupid that of the hundreds of kids in school in this dump you could count those in grammar schools on the fingers of one hand?

The only exception to the unease, concern and criticism I found amongst both parents and pupils was in the area of further education. The people attending further education institutes, especially Handsworth Technical College, were in the main very impressed with the staff and with the work done there.

YOUTH FACILITIES

One of the comments I heard most frequently from both young and old was that young people felt hemmed in in Handsworth – nowhere to go to, not enough to do by way of entertainment and activities.

Some youngsters simply ridiculed the idea of youth clubs. An even greater number felt that not only were there not enough youth centres, but not enough of the right type, offering what *they* considered to be relevant facilities.

To a majority of those attending youth clubs the youth club was the only place they could go to. It was also the only place their parents would allow them to go to. But even teenagers who are regular members of youth clubs (and a number of those who used to attend at one time) complained of authoritarian and paternalist youth leaders and club structures. What they clearly wanted was a more unstructured setting within which they could promote more spontaneous activity.

One youth leader, it is fair to add, argued that he had tried the unstructured approach, but that this had produced the complaint that the club was boring and that he was not doing enough. As a result, he found members saying that they went to the club because they had rather be there than at home, not because they liked the club.

For many youngsters, however, *the* club in the area is Handsworth Park. The groundsmen at the Park talked of hundreds of youngsters using the Park during the spring and summer months, especially when the schools and youth clubs are closed. This in itself is a distressing comment on the absence of facilities in the area.

HOUSING

Many West Indians, in particular those who have been in Handsworth upwards of five years, own their houses. The one-family, owner-occupied houses are usually very well-kept. In some cases, however, the combined effects of low salaries, hire-purchase commitments, higher down payments and low mortgages makes it economically impossible for owners to keep their property well preserved.

Multi-occupied houses give rise to the greatest concern. Occupiers complain of exploitation by landlords, of lack of adequate space and facilities, of too many people sharing basic amenities. It is important to add that when these properties are purchased they are already in need of extensive repair and, in many cases, renovation. It is, therefore, all the more difficult for people with few resources to refurbish such properties adequately.

As for rented property, landlords in many cases fail to provide adequate basic amenities, in the knowledge that in the last resort tenants admit, however reluctantly, that were it not for the grace of the landlord they would be out on the streets. Most tenants feel it is dangerous to complain or to take up the matter with the Rent Tribunal or with officials, for there is the constant fear, 'What if I and my children find ourselves on the streets?' or (if the landlord does not go as far) 'What if he decides to make life unpleasant for us?'

I found a number of cases where the non-resident landlord had empowered the 'non-complaining' tenants to keep a close eye on the more 'fussy' tenants who demanded fairer treatment. These invariably ended up in household disputes in which the absentee landlord himself was, of course, never directly involved.

The housing situation is plainly one of the root causes of the social tensions and individual problems in the area. My attention was drawn to twenty girls who, on reaching puberty, had felt that they had to leave home and go to live with friends because, for obvious reasons, they could no longer live in the same room as their parents and younger siblings. The parents themselves are usually struggling to make ends meet and scarcely have the resources to cope with the problem of inadequate living space.

A recent report in the *Birmingham Evening Mail* described how a group of black children on their first day at school were seen huddling together in one corner of the playground, unable to make use of the open space of the playground and unwilling to disperse. An educational psychologist suggested that play-space itself was a novelty to children who came from homes where there was no space available for play. I myself observed a boy of nine who, on being taken to the home of a social worker, spent the first fifteen minutes running up and down the stairs, shouting 'Isn't it clean! Isn't it clean!'. The child lived with his parents in an attic room up three flights of stairs in a multi-occupied house. He was not allowed to play on the stairs or the landing. The room was at once bedroom, kitchen, living room and the father's radio and television repair shop. The mother had to go down three flights of stairs to fetch water. There were about four square feet of open floor space, and the child constantly played on the double bed which his invalid mother occupied most of the time.

It says little for the stability of family life in such housing situations when, on being asked why they hang around street corners or cafes, youngsters invariably say that they 'live on top of each other so much at home' that they would sooner be out in the streets until bed-time.

WORK

The area of employment is one which gives rise to a great deal of discontent and bitterness, although statistically the situation does not appear at all bad. By mid-December 1969 I had interviewed 35 youngsters under 20 who had not yet been placed in jobs. Of the youngsters I interviewed, 70 had been helped to find jobs by the Youth Employment Office, and praised the service for its efforts. But from these, as from the 35 unemployed, the major criticism was not so much that they could not find jobs as that the jobs did not conform either to their abilities or to what they particularly wanted to do.

While the overall statistics show a relatively low unemployment rate amongst black youngsters, in my view these statistics mask the severe degree of job-dissatisfaction amongst these people. We should be much more concerned about the fact that many of them are dissatisfied with their jobs and their job-prospects, and that most of them are unwilling to be stuck in a 'tedious boring job with no future' for the rest of their lives. I may say in parenthesis here that no one should make judgements about youngsters who kick over the traces and get into trouble with the authorities until we have considered what the world looks like to a youngster who has nothing in front of him except the prospect of 40 or 50 years as an unskilled labourer.

AN INTERIM SUMMING-UP

It should be obvious that this report is not meant to be an objective and scientific survey. I had neither the time nor the resources for such a study. It is instead an attempt to draw a picture of Handsworth as the people concerned saw and experienced their area.

I think myself that it contains the seeds of a potentially dangerous racial situation. But even if it is felt that the evidence produced in this report does not warrant such a pessimistic conclusion, it still remains true that we ought to be just as concerned about the fact that hundreds of youngsters feel that this society has very little to offer them, that the future holds very little promise and meaning for them, that they constitute a people without rights. No programme of action for the area can afford to neglect these facts.

Nor can we neglect the implications for race relations. At the moment we see black Handsworth being made the scapegoat for the deprivations of the area. Given the leaven of discontent amongst black youngsters, they will not accept the role of scapegoat for much longer. Indeed it is only too likely that they will come to see white society as such being responsible for their own second-class status, although white Handsworth is as much the victim of neglect and deprivation as black Handsworth.

My total impression of Handsworth – as the residents see it and as it is presented in the press – is that an excessive preoccupation with the symptoms of neglect have diverted attention effectively from the root problems themselves. If the discussion of Handsworth is carried out day in and day out in terms of crime and the breakdown of law and order, it will become impossible to begin to discuss the real problems of the area – the sheer deterioration in the quality of life, the perennial lack of basic resources and amenities, the sense of being *de facto* second-class citizens, the sense of hopelessness – which underline the tensions, conflicts and the law-breaking of the area.

The situation calls for immediate action on the part of local and central government who have for too long been seen to have failed in their duty to Handsworth and to areas like Handsworth.

Socially Deprived Areas

Robert Holman

Reprinted with permission from *Socially Deprived Families in Britain*, Bedford Square Press, revised 1973, pp. 153-7

Differences between regions in Britain are recognized in connection with certain measurables. It is known that housing conditions tend to be better in the south-east; that children tend to weigh more, and general practitioners be proportionately more in abundance in London and the south-east; that Ulster and the north-east have a higher rate of unemployment, and so on. The Government has commissioned regional plans and inaugurated new regional machinery in the economic planning councils and planning boards in efforts to encourage economic growth in certain regions. But regional studies have failed to identify the comparatively small areas of intense deprivation. This requires highly specialized studies of communities, which have been notably lacking in post-war Britain. A partial rectification is now occurring and, apart from the completed studies mentioned below, there are on-going studies of parts of York, Liverpool and Newcastle.

The study of St Ann's by Coates and Silburn revealed a high incidence of the types of social deprivation with which this study is concerned – an incidence obviously much higher than in other parts of Nottingham.

The study on parts of Notting Hill in the Borough of Kensington and Chelsea showed a similar concentration. The Borough as a whole has 26·9 per cent of its resident population born outside of the British Isles, compared with 3·6 per cent for England and Wales. In the wards actually surveyed the tenure patterns were owner-occupied 8 per cent, compared with 43·2 per cent for Greater London; local authority housing was 5·4 per cent compared with 21·6 per cent; privately rented unfurnished accommodation 42·8 per cent compared with 28 per cent; privately rented furnished accommodation 35·1 per cent compared with 4 per cent. Overcrowding was intense, with over 33 per cent of all households living at more than 1·5 persons per room, 13·1 per cent of households had no access to a fixed bath or shower, and a further 53·3 per cent shared a fixed bath or shower. Inhabitants were also characterized by low incomes, especially amongst large families.

Rex and Moore's research on Sparkbrook in Birmingham has been severely condemned on methodological grounds. Nonetheless it shows how one part of Sparkbrook is characterized by a comparatively high incidence of immigrants and overcrowding.

It must be added that the areas surveyed so far are ones with a number of voluntary agencies, especially community work bodies, working in them. Indeed the surveys may have occurred there because these areas were 'fashionable' deprived areas. It is likely that studies of places less attractive to social workers may reveal even worse situations.

The Plowden Report undertook valuable research from an educational angle by correlating certain social symptoms with certain geographical areas. It listed indicators of deprivation as being clustered in certain deprived zones, especially inner ring areas. This research, described in Vol. II of the Report, included a study in the Midlands of the social services available to primary school children in different types of area. In the inner ring area they found that a much higher percentage of the children had to be visited at home by the social services for cases where the child's 'health, social adjustment or educational performance appeared to be suffering because of adverse home or other social factors', than in the small town and county area also studied. Significantly, children in the town's outer ring, mainly composed of council estates and often families rehoused from the inner ring, displayed far fewer problems, so indicating the probable positive 'influence of housing conditions and general environment'. In addition the city area suffered much more from shortage of social workers than the county or small town.

Putting together the above studies, and using material available from the census and from local authorities, there appears a strong case for saying that socially deprived families are frequently found in confined geographical areas identifiable by certain physical and social characteristics, some of which are as follows:

(1) A geographical location between a city's business centre and the outer suburban areas. Frequently called 'twilight zones' they have been left behind as the business and outer rings have been developed.

(2) A relatively high number of immigrants. A further example of their concentration is found in the Yorkshire town studied by Karn, where 54 per cent of its coloured immigrants were in two of the town's 21 enumeration districts. Immigrants are not necessarily an indication of a deprived zone, and it would be a mistaken policy to give extra aid to areas simply because of their statistical preponderance. Indeed, many immigrants have given an area stability, and possess skills and leadership potential. On the other hand, their frequent lack of earning power, plus a lack of residential qualifications for council housing, does often drive them to the cheapest private rented housing commonly found in the twilight zones.

(3) Housing conditions characterized by overcrowding and a lack of amenities. The housing stock is frequently of older, often Victorian houses. As Spencer points out, age of dwelling stock is highly correlated with levels of obsolescence and lack of amenities. This is likely to be privately rented property, which also displays the more adverse housing factors, although they do provide a greater variety of types and sizes than council or owner-occupied houses.

(4) Higher than average proportions of unskilled and semi-skilled workers.

(5) High...
supplements...
(6) A higher t...
(7) Comparatively large...
(8) A lack of play space and recreation... ...ies.
Soho ward in Birmingham, an area with large num... the
children, immigrants and overcrowding, has no public play
space. In 1963 in North Kensington, London, up to 80 per cent
of children aged two to five had 'nowhere to play'.

(9) Poorer health than is found in the population as a whole.
Dr Wilson draws attention to Dr Asher's research in Birmingham, which found the number of untreated defects in primary
school children greatest in the school serving an area of 'many
decrepit houses, shifting populations, and many problem
families', so that nearly one-third of the inner ring school had
untreated conditions or defects. Noticeably, inner ring areas
are also characterized by higher infant mortality rates.

(10) A high incidence of child deprivation and delinquency. Dr
Wilson establishes that delinquency and truancy correlate with
'slum' areas. Another indicator is the number of children who
have to be taken into the care of or are supervised by children's
departments. Thus statistics kept by the Birmingham City
Corporation show wards with the other characteristics of this
list to have many more children taken into care or supervised
than council estates and suburban areas. Plowden suggests also
that they are characterized by high rates of poor school
attendance and truancy.

(11) There is also some evidence, as in the Plowden Report, that
the areas have the worst social services. The schools tend to be
older and classes larger, the staff turnover rate greater, the
number of nursery places fewer. J. W. B. Douglas, in his study,
says that children on council estates possess better education
chances because they have both better schools and better
housing. It also appears that trained social workers are also at
a minimum, perhaps being attracted to more pleasant surround-
ings, while day care in the form of day nurseries and play
groups are conspicuous by their absence.

It is not claimed that socially deprived families are only in areas
with the above characteristics. On the contrary, some are found

on council

generally ...unities. Although one result is that the families are

in parti...

are....ed in a circle of poverty, at least their location, if identified, ...ly in suburban areas. But ... for such families to be concentrated ...able areas which come to be called deprived should allow local and central government to allocate extra resources to them on an area basis.

Further Reading
The Deprived: Groups in Need

J. BRADSHAW, 'The concept of social need', *New Society*, vol. 19, no. 496, 30 March 1972.

E. EVASON, 'Measuring Family Poverty', *Social Work Today*, vol. 4, no. 3, 3 May 1973.

B. GLASTONBURY, *Homeless Near a Thousand Homes*, National Institute for Social Work Training Series, Allen & Unwin, 1971.

J. GREVE et al., *Homelessness in London*, Scottish Academic Press, 1972.

V. GEORGE and P. WILDING, *Motherless Families*, Routledge & Kegan Paul, 1972.

R. HOLMAN et al., *Socially Deprived Families in Britain*, Bedford Square Press, 1973.

D. HUMPHREY and A. JOHN, *Because They're Black*, Penguin, 1971.

B. JORDAN, *Paupers: The Making of the New Claiming Class*, Routledge & Kegan Paul, 1973.

K. SLACK, *Social Administration and the Citizen*, Michael Joseph, 1966.

Chapter Three

Meeting Needs

The experiences of the 1930s made clear that an unfettered system of capitalism resulted in extreme sufferings and unmet needs for sections of the population in comparison with others. Noticeably, propaganda during the Second World War promised that victory would be followed by changes to ensure a better Britain for all. Consequently, the immediate post-war years witnessed extensive social legislation aiming to lessen social differences by intervening into the free market mechanisms which dominated the economy. The three forms of intervention, or three approaches to meeting need, were: the installation of a comprehensive social security system, the wider application of planning, and the expansion of social work. The readings in this chapter will illustrate their scope, advantages and limitations.

SUPPLEMENTARY BENEFIT

The war-time Beveridge Report, *Social Insurance and Allied Services*, proposed to help those in financial need by three types of benefit: children's allowance for all families with more than one child, social insurance dependent upon the payment of previous contributions, and national assistance for those shown by a means test to have no other sufficient means of support. The ensuing Family Allowance Act (1945) and National Insurance Act (1946), in combination with full employment, were expected to provide incomes of such a level that few would require the safety net of the National Assistance Act (1948). In fact, the low level of family allowances and large variations in rents (of which National Insurance takes no account) resulted in many dependent upon National Insurance benefits needing national assistance as a supplement in order to reach a subsistence level. Moreover, the unemployment of sections of the population not eligible for insurance benefits, or whose contributions had expired, further swelled the number in poverty, as enumerated in the previous chapter.

In order to reduce the sharp distinction between insurance and means-tested benefits, the Ministry of Social Security Act (1966) amalgamated them under the now Department of Health and Social Security. Nonetheless, within this framework the Supplementary Benefits Commission (SBC) was created to administer Supplementary Benefits (which replaced the term national assistance) separately.

Advantages of Supplementary Benefit
The British social security system is frequently compared favourably with that of the USA. Being a central Government responsibility, the SBC does ensure that similar basic rates are paid throughout the country. It thus avoids the variations and problems of transferability of benefits which can occur where it is run by a multitude of different local authorities. In addition, the SBC claims to combine, in the words of its chairman Lord Collison, 'basic rights with the flexibility which discretion affords'. The first reading, from an official publication, gives not only the basic rates of Supplementary Benefit but also explains that certain discretionary payments may also be available. These payments are intended to allow officials to take individual needs into account but in order to avoid too much variation they are guided by codes whose detailed instructions are kept secret. The individual relationship between officials and claimants should enable the latter to receive, again to quote Lord Collison, 'courtesy and understanding'. But others see it primarily as a means of detecting and deterring those who make false claims. The Fisher Report, *Abuse of Social Security Benefits* (1973), approved fully of an effective system to prevent claimants receiving too much money.

Criticisms
Three major criticisms are made of Supplementary Benefits. The first, concerning the inadequate level of its rates, was made in the previous chapter. The second, illustrated by the paper

from **Nick Bond**, claims that many recipients do not receive their full dues. His research detected that significant numbers could not check their benefits as they were unaware of the basic rates and, at times, found officials unwilling to provide this information. An even greater proportion did not know of the existence of discretionary payments and many were ignorant of their right to appeal against official decisions. Consequently, over half were actually receiving less than their full entitlement and, if Bond's research has a general application, it would appear that under-payment of claimants rather than abuse by them is a characteristic of the social security system.

At least, all the persons in Bond's survey were receiving some benefit. Others may refuse to claim at all because of the stigma. It is this stigma associated with means-tested benefits which constitutes the third criticism as discussed in the reading by **Sheila Kay**. Means testing requires submission to an official investigation which appears to question the claimants' characters as well as their finances. This position of enforced dependence, according to the America writer, Haggstrom, reinforces the poor's feelings of powerlessness and is destructive of their self-respect. Kay takes the argument further by showing how it also exposes the claimants to condemnatory treatment from other members of society who stereotype them as 'spongers', 'layabouts' and 'the irresponsible'. In response, those in need may either accept their inferior position and act in accordance with societal expectations or may flee from the stigma by refusing to apply for financial help.

The criticisms are usually accompanied by suggestions for reform. As mentioned, the Child Poverty Action Group, of which Sheila Kay was a member, has campaigned for greater reliance on universal rather than means-tested benefits. Later, Chapter 6 will describe efforts to encourage the deprived to more fully use the Supplementary Benefits system. The final chapter will consider more radical proposals to reduce the numbers of those having to apply to the SBC.

PLANNING

Planning, according to Gans, 'is a method of public decision-making which emphasizes explicit goal-choice and rational goals-means determination, so that decisions can be based on the goals people are seeking and on the most effective programmes to achieve them'. Almost any managerial activity could fit into this definition but, more specifically, the term planning usually encompasses the decisions associated with professional planners. Local authorities have had considerable involvement in planning since the Town and Country Planning Act (1947) gave them the extensive negative powers of granting or refusing planning permission on land and building use to match their positive powers to develop (or re-develop) parts of the environment. More recently the Town and Country Planning Act (1968) has obliged them to stress economic aims as well as land utilization in their developmental plans while the scope of planning has been extended by planning councils with a regional brief.

The case for planning

Although the extent of planning which is desirable is still a political issue, the necessity for some planning is not disputed. The selection from **Longman** succinctly argues its advantages, citing the growth in population, in human expectations and life complexity as requiring planning to reduce chaos and to distribute goods more fairly. It assumes that free market mechanisms do not adequately distribute the use of resources such as houses, land, roads, etc. and that planning is needed both to resolve conflicting demands and to maximize their effective use.

Criticisms

Planners can point to exceptional achievements – miles of road, bridges, thousands of dwellings. Their technological expertise is such that major disasters, such as Ronan Point, are rare. Yet planners are currently under attack, being blamed for traffic congestion, 'soulless' estates, the shortage of land for development and the consequent high house prices. Leaving

these aside, t...
three general tr...
  Firstly, planning...
aspects. Many local ...
estates without conside...
recreation and communit... ..., in his reading,
indicates that whole deprive... ...ourhoods have been
demolished and moved to new areas although residents valued
their old communities. Indeed, studies suggest that
re-development can precipitate social problems. Children must
adapt to new schools, workers face higher fares to reach work,
families meet the higher rents of new houses. (Moreover,
Ungerson's research confirms that not all individuals in
re-development areas are eligible for new housing with the
most vulnerable forced to move to other 'inner-ring' locations.)
Underlying much re-development is the belief that social
malaises will disappear in a new environment. Gans, in a
recommended book, calls this the 'fallacy of physical
determinism' which under-estimates the extent to which people's
behaviour is shaped by social, cultural and economic forces
outside of their own houses. The argument is not that people
should not have better environments but that other changes
are also needed in order to improve their social welfare.

  Secondly, and related to the above, planners are criticized
for ignoring poverty. A theme of Pahl's contribution is that
the physical focus has blocked consideration of the unequal
distribution of power which determines wealth and poverty in
society. Similarly, Gans in America urges planners to tackle
poverty which is 'the major problem to be solved if cities are
going to provide the quality of life which planners are
seeking'.

  The creation of roads, estates and yachting marinas may
bring professional prestige even if not helping the deprived.
The third criticism is that planning serves the interests of
planners not those planned for. Broady, in a penetrating
analysis, has ironically observed, 'the people as recipients of
that service are – and perhaps should be – passive, inert and
acquiescent in accepting the professionally administered services
in the conduct of which, for the most part, they can have only

Signs of Change

participate
explains,
the most
124
...ent'. In short, Longman
...ted by planning decisions do not
...aking.

...hange

...nning professionals and committees have not wholly
ignored the complaints. Smith's reading describes the intention
of one chairman of a city planning committee to emphasize a
policy of improving deprived neighbourhoods rather than
bulldozing them away. Elsewhere, Cullingworth recently has
drawn upon his extensive knowledge to comment, 'Physical
planning documents decreasingly deal solely with urban form,
land use, the layout of roads and the juxtaposition of
buildings . . . The implicit aim of improving social well-being
is becoming more explicit.' Certainly advance reports of the
North West Strategic Planning Team indicate a concern with
improving local services to improve the general quality of life
of a depressed region.

Perhaps most significant of all, the need for public
participation in planning is being more widely recognized.
The Skeffington Report, *People and Planning* (1969), set up by
the Ministry of Housing and Local Government, recommended
that the public be kept informed of the preparation of local
plans, that they be invited to discuss them before final decisions
were made and that, where available, alternative courses be
presented for public views. In addition, the Report wanted
community forums to enable local organizations to discuss
planning issues and community development officers to secure
the involvement of people not in organizations. It is true that
these proposals have not been fully implemented, that some
local authority representatives and officials regard participation
as too time-consuming, and that participation can have varied
meanings. Nonetheless, the emergence of community groups
to challenge – often successfully – official decisions has three
implications. It demonstrates that those affected by planning
decisions can exert an influence; it reflects a development (also
seen in Supplementary Benefits and social work) of recipients
refusing to accept professional supremacy; it means that some
of the power previously held by politicians and professionals
passes to those involved in community activities.

The criticisms – often by planners themselves – reveal that planning is not a value-free activity. It is part of a political process which may uphold traditional physical planning or attempt to promote social equality. At least the greater participation of the public should encourage planners to consider the social implications of their decisions, enable them to take more factors into account, and help make explicit the values on which decisions are being based.

SOCIAL WORK

The annual report of the Department of Health and Social Security revealed that at the end of 1972 local authority social service departments employed over 15,000 social workers and a total staff force approaching 135,000. These numbers, which exclude social workers employed by other agencies, show a rapid rise from pre-war days and lend force to the contention that in post-war Britain social work within the personal social services became regarded as a major approach to meeting need. The Younghusband Report, *The Employment and Training of Social Workers* (1947), which strongly influenced thinking, described the social worker as being 'concerned with remedying certain deficiencies which may exist in the relation between the individual and his counterpart' in order to assist 'the individual or group of individuals to make the best use of [these] resources and to achieve a better degree of personal development and a more satisfying adjustment to the social environment'. Attention was drawn to the possibility of changing environments and social structures but it was the report's emphasis on the individualizing aspects which reinforced contemporary trends in social work. The growth of local authority children's mental health and welfare departments (as well as settings for probation, medical and psychiatric social work) created a demand for caseworkers. A widespread assumption was that the central Government's social security services could deal with income-maintenance needs leaving local authority and voluntary social workers to concentrate on personal and emotional problems through an individual relationship.

Social Work Developments

The 1950s and 1960s witnessed many developments. Social
work agencies grew from insignificance – the first children's
officer in one town was initially allocated a desk in the typing
pool – to large organizations with, in some instances, senior
staff responsible for the management of thousands of
employees. Accordingly, social workers had to fit their skills
to the statutory and organizational demands of their agencies.
Many more social workers were trained, a development which
reflected their increasing professionalization culminating in the
amalgamation of most social work associations into the
British Association of Social Workers with a membership, in
1973, of 11,500.

Professor Halmos, in a book recommended at the end of the
chapter, interprets the expansion of social work and allied
professions 'as a new social factor of considerable influence on
the cultural and moral changes in twentieth-century western
society'. He believes it restores the values of love, humility and
respect in an inhuman age. His claims have been contested and
many social workers would probably prefer to point to the
value of their profession in supplying specialized skills for the
emotional and psychological problems of foster children,
delinquents and the mentally ill. Certainly, Holman's
comparative study of local authority and private foster children
establishes that those receiving regular help from social workers
are significantly more likely to obtain suitable foster parents,
experience less emotional deprivation and be less liable to
sudden and multiple removals.

During the 1960s, social workers became more involved in
the provision of material aid as legislation and policy enabled
them to help children in their own homes and to keep the
mentally disordered in the community. The Children and
Young Persons Act (1963), for instance, gave local authorities
a duty to prevent children having to come into care and to do
so by providing material or financial help. The selection from
Heywood and **Allen** has been included precisely because it
studies how social workers use that Act and so how they
reconcile their skills in inter-personal relationships with the
giving or withholding of money. Some considered that
financial concerns spoiled the casework relationship, others saw

it as a practical means of help. Further, the major finding that
material help was not for income-maintenance but for
emergencies, such as preventing evictions or the cutting off of
electricity, may indicate support for the contention of Professor
Meyer, in another recommended book, that, as social workers
cannot eliminate poverty, their role is to make life more
tolerable for its victims.

A Critique of Social Workers
Any complacency felt by social workers has long since been
shattered by a growing critique which found strong expression
in a pamphlet by **Adrian Sinfield**. Reviving earlier attacks from
Barbara Wootton, his charges came with extra force by
appearing in the wake of the *Seebohm Report's* recommendation
to amalgamate most local authority social work services into
one social service department. The final selection in this
chapter reproduces part of Sinfield's work.

Initially, Sinfield questions the Seebohm committee's
uncritical acceptance of social work. He explains that little
research exists to substantiate the effectiveness of casework –
the predominant social work method. He argues that individual
therapy, which concentrates on psychological change, is of
little avail to persons lacking money or housing, particularly
when their deprivations result from social and economic forces
beyond their control. He then criticizes social workers on
three grounds: that they offer therapy not material goods;
that they lack knowledge about welfare benefits for which
clients might be eligible; and that by persuading clients to
'tolerate the intolerable' they act as agents of social control
and so lessen the prospects of radical social reform.

Sinfield has not been alone. George and Wilding's research
detected motherless families needing financial aid and day-care
facilities instead of kind words. Glastonbury's study found
'some reluctance on the part of professionally trained caseworkers to undertake full responsibilities towards homeless
families'. It is even argued that the casework relationship
can reinforce poverty by emphasizing the dependent position
of the poor.

There have been replies to the charges but it must be noted
that Sinfield is not attempting to abolish casework. Rather he

claims that frequently social workers use it inappropriately.
More positively, he encourages them firstly to deal with clients'
immediate difficulties – such as a child's problems at school –
rather than probing into their personalities and secondly to
actively inform them of the welfare benefits they can obtain.
Although Sinfield forcibly argues that social work has political
connotations, he is less clear on how social workers can be a
political force striving for the abolition of poverty. Chapter 6
illustrates that social workers can and do take direct action
but many of their profession are uneasy about such
developments. They would place their faith in organizational
reforms to improve the quality of services to meet clients'
needs.

Supplementary Benefits Department of Health & Social Security

Reprinted with permission from Department of Health & Social Security, *Family Benefits and Pensions*, H.M.S.O., 1974, pp. 3-7

What supplementary benefit is
Supplementary Benefit is different from the other social security cash benefits. Its purpose is to provide income on a non-contributory basis for people who are not in full-time work and whose income (if any), whether from benefits or from other sources, is not enough to meet their requirements. This benefit, therefore, supplements other State benefits or private resources. The Supplementary Benefits Handbook, published by Her Majesty's Stationery Office, goes into more detail than is possible in the paragraphs which follow.

Supplementary Benefits are payable as a right to people in Great Britain whose incomes are below the level of requirements approved by Parliament. Supplementary pension is for people over the minimum pension age (65 for men, 60 for women). Supplementary allowance is for people aged 16 or over but under pension age.

Those entitled
People are entitled to benefit if they are not in full-time work and their resources are less than their requirements. Anyone over 16 and under 65 (60 for women) and fit for work may have to register for work at the Employment Exchange as a condition of receiving benefit.

How benefit is worked out
The amount of Supplementary Benefit payable is worked out by taking a person's 'requirements' according to the scale rates plus an addition for rent and any special additions the person may be entitled to, and deducting his income from the total.

The requirements and income of a married couple in the same household, and those of any dependent children living with them, are counted together and only the husband can claim. A couple who, although not married, are living together as man and wife are normally treated as if they were married.

CALCULATION OF REQUIREMENTS

| Weekly scales | Ordinary scale | Long-term scale* | |
		Claimant (and wife) under 80	Claimant (or wife) aged 80 or over
	£	£	£
For			
Married Couple	13.65	16.35	16.60
Single Householder	8.40	10.40	10.65
Any Other Person			
18 or over	6.70	8.40	8.65
16 to 17	5.15	–	–
Dependent Child			
13 to 15	4.35	–	–
11 to 12	3.55	–	–
5 to 10	2.90	–	–
under 5	2.40	–	–
For the Blind			
married couple			
one blind	14.90	17.60	17.85
both blind	15.70	18.40	18.65
single person			
18 or over	9.65	11.65	11.90
16 to 17	6.05	–	–

* The long-term scale rates apply to (1) supplementary pensioners and (2) people under pension age, except the unemployed, who have received Supplementary Benefit for a continuous period of two years or more. These higher scale rates include a margin of 50p (75p for the over 80 rate) towards special expenses.

[These rates were current in 1973 and have been included to illustrate what at that time was taken to be an acceptable level of income.]

Attendance allowance

The requirements of a person who is entitled to a national insurance attendance allowance are increased by the amount of the attendance allowance payable.

Rent

To these basic requirements should be added:

An amount for rent. A householder's addition for rent will generally be the full amount of the rent and rates (but see below). If a person owns the house in which he lives, his outgoings, including payments of mortgage interest – but not of capital – and rates, etc. will be treated as rent.

The rent addition will be less than the full rent if this includes such items as heating or lighting, if it is unreasonably high, or if there are any payments from sub-tenants. Part of the rent may be attributed to other members of the household who are not dependent on the householder.

Rent rebates or allowances and rate rebates are not normally made available by local authorities to people who receive Supplementary Benefit for continuous periods of more than eight weeks. When someone claiming Supplementary Benefit already has a rent rebate or allowance or rate rebate, the relevant amount is deducted from the amount to be added for rent in the Supplementary Benefit assessment.

If a person lives as a member of someone else's household, a standard amount of 90p will be added for rent.

If a person is a boarder and pays an inclusive charge for board and lodging, his weekly income level will be the amount of his board and lodging charge, up to a reasonable figure, plus £2.70 a week (£3.05 for long-term beneficiaries) for personal expenses.

Special expenses

A weekly addition to requirements can be made where there are exceptional circumstances, for example, where a diet or domestic help is needed, extra heating is required on account of ill-health or poor accommodation, or extra expenditure is necessarily incurred in centrally heated accommodation. The long-term rate of benefit already includes a margin of 50p (75p for the over 80 rate) towards special expenses and this will be deducted from any additional requirements other than for heating or for special expenses of children.

CALCULATION OF RESOURCES

Income

In working out the resources different kinds of income are treated differently:

(1) Earnings. The first £2 a week of any part-time earnings plus the first £2 of a wife's earnings are not counted. But only £1 a week of a claimant's part-time earnings can be ignored if he is unemployed and registering for work at the Employment Office.

(2) Family allowances and most national insurance benefits and maintenance payments, whether voluntary or under Court Order, are taken into account in full.

(3) Disablement and war widow's pensions. Up to £2 a week will be disregarded.

(4) Other income. The first £1 a week of the total of any other income, including any assumed income from savings and other capital (see below) will not be counted.

The total which can be disregarded from (3) and (4) together is limited to £2.

Savings and capital

If a man or his wife owns the house they live in, its value will be ignored. Other savings, such as money in the National Savings Bank or Building Societies, are treated as capital. If a man and his wife and dependents have, between them, capital of less than £325, it will be ignored and so will any income it produces. If capital amounts to £325 or more, the actual income from it will not be counted, but a weekly income of 5p for each £25 between £300 and £800 will be assumed. On capital over £800 the assumed weekly income is 12½p on each £25, on the basis that a person can reasonably be expected to draw something from capital over this amount for normal living expenses.

How to claim

Leaflet SB1 which includes a claim form is available at any Post Office or local Social Security office. Unemployed people should claim on form B1 obtainable at an Unemployment Benefit Office of the Department of Employment (where leaflet SL8 which gives them further guidance is also available). Information about a claimant's circumstances is needed so that the amount of the benefit can be worked out. This information will, of course, be treated as confidential.

How payment is made
Payment will usually be by means of a book of orders which can be cashed at the chosen post office; but for the person who is unemployed and required to register for work payment will be made through the Unemployment Benefit Office of the Department of Employment. It is often possible to pay a supplementary pension combined with a retirement pension on a single order book.

Appeals
A claimant has the right to appeal to an independent Appeal Tribunal if he is dissatisfied with the decision on his claim or with any condition attaching to the award of benefit.

Exceptional needs
If a person has exceptional needs, lump-sum payments may be made in certain circumstances. Such payments may be made, for example, where a person has inadequate stocks of bedding.

Emergencies
In an emergency such as flood or fire the local Social Security office will usually help in the task of relief. They can also help in less serious emergencies: for example, some payment may be made (and subsequently recovered) when a person has lost wages by being unavoidably prevented from going to work, or when he is in some other temporary emergency, and has insufficient resources for his immediate requirements.

Entitlement to other benefits
People and their dependents receiving Supplementary Benefit are also entitled to exemption from payment of the charges for prescriptions, wigs and fabric supports (or to a refund of charges paid) and to an additional payment to meet any NHS dental and optical charges they incur; children under school age and expectant mothers are also entitled to free milk and vitamins; children at

school do not have to pay for school meals; members of the family attending hospital for treatment may claim a refund of fares.

Knowledge of Rights

Nick Bond

Reprinted with permission from *Knowledge of Rights and Extent of Unmet Need Amongst Recipients of Supplementary Benefit,* Coventry Community Development Project, 1972, pp. 1-9

The Supplementary Benefit system in this country exists as the final safety net in our income maintenance strategy. The scale-rates for benefit are based on estimates of minimum subsistence-level needs. Consequently anyone who slips through this safety net, even partially, will be forced to live at a level below that which the State considers no one should fall. The Supplementary Benefit system fails in its purpose, therefore, to the extent to which those who are entitled to receive help through this system fail to receive their rights. Because of its function as the final safety net the Supplementary Benefit system, of all our systems for maintaining income, should be the most sensitive in locating need and the most foolproof in its operations to meet need.

THE BACKGROUND TO THE SURVEY

In June 1970 a shop-front Information and Opinion Centre was opened in Hillfields, an inner-city area of Coventry, chosen as the focus for part of the national Community Development Project. During the first 12 months numerous enquiries and complaints concerning entitlement to Supplementary Benefit came to light at the Information Centre.

As a result of dealing with a number of similar cases, workers at the Centre began to speculate about the extent of ignorance among recipients of Supplementary Benefit of their basic rights to entitlement. Moreover, they began to wonder whether the cases that came to their attention really were the few 'unfortunate exceptions', as often claimed by officials of the Department of Health and Social Security, or whether such cases of claimants failing to secure their full entitlement were in fact more common than generally realized by the public at large and the Supplementary Benefit Commission (SBC) in particular. In an effort to discover answers to these questions it was decided in June 1971 to conduct the action-survey described below.

THE PURPOSE OF THE ACTION-SURVEY

(1) To discover among a sample of recipients of Supplementary Benefit below pension age:
- (a) the extent of knowledge of basic rights connected with Supplementary Benefit.
- (b) the extent to which claimants in this sample were not receiving their rights.

(2) To help any claimants who were not receiving their full entitlement to Supplementary Benefit to claim it.

Advantage was taken of a sampling frame provided by a 1 in 6 household survey of the project study area conducted by the CDP Research Team. The sample comprised 40 claimants representing 93 per cent of all claimants under pension age identified by the 1 in 6 household survey.

THE RESULTS OF THE SURVEY

Knowledge of Basic Scale Rates

The answers revealed an extensive lack of knowledge about this most basic information. Seventeen (42·5 per cent) of the sample did not know if their basic Supplementary Benefit was correctly calculated or not. Thirteen of these did not know how to find out; four thought they could find out by asking at the Supplementary Benefit Office. A further 11 (27·5 per cent) of the sample thought their benefit was incorrectly calculated. Eight of these did not know how to find out; three thought they could find out by asking at the Supplementary Benefit Office. One had tried this but said that he got no satisfaction. Moreover, of the 12 (30 per cent) who thought their Supplementary Benefit was correct, 10 did not in fact *know* if it was correct; they merely assumed that the Supplementary Benefit Office would not make a mistake.

Altogether only two (5 per cent) of the sample were certain that their Supplementary Benefit was correct; 38 (95 per cent) simply did not know.

No one in the sample suggested writing to the Supplementary Benefit Office asking for a written statement of how their benefit was calculated. None seemed to realize that they had a right to receive such a written statement. None suggested checking with Form S1. This form is obtainable at any post office but not, inexplicably, on display at any Supplementary Benefit Office. Presumably many of the sample were unaware of its existence.

As a result of being interviewed eight individuals wrote to the Supplementary Benefit Office asking for a written statement of how their benefit was calculated. In each of these cases there appeared to the interviewer to be the possibility that the calculation of benefit was incorrect. Only two received a written reply. The others were told verbally by a visitor that their allowance was correct – a procedure which is far more difficult to check or challenge.

Knowledge of the Discretionary Powers of the Supplementary Benefit Commission to meet need in special circumstances

For the large proportion of claimants who are dependent upon Supplementary Benefit over a long period of time (70 per cent of the sample) it is particularly important that they should be aware of their entitlement to the discretionary grants and additions available, since it is widely recognized that, whilst it may be possible to manage on the basic Supplementary Benefit allowance for a short period, the longer dependence continues the more difficult it is to cope both practically and psychologically.

(1) *Special Needs Grants* (SNGs). These grants are lump sum payments intended to meet need in exceptional circumstances when there is no other way of preventing hardship and to meet the costs of any essential expenditure which is not provided for in the scale rates, e.g. the cost of providing or replacing large items of essential household equipment such as a bed, bedding or cooker.

As revealed in the answers 20 of the total sample (50 per cent) had never heard of these grants. Moreover, of the 19 (47·5 per cent) who had heard of SNGs only 13 (32·5 per cent) of the total knew how to apply for them. Of these 13 only one suggested the method of claiming that would seem to be most certain of response, i.e. to make a written application. Of the remaining 12, 10 suggested asking at the office and two asking the visitor. Altogether 27 (67·5 per cent) of the sample had no idea how to apply for this important discretionary grant.

Moreover, in the sample there appears to be a significant connection between knowledge of how to apply for a SNG and the receipt of a SNG. Of the 13 who had heard of SNGs and knew how to apply, 11 had applied at some time and two had not. Of these 11, 10 had received a SNG at least once.

Similarly, there appears to be a significant correlation between lack of knowledge of how to apply for a SNG and the failure to receive a SNG. Only three of the 27 who did not know how to apply for a SNG had received a SNG as a result of an initiative from the Supplementary Benefit Office. During the survey 15 claimants applied for SNGs (i.e. were judged by the interviewer to have special needs). Seven of these knew in principle how to apply, but had not done so; presumably because they did not realize they could apply (or did not have the confidence to apply) for the particular special need they revealed to the interviewer. The others did not know how to apply.

(2) *Discretionary Weekly Additions* (DWAs). Ignorance concerning this discretionary benefit is even more widespread than that surrounding SNGs. Altogether only 10 (25 per cent) had heard of this discretionary allowance and only six (15 per cent) how to apply for it. All six suggested contacting the Supplementary Benefit Office in order to claim. Not one suggested the method of claiming that might be thought to be the most dependable – i.e. claiming in writing. As a result of being interviewed four claimants applied for DWAs. None of these four had heard of these additions. These payments are made weekly to the claimant on top of his basic scale rate and are intended to meet the costs of any essential recurring expenditure which it is recognized as not provided for in the scale rates, e.g. the costs of providing a special diet or extra heating for the sick or infirm.

Knowledge of Supplementary Benefit Appeal Procedure

Seventeen (42·5 per cent) of the sample did not know that they could appeal against decisions of the SBC. Thirteen (32 per cent) thought they knew how to appeal but *in fact only 6 (15 per cent) of the total sample knew the correct method of appealing,* namely to write to the Supplementary Benefit Office or fill in an Appeals Form. Moreover, only four (10 per cent) of the sample knew that it was possible for someone to speak on their behalf at a tribunal. Altogether only two (5 per cent) of the sample had ever appealed. However it cannot be assumed from this that there is widespread satisfaction concerning Supplementary Benefit payments: when asked if there had been any occasions in the past when they would have liked to have appealed against a decision of the SBC if they had known how to go about it, 12 (30 per cent) quoted specific instances when they would have appealed. It appears that knowledge of appeal procedures is a more important variable in determining whether an appeal is made than whether a claimant feels he has ground for appeal.

Altogether 11 (27·5 per cent) of the sample were thought by the interviewer to have grounds for appealing; eight (20 per cent) actually appealed. A further three were advised to appeal but they preferred not to. Of the eight appeals against decisions of the SBC four were resolved in the claimant's favour without going to Appeal. Four went to Appeal and in three of these cases a determination was made in favour of the claimants (a success rate of 87·5 per cent). These figures compared with a national appeal rate of less than 1 per cent and a successful national appeal rate of approximately 20 per cent of all appeals made.

EXTENT OF UNMET NEED REVEALED BY THE SURVEY

Receipt of certain rights associated with the receipt of Supplementary Benefit

(1) *Free Prescriptions.* Eight (20 per cent) of the total sample in fact paid for prescriptions. Two of these knew that they did not have to pay but preferred to do so in order to avoid embarrassment. The other six (15 per cent of the sample) did not realize that they could get prescriptions free.

(2) *Free School Meals.* Of the 19 families with children at school four (21 per cent of those eligible) did not receive free

school meals. Of these one did not realize that his children could receive free school meals. One preferred his child to come home to dinner – he thought he was too young to stop. Two said they preferred to pay for school dinners so that their children should not feel different from other school children. Both of these were mothers of adolescent girls.

The total number of children not receiving free school dinners in these four families was five, i.e. 11·4 per cent of the 44 children eligible. This represents a loss of assumed income of 60p per week for three families and £1.20 for one family.

Failure to receive rights as a result of administrative errors

(1) *Receipt of Free Milk Tokens.* Failure to receive free milk tokens represents a serious loss of income for claimants with children under five. In the sample three (21 per cent) of those claimants eligible had been without milk tokens in the period immediately prior to the survey – two for about three months and one for four weeks. All of these three claimants were unsupported mothers. This represented a total loss of income of 77p for one family, and 38½p each for the other two families. An average loss of income of 51p per week. This failure is a result of simple bureaucratic incompetence. The tokens are given as of right and should involve no need to claim for those entitled. All three claimants successfully claimed payments in cash to the value of the tokens they had failed to receive.

(2) *Other Administrative Errors.* One of the sample was found to be receiving an incorrect basic supplementary allowance. This was 45p below the correct scale rate.

One severely handicapped man had been granted £10 to purchase a gas fire in December 1970 but the grant had not arrived by the date of the survey (16.6.71). The grant was sent with apologies as soon as the matter was drawn to the attention of the local office.

In total therefore five of the sample (12·5 per cent) were found to be receiving less than they were entitled to as a result of administrative errors.

Failure to receive SNGs in cases of special need

As a result of the survey 13 (32·5 per cent) of the sample applied for SNGs and 10 (25 per cent) in fact received these. However, none of the three whose applications were refused appealed. Assuming two out of three of these would have won their appeals it could be estimated that 12 (30 per cent) of the sample in fact had a special need at the time of the survey but failed to receive a grant to meet that need.

Failure to receive DWAs in circumstances of special need
Altogether four (10 per cent) of the sample applied for DWAs. Three of these were granted. The other was refused but the claimant did not go to appeal. At least three (7·5 per cent) of the sample therefore were entitled to DWAs at the time of the survey (and at the time of their original interview with an SBC official) but had failed to receive such a grant.

As a result of the survey 16 (40 per cent) of the sample received cash grants either to meet special needs or to rectify mistakes made by the SBC. The total amount of cash received in lump sum payments was £148.27 – an average of £3.70 per claimant in the sample. In addition five claimants (12·5 per cent) had their weekly rate of Supplementary Benefit increased. Three of these had their weekly rate of benefit increased by DWAs averaging 53p per claimant. One claimant had a weekly increase of 45p as a result of the discovery of an administrative error and one claimant received a weekly increase of 25p as a result of notifying the SBC of changes in his circumstances.

Altogether nearly half of the sample – 18 (45 per cent) – received additional resources as a result of being interviewed. In other words, *at the time of the interviews approximately half of all the claimants in the sample were failing to receive their full entitlement.*

Problems of Accepting Means-Tested Benefits

Sheila Kay

Reprinted with permission from 'Problems of Accepting Means-Tested Benefits', in D. Bull. (Ed.), *Family Poverty*, Duckworth & Co., 1971, pp. 29-32

Stigma not only affects those with a problem, who have to live with the feeling of being shameful or different, but it acts as a warning to others who might have the problem but narrowly escape or hide the fact. It also affects the reactions of other people towards the stigmatized. The older terms – pauper, criminal, lunatic, prostitute; the modern terms – layabout, juvenile delinquent, ex-mental patient, unmarried mother and coloured immigrant, call up a series of stereotypes of irresponsible people lacking in the accepted standards, collectively different and to be treated with suspicion and reserve, and in particular, having their right to maintenance in financial need, sickness or unemployment put under a microscope.

THE EFFECT OF STIGMA

Fear of being 'branded' in this way involves those in need of help in a range of emotional reactions, from shame and refusal to apply, through confusion about requirements, resentment and 'hostility towards a system which deliberately and continually creates the role of suppliant', through desperate efforts to tap every source, to fight or flight. The fight may be constructive, or it may be expressed in 'putting one over' on the authorities; the flight may be into apathy or, by 'doing a moonlight flit', escaping from rent arrears and debts. The fear may not be justified, and a sense of relief and restored self-confidence is experienced if a considerate hearing, followed by help, is given. In others who do not apply for help, their ignorance of benefits available may be the chief reason why they adapt to a restricted life and defend themselves and their children against disappointment by reducing their demands on life compared with those around them, thus giving the appearance of apathy.

In both of the Merseyside CPAG Welfare Rights projects, we have found confirmation of this consciousness of stigma again and again. In the second study, a small proportion of those who knew about the benefits said they would not claim them, even if they were eligible:

> The reasons for this reluctance to apply for what are rights varied considerably, but could be divided between four groups: (1) those who felt, with regard to education benefits, that their children would be jeered at if they received them; (2) those who preferred to be independent and manage somehow by themselves; (3) those who felt the 'red-tape' involved in applying was not worthwhile for the small return; (4) those who had been refused on previous applications and refused to be 'humiliated' again.

In the first study, there was a core group of about one third of those in poverty who were receiving Supplementary Benefits and who knew about many other benefits such as free welfare foods, school meals and clothing, though not often about rent rebates. Then there was a group of working men's families – low paid labourers, drivers, etc., who knew very little of these rights and viewed their acceptance with considerable doubt; not that they were free from financial anxiety, for one docker said that only the recent strikes, giving him an increase of over £3 per week, had enabled him to look forward to rehousing with its prospect of a rent increase. A third group included a number who refused or were initially hesitant to complete the questionnaire and several who declined help in applying for benefits for which they appeared to be eligible. Many of these were retired people who 'did not discuss their business with anyone'; at least two of them were drawing £4.50 retirement pension plus £1.50 per week out of savings to pay the rent, rather than claim a supplementary pension.

One young woman refused to talk to the student who first called on her, but eventually opened the door to 'someone older':

> After being reassured about confidentiality, she explained that she did not want her neighbours to know she was unmarried. She had two children, and was living on Supplementary Bene-

fits and having some difficulties in managing, but the older girl who was at school either came home for lunch or paid for dinners. When we discussed free dinners, both she and the little girl assured me that everyone in the class had known about it when she was getting free dinners the previous year and the child could not face it again. Although I dropped the subject, I must admit I doubted that everyone knew, until some weeks later in the summer of 1968, my own child of seven volunteered that yellow tickets were for those who paid, and pink tickets were for the free dinners, at school.

This is an example of stigma having a twofold effect: it was painfully disadvantageous to the child who bore it, and the knowledge of her reactions might affect her classmates' willingness to accept free meals, so that it was also a deterrent to the population at risk. The disadvantage of being in poverty and asking for help includes loss of privacy in one's private life and relationships, and in one's financial affairs, and may include loss of confidentiality about other things. Dennis Marsden, in *Mothers Alone*, discusses the effect of stigma upon mothers without husbands in their homes. Not only were many of the mothers conscious that their single, divorced, deserted or widowed state led them to be regarded as 'easy meat' by male acquaintances, visiting tradesmen and callers; but 'fears of the woman's possible cohabitation caused officers [of the then National Assistance Board] to treat a large proportion of the mothers with suspicion'.

If there are grounds for such suspicions, their chances of achieving a more regular way of life were illustrated by one mother who asked advice of CPAG, and complained that she was 'always having her money stopped' although she had three children.

She was concerned that a strange visitor had called, saying he was from the Ministry of Social Security, though he 'only had a little black book and not the usual case sheets'. When she asked for identification, he laughed and said she knew very well, so she refused to answer any more questions, whereupon he referred, in front of a neighbour and the eldest child aged nine, to the fact that she had a police record. She said she was going to consult a solicitor; she was sick of being hounded for a conviction seven years ago 'when all [she] had done was stand talking to a strange man in the street'; since then she had several times been questioned by the police when she was out of doors in the evening, and an official had once met a request for a clothing grant for the children with the suggestion that she 'go out and earn it'. She existed, one felt, in an embattled relationship with the authorities who she felt drove her into the way of life she still denied, and about which she felt extremely ambivalent.

Social Planning in an Urban Community

Ford Longman

Reprinted with permission from 'Social Planning in an Urban Community', *Social Service Quarterly*, vol. XL, no. 3, Winter 1966-67, pp. 99-101

Whether we like it or not, we live in an age of planning. The complexities of modern life are such that only by planning can we produce order from chaos and if we are to derive the maximum benefit from planning techniques, we need to understand the nature of the beast and come to terms with it.

We as a nation are faced with a number of domestic problems of the first magnitude, virtually all of which are found together in conurbations and which deserve our closest attention. I am deeply concerned that in tackling these problems we should get our order of priorities right and that we should see more clearly what are the social aspects of planning.

Perhaps the most relevant fact underlying the next thirty-five years is that the population of these islands is likely to rise very considerably. The Registrar General's projections assume over eight million more people by 1981, and over seventeen million more by the year 2001.

On top of this, people have come to expect – as of right – higher standards of living and increased leisure. Not only are working-class people adopting middle-class standards in ever increasing numbers, but they are adopting middle-class standards of mobility.

All these factors combine to place a tremendous strain upon the national stock of houses and upon the means of building them. It is now generally accepted that we must step up production to around 500,000 dwellings each year. Of these about half – or 250,000 per annum – will be required to meet new demands, to allow increased mobility and to take account of present over-crowding and multiple occupancy. The remaining quarter-of-a-million dwellings will be required to replace existing worn out properties.

On top of this we are becoming increasingly dependent upon immigrant labour, chiefly from the Commonwealth. Without these immigrants neither our hospitals nor our transport system, for example, could continue to function. We are indebted to these people, and they deserve every consideration. But the absorption and integration of these immigrants, and particularly coloured immigrants, is not easy and – coupled with the housing shortage – could lead to grave social problems.

It is useless tackling difficult questions such as these on a piecemeal basis; we have got to be able to make land available for housing and industry and have got to be able to do it on a scale undreamt of before. And it is no use blaming the building construction industry granted that, with comparatively few notable exceptions, the industry simply is not geared to present needs – but then, neither are we.

Moreover, the urban pattern has got to make good sense and the people – including the extra seventeen million – have got to be fed. We cannot ignore the economics of agriculture, nor can we ignore the physical environment, for people will no longer put up with inferior conditions.

REGIONAL PLANNING

With the publication of the Government's National Plan last autumn, regional planning councils and boards were provided with an overall framework for regional economic development looking five years ahead. The initial emphasis is being placed upon the industrial and economic aspects of planning, since it is upon increased production and exports that national prosperity larily depends. The social aspects of planning are, however, no less important, simply representing different facets of the totality.

Of course, economic growth and industry and transport are of basic importance for community growth. What interests people most are housing, education, health services, facilities for culture and recreational activities and like matters. And, moreover, they want all of these services near to their place of work. This is a tall order – but it is what planning is about – at least in part.

All this involves a multiplicity of interests, giving rise to a complicated pattern of interaction. To take just one example: no less than fourteen government departments are closely involved in regional planning. The number of permutations and combinations of involvement are legion – as are the possibilities of conflicting interests!

It is vitally important, therefore, that *all* those who have a part to play should be reasonably conversant with what others in related fields are seeking to achieve.

If our plans are to be really effective, we need to take a long, hard and wholly realistic look into the future. We need to think – and encourage others to think – seriously about the sort of New Britain in which we want to live. Planning should be our servant, not our master. Our environment should be built for us and not we moulded to fit our environment. We need to plan for twenty, thirty and fifty years ahead. It is not any more difficult in the long run to plan coherently and constructively than it is to live from hand to mouth and from year to year – each successive *ad hoc* decision making it ever more difficult to reach sensible conclusions in the end.

The development of our environment on the scale we have been talking about confronts us immediately with yet another problem: that we have totally inadequate numbers of professional men of the necessary quality for the needs of today, let alone tomorrow. We must have these people and this in turn raises an educational and a training problem as well as a whole series of questions as to whether we make the best use of their time and their talents.

SOCIAL PLANNING

In developing our environment and in meeting our social needs we need to give as much thought as possible to standards of provision and design, both in replacing existing defective services and in providing new services to meet increased needs.

Our social planning must take account, too, of needs which arise as the consequence of decisions taken in the fields of physical, economic or industrial planning, and in the field of social planning itself. To take but one example: what does it mean in human terms if you move large numbers of people from a district (however poor and ill favoured) and rehouse them on a vast new housing estate, or in blocks of high flats? What happens to their lives, and to those of their neighbours and their relatives? Does life become restricted? Do *things* become more important than *people*? Do you, among other things, end up with an inordinately high proportion of families and individuals with problems with which they cannot cope?

These problems, and others like them, are not academic – they are very real and they impinge on the lives of all of us.

Again, there are many other questions to which we need answers. For example, should you take work to the workers or vice versa? And what are the implications in social (and financial) terms? What is the impact on people's lives of the terrific mobility within industry today? What are the effects of retirement policies, or of administrative and technical developments? How often do we really get down to studying the needs and aspirations of the individual men, women and children involved? Have we any real understanding of who they are or, more fundamentally, who they should be if the resultant community is to be a balanced one?

In much of our social planning we still think in terms of a conventional family unit of a married couple with two or three growing children, and, possibly, an elderly relative; if we are enlightened and progressive, we provide something for the elderly and the aged! But large sections of the community all too often remain outside; single people of all ages (including students of all kinds) and many of them desperately lonely – immigrants – young marrieds – large (and often poor) families – the chronic sick – fatherless families – shift workers and mobile workers, and so on. All these have *special needs* which, let's face it, receive scant attention, but to which social planning should give full weight.

Coupled with these difficulties are those arising from lack of effective communications and from poor co-operation. Do people in each social service really know what other services are also operating in the same area, how they are organized and whom they can contact with confidence?

And there is a corollary to this: do too many workers in the social services assume that other people are not interested in what they are doing and so grow increasingly insular? And is there not scope for pooling and disseminating information and expertise?

Whose City?

Ray Pahl

Reprinted with permission from 'Whose City?', *New Society*, vol. 13, no. 330, 23 January 1969, pp. 120-22

What is to become of the city? Intellectuals scorn the neatness and order of skilled manual worker or lower middle-class housing in new towns or spec-built estates, and deplore huge, 'inhuman' blocks of flats. But at the same time they feel angry or guilty about overcrowding and poverty in Notting Hill or Sparkbrook. They are not sure whether the car must adapt to the city or the city to the car. Their attitude to the London motorway box seems to depend more on whether it affects their local area or on whether they have recently been ensnarled in crawling traffic for hours, rather than on any clear vision of what the city might or should be.

The attitudes of middle-class radicals to many other urban problems are highly ambivalent. Commuting, urban renewal, the location of the third London airport, urban poverty, mobility and congestion are all irritatingly confused issues on which the progressive line is not at all clear. Attempts to stay in London, by making such areas as Islington fashionable, are a potential source of guilt ('taking away houses from those in greater need'). The only comfort is that those who have done up cottages in the country are probably suffering from a similar sort of guilt.

There has been a recent spate of television programmes and articles by various pundits giving 'personal views' about the dreary creations of the planners and architects, particularly when seen in contrast to the lively, human, squalor of the streets of Soho and Chelsea or the excitement of the great mobile life of California. There is a pathetic demand for a visionary, who can explain in one Sunday supplement how we should all live; and yet at the same time there is a sort of underlying resentment that the richness, diversity, variety, etcetera, or 'real human life' should be squashed into the moulds devised by planners, who, by implication, are all unimaginative technocrats. Planners are expected to make our life 'better', but if they succeed they may be resented – because people are thereby being deprived of the freedom to plan their lives for themselves.

It seems that we are as uncertain of the problems as we are of the solutions. We know that there are slums; we know that the population is increasing; we know that the basic physical infrastructure is ageing and will have to be renewed; we know that our urban roads are congested; and yet we don't know which aspect of these various issues is 'the real problem'. New towns and new cities can help siphon off young, skilled, energetic people from existing cities. But they are far from complete solutions, since it is those most in need of help who are left behind. When the transportation technocrat is not sure what to feed into his computer, and the playwrights' and novelists' visions don't go much further than a few bustling streets in certain parts of London, maybe the third culture, sociology, will provide the answers?

Surely the sociologist can tell us what people will want – not only now, but in 1984, the year 2000, or whatever year it is to which we have to fix the long-term financial budgeting? But the sociologist wriggles. He argues that it is for him to analyse the implicit goals of different groups in society – how they conflict and what the unintended consequences of planning decisions might be – but not for him alone to prescribe these goals. He is a member of society as much as anyone else.

However, if pressed, the sociologist will say that physical arrangements have very little effect on social arrangements. Renewing the physical environment of the urban poor does not eliminate the causes of their poverty. The poverty is largely the result of the distribution of power in society and this distribution is preserved by powerful interest groups and finds expression in spatial and physical terms in the city. The elimination of poverty necessitates a voluntary abdication of some power by the affluent majority in favour of the poor minority.

Even though buildings and land use have very little effect on people's behaviour, this is not to say that the actual house that people live in is not very important. It is hardly an agent of social change, but it is still a much more important environment than the locality. People's *social world* is best conceived of as a social network of linkages, which is not necessarily based on locality.

However, physical planners have enough of the conventional wisdom to know that ultimately they must be concerned with social welfare in the broadest sense. Certainly, some might argue that planning is simply an end in itself rather than a means to an end. Neatness, tidiness, orderliness and planning in general may be defined as good, in some abstract sense, no matter what the people being planned may think. But the current vogue is 'participation', the Skeffington committee on public participation in planning is sitting, and so even the most enthusiastic 'drains man' or rule-book backwoodsman is probably prepared to make some small gesture towards public participation.

I have been stimulated to consider these issues by reading *People and Plans*, a collection of essays on urban problems and solutions, by Herbert J. Gans. It seems to me that, particularly for us in Britain, Professor Gans's essays could not have been published at a more opportune time. As both a sociologist and a qualified planner Professor Gans has had a long and distinguished record of research, and his books on *The Urban Villagers* and *The Levittowners* were valuable contributions to the ethnography of contemporary America. More recently he has been actively engaged in advising Government committees on the nation's so-called 'urban' crisis. Few people are as well qualified, either here or in America, to discuss the relationship between people and plans.

Furthermore, Gans is prepared to forsake academic detachment and make clear suggestions on policy. He argues consistently that planning must be *user*-oriented – it is for people, not for planners: it ought to be *compensatory*, so that those who get the fewest rewards from the private sector ought to get most from the public sector; finally, it ought to be more concerned with the established needs of *today* rather than with the hypothetical needs of the future. The problems of urban slums are greater than the problems of the aesthetics of urban sprawl. He is more concerned with the *processes* than with the symptoms they create, and traces back the causes of urban poverty to the social, economic and political structure of the society.

There are some 30 or so essays collected in this book ranging from satirical or polemical pieces aimed at a popular audience, to summaries of the sociological literature on a topic prepared for planners or social workers, and to scholarly papers, such as his critique of 'Urbanism and suburbanism as ways of life'. It is hard to think of a better book to recommend to all the planners and architects who are increasingly wanting to know what the contribution of the sociologist to their field is or could be. There is much that is wise; it is cogently expressed and it provides a fine contribution to the sociology of planning in its widest sense. Nevertheless, the book ends on a deeply pessimistic note, as Gans doubts whether the war on poverty and segregation can be won and raises the question whether the new, affluent suburbia has been achieved at the cost of withholding opportunities from the poor and non-white.

One fears that some British planners may be acting out a script which was written in the United States in the 1950s and is now increasingly outdated. The fashion in America was then to concentrate on transportation facilities, and teams of transportation experts, with economists and operation researchers, programmed their computers with alternative simulation models: thus, given the simplifying restraints of the exercise, they were able to formulate a number of alternative schemes. It would be sad if a decade later some British planners are still expecting too much from this new technical expertise, while a large part of the American planning profession has moved on to a greater concern with *social* objectives and the most rational and effective way of achieving them.

Professor Gans describes these changes in his essays on the 'Sociology of city planning' and on the 'Goal-oriented approach to planning'. In an essay on 'Culture and class in the study of poverty', Gans attacks the notion that the poor are condemned to remain so, trapped in a culture of poverty. 'If the culture of poverty is defined as those cultural patterns which keep people poor, it would be necessary to include in the term also the persisting cultural patterns among the affluent which, deliberately or not, keep their fellow citizens poor. When the concept of a culture of poverty is applied only to the poor, the onus for change falls too much on them, when, in reality, the prime obstacles to the elimination of poverty lie in the economic, political and social structure that operates to increase the wealth of the already affluent.' It is at this point that the British planner may begin to assume that the discussion is no longer relevant to him.

This is the tragedy of the British situation: it is tragic for the people that the planner sees his job in such a limited way; and it is tragic, too, for the planner that his best efforts are frustrated by forces which he defines as being outside his dominion. Thus he may build houses, only to find that those for whom they were built cannot afford to live in them because wages locally are low (Manchester Corporation reported last week that this is the situation in its newest estate, at Whitefield); or he may help to create jobs, only to find that he has condemned those who fill them to overcrowded housing because local land values are so high that housing is scarce.

However, we in Britain are fortunate in that we have the example of America to learn from. There, too ready an acceptance, both of the most easily applicable techniques and the values of the most powerful groups has led to the situation in which they have, for example, splendid freeways, which simply enable the middle-class to ride past the poor more rapidly. Making physical changes without parallel changes in the social structure may serve to add to the problem by drawing sections of the population further apart. Clearly no one wants British cities to be centres of poverty and racial intolerance. However, there may be some danger that if British planners feel that their main task is to concentrate on the future and to spend their time worrying about the provision of motorways and yachting marinas in 1991, they may take attention away from present problems and so, indirectly, help to make them worse.

Similarly, if they concern themselves with large areas, which have no elected representatives – such as regions – they can avoid facing local problems by claiming that they are not relevant at the larger level. Thus planning as an activity can continue indefinitely, without having to face the conflicting goals of the present at the scale on which people live. Method-oriented planners can easily lose sight of the goals, and the question which Gans poses in the American situation is equally relevant here. 'Who plans, with what ends and means, for what interest group?'

Yet Gans is one sociologist who cannot be criticized for being negative and for providing no positive suggestions. If only for his chapter on 'Planning for everyday life and problems of suburban and new town residents', any new town social relations officer should have the book on his desk. It should be standard reading for all community activists from Glenrothes to Solent City.

The British situation is very different from that in America, but is nevertheless disturbing. Not only are planners coming increasingly under attack through the mass media at the national level but also they may feel threatened and insecure at the local level as their professional isolation is invaded by public participation. There may thus be a retreat to defending bureaucratic procedures at the very time that a more outward-looking concern with social processes is needed.

The planners are being urged to devise means to achieve social goals, but neither they (nor the sociologists) can determine a community's goals. These goals may be explicit – an economic growth rate of 4 per cent, a modern, nation-wide transport network, a minimum standard of living which is above the poverty line; or they may be implicit – more choice for the affluent sections of society, fewer constraints placed on the poorer sections, and so on.

The will of the community is mediated through the political process, so that those with the most power set the goals, which makes the planner simply the tool of the elite. This is why, in America, the profession is becoming politicized. The progressives want social planning to reduce economic and racial inequality; the conservatives want to defend traditional physical planning and the legitimacy of middle-class values. A third group wants to plan for all interest groups, but is split over whether to work for or against the establishment.

All planning is social planning, and while geographers and transportation experts have an important role in the planning process they should not be the tail that wags the dog. In America, as Gans says, 'the city planner is no longer a non-political formulator of long range ideals, but is becoming an adviser to elected and appointed officials, providing them with recommendations and technical information on current decisions.' Urban renewal should be seen as a way of dealing with the processes which force people into slums: land-use studies are becoming less relevant as planners concern themselves with the provision and use of social services and the economic and political consequences of the policies they recommend.

The crucial lesson for British planners is to learn their limitations, and to make these limitations more widely known. The public, seeing, for example, the physical environment in decay, mistakenly assumes that the solution lies in physical renewal alone. However, the planner finds that the amelioration of one problem brings about a deterioration in another sphere, for he is dealing all the time with symptoms not causes.

If the planner analyses the social and economic origins of the problem, he might wish to suggest quite other solutions, even if it were outside his scope to implement these solutions. The danger is that his regard for his professional position will make him disregard the most relevant policies in favour of policies within his field of competence. The planner cannot be the *deus ex machina* of the urban condition. The trouble is that neither the planners nor the people are facing up to the fact that our power to alter the physical environment is greater than we can cope with. Participation implies that people should not only take part in making decisions about the physical environment, but should also take responsibility for the values implicit in planning decisions.

In this sort of situation it is simpler to do what can be done most easily, even if it is expensive. Enormous sums of money are being spent by planners on traffic surveys and transportation studies, but as we concentrate on physical mobility we completely ignore social mobility. Hence we do not know whether our urban areas are collecting an unskilled rump with little oppor-

tunity for occupational mobility. We do not know how easily
coloured immigrants are moving up the occupational hierarchy.
Published plans make pious statements about social goals and
social objectives but no long-term social research, such as a
continuing monitoring programme on social mobility, is being
planned. There are, however, signs that the Central Statistical
Office will initiate work on social indicators and this would be a
welcome and much needed task.

Professor Gans's book has prompted these thoughts because I
feel that in Britain, too, the physical city with its physical
problems has been overstressed. The city is essentially a social
entity – the product of a particular society at a particular time.
It is partly because the Americans saw the city in terms of
accessibility, and urban renewal as a way to more profitable uses,
that they have got into their present confusions.

In Britain we more readily accept positive discrimination – we
already have the educational priority areas, the urban programme
and so on. Despite this we still tend to get carried away by the
discussions of the physical forms and sometimes neglect to discuss
the social goals we are aiming to achieve. Professor Gans says,
'I want immediate change that improves the conditions of the
deprived immediately.' Are we sure that we have our priorities
right in this country? The city is what society lets it be.

Knocking Down is not Solving Problems

Peter Smith

Reprinted with permission from 'Knocking Down is not Solving
Problems'. *Municipal Review*, vol. 43, no. 514, October 1972,
pp. 291-3

Deprivation, poverty, unemployment, vandalism. The stories,
gleaned from just one edition of one day's local newspaper, reflect
some aspects of the crisis that faces Birmingham and every other
major city in the country.

Birmingham has a three-pronged attack under way against its urban renewal problems. Like other authorities, the city is preparing its strategy plans for housing; it is co-operating with the Home Office in one of 12 Community Development Projects planned for various parts of the country; it is working with the Department of the Environment on the Urban Studies Project.

The housing strategy is being prepared in response to a call from the Government for local authorities to review existing housing stock, both public and private, investigate the age, condition and tenure of the housing, assess future housing needs and prepare a strategy covering the whole spectrum – slum clearance, new building both for letting and sale, replacement of demolished housing, provision of specialized housing and improvement schemes.

The aim of the Community Development Projects is to discover how far the social problems experienced by people in a local community can be better understood and resolved through closer co-ordination of all the agencies in the social welfare field, together with the local people themselves. The method used is to carry out research experiments in selected urban areas and feed back the lessons learned into social policy, planning and administration both at central and local government level.

The Urban Studies Project will involve 'practical work on the ground' largely financed by the Department of the Environment and involving work extended over a number of years.

I talked about the city's deprived areas with Cllr Shuttleworth. Earlier in the day I had taken a long walk in the Handsworth area that Cllr Shuttleworth has represented on the city council since 1970. It is a typical 'middle ring' ward of long terraces, cosmopolitan shopping centres, demolition sites and rebuilding. Birmingham has many areas just like this one.

'The city has 82,000 homes built before 1901 – that's 25 per cent of the housing stock', said Cllr Shuttleworth. 'And there's another 32,000 homes built between 1901 and 1915. The City has already cleared 54,000 houses. A lot of the back-to-back houses have gone.

'But new concepts are needed. Now we are faced with the obsolete housing which is often structurally sound but not up to modern standards of amenities.'

People who live in places like the physically most deprived areas of Handsworth want, in the main, to stay where they are. 'You haven't the density problems, it's cheap, you are near your families and friends, often your place of work is not far away and there is easy access to the city centre and all its facilities', explained the councillor. And living on one of the city's bright new estates is just not on for many of them. The housing is too expensive, the estates are far from the jobs, transport to work and to the city's wonderful central shopping areas is costly. Little wonder then that people prefer to stay put.

The crux of the whole urban renewal problem is how to make the old, central areas fit to live in. And Cllr Shuttleworth sees the return of 'confidence' to such areas as one of the keys to the renewal process. 'Our job is to put back confidence into these areas. The days of massive redevelopments are at an end. They were necessary because of the very nature of the problem. Now with the General Improvement Areas we can deal with the environmental quality of an area.

'There is a myriad of small communities in areas like this. People tend to think of a city the size of Birmingham as being a huge place where the individual is completely lost. But there is as much a community feeling in these areas as you get in the traditional villages. You want to keep these communities together as much as possible. Of course there will still be pockets of housing that will simply have to come down. But these cleared areas can be developed in such a way as to benefit the surrounding community area . . . with warden housing for the elderly, for example, or with play areas . . .

'There is great uncertainty in these areas. People cannot sell their houses because they do not know what is going to happen', said Cllr Shuttleworth. This is one of the fundamental causes of the lack of confidence which Cllr Shuttleworth sees as a major cause of deterioration. So the city council is preparing a programme for urban renewal, for clearance and improvement areas. Co-operation between the council and landlords and tenants is seen as a major ingredient in the recipe for success; the council working out its responsibility for the physical environment of an area in tandem with the landlords and tenants working out their own responsibilities for the state of the homes.

'We believe that with co-operation between the people and the council in this way, investment in these areas will start flowing in

again . . . It's not just a once and for all effort. You put in the
capital to create confidence but you have then got to pay out
money to maintain confidence. Traffic management is important
in this. And decay can bring down an area very rapidly. Maintenance is important then, and that's a question of money. If you
have dereliction no one can be surprised by vandalism . . .

'The city council has got a lot of land waiting for development.
What we are trying to do is to try and clear the debris and
dumping that has been going on; grassing some areas, putting in
temporary car parking in others, turning still more into play
areas. It's small things that people are concerned about. We are
looking at ways of minimizing disturbance, by rationalizing
compulsory purchase procedure for example.'

Apathy is the great enemy of the confidence that is needed if
ageing urban areas are to get a new lease of life. Helping people to
feel a concern for their areas, to feel that they can influence what
is happening in them, to feel that they can better themselves, their
homes, their communities, is the major aim of the Community
Development Projects. But the Birmingham Project itself will be
an intensified one, confined to a community of 10,000-15,000
population. The City Council is already encouraging participation in planning and redevelopment in other city areas.

So far the city council's contact has mostly been through community action groups, some of which have retained professional
advisers. A bi-monthly *West Midlands Grassroots* magazine offers
a forum for the exchange of views, often critical, between the
community action groups and the council.

Cllr Shuttleworth hopes that new points of contact will emerge
from the Community Development Project. He would like to see
independent community welfare officers acting as catalysts in the
priority areas, getting people involved and being activists themselves. It is a role that more and more social workers employed
by local authorities up and down the country are feeling called
upon to fulfil with a resultant three-way strain on their loyalties to
client, council and departmental superiors. Cllr Shuttleworth's
idea for independent professional activists would at least resolve
some of these strains on loyalties. It would also remove another
big danger inherent in present trends. This is the danger that
social workers will feel obliged out of loyalty to their clients to
undermine the democratically resolved policy of the employing

authority where this policy seems to run counter to the immediate interests of the client.

The Community Development Project which Geoff Green is directing will be based on a community where 50 to 60 per cent of the population is coloured. It is an area of high social deprivation where new tactics and approaches will be tried. The Action Team, backed up by a Research Team of academics waiting to evaluate results, is to be concerned in all aspects of urban problems; industry, transport, race relations and the physical environment. The project will be managed by a group of 12 city councillors. For historic reasons – the decision by the then controlling group that the project should be linked with the social services department – six of the managing group will be from the social services committee. The remaining six will come one each from the other key committees.

Geoff Green sees the Development Project's task to help councillors as well as electors. 'The councillors are central figures in all this. We shall be trying to service them and enable them to be more efficient, to give them a means to communicate with the people and to provide them with better information on which they can make their decisions. Local government action must be geared to the needs of the people and not indulged in to fulfil the internal desires and needs of a particular department.'

New approaches and new alternatives must be generated. The urban crisis is not something that can be met in the next few years and cured for all time. The seeds of the crisis are going to remain far into the foreseeable future. Cllr Shuttleworth again: 'I foresee urban renewal as a major function of local government, in the same way as education and social services, and for as long as there is local government.

'Knocking down is not solving problems. Once the present priorities are met, a short lull can be expected until 1990 when we shall have to face the problems of the inter-war housing. We are already tackling rehabilitation of our first council housing estates.'

Financial Help in Social Work

Jean Heywood and Barbara Allen

Reprinted with permission from *Financial Help in Social Work*, Manchester University Press, 1971, pp. 70-74, 76-78

We undertook this study because there was a good deal of concern and confusion in children's departments about the giving of financial aid. This concern was natural, despite the limitations set by Section 1 of the Children and Young Persons Act and the guidance offered in the Home Office memorandum, since many social workers and social administrators had no previous experience or theory to guide them about dispensing money.

> The Home Office memorandum on the Act stated that Section 1 does not give power to intervene in family difficulties or domestic problems unless there is some reason to suppose that this may create the risk of children having to be received into or committed to the care of the local authority, nor does it give power in any circumstances to impose guidance on parents who are not willing to receive it.

Financial or material help, therefore, must clearly be part of a casework plan in which parents co-operate to prevent the children being received into the care of the local authority or committed by the court. Because casework is so specifically individualized the giving of such help within the overall plan *must* be discretionary and not subject to eligibility rules. Here is an example (given to us by a worker in a Family Welfare Association) showing the advantage of a social work agency having discretionary power to give aid at the appropriate moment:

> Let me give you an illustration of a family with two young children and parents in their 20s. Father had a steady job and income. He undertook to buy a small house, had to furnish it, so he committed himself to HP. He became sick with an ulcer, was off work for months. His debts mounted. He felt hopeless. He became increasingly paralysed by feelings of inadequacy and so quite incapable of looking at his difficulties. The

mortgagor's warnings provoked no real action other than that of apparent indifference and irresponsibility. Likewise electricity bills and rates demands. The furniture was repossessed. The father felt more guilty and became more paralysed. A third child was born. A health visitor contacted an agency. Could we get the electricity on for the sake of this third child, who was currently in hospital? When the caseworker visited, he found this paralytic, irresponsible father making inappropriate schemes, agreeing over-readily to suggestions from the caseworker and then not acting on them. The father was physically almost ready to return to work but so overwhelmed by the difficulties that he was not really able to regard this as very hopeful and constructive. The caseworker, after deliberation, decided not to seek financial help at this stage, since the cost of getting the electricity on might be the further depression of the father and so might not help in the long run. The family caseworker decided to play for higher stakes first. He returned to the father and talked with him about his feelings at being off work for so long, at not being able adequately to care for his family, at seeing their conditions deteriorate, at being hounded by creditors, at being helpless. The father's reaction was much warmer, less guarded. He responded to this approach to the essential man in an almost impossible situation through little fault of his own. In a short while he returned to work, emotionally supported through the difficult first three weeks before he drew a full week's wages. Meanwhile he was able to adopt a much more positive approach to his financial difficulties, and in view of this and the fact that the new-born baby was coming home, the caseworker sought a grant to enable the electricity supply to be reconnected. The committee sanctioned it and the family was much encouraged. The outlook was much more promising. Clearly, there is a great advantage in aid and casework coming from the same source and not really being available to the client as a right – in those circumstances where there are the special kinds of needs that I have been discussing.

Nevertheless, it was the absence of precise eligibility rules, the apparent arbitrariness of decisions, the responsible nature of public accountability, the stigma imposed by society upon their particular clients, the history of charity as opposed to rights, and additional feelings about giving or withholding money, which made the problem so acute for the workers. They were engaged in an exercise illustrating the classic dilemma and dynamism of social work (too seldom acknowledged): how to meet the needs of individual clients within the structure and framework of a social policy which must also be determined by the resources of money, skill and knowledge available at any time. These needs and resources are held in tension while the client is helped, but the dilemma itself goads social workers to contribute to the development of social policy and so to lead forward into social change.

Our local study of the kinds of families who were helped, the kind of help given, and our very tentative assessment of its effectiveness, served to underline some general facts we know from the national statistics. We found, for example, throughout the region a wide variation in the areas between the expenditure (as much as between £0.7 and £18 in the amount spent per thousand of the population under 16, for example) and an overall increase in the amounts given during the period 1964-9. Reports from the Advisory Council on Child Care show that financial and material help given by children's departments increased substantially during this period, even taking into account the falling in the value of money. The rate of increase of cash assistance has been about £58,000 per year, rising from £88,000 in 1966 to £202,900 in 1969 – an increase of 200 per cent, mainly in expenditure on rent, domestic services and household requirements. Although the pattern differs from authority to authority, there is some evidence of a national trend towards more help being given in the form of loans. In our study, however, a pattern of loans gave way to a pattern of grants. There is also evidence in our study of the way in which not only the amount but also the manner in which cash assistance was given was determined, as far as help with rents went, by local housing problems and policies in the first instance, and subsequently modified by the local practice of the child-care workers and the response of the clients to the help they offered. Nordale was perhaps the clearest example of this, though each area showed a sensitive modification in the light of the local situation. In contrast, our study also showed the reluctance of local children's departments to indemnify public utilities. Even though families incurred debts because their gas and electricity bills were unpaid it was not usual for grants or loans to be given for the purpose of clearing these debts.

More important, our study brought to life the encounter between families with problems and the social workers' use of financial and material aid in supporting them. We studied how the workers responded to the challenge of this, and saw how their response in turn influenced the development of new policies.

The two major purposes of using financial aid were found to be, first, to keep families in their home, and second, to provide food in emergencies. All the departments in our study used their new powers under the Children and Young Persons Act to ensure the provision of a house for families needing one, seeing this as the first step in prevention, insuring their clients against eviction and homelessness, which drastically disrupt family life. Because so many of the families were the concern of the housing committee and were already in council houses, the children's departments' powers largely took the form, in our study, of indemnifying the housing committee against loss through families who were not paying their rent. Alternatively, we have seen that one local authority had earlier allowed its children's committee to acquire property of its own which the department could then re-let as a preventive measure. This housing welfare function was temporarily taken over by children's departments as part of their work to ensure the prevention of neglect, but, except in Angleshire, this did not involve the most frequent form of expenditure under the Act, and, as we have seen, it was found that the casework support and help of the child-care workers was an important factor in enabling the rent to be paid. The most frequent form of financial aid was used as a crisis response and was a grant or loan for food in all the areas, except Angleshire, where the main expenditure was on grants or loans to cover rent. The special problems of Angleshire in the field of housing welfare have, however, already been mentioned.

A further very important fact which emerged from our study was that many social workers believed that dealing in cash confused their role and had no positive contribution to make to their casework. This was a very real concern to them, and was revealed to our researcher in the discussion about giving and withholding money and the budgeting involved in the rent guarantee scheme. Emphasis on budgeting was actually written into the guarantee scheme in the Welsh county, but was implicit in the work of all the other departments we examined. However, when the child-care workers were interviewed the majority said they did not help clients with budgeting in detail, but only in the ordering of priorities for spending. A minority of older workers saw budgeting as a positive way of helping the clients. The majority, however, mainly young workers, expressed hopelessness about enabling a family to budget on a low income. Some were upset at the prospect of budgeting for clients because they themselves had no need to do this on their own income. In interviews with the workers our researcher examined the problems they themselves experienced around the power to give or withhold financial aid and the necessity to collect money and debts from clients. There was a wide range of feeling. Some said they had no problems at all; at the other extreme were those who wished the department did not have this arbitrary power. The most problematic area was that of collecting loans made by their own department and, perhaps because of this, we found loans were collected haphazardly on the whole. When money had to be refused, workers almost invariably offered some alternative help, such as referral to another agency, or offered a different solution to the problem. On the rare occasions when neither alternative was open, workers expressed feelings of real distress and fell back upon departmental policy about giving money. A clear-cut direction – for example, that no grants are given at all – seemed more supportive to the worker in that it absolved him from having to exercise arbitrary power.

Giving aid did not evoke as much feeling as withholding it, but there were marked variations between workers as to whether the giving of aid was good or bad for the client. Workers were aware that their feelings could sometimes affect their decision about what kind of help it was appropriate to offer. The discussion of this whole subject was often painful to the workers and we appreciated the self-insight and openness which they shared with our research worker.

We have seen that the social workers' main task was to assess the situation and whether it would be appropriate to use their new powers to help the client in the light of their goal. The way they approached the problem was influenced by local situations, particularly by the local housing management policies or lack of them. The circular of guidance issued by the Home Office after the passing of the 1963 Act, to which we have frequently referred made reference in para. 12 to the possibility of contribution towards the expenses incurred by housing authorities and the prevention of eviction, but the children's committees each developed their own form of liaison which was intended to be of mutual benefit to each department, as well as to help the families to keep their homes and cope with their family responsibilities. Following this, the workers had to decide in which cases help should be given. In social work this is a very old question. At one time it took the form of distinctions between the 'deserving' and the 'undeserving' poor, with overtones of moral judgements about the undeserving who did not respond to social pressures. We chose to ask the workers when they considered financial help was *appropriate*; their answers reflected what the joint wisdom of the department considered appropriate as a result of its experiences.

They showed that the assessments of appropriateness were strongly influenced by the experiences of senior staff and their interpretation of the Act. Grants, loans or guarantees were given where there were large families; where there was a possibility of collecting a loan back because the client was responsive to casework help; where there was no alternative accommodation; where families had severe physical or mental handicaps; where there was no other means of preventing the children coming into care; where the cost of children coming into care would be saved; where families were really trying to help themselves; where the family was in a crisis in imminent danger of disintegration; where parents were good managers. These were the conditions where help was thought appropriate. Were the workers right? In the short-term they were. In the long-term it is impossible to tell, but, on the whole, workers felt that their limited financial aid was less effective than their supportive casework. Workers were clearly haunted and troubled by the old spectre of the 'deserving' and the 'undeserving' poor, and their insecurity really came from being faced with clients in desperate need. Workers wanted to help them all financially but were unable to justify doing so, particularly in the long run, because they knew that financial help *by itself* would not guarantee that they would achieve the goal.

What recommendations can be made from this research, this description of the way some local children's departments operated? We see departments tackling a new dimension of work. How did they set about establishing policies? What factors were important in modifying the policies in the light of the field workers' experience?

First, we saw the importance of good internal communication within the departments. The support and guidance of senior staff were very effective in enabling workers to come to decisions, and there was machinery for discussion, consultation and approval at all levels in all the departments. This was important in sustaining the morale of workers in a difficult job, and enabling them to think through the effect of what they were doing.

Second, we saw the need for co-operation and mutual understanding between the children's department and outside agencies. The *effective* giving of financial and material aid within the context of the Act was dependent upon the mutual understanding of the different roles of the child-care workers and officers of the housing department, Social Security and so on. Where this understanding was good they were able to develop complementary policies, bearing the other agencies in mind. This made for more effective support for the client and a more economical organization of joint resources.

Third, we see the need for the social workers continually to be aware of what they are doing, to take stock and consider where their policies are taking them. This, as we have seen, can lead to the development of change within the services arising out of the 'grass roots' experience of the workers and the continual monitoring of the effect of their work.

Finally, we see a need to face the dilemma of social work – reconciling needs and resources – and to think through the role of the social worker. By its very nature it must be a role of uncertainty, stress and change, and workers have to find their own ways of dealing with the anxieties consequent upon this. But the dilemma has an inherent dynamism which makes it impossible for social work to stand still while services develop and legislators legislate. Social work seems inseparable from the development of changing policies based upon people's needs.

Which Way for Social Work?

Adrian Sinfield

Reprinted with permission from *Which Way for Social Work?*, Fabian Society, 1969, pp. 6-8, 10-13

Implicit in much that is said about the services provided by social workers seems to be the assumption that anything is better than nothing. This is linked to the fact that, because most social workers feel themselves overworked, they do not very often stop to consider what their work is achieving nor whether it should be redirected. And because they are overburdened, they have little opportunity to follow the experiences of their clients; and they seem even less likely to do this when responsibilities cross jurisdictional boundaries. As the American poet Robert Frost said 'It couldn't be called ungentle, but how thoroughly department-mental'. Though of course, we hope that co-ordination will at least put a stop to this fragmentation of responsibility.

The Seebohm Report never appears to question the efficacy of social work. Yet this question cannot be ignored if we are to decide whether the Seebohm proposals are adequate. This crucial issue has received scarcely any attention from the social work profession, though without a clear and positive answer the necessity for social workers, and more of them, must remain largely a matter of faith.

'GIRLS AT VOCATIONAL HIGH'

In the United States there have been more attempts to evaluate social work and measure its effectiveness. The best known is probably *Girls at vocational high*, an examination of the effect of social work counselling on some 200 teenage girls with a control sample of the same size. I shall describe this study in a little detail because it seems to illustrate some of the basic problems facing social work in all countries.

The very cautious conclusion of the book was that 'on these [objective] tests no strong indications of effect [of counselling] are found and the conclusion must be stated in the negative when it is asked whether social work intervention with potential problem high school girls was in this instance effective'. There was a marked discrepancy between the results of the objective tests of progress and the subjective evaluation of the social workers involved: this led the investigators to compare the workers' evaluation with the familiar 'the operation was a success but the patient died'. The social workers in fact tended to pay more attention to the ways in which the girls actually behaved during their counselling sessions rather than to the effect of the counselling on behaviour outside these sessions. This is a danger of the psycho-therapeutic process when the social worker may become so engrossed in building up a relationship that he may lose sight of his reason for doing it.

Many criticisms can be, and some have been, made of the study both in its methodology and its theoretical analysis. Of course, too sweeping claims have been made for its findings which have been extended to cover – and denounce – the whole of social work. The blame here must lie not just with the publicists but with a profession that has persistently failed to evaluate its own efficacy. This failure to validate techniques can be partly explained, I think, by the fact that many social workers have come to regard themselves as checking their own work in the process of casework counselling itself and in the course of discussion with colleagues and supervisors. The criteria for 'success' therefore are their own and not their clients'. For many the journey – the casework or group session – has almost certainly become the goal. Clients who are unwilling to discuss their difficulties in this way are classified as 'unco-operative' or 'lacking in insight'. Some talk of a client's 'willingness to use the casework relationship' or his 'ability to use the service'. In the last resort then it may be seen as the client who is the failure.

The social worker's own insights into the individual's problems may often be determined by the techniques employed. *Girls at vocational high* revealed very clearly that the use of different social work techniques led the social worker to change *her* view of the client's situation, and so brought her to consider different ways of solving the client's problem. In individual casework the social worker was more likely to assume that a client was magnifying or distorting the problem in some way. In group sessions the worker was compelled to recognize that what the client said was true, as in these sessions, the girls had a greater opportunity to 'bring in their world'. 'When all or a majority of members of the group, in spite of differences in their psychological make-up, almost simultaneously described situations of external stress in similar ways, the worker herself came to view the problem differently . . . Discussions of violent acts – suicide, gang warfare – occurred frequently in the group sessions. However in the group setting it seemed clear to the leaders that talk about such things was more related to actual happenings than to the girls' inner preoccupations with such events.'

In some ways the authors come close to reversing the conventional wisdom of 'treating' the deep-seated internal causes and argue for treating what is often called the 'presenting problem'. They argued that social workers need to pay much greater attention to possible environmental changes in helping their clients. 'Should we expect weekly interviews with case-workers', the authors ask, 'or weekly counselling sessions in groups, to have critical effects when situational conditions were hardly touched?'. They lay stress on the importance for the social work profession of developing means of bringing about changes in the social conditions rather than trying to help clients by 'indirect efforts through influences on internal psychological states'. Helping a girl to stay on and get through school with material assistance is given low priority by the social workers in the study but failure to achieve this may make other desirable objectives even less attainable. Altogether this study emphasizes the need not to let casework roles get out of proportion and the need to attempt new, and as yet less professionally fashionable, methods of help.

THE DEFINITION OF SOCIAL WORK

Social work might better be understood in social terms and not only socio-psychological terms. A social worker imparts information about rights, makes services available, helps to communicate needs to those in authority, and encourages action by the individual, family and group on their own behalf as well as on the behalf of the community. The advantage of this definition is that it suggests the role the social worker can play in the community whatever type of social work or organizational attachment.

This moves the emphasis away from the skills and techniques used and towards the objectives of the worker. In fact, although the social worker is trained to make contact with his 'client', studies such as *Girls at vocational high* show how his understanding has been limited by his skills. As Forder says in his new edition of *Penelope Hall's Social Services of Modern England*, 'information about the social services has been poorly disseminated; the social and psychological barriers that prevent people from using them have been ignored; professional workers have often been more concerned to have "co-operative" clients on whom to practise their skills, than to draw their clients into active cipation in the aims of the service; those who have been unable to make effective use of the service have been too readily labelled "unco-operative" and rejected on this basis. Criticism of the services by the customers, even constructive criticism, is not generally encouraged and usually resented.'

BLOWING IN THE WIND

How far does the current narrow interpretation of this role and the lack of facilities and the inadequate services and resources available to him, leave the social worker with an acute sense of helplessness? This is a question that many social workers are greatly concerned about but so far there has been little attempt to bring this to the notice of a wider audience. With the exception of often rather oblique comments in chapter XIII on housing, the Seebohm Committee scarcely raised this issue.

Indeed many social workers do see themselves as faced with the task of persuading people to tolerate the intolerable. They become agents of control or 'social tranquillizers'. Despite their frustration most stay on in the hope of making the best of a bad job. Their dissatisfaction however is often evidenced by the vigorous support given by many social workers to such organizations as the Child Poverty Action Group and the Disablement Income Group, both established in 1965.

At the same time, there are many social workers who disapprove of such activities and some senior workers in children's departments have regarded attempts by younger colleagues to obtain written explanations of Supplementary Benefit assessments as 'militant'. Some social workers whom I met in the last few months did not even know of either of these groups and had no idea what was meant by for example the 'wage stop', (the procedure whereby Supplementary Benefit – formerly National Assistance – is not paid above the level that a man, unemployed or temporarily sick, is expected to receive in net wages even if his entitlement, because of a high rent, large family or some special need, is higher than this). Some 28,000 families headed by an unemployed man had their allowances reduced for this reason in February 1969.

SOCIAL WORKERS AND THE ATTACK ON INEQUALITIES

In examining the role of social work in a modern industrial and still class-bound society, it is vital to analyse its relevance to the basic issues of inequality and privilege. It is still widely believed that the social services, as the other parts of the 'Welfare State', are instruments of redistribution reducing inequality. A typical and recent statement of this view was made by T. H. Marshall, formerly Professor of Sociology and Head of the Social Science Department at the London School of Economics. 'The social services proper – in health, welfare, education, housing, etc. – have undoubtedly had a profound effect on the distribution of *real* income'. This seems clear and categorical enough, but a few sentences later Marshall changes his position remarkably. 'This has been their aim . . . it is hard to say how much progress has been made'.

No doubt they are redistributive, as are any other allocation of services or resources in kind. The important question is not 'Do they redistribute?' but the much more complicated set of questions 'In what directions do the social services distribute and redistribute? To what extent? How? And for how long, and with what effect?'. The answers to these questions then need to be set against the intentions in policy as to the extent and direction of redistribution. The Seebohm Committee disregarded these questions in deciding what constituted an 'effective family service'.

Yet it is vital to know the actual effect of social workers in distributing resources in kind in a society which is still more or less rigidly stratified by class and where there has been no significant downward redistribution of earnings since the beginning of this century. As long ago as the census of 1911 the proportion of average earnings received by unskilled and semi-skilled working men was the same as it was in 1960 – about 79 per cent and 86 per cent respectively. There have been fluctuations since 1911 but two world wars, a cold war, the depression of the 1920s and 1930s and the introduction of the social welfare legislation after 1945 has not lessened occupational differentials at all between the main groups. In 1911 the average unskilled man's wage was 31 per cent of the average manager's, but by 1960 this had fallen slightly to 29 per cent. If one considers that in the 1911 census, aeroplane pilots and aviators were grouped with acrobats, magicians and conjurers in the same occupational category headed 'performer, showman', one has some idea of the vast changes that have occurred over this period. These have nevertheless done very little to alter the differences between the main groups in the socio-economic structure of Britain.

In 1955 Richard Titmuss questioned the extent of redistribution by government and the reduction of inequalities by all forms of social services in 'The social division of welfare'. In the last ten years an increasing amount of evidence has been published revealing that the total resources of many are well below the average standard of living. In 1960 as many as one in eight households existed at a level no better than that of the recipients of National Assistance.

The apparent lack of interest on the part of social workers in the command of resources – or at least the vocal or literary members of the profession – must be related to two facts. Until very recently few were aware of the persistent inequalities in the distribution of resources and opportunities that survived the introduction of the 'Welfare State' and even today many social workers seem to see little relevance in the problems of inequality or the stratified class structure within which they are working. They do not pay sufficient heed to the possible connections between simple lack of resources and personal and family 'disintegration'.

Secondly, many social workers and social administrators have consciously striven to escape the image of charity workers amongst the poor, and some seem to have believed that in this way they could best improve the standing of their own discipline. They have welcomed the 'Welfare State', worried about the effects of over-dependency resulting from its 'feather-bedding', and departed to fields of research and practice more in touch with the 'better classes'. The poverty they did see they tended to dismiss as due to the *misuse*, rather than the *lack*, of resources. Indeed, it can be argued that the emphasis on psychodynamic techniques in social work in the 1950s did much to make the poor 'silent' or 'invisible'.

The Chairman of the Seebohm Committee, however, estimated that poverty and bad housing 'probably cause something like 60 per cent of the work that is now carried on by social workers'. Now this sort of statement backed up by evidence could be of great help in establishing the priorities for action for the social services. It also supports very strongly the view that much social work activity is simply a holding operation. If the energies of social workers are directed more towards the poor, there are strong grounds for thinking this leads more to social control than to social welfare and any redistribution of resources. It is a pity that there is no such comment, or evidence for it, in the Seebohm Report. Given a different emphasis and a greater concern with material and environmental causes of family break-down and individual frustration, the profession of social work might well have played a leading role in making society aware much earlier of the persistence of poverty. Instead, the major social work discovery of the 1950s was the 'problem family' with an emphasis on the problems that came from within. It was left to others to pursue the questions of the level of social security payments and of individual rights.

Further Reading
Meeting Needs

M. BROADY, *Planning for People*, Bedford Square Press, 1968.

B. CULLINGWORTH (Ed.), *Problems of an Urban Society*, vols. 1-3, Allen & Unwin, 1973.

H. GANS, *People and Plans*, Pelican, 1972.

W. HAGGSTROM, 'The Power of the Poor', in F. Reissman (Ed.), *Mental Health of the Poor*, Collier-Macmillan, 1964.

P. HALMOS, *The Faith of the Counsellors*, Constable, 1965.

J. HEYWOOD and B. ALLEN, *Financial Help in Social Work*, Manchester University Press, 1971.

R. HOLMAN, *Trading in Children, A Study of Private Fostering*, Routledge & Kegan Paul, 1973.

C. MEYER, *Social Work Practice*, Collier-Macmillan, 1970.

Report of the Committee on Local Authority and Allied Personal Social Services, (Seebohm Report), HMSO, 1968.

O. STEVENSON, *Claimant or Client?*, Allen & Unwin, 1973.

C. UNGERSON, *Moving Home*, Occasional Papers in Social Administration, no. 44, Bell, 1971.

Chapter Four

Purposes and Priorities

The readings to date generally have accepted that the social
services exist, to quote the Seebohm Report, to find 'ways of
helping those in need'. As was explained in Chapter 2, the
actual definition of individuals' needs is a complex matter but
beyond this some commentators have insisted that the services
are concerned with purposes far larger than the requirements
of a minority of needy individuals. The question thus is raised
– what is the purpose of social welfare?

PURPOSES

The assumption that social welfare provisions represent an
altruistic and collective response to individual suffering must
be put against the fact that major developments have occurred
at times of national crises. Certain early reforms aimed to
raise health standards came not from concern about the sick
but because fears were expressed that the nation would
lack fit soldiers. During both world wars, promises of social
reforms were offered in order to convince civilians and soldiers
that sacrifices were worth making. In other words, in these
respects the purpose of social welfare was not care for the
most deprived sections of the population but a wish to uphold
what was regarded as the well-being of the nation as a whole.
Similarly, the purpose of educational and health services may be
that of providing well-trained and healthy workers able to
more efficiently promote economic growth. The reading by
Greve demonstrates that social welfare may have many varied,
even conflicting objectives. It is even possible that far from
promoting radical changes, social welfare concessions may be
made, as Greve explains, as a sop to forestall unrest and the
possibility of more profound changes.

The varying conceptions of the purpose of social welfare

stem, as Greve makes clear, from the different values held by individuals. His own value system means he is not prepared to accept that social welfare should promote economic growth regardless of the interests of individual members of society. For instance, social welfare should provide for the needs of the elderly and the unemployed even though they are not economically productive. Again, his values lead him to regard social welfare as a means of promoting social change rather than of conserving the *status quo*. Greve believes that such objectives are contained within a United Nations definition which states the purpose of the social services as 'helping towards a mutual adjustment of individuals and their social environment'. To this, he adds the very important rider that society must also adjust to individuals. But what adjustments should be sought? Greve answers that the adjustments should enable 'the person concerned to participate more fully and satisfyingly in society'. The reply serves to provoke another question: what is full and satisfying participation? Greve's reading provides a generalized answer. He believes that social welfare should not merely take people above the poverty line but should promote a more equal society. It is only in these conditions that all members have the chance of participating fully in the social and economic life and benefits of society. In short, the purpose of social welfare then is re-distribution. It aims to transfer resources from one section of society to another.

In practice, the overall purposes of social welfare have to be translated into the objectives of particular agencies and then into the roles of their workers. The reading by **Butterworth** is included to illustrate the dilemmas in this respect faced by the workers of Community Relations agencies. The overall purpose of their agencies might be defined as 'helping immigrants to adjust to society so that they might participate fully and satisfyingly in community life'. But once in action, the workers interpreted their roles in many different ways. Some were seen (or saw themselves) as leaders of local black groups, others as stimulating the formation of such groups, others as minimizing the problems the groups posed for the rest of society, others as influencing wider social reforms aimed to ease the lot of newcomers, and others as helping individual black persons with their personal problems. The ambiguity of goals, the unclear status of the agencies, the conflicting and differing value judgements made about black persons and the changing nature of public moods towards immigrants, all served to confuse the workers. Butterworth offers no pat solutions but argues that to be more certain of their position and thus be more effective, the community relations workers require knowledge of the social and economic situation in local areas both as it now is and how it is likely to be in the future. He further explains that they need a status within the overall structure of social welfare and the capacity to set objectives which can be achieved by their resources. Only then, he claims, can purposes be clarified and methods shaped to reach them.

PRIORITIES

Greve states that social policy may identify the purpose of social welfare but that real policy is what is actually implemented. Two factors, in particular, serve to constrain the full execution of purposes. Firstly, and obviously, the resources accorded to the social services are limited in amount. Secondly, the demands made on the services vary over time in nature and strength. The purpose of social welfare embrace, amongst many others, the unemployed, the disabled and the elderly. But in periods of high unemployment demands for attention are heaviest on the income maintenance services. Then, say, a new act and consequent publicity lead to extra requests from the sick and disabled. Next, demographic changes mean an increase in the proportion of elderly in the population and heavier calls on pensions. Similarly, fluctuations in the birth rate, the patterns of family formation, the age of marriage, the rates of immigration and migration, all can influence the extent of social need and so change the force of the demands made upon the social services. With so many pressures on limited resources, the providers of social welfare therefore have to establish an order of *priorities* as to which demands will be met and, as a result, what kind of services will be offered. For instance, at government level a debate has occurred concerning the proportion of resources to be allocated between, on the one hand, residential units (such as hospitals and old people's homes) and, on the other hand, community services to keep people in their own homes. In general the desirability of the latter has been accepted as an objective, as a means of maximizing people's satisfactions. However, in the immediate situation money has to be directed into existing plant – often expensive-to-run Victorian buildings – just to cope with present inmates. Moreover, many present staff have been trained within these institutions and to train them or to recruit new staff with community skills would involve an enormous outlay. Thus a compromise has to be reached between stated purposes and practical constraints. To take another example. A Social Service Department's committee may understand that preventive work is required to forestall the rise of family breakdowns. It believes that community and group work is needed to achieve this aim. However, the department is being bombarded with immediate crises which have to be dealt with at once. Skilled case workers are available to deal with these types of problems but the department is unable to recruit community and group workers. Consequently, the department has no option but to put its preferred objective lower in its ranking of priorities.

The manner in which agencies deal with the problem of priorities is the subject of the reading by **Parker**. Usually social service organizations cannot control the demands made for their goods or benefits by the use of the price mechanism – as happens in a free market situation. Instead, they can adopt, as Parker reveals, two basic ploys. They can attempt to control demand by deterring people from approaching them, by imposing eligibility requirements, by delaying action or by refusing to advertise their services. By the use of these mechanisms, client pressure can be diverted away from services which are not being awarded priority. In addition, or alternatively, the agencies may ration out their resources by diluting the overall standards of their services.

Clearly, the use of priority ranking or rationing techniques has an adverse effect on clients considered of low priority. But they also contain important implications for social workers and for the organization of the agencies themselves. Parker points

out that the rationing of services and its consequent lessening
of pressure on social workers may serve to create the
environment in which they have the time to develop their
professional skills. Yet the same workers may feel that a denial
of service to clients conflicts with their professional
commitment to serve all those in need. Similarly, their agencies
also meet a dilemma. A scarcity of resources make it imperative
that different organizations should co-operate to make the best
use of them. Yet the same scarcity sharpens the competition
between them for the same resources. The argument that
legislative reform was required to impose co-operation between
different welfare agencies was a powerful one in the case that
eventually did lead to the Seebohm Report and the
re-organization of local authority personal social services as
will be discussed in the next chapter. In the meantime, it is
well to note Professor Greve's questioning of the assumption
that social services should accept their existing limitations. He
describes, for instance, how resources also go to prestige
showpieces for the armed forces. The implication of his
remarks is that social service administrators and social
workers should be claiming these resources for their
agencies. If they fail to make such claims they are pushed into
the position of modifying the overall purposes of social
welfare and implementing rationing procedures which can only
partly reach the desired objectives.

WHOSE SERVICE?

Given the differing views on what constitutes the purposes of
social welfare and the compromises and modifications resulting
from setting priorities, it is timely to ask the question – for
whom does social welfare exist? Recently, a number of
publications have argued that the social services tend to favour
higher income groups at the expense of the more deprived.
For example in the National Health Service, Howlett and
Ashley argue that middle-class patients have a greater chance
of obtaining the best treatment – such as from teaching
hospitals. The Child Poverty Action Group made a strong
claim that the social reforms of the Labour Governments of
1964-70 actually worsened the position of the poor. In a

stimulating study, Mandell has shown that child welfare
services provide excellent services for middle-class adopters
but give inferior aid to poverty stricken parents trying to retain
the care of their children. Yet other writers have argued that
the interests of clients have been placed beneath those of
officials and professionals.

Parker's reading makes clear – as did that of Bond in
Chapter 3 – that officials in social security offices or housing
departments may inhibit applicants from securing their rights
by displaying hostile or patronizing attitudes. The suggestion
is that officials are sometimes judgemental about, for example,
applicants whom they regard as 'scroungers' and therefore
deny them access to discretionary benefits. Such officials have
the difficult task of making decisions about who receives what
level of benefits, of attempting to eliminate abuse of public
money and of maintaining what Weber called the bureaucrats'
'formalistic impersonality'. Nonetheless, the evidence is strong
that in some cases the administration of a welfare agency is
manipulated to suit the values and prejudices of its officials
rather than serving the needs and rights of clients.

It is sometimes argued that social security and housing
officials would display more liberal and understanding attitudes
if they received training akin to that of social workers.
However, the reading by **Arthur Keefe** presents the case that
even social work agencies may not be orientated towards the
needs of clients (or customers, as he calls them). A major
reason for this, he explains, is the desire of social workers 'to
be awarded a professional status' which results in attention
being focused on the requirements of an occupational group
rather than on its clients. It could be countered that professions
bring a number of positive benefits such as a uniform
standard of training, an ethical code of behaviour and the
advancement of professional skills. But, in regard to social
work, there could be at least three adverse side effects. Firstly,
professionalism may imply that many social workers have the
right to make decisions *for* certain clients. Such decisions
may involve the future place of residence of deprived children,
the kind of services to be made available to (or withheld from)
the community, the assessing of which individuals should be
awarded casework or material help. Moreover, rarely is there

effective provision for clients to appeal against such important judgements. Secondly, Keefe stresses that the very process of making decisions for clients may reinforce their own inferior position in society. If a part of their general deprivation is a lack of control over their own lives and environments, then the taking of fundamental choices about the direction of their futures without their involvement only serves to heighten their powerlessness. Thirdly, it is worth pointing out that any professional obsession with individual cases may prompt social workers to measure progress in terms of the development of minute occupational skills rather than according to broad social trends. As A. N. Whitehead formulated the issue nearly fifty years ago:

> Each profession makes progress, but it is progress in its own groove . . . The dangers arising from this aspect of professionalism are great, particularly in our democratic societies . . . The rate of human progress is such that an individual human being . . . will be called upon to face novel situations which find no parallel in his past. The fixed person for the fixed duties, who in older societies was such a godsend, in the future will be a public danger . . . In short, the specialized functions of the community are performed better . . . but the generalized direction lacks vision . . . We are left with no expansion of wisdom and with greater need of it.

Keefe's answers to the dangers are proposals for greater participation of clients in agency practice. He suggests a panel which would include consumer representation. The panel would be empowered to hear objections to the decisions made by social workers and to feed general policy proposals into the local authority committees. Thus it would cope with individual cases and overall trends. Two criticisms might be made of Keefe's plans. Firstly, he does not overcome the possibility that the local authorities might appoint client members whom they knew would acquiesce in social work decisions. Secondly, individual client members might not be able to maintain an independent line if outnumbered by other representatives. The Coventry Community Development Project has reported that local representatives, when incorporated into a large committee of councillors and officials, tend to take on the latter's roles and attitudes. Client representation can then become a means of manipulating the consent of the deprived. Despite these objections, it cannot be denied that consumer involvement is on the increase. Indeed the Gulbenkian Report of 1973 noted that between 1968 and 1973, there was a rapid increase in clients' groups organizing around a specific need and resident groups organizing around a locality. This growing involvement of client and community organizations would seem to confirm Keefe's belief that participation can be one way of ensuring that professional power is modified and exercised in a responsible manner.

The behaviour of professionals and officials are not the only forces operating to deflect social welfare agencies away from their original purposes. Kahn's reading, based on a paper to the National Standing Conference of Citizens Advice Bureaux, illustrates that the location, the practices and procedures, indeed the whole administrative framework of agencies, also determine whether those most in need are reached or not. He points to American criticism that techniques and methods employed in health, education and social casework agencies discourage less privileged groups from obtaining services and benefits. Access is denied to these consumers and Kahn then draws upon his American experience to describe how some social workers attempted to counter these effects by 'reaching out' into the community to find those in need and, if necessary, to act as advocates on their behalf. They enabled clients to manoeuvre around the 'bureaucratic structure, professional ritualism, unnecessarily restrictive guidelines, *de facto* discrimination, cultural chasms, problems in communication, practical obstacles which stood in the way of expression of one's needs or assertion of rights'.

It is not enough to rely on the enterprise of a few social workers to overcome access barriers. Kahn reasons that access facilities must be given an organized and institutionalized framework. He therefore proposes the establishment of independent 'access centres', existing to inform clients about and to help them obtain their many and varied rights. More generally, the centres could function to expose and challenge the rationing devices – as described by Parker – which agencies use to limit demands and control resources. Although the access services would be available to all, Kahn believes they should be given priority in areas where residents receive the least help from the social services.

Kahn's proposals may be criticized – as he acknowledges – on the grounds that the new centres might divert resources away from current agencies which are already short of funds. But he argues convincingly that if the centres involved local citizens as well as professionals they would be in a strong position not only to improve access but also to identify defects in social welfare provisions and to call for improvements. In other words, they would serve to make a case for extra resources. These contributions, if successful, would then support Kahn's main point, namely that the redistribution of social welfare goods will be achieved not only by new laws but also by arrangements which facilitate access to existing benefits.

The readings in this chapter demonstrate some of the difficulties of identifying the purposes of social welfare. Even if agreement is reached, the shortage of resources and the varying nature of demands mean that priorities have to be established which, in turn, limit the achievement of the objectives. The resultant rationing techniques combined with the influence of professional and official interests can result in clients' needs not being met. Clearly, the organizational structure of the social welfare services will play some part in defining purposes, determining priorities and assessing who benefits from available resources. The following chapter will examine the organizational structure in more detail.

Comparisons, Perspectives and Values

J. Greve

Reprinted with permission from *Comparisons, Perspectives and Values,* An Inaugural Lecture, University of Southampton, 1971, pp. 2-9

I should like to begin by quoting from a report published in the *Guardian* just over two years ago:

> Hyde Park Barracks—
> . . . the new £3.6 million immaculate brick and concrete complex with accommodation for 273 horses and 514 soldiers is lined up for inspection by the press.
> Selected . . . horses from the Household Cavalry have been brought in for a preview of their new air-conditioned stalls . . . saddles and tack are displayed in separate rooms away from the ammonia-laden air: all ducting has apparently been sprayed with chlorinated rubber to avoid corrosion. Dung chutes link to tracked trolleys which collect profitable loads for sale to cultivators outside London. The upper level stabling is reached by a gently sloping ramp fitted with electric coils to melt potentially dangerous ice in winter.
> The accommodation for 284 young troopers is not quite so spacious with four men to a room, although there are plenty of specially designed cupboards to cope with the storage of ceremonial helmets, swords, and boots.

I have quoted from this newspaper report because it raises a number of questions relevant to social policy. Before going on to refer to some of them, however, I want to say something by way of definition about social services, social policy and administration.

A United Nations report defined a social service as:
an organized activity that aims at helping towards a mutual adjustment of individuals and their social environment. This objective is achieved through the use of techniques and methods which are designed to enable individuals, groups, and

communities to meet their needs and solve their problems of
adjustment to a changing pattern of society, and through
co-operative action to improve economic and social conditions.

This involves

   . . . a variety of governmental and non-governmental activities
in a number of fields.

No definition can be entirely satisfactory which tries to
encapsulate a remarkably heterogeneous collection of aims and
services – particularly when viewed on the international plane –
but the UN definition is better than most, and it makes some
important points which are not always appreciated by professionals and administrators who man the social services, still less
by the actual or potential clients or consumers (usually because
no one has told them).

The first point advanced by the definition is that the provision
of social services is not simply a transaction in which a passive
client receives bounty (in the form of cash, kind or counselling)
from the rest of the community. Nor, as many still think, is a
social service concerned to get people to adjust unilaterally to
society or to their possibly squalid environment (and to count
their blessings) – though assisting people to adjust to reality *is* an
important function of some of the counselling and treatment
services on (ideally) quite proper grounds relating to health and
further personal development. Where possible, however, such
adjustment should have a constructive aim and be no more than
a stage towards the principal goal of enabling the person concerned to participate more fully and satisfyingly in society.

But society must also adjust to the individual. This is the
second point in the definition – and 'society', for this purpose,
must be taken as including housing and the wider physical
environment.

A further point to be noted is that social services aim to assist
groups and communities, not only individuals. And again the
passage quoted emphasizes the need for *mutual* adjustment – by
the larger society as well as by its members, whether singly or as
groups and communities.

The final point in that passage which I want to highlight
reinforces what has already been said. It is that social services

have a positive, developmental function 'through co-operative action to improve economic and social conditions'.

We have passed the stage in this country – though only since 1945 in any general sense – when the main aim of social services was to provide rescue or subsistence level aid: essentially, emergency aid to restore people to adequate physical functioning and prevent them from falling into a condition which, from economic or physical cause, endangered health or life. Hence the dominance in pre-war social services of health insurance, the 'dole', 'relief' measures including free school meals for children with soup kitchens for their older relatives, and housing for the 'working classes' – accompanied from the mid-thirties by a major slum clearance campaign – delayed for some years on grounds of economy, but which once started quickly reached a faster rate of demolition and replacement of 'unfit' housing than we have been able to achieve since.

Despite the enormous scale of acute social and economic dislocation and distress between the wars, social policy occupied little parliamentary time, and did not figure prominently in public discussion. Some might argue that it was because of the dire economic conditions that social services were not expanded as rapidly as we might now consider desirable or essential. It is a plausible view and, no doubt, has an element of truth, but it is over-simple, for other factors were also important, among them the persistence of a strikingly hierarchical social structure which sustained, and was sustained by, values and attitudes which were not merely outdated by the social changes that accompanied and enabled industrialization, but were pernicious in their effects on the well-being of millions in the 'lower classes'. Nourished by these prejudices, or in deference to them, were a lack of sympathy for and resistance to social reform. A study of the social and political history of this country from 1900 to 1945 frequently reveals a degree of incompetence and callousness which at times t kes the breath away. One of the official histories of the war – dealing with social policy – describes the ineptitude, incomprehension and obsessional bureaucratic behaviour which all too often characterized governments' relations with hundreds of thousands of uprooted children (the evacuees), bombed-out people in the devastated poor quarters of cities, and even the local authorities. It was a desperate period in which the poor helped the poor, the rich looked after themselves, and government servants often failed to look after anyone.

A third obstruction to the expansion of social services during the inter-war depression was the fallacious pre-Keynesian economic doctrine that public spending should be cut back during a slump – thus reducing investment and consumption even further: analogous to prescribing accelerated starvation as an effective cure for hunger. Geddes, in 1922, swung his axe with total disregard for economic logic or social justice.

Apart from cuts in the army, and navy, the committee (on government expenditure) recommended economies in educa-tion* and public health; reductions in teachers' salaries; and the abolition of five government departments including the ministry of transport and the ministry of labour.

* In 1922 a quarter of all classes (in the public sector of education) had more than 60 pupils. 'The highest ambition of educational policy between the wars was to reduce the classes to under 50.' It failed.

Put most simply, social policy is concerned with the improve-ment of the conditions of life of the individual, but that is not saying very much. What are commonly thought of as the social services – health, welfare, social security – occupy only part of the thinking of social policy, and comprise only part of the growing variety of direct and indirect means deployed by government (increasingly) and by voluntary agencies. The following are also to varying degrees linked with or part of the broad sweep of social policy – and the list is not complete: law, education, housing, environmental planning; the control and elimination of pollution; countryside parks; the provision of open spaces in congested urban areas; adventure playgrounds, pre-school playgroups; the treatment and rehabilitation of offenders; relations between police and public, especially in poorer districts; community (or race) relations; the Arts Council; financial support for theatrical groups and exhibitions of visual arts in socially 'deprived' areas; wages councils; measures to assist 'special' or 'depressed' areas; 'new' and 'expanded' towns; grants for the improvement of houses and environments; language classes for immigrant mothers; fiscal policies, direct taxation (indirect taxes are generally regressive); and subsidized transport.

The social services have three aims: curative, preventive and developmental. They are assisted in these, directly or indirectly, by an extensive network of other measures aimed at giving support or creating a framework within which the services can operate more effectively. In these ways social, economic and environmental policies have become increasingly intermeshed and interdependent. The 'success' of one area of policy depends on the effective functioning of another. The major connections between social security, housing, health services, education and a productive economy, have been documented fully enough elsewhere not to require spelling out here.

For the purposes of analysis and study a distinction can be made between 'social policy' and 'social administration'. Broadly it is a distinction between the 'what' (and 'why'), and the 'how'.

Social *policy* is concerned with aims and functions, but real policy – as opposed to stated policy – is what is actually implemented, which may differ from what was intended, let alone promised. Social policy is about individual and social needs and aspirations; about priorities, and the allocation of resources to meet needs, to reduce deprivation and to provide opportunities for people to gain greater control over their lives and environments.

Social *administration* is the machinery or processes by means of which policies are implemented. It should be acknowledged, however, that the machinery and the processes by which it operates contribute to policy in two principal ways:

(1) by helping to determine or shape it – for example, via the local authority official, social worker, or civil servant as advisers or advocates;
(2) by interpreting and modifying policy decisions, legislation or regulations, especially in those services which provide for the exercise of discretion – as in supplementary benefits; personal social work; most local authority services; and in the administrative levels of the civil services.

In practice, social policy and administration cannot be separated, for they are parts of the same set of activities. Policy has little meaning without having a vehicle of administration to carry it out. Administrators act according to policies – their own or somebody else's, and usually a flexible mixture of the two. The policies may be incremental and *ad hoc*, or comprehensive, clearly defined and prescriptive, or simply evolve from the continuous interchange between administrators. They may be frankly ideological or apparently unideological – an eclectic and pragmatic culture from which policies evolve and adapt in some kind of organic process. But, whatever their origin, whatever form they take, they are suffused with values. Their aims, means, and predicted (or hoped for) outcomes, are all determined and assessed by value judgements.

To return briefly to Knightsbridge Barracks. I do not wish to explore this example much further, but it serves to illustrate the way in which alternative uses of resources provoke comparisons and precipitate questions about social priorities and political values; the more so when the choices are being exercised by governments as in this case.

Just two comparisons:

First, the £3·6 million invested in the construction of the barracks happened to equal the amount spent in the first two years (1968-70) of the Urban Aid Programme which had been set up to deal with the acute social deprivation in urban areas.

Secondly, at the time the barracks were being opened some 9,000 homeless people were living in local authority temporary accommodation in inner London alone – many in humiliating conditions – and others were scattered widely in a variety of accommodation elsewhere: in lodging houses, cheap hotels, huddled on benches in railway stations, in parks, motor-cars, derelict houses, or bedded down under newspapers and corrugated cardboard in doors and alleyways throughout the metropolis. The numbers of homeless in London and the rest of the country had been rising sharply for over ten years, while the output of housing in London – including council housing – had been falling for two years or more. In fact, the total number of dwellings in London had been falling since at least 1961 – the average fall for the Inner London Boroughs for the period 1961-5 was 8·5 per cent of the stock. Over 1·3 million people were living in what were officially defined as 'housing problem areas'.

The kinds of questions which are pertinent in the context of social priorities, but unlikely to be given serious attention by government or architect*, include:

What was the case for building a new and expensive barracks on a prime site on some of the dearest land in the world?

Did it, for example, rest on the social function or economic utility of the Household Cavalry?

Was it on grounds that 514 soldiers and 273 horses in the middle of London are essential to the defence of the capital, or to the protection of the Royal Family and Crown property?

Can the decision be justified on the imputed foreign currency earning value of the Household Cavalry as a tourist spectacle? (Such a proposition should be looked at with scepticism, for the diseconomies of tourism in Central London are considerable, and the ramifications in terms of housing for hotel and catering staff [predicted to increase by up to 20,000 a year for the next few years], the cost of providing hotel beds and ancillary services, traffic congestion, wear and tear on irreplaceable national monuments, are widespread. The disbenefits of tourism are borne mainly by the general public – as social costs – neither hotel owners nor tourists meet the true costs of the tourist trade.)

In the newspaper report the architect is quoted as saying:

*The architect is a servant, a tailor, who cuts and measures the thin chap or the fat chap and tries to make him comfortable. He is not a reformer.

I regard this as a somewhat disingenuous view which ignores considerations of the architect's social responsibility and professional ethics – a matter of particular relevance for an architect whose work and reputation are derived overwhelmingly from large-scale projects in the public sector.

This architect's reported view may be contrasted with that of his even more eminent colleague Walter Gropius who said:

In the struggle for more effective urbanistic [sic] planning and design which would restore a sense of identity and balance to the total fabric or a city or region, we must strengthen the fading image of the architect as a man who helps his community achieve these aims. It isn't enough for him to be rushing on stage with a fancy proposal that promises nothing so much as a monument to his own ego.

These kinds of questions are difficult (often leading to elusive or intangible conclusions). They touch upon social and political values, public regulation or control over the disposition of resources, the means and limits of such intervention, the conditions under which it is appropriate or acceptable, the transferability or alternative uses of finance, materials, manpower, and land. Of relevance as a question of social – or, for that matter, economic – policy is not only *would* the resources devoted to Knightsbridge Barracks have been used for, say, housing, schools, a hospital, or other forms of social provision, but ought they to have been so used? The problem of how to choose between a number of competing uses, what criteria should guide the choice, and how valid the choice might be, are part of the continuing debates of social policy and must necessarily remain so.

There can be no ultimate, unquestionable validity in these kinds of choices – if only because the social and economic context within which policy operates is continually changing. Indeed, the implementation of a policy decision by modifying the input of resources in a given situation changes that situation to a greater or lesser degree. Thus, what is – or, at least, is seen as – sensible policy at one point in time may be inappropriate or irrelevant – or regarded as such – a short time afterwards. But perceptions of what is 'sensible', 'appropriate', or 'relevant', depend heavily upon the availability of information, and upon its interpretation, which is influenced by the attitudes and values of the interpreter.

Different sets of values shaping the evolution of social policy – and the way it has been implemented – have been decisive at different times. Sometimes one value or motive has been dominant, sometimes another. Usually, however, several motives have been at work simultaneously. The following factors have been important determinants of social policy in this country.

(1) Fear of unrest or revolution – in the nineteenth century and again after the First World War.
(2) A recognition of the need to create a stable and conducive social environment in which industry and commerce could flourish.
(3) Military and economic rivalry. The former has receded in importance since the Second World War, but economic

rivalry has remained an effective spur since at least the time of Disraeli's emulation of Bismarck.

(4) Humanitarian concern – not always purely altruistic, sometimes linked with sound business sense that healthy, adequately fed, and decently housed people not only suffer less, they are more reliable time-keepers and produce more. Human kindness has played a role in the development of social policy in Britain, but it is significant that the pressure or initiative for reform rarely originated with the government or its advisers – on the contrary, they usually resisted pressures as being inopportune or too costly – and it is also significant that major advances in social policy came after wars or periods of appalling social distress. It was only after the Second World War that the emphasis in social policy shifted from the alleviation of blatant social and economic deprivations to a concern with development and the construction of a range of comprehensive, interlocking services, in a succession of social, economic, and physical planning policies.

(5) Rising material standards and rising expectations among the mass of people, both of them associated with economic growth, fairly full employment, and substantial increases in real wages since 1939, have contributed to improvements in the quantity and quality of social services.

(6) Administrators, politicians, 'professionals' in the services (and their professional organizations which have grown remarkably in size, competence and political influence in recent years), have become more active and effective in promoting innovation in social policy. The climate has changed since the war. Social policies are now much more prominent in the public's consciousness, they and their defects figure much more centrally in political debate, they are expanding comparatively steadily in spite of occasional setbacks, they are attracting personnel and material resources on a scale undreamed of a decade or two ago. All major political parties now recognize that social services are indispensable parts of the structure of modern society. The debate nowadays is not about their abolition, but much more about how to make them more effective – including more cost-effective.

The magnitude of the shift in political and social perspectives should not be underrated. As far as social policy is concerned the Second World War was of greater significance than the First World War. But government failure to redeem its promises after 1919, and the bitter experiences of the depression years, helped to make it so. In that sense the Second World War completed the destruction and discrediting of Edwardian England, with its bourgeois pretensions and imperial illusions, and the self-conscious social disdain that warped government for so long. It was still influential during the early years of the Second World War, but it never recovered from the twin blows of war and the 1945 election.

Dilemmas of Community Relations

E. Butterworth

Reprinted with permission from 'Dilemmas of Community Relations', *New Community*, vol. 1, no. 3, Spring 1972, pp. 205-7, & vol. 1, no. 5, Autumn 1972, pp. 435-38

Community relations is faced by a number of particularly noticeable dilemmas at the present time. Any structure which contains a mixture of central and local interests in the decision-making is bound to find it difficult to pursue clear and coherent policies. The danger in such a complex structure is that the problems which arise from keeping those diverse interests happy, with the enormous range of motivations which are present and which influence the goals which are considered desirable, will take precedence over the interests which the structure is designed to serve.

STAGES OF SETTLEMENT AND STYLES OF WORK

I should like to single out from a range of dilemmas those which concern styles of work, and in particular to ask whether those styles, and the assumptions which inform them, are appropriate for the practice of community relations in the future. By way of preamble, we must ask how far there are different priorities, and even different tasks, as between one area and another. Despite the existence of some features which are general for relations in Britain, there are also significant differences. These arise from the interplay of a number of distinct variables, among which are the stages of settlement which have been reached by different ethnic minorities, the density of settlement, social mobility within the minorities, the leadership available to them, the sources from which leaders derive their support, and the relationships established with the power structure. Obviously, the issues are relatively simple if only one minority is present, though that does not mean they are easy to resolve. But if there are several minorities, then we must move away from a fairly straightforward view of what needs to be done to one which takes into account inevitable tensions and conflicts of interest and focus.

The stages of settlement with which community relations work has been concerned so far can be characterized in a very general way. Stage I – all-male immigration; Stage II – the arrival of an increasing number of women and children; and Stage III – long-term settlement. The first two stages are ones to which the term 'immigration' can be applied, in that many of the issues which are of most concern relate to adjustment to British society. Progression through the stages has gone on at different speeds in different parts of the country – fastest in Greater London and the West Midlands, and slowest in the north. Moreover, there is considerable variation in the way it happens as between one ethnic group and another, and between sub-groups within a particular group. The pace of the move from one stage to another depends on such factors as the experience of the group with which we are concerned, and the length of time it has been in that particular town or city. Little work has been done so far on the moves from areas of primary settlement, to which the original migrants came, to areas of secondary and later settlement. This can occur both within towns but also between towns.

Taking the main ethnic minorities, the West Indians have progressed furthest from Stage I, the Indians next, and the Pakistanis least far. If we now distinguish between Pakistanis and Bengalis, then the latter are more likely to be in or near Stage I than Punjabis or Kashmiris. In Stage III there will be much more preoccupation with social justice, opportunities and aspirations.

The move is away from an occupation with basic minimum stand-ards and requirements to a concern at Stage III with citizenship and its rights and obligations.

I think there are practical ways of distinguishing between the stages which have been reached in different towns and among different groups which would allow us to put the towns into categories which would reflect the stage reached and the appropri-ate methods of work, and also perhaps the level of resources that would be necessary. Usually, one finds sub-groups within the minorities in all three stages, but the balance will have changed dramatically within the past decade. Once the 1971 Census material is available, this kind of analysis can be undertaken.

The proportions in age and sex groups provide a reliable guide in distinguishing between Stages I and II, together with evidence about the duration of settlement in that town. The distinction between Stages II and III depends on length of residence and on the proportion of children either brought to Britain from their parents' countries of origin or born here to these parents. Once the number of children born in Britain exceeds the numbers coming in, which is true almost everywhere now, the move towards the time when the British-born will outnumber those born elsewhere will accelerate rapidly. This has implications for community relations that need to be anticipated before the event.

THE 'HARMONY MODEL'

The ideology on which the assumptions and official practice of community relations are based is to be found explicitly in the history of the CRC* and its predecessors. The Report of the CRC for 1968-9, for example, suggests a 'basic aim of harmonious community relations . . . which can be pursued steadfastly in the face of whatever tensions and conflicts may arise in future from various sources'. The implication seems to be that these tensions and conflicts arise from outside the structure, not within it. The reasons for the emphasis on a model which stresses harmony of interests and 'community' are not hard to find. It appealed to the notion of organic social change and the 'British tradition'. It may thus have made the political problem of securing the acceptability of the structure an easier one. It promised little that was specific,

* Community Relations Commission

so could be seen as offering many things in the way that most structures do. It was in line with traditional practice in most voluntary social movements, and in particular of the Councils of Social Service. Finally, it argued that since the main problems were those of the 'adjustment' of immigrants, the model was quite valid.

How adequate is a model based on harmony for community relations? It is part of my argument that it has some relevance for the first two stages of settlement outlined above, and less for the third and any subsequent ones; but there are two qualifications which have to be made to this statement. In the first place there is a vast difference between the way harmony may be viewed by those in different parts of the structure. Secondly, it is the whole apparatus surrounding the concept, and the ideas and practices which have been linked with it, that are the source of many problems arising from it.

It is possible to assume a goal of harmony whilst at the same time recognizing that the means to achieve this may involve some conflict. Unfortunately, it is often assumed that *everything* – goals, methods, the personality of the full-time officer, the initiative – has to be acceptable. Nothing less likely to encourage effective action can be imagined.

As David Donnison has pointed out: 'British politics, particularly at the local level, are "machine" politics: civilized and honest on the whole but machine rule nonetheless.' Yet the myth of British local government does not rest on a notion of a small core of people in power running the system; it depends on a notion of political man and representative democracy deriving from the nineteenth century, whereby the exercise of power is open, governed by rational principles and where the individual citizen can have his grievances resolved and play his part in the processes of government. Even now one can meet people who think this is a reality. In all this I am not discussing the effectiveness or otherwise of our system; I am pointing out the gaps which exist between the myths and the realities.

It is no accident that a preoccupation with harmony arises from those who are concerned to preserve what they have, are satisfied with things as they are, apart from some marginal adjustments, and are in decision-making positions, or who feel that the networks of influence to which they have access, will be responsive to their needs. As the American community organizer,

Saul Alinksy, pointed out when he was taken to task for his acceptance of conflict and failure to promote reconciliation: 'In the world as it is, "reconciliation" means that one side has the power and the other side gets reconciled to it.' In reality, the worlds of economic and political man are inhabited by vested interests, monopolies, and differential access to resources, whereas harmony implies a company of equals.

The model based on harmony does not take into account the full implications of the disadvantages which arise from the structure of society. If it is 'people' that matter, then they must be looked on as individuals rather than as groups or aggregates. This is intended to make the approach to them more humane, immediate and sympathetic. The effect is often quite the reverse – to blur and conceal the in-built disadvantages. Among the more unrealistic of myths (if such a term can be used of them!) are those which suggest that the rewards of high social status go to those who practise the 'Protestant' virtues of thrift, hard work, and the rest. If we accept that the ethnic minorities with which we are concerned are disadvantaged, then this has implications which ought to be important for community relations policies.

INADEQUACIES AND EASY OPTIONS

The harmony model is often stronger on hope than it is on performance, since its goals are *process* goals: that is, more concerned with such long-term consequences of bringing people together as the development of self-help, more co-operative attitudes, and better community integration. It is not usually strong on the assessment of performance – nor indeed is this ever an easy matter. The harmony model is preoccupied with generalities about what is assumed to be in the hearts and minds of men rather than interested in asking awkward questions. If a play-group is started, then it is normal to take pride in this and the way in which people have co-operated to make it possible. At the same time, quite apart from the numbers of children who may be involved during the sessions, there are other questions about how satisfactory the sessions are, whether they provide the children with what they require, how far the mothers of the children are involved (and whether in organizing or merely menial capacities); in short, what are the wider implications of what is being done? It is easier to make quantitative than qualitative judgements. Moreover, questions about whether resources could be better employed may never be raised. The fact that something tangible now exists where it did not do so before is the proof of success. This compounds the view that it is better, and safer, to create objects that others can see – such as centres of various kinds, which one may then spend most of one's time, energy and money keeping going, irrespective of how irrelevant or unsuccessful the project is turning out to be – than to put resources into organizing and co-ordinating existing efforts and retaining flexibility of response. There are many cautionary examples to illustrate these points, and it is not necessary to live where large numbers of churches have become redundant, and their use has been changed, to appreciate the significant underuse of many public buildings, both now and in the past. It is, however, usually much easier to raise money for these traditional purposes. There are occasions when new buildings and services need to be provided, but the chance of doing this must rest on a strong body of existing support, or the reasonable expectation of one. Much depends on our perception of the community, and its potential.

What I am suggesting is that there is no necessary relationship between the intensity of social needs and the resources available to meet or to be allocated to them. Rather is there an inverse relationship, if it exists at all. The dilemmas here are that we shall be more unpopular if we tackle serious problems rather than minor ones which offend few vested interests; more unpopular if we act rather than talk, such problems as poverty, poor environment, and discrimination, find less response, for example, in the voluntary sector than those which call upon feelings of human pity and sympathy for individuals whose plight is particularly dramatic and hopeless. There is more likelihood of raising money for a kidney or heart machine than for tackling general social problems which affect large numbers. This may in part be the fault of the way in which the issues are presented. It will certainly reflect prevailing social attitudes, for these have a great bearing on what people are prepared to do.

Constraints and dilemmas arise from the *ad hoc* ways in which CROs and their predecessors, the liaison officers, came nto post and the work began. This has helped to form a view of the CRO as a kind of fire prevention officer, always at the mercy of events and unable to control, anticipate or plan for them.

A CRO has often started by setting up in an office and finding, over time, that people come to him with particular kinds of problems with which they need help. This is often, and wrongly, given the umbrella term 'casework', although it is by no means the same as the casework practised by professional social workers. What this kind of work in community relations requires is a knowledge of the system, of the availability of services of which the client is ignorant and which he needs, and the capacity to take enormous time and trouble with all the problems that arise. A lot of this experience has been positively helpful to the CRO. He contacted officials on behalf of his clients and thus became known to them; he lobbied on their behalf and helped them to prepare their cases. Their concerns took priority and some CROs spent enormous amounts of time on cases where, for example, members of the client's family were being denied entry to Britain. They were right to do this. It served two main purposes: the first was to show concern for the individual and the second to make the existence of the CRO better known. The context was that no other organization would be able to offer this help, something which was true until recently.

One could make a distinction in the work between cases where there was lack of knowledge and those which arose through discrimination and denial of rights. Although in theory the second kind of cases came within the scope of the Race Relations Board, it was not uncommon for CROs to take these up in spheres such as employment and housing and attempt to do something about them (until 1968 the Race Relations Act did not cover these main areas of discrimination). It could be argued that the knowledge which CROs gained of the community in consequence of these activities, and the knowledge which the community gained of the CRO, was essential to establishing an effective working relationship. Yet the consequences of this emphasis in the work were several. The CRO became known to many people but with a particular kind of orientation in mind. An image of him was created which made it more difficult for him to move into new areas of work (as identified, for example, in the eleven-point job description set out by the Community Relations Commission), from the viewpoints of those in the official hierarchies of departments and agencies, his committee members and his clients. To continue the process of grievance-solving effectively, in a situation where more clients were appearing, became increasingly difficult, particularly where other aspects of the work were developing. Furthermore, once CROs were proficient and developed expertise in this, it has been difficult to prevent it becoming or remaining a continuing and even a dominant part of their work.

This was not the only kind of problem to arise. In particular, some CROs, members of minorities themselves, operating in areas where the main or sole minority was a different one, have faced complex and difficult situations. Questions of how the CRO was perceived, relating not just to the structure of community relations and central and local government, but also involving his or her personal and ethnic background, have been the source of continuing dilemmas affecting the work, and have influenced the choice of priorities and the style of the operation. Since the CRO in most areas had few resources, apart from an office and some secretarial assistance, often part-time, much more depended on him personally than would be the case in a situation where there was a bigger staff and more resources. It may not be too far-fetched to think of him at this stage as exercising a kind of pastoral care on the analogy of the local vicar, at times with custodial overtones!

LIMITATIONS OF FIRST-STAGE ROLES

In Stage I, then, apart from the taking up of individual cases, the CROs role has, in the main, been a relatively limited one. There were unlikely to be many other issues in which the CRO was used other than as a source of information about the conditions in which the minorities lived, or the agencies to which particular issues or problems could be referred. He was seen, therefore, as a channel of information between them and the power structure. He was, however, concerned to emphasize the relevance of community relations work and its importance in the town in which he worked, and accepted invitations to speak to local groups about the main issues as he saw them. He was also present at committees or meetings, often of marginal or no relevance, as an embodiment of how important community relations was thought to be. The whole concept of the job which arose at this time was of selfless dedication, reflected above all in the amount of time the officer spent at work. In face of a range of competing, and sometimes conflicting, demands on his most precious resource of all, his time, it is not surprising that the turnover of those in post was high.

Speaking to local groups too, may be seen as fulfilling the function of public education built in to the role of the CRO. In so far as no distinction was made between the groups in the community whose opinions were more or less important, or between the degrees of intensity with which views about the minorities were held, such talks could have only a minimal effect. This, too, could become something which the CRO enjoyed doing, and which he continued to do long after he was known within the area and long after the advantages of this rather diffuse 'educational' activity had disappeared.

ALTERNATIVES AND CHOICES

Such main activities were, I suggest, inherently dangerous for the future, in that the assumptions made then about the role of the CRO, arguably of prime importance in Stage I, could be carried over into stages where they were less relevant, and possibly even harmful, to group relationships. To add to the difficulties of creating a policy and an organizational image, the second stage of settlement, with wives and children coming over, further increased the number of cases with which the CRO had to deal.

There were two alternatives at this time for most CROs. One was to refer people to individual departments of the statutory services, thereby recognizing that the clients were citizens and were entitled to redress in the normal way. Such a decision could make the position of the clients worse in a number of respects, simply because lack of knowledge of the whole apparatus of the Welfare State compounded the disadvantages which all clients experience. The second was to attempt to create an organization or an advisory group which, though possibly linked to the CRO and his committee in various ways, could undertake the tasks which he had initially performed.

This leads us to the problem of effectiveness, which raises another crunch question about the CRO and his method of operation. Given that his responsibility often extends to tens of thousands of people, that his resources are relatively small and his time limited, he has to choose between being a front runner on a few issues or organizing himself and his set-up in such a way that he creates an effective structure of advisory panels and of groups, without having too much oversight of them.

It can be argued that individual cases are still there, and that if the CRO does not deal with them no one else will. If this is the case, and it is in some places, then a choice will have to be made. Every time a priority is decided, then the work changes in emphasis, and a number of people will be dissatisfied because they are not convinced that this is desirable or necessary. If they include the chairman or important members of the executive, then other dilemmas arise.

At Stage III, I suggest that work on cases becomes virtually redundant, and that policy issues and providing resources for developing new approaches, including radical ones, should become much more important. There are indications that this is beginning to happen. It is, however, a move from a 'personal' involvement to a structure of organization which may seem, to any individual requiring help, to be a faceless bureaucracy.

PLANNING FOR THE FUTURE WITH CLARITY

Important and rapid changes have taken place and continue to take place in the situations of the minorities and the majority, and their relationships, and in the requirements, style and objectives of community relations work. How far do those in decision-making positions on local councils or committees acknowledge this and take account of it in their determinations of priorities? How far do they, given greater resources, want the same as they have now, only more of it?

Priorities in the future should revolve around the need to give groups the opportunity to act effectively on their own behalf, and the range of what is considered appropriate should be extended beyond play-groups, language-classes and similar forms of provision, to support and services which can help groups to be more effective on their own behalf and to build a source of power either through their own efforts or, more likely, by coalitions with other groups. Ways of achieving these objectives are being developed, and they need to be more widely known and copied. These are not the only issues, but they are some to which we should give attention in trying to resolve present dilemmas.

Finally, we must be clear what we are planning for in the future. This will not be without all kinds of stress and tension, as groups organize to achieve their rights. Without stressing American analogies, and even being sceptical about them, we can still take note of Aaron Wildavsky's cautionary recipe for violence, which has at some points a familiar ring:

Promise a lot; deliver a little. Lead people to believe they will be much better off, but let there be no dramatic improvement. Try a variety of small programmes, each interesting but marginal in impact and severely underfinanced. Avoid any attempted solution remotely comparable in size to the dimensions of the problem you are trying to solve. Have middle-class civil servants hire upper-class student radicals to use lower-class Negroes as a battering-ram against the existing local political systems; then complain that people are going around disrupting things and chastise local politicians for not co-operating with those out to do them in. Get some poor people involved in local decision-making, only to discover that there is not enough at stake to be worth bothering about. Feel guilty about what has happened to black people, tell them you are surprised they have not revolted before; express shock and dismay when they follow your advice. Go in for a little force, just enough to anger, not enough to discourage. Feel guilty again; say you are surprised that worse has not happened. Alternate with a little suppression. Mix well, apply a match, and run . . .

Social Administration and Scarcity

R. A. Parker

Reprinted with permission from 'Social Administration and Scarcity: The Problem of Rationing', *Social Work* 1967, vol. 24, no. 2 (April), pp 9-14.

I

Needs are potentially infinite; resources always limited and therefore scarce. This is, of course, one of the major problems which economic organization has to solve. In the free market situation, as any student of economics will know, the difficulty is overcome by resort to the price mechanism. However, unlike need, demand at a particular price is finite and theoretically measurable.

The social services have two important characteristics which distinguish them from the free market services. First, they tend to meet a range of needs which society and the individual usually regard as basic or urgent, yet expensive to provide. Second, they largely eschew the price mechanism as a means of distributing and allocating services. The universal problem of balancing scarce resources against prolific needs nevertheless still has to be resolved. Its dimension can only be significantly reduced if some need is unmet or resources increased.

One way in which needs have been controlled is by assuming that they do not exist, or that they are not the proper concern of public provision. Their satisfaction is then left to the market and the individual's ability or willingness to pay the price. Although the State's responsibility for the provision of many social services has increased many people still hesitate to use them, and this very reluctance has restricted the demands which they make. In these circumstances it has been easier to strike a balance between apparent need and resources. Similarly, in earlier forms of organized social provision, whether administered by the State or by voluntary bodies, needs could be adjusted to resources because they were not met as a universal right but upon the fulfilment of certain conditions. Recipients might be obliged to establish that they were deserving or be tested to ensure their eligibility for the service.

With the growth of 'welfare', organized by the State on the basis of mandatory and universal services, the possibility of limiting needs by ignoring them declined. Furthermore Government was made fo cibly aware of the range of unmet needs, as well as new ones, by urbanization, the emergence of organized labour, economic depression, war and a multitude of other factors. The rate at which demands upon the social services grew after the 1945 war caused some to shout 'abuse', others to wonder at the extent to which urgent needs had previously been stifled; and yet others to try to estimate the potential size of the latent but legitimate demand for social services. These demands have certainly increased and the standards offered have risen. Relatively more resources are now being consumed by each recipient than in the past.

II

One is impressed by the variety of ways in which this problem of scarcity is dealt with in our social services. Of course, the panacea is seen as more resources but although this will ease the problem, at least temporarily, it will not eradicate it. Indeed the mobilization of additional resources is usually a slow and often unpredictable affair, and achievements usually fall short of the target. For these reasons the demand for a service normally needs to be restrained, or its nature and quality modified. The aim of this section is to examine the manner in which this occurs.

Deterrence
In the first place there is still *deterrence*. It may take the form of traditional 'less eligibility'. This can be seen in the administration of much part III accommodation for homeless families. Conditions are *supposed* to be uninviting, and this is reflected in the poor standards of the buildings and their amenities as well as in the rules which exclude husbands. It is feared that were such accommodation to be improved it would become more attractive than the housing conditions under which many families have to live. There is the related fear that better standards would encourage some families to seek the speedier allocation of a council

house by way of homelessness. Of course, such a possibility is only likely to occur whilst there remains an unmet demand for reasonable housing.

But it is not only in administrative policies that deterrence occurs. The manner in which applicants are received may easily deter the apprehensive or uncertain. Officials, official buildings or official forms may prove daunting and awesome. The unmarried mother may have to screw up her courage to apply for Supplementary Benefit and be sharply aware of a censorious tone or implied disapproval. Her first contact could be her last. Similarly the discharged mental patient may dread an initial visit to the employment exchange, and even a slight rebuff could be sufficient to deter him from seeking further help.

It may also be the past character of a service which acts as an important deterrent. How people *imagine* they will be treated, and what they *believe* they are entitled to may reflect the experience of a previous generation, and effectively stop them seeking assistance. Likewise it is important whether or not they feel the service carries the stigma of social inadequacy, failure, or charity.

Eligibility

Deterrence may or may not represent an explicit policy; usually not. But it does occur and its effect is to suppress some demands upon the social services. *Eligibility* bars on the other hand are normally explicit, and frequently define the limits of the service in a quite precise way. With voluntary societies religious affiliation may be the criterion. Age is a common boundary in many services and so is the diagnosis of a specific condition or problem ('We only take boys who are severely disturbed but have IQs of over 120'). The strict categorization of the needs which a service will meet is an important means whereby it can control the demands made upon it. In the field of housing, residence qualifications are still common and serve to check the size of waiting lists, particularly in areas of high immigration.

Eligibility is part of the somewhat wider process of *deflection*. Some need can be deflected from one organization to another. This may be rationalized in terms of administrative boundaries, financial responsibilities, or the greater appropriateness of the other service. The phenomenon is not unfamiliar in the relationship between districts and counties, central and local government,

local authorities and the regional hospital boards or statutory and
voluntary organizations. In some cases there is the additional
possibility of deflection from the public to the private sector, as
with day nurseries or foster parents.

Delay

Then, of course, there is rationing by *delay*, which may be either
organized and explicit, or unplanned. Typically it takes the form
of a waiting-list or queue. Restraining demand by delay enables a
policy of universal access to be maintained whilst taking account
of the realities of the supply side. It can also be an important way
of keeping standards at a reasonably high level. The general
practitioner may please those who are waiting by dealing
expeditiously with his surgery patient; once inside the consulting
room however, the patient is only too anxious for the doctor to
take his time, be painstaking, and thorough.

Delay may also become a deterrent; two hours spent sitting in
an out-patients' department is a cost which once experienced may
deter patients, except in serious circumstances. Waiting-lists may
also shrink as a result of what is now respectably termed spontaneous remission. Time spent on the list, as John Stroud so
nicely shows in his novel *The Shorn Lamb*, may appear to be a
therapy in itself.

About a week later I [a child-care officer] was passing a dark
grocer's shop in the High Road when out came a fat, sad-
looking woman, Miss Niff, the Social Worker from the Clinic.
When she saw me she hailed me with a mournful hoot.
'Hilloo, Hilloo! I vos going to tiliphoneyou!'

'Oh, yes?'

'Our leedle friend Egbert,' she said, falling into step beside
me and nodding her head sagaciously. 'Yis. Vell, ve haf seen
through *him*!'

'Oh, have you?' I said disappointed. I'd known him for a
couple of years and I couldn't see through him. I felt ashamed
and chagrined that Miss Niff could do better than I could.

'Ho, yiss,' she said, still nodding, 'Hev no fears. Shall I tell
you vot ve propose to do? Ve are going to put Egbert on the
vaiting-list.'

'My word!' I said, adding cautiously: 'Is that good?'

'Ho, very good,' she said. 'Very effective, it is a method of treatment with a very high success rate: ve put them on the list and by the time they are actually seen at the Clinic nearly ninety per cent are cured.'

Misunderstanding

Of course, if people misunderstand the function of a service or do not know of its existence they are unlikely to apply. The recent rate rebates fiasco is good illustration, as is national assistance. Indeed in the last NAB report it was pointed out 'that many pensioners [who had not applied] had not properly understood the provisions of the assistance scheme about such matters as the possession of savings (including owner-occupied property), income which is disregarded and the effect of sharing one's house with a relative in well-paid employment'. The idea of a campaign to 'sell' a particular service is not always welcome: understandably so, for it might prove impossible to cope with any sudden increase in demand without a simultaneous increase in resources. Such reluctance to advertise a service fully is often justified by the comfortable assumption that those *really* in need will find out about the service soon enough; an attitude which hardly squares with any attempt to promote a preventive approach in the social services.

Although the social services are characterized by the rejection of price criteria as a basis for distribution, some charges are still made: notably for council houses, residential accommodation, home helps and, until recently, prescriptions. What direct effect this has on the level of demand is difficult to assess; but, equally important, prospective users may be deterred by what they *think* they are going to be charged. Assessment scales are rarely comparable, simple or fully public.

Dilution

A general alternative to restraining demand for a service is *dilution*. There are many variations upon this theme. If more has to be done with the same resources standards have to be lowered and the service spread more thinly. In the home help service, for instance, extra demand is not often deflected, turned away or kept waiting. Instead the amount of time allocated to each recipient is reduced. The annual report of the County Medical Officer of West Sussex provides another example of this process. It gives an account of the work of one child guidance clinic: 'The . . . clinic is at present a first-aid centre, due to lack of staff. It is kept going largely because those who *are* available are prepared to exchange roles as and when necessary, and do what *can* be done rather than what they know *should* be done'.

Different services will be obliged to adopt some of these strategies rather than others becauseof their history, their degree of specialization, public opinion, statutory responsibilities, or the character of their work. The child-care service, for instance, can rarely ask deprived children to queue for its service, similarly no child can be denied education after the age of five. In contrast waiting-lists are a traditional feature of local authority housing.

The rationing of services
There appears to be a growing disquiet, however, about the existence of deterrence, delay, deflection or public ignorance of the social services. Indeed this is illustrated by the setting up of the Seebohm Committee, with its brief to look at possible ways in which the personal social services can be reorganized to better effect, as well as events such as the recent outcry about the treatment of homeless families. But as one method of controlling demand is rejected as socially undesirable another has to be found *even* with increased resources unless, that is, a lower standard of service is offered. Doing away with eligibility criteria, for instance, may be laudable but a further dilution of the service may occur as a result; services may be provided in a less deterrent manner but a greater use of waiting-lists may be required in consequence; or a service may become better known but the staff forced to defend themselves from the extra work by giving less time to each client. Enoch Powell has pointed out in his recent pamphlet *Medicine and Politics* that there is 'the political convention that the existence of any rationing at all must be strenuously denied'. He goes on to make the important point that the 'worst kind of rationing is that which is unacknowledged'. There is advantage in it being conscious and explicit and in it occurring *before* the service is offered. Otherwise some form of rationing will emerge (by default) through the manner in which the service is provided. Where this happens those who are most easily deterred, least articulate, worst acquainted with the service, least able to wait, or who fall outside the conventional categories

of eligibility will tend to be penalized. The recent Plowden Report on primary education suggests the designation of 'educational priority areas' where social and educational conditions are worst. This would be an example of deliberate allocation before actual provision. Such methods as these may ensure positive discrimination towards under-privileged groups, whereas rationing which is allowed to emerge in the day-to-day work of an organization tends not to do this. A share of any service needs to be specifically earmarked for those least likely to consume it if left to press their own claims in a rationing situation. Such developments would bring the questions of the distribution and allocation of services back into the company of major policy issues; which, after all, is where they belong.

III

All social service organizations face the problem of scarce resources, albeit in varying degrees. This not only creates problems of general policy but also difficulties in the day-to-day work. Some of these problems are discussed in this last section.

The effects of professionalization

Social welfare organizations are becoming increasingly professional in outlook, aspiration and staffing. Professional identity and ambition, however, are both closely associated with the quality of the service offered. An individual worker's skill and knowledge will be improved and sharpened by careful and intensive work. Indeed the struggle for professional status is unlikely to be won when standards of work fall short of what it is known could be attained. Hence the professional, or aspiring professional in the social services will frequently face a dilemma. Standards of practice tend to rise when demand is carefully sifted and held back, particularly so in social casework, medicine or education which are all labour intensive and time-consuming disciplines. But anxious to meet need wherever he finds it, or faced with an unregulated demand, the professional is obliged to lower his sights. Where this happens he may become disenchanted and experience a perpetual state of conflict about the courses of action open to him. He may despair of the relevance of his training faced with situations in which it cannot be fully or appropriately used. In conditions of excessive scarcity little difference may be apparent in the performance of the trained and the untrained and the sceptics may see their worse doubts about the value of training fulfilled. Trained staff may be tempted to leave the work altogether or seek jobs in more clinical and specialized situations where a highly selective service is able to sustain high standards.

Administrator v. *fieldworker*
In situations of scarcity there is also likely to be an inherent conflict between the administrative side of the work and the field work side. Some rationing of the organization's resources will have to occur prior to the provision of the service. Senior staff will necessarily be concerned with allocation within the whole organization and as between all the consumers. They will have to maintain some sort of parity between one district and another; between this worker's requests and the next, or between one client and another. The fieldworker on the other hand, professionally trained and with quite proper aspirations about the sort of service he wants to provide, will wish to obtain as large a share of the organization's resources as he judges a particular case requires. He will not be over-concerned with questions of general distribution, although, of course, in his work he too has to allocate his time and energy according to some set of priorities. Nevertheless the orientation of the fieldworker and the administrator, even though they be broadly agreed about ultimate ends, is likely to be dissimilar.

Co-operation and planning
Co-operation in general is likely to be more difficult to achieve the greater the scarcity. Co-operation usually requires one person, or organization, to adjust their priorities to accommodate another. In doing this the co-operative person frequently creates other problems for himself: there is a cost, in terms of alternatives foregone or work not done. The organization with the more favourable balance of resources is more likely to be co-operative; it possesses more elbow-room. Likewise an organization whose basic 'factor of production' can be stretched is likely to be better placed in this respect than one in which this cannot be done. A casework agency, for example, which depends very largely upon manpower can usually stretch its service, at least temporarily, by

way of overtime, Saturday work and so on. A housing department on the other hand cannot stretch its stock of houses even temporarily. This affects its ability to be co-operative.

Shortage also affects planning. It often obliges both organizations and individuals to provide essentially short-term solutions to what are really long-term problems. This is uneconomical and often inappropriate. For instance, if there are insufficient domiciliary services for the prematurely ageing who have no family to look after them, people in their late fifties may be taken into residential accommodation and proceed to block a place for twenty-five or thirty years. Shortage, of time to think and plan in particular, makes most problems immediate and short-term.

It is also important to recognize that if staff are placed in a situation where they face the prospect of an impossible or unacceptable work load they will find ways of reducing the pressure. They may narrow their conception of the job and its objectives, with the consequent danger of red-tape; they may adopt unco-operative or deterrent attitudes; they may slow down; suppress information which creates work; go sick, or resign. If the organization has no general rationing policy individual workers will have to develop a system of their own, which may or may not accord with the spirit of the service, and may be more or less idiosyncratic.

Conclusion

One of the principal tasks of chief officers, committees or boards of governors is to fight for additional resources. But however successful they may be in this they also have the task of deciding the main rationing procedures which will be adopted in the services for which they are responsible. This is a matter of policy. The existence of 'universal provision' has unfortunately seduced many into believing that the problem of rationing no longer arises. As a result its political and administrative implications tend to have been side-stepped, and the problem all too often allowed to resolve itself without conscious planning or public debate – often to the detriment of the weakest and most needy.

Is the Customer Never Right?

A. Keefe

Reprinted with permission from 'Is the Customer Never Right?',
Social Work Today, Vol. 1, No. 11, February 1971, pp. 23-28

A consideration of the ways in which developments taking place in social work tend to restrict the liberty of the individual and an attempt to suggest how this may be avoided.

INTRODUCTION

The recipients of social work services are very often the socially deprived. Social workers call these recipients their 'clients' which makes them feel that the service offered is a professional one and one which the 'client' chooses to avail himself of and even has control over.

I would argue, however, that our relationship with our 'clients' is in most cases quite unlike that in any other professional relationship in that the degree of choice exercised by the 'client' is usually limited and quite often non-existent. Indeed, I would contend that social workers collude with society in denying their 'clients' certain basic liberties.

In this article I intend to show:
(1) that the client has had little opportunity to participate in planning the development of the social services;
(2) that wide discretion is exercised by social work departments at present and will increase still further in the future;
(3) that the extent to which the client can dispute a decision made concerning himself or his family is limited at present and that the trend of the changes taking place in the legislative and organizational framework of the social services seems likely to decrease such opportunity still further;
(4) that decision-making in social work departments is complex and inevitably very subjective;
(5) that it is possible to incorporate a scheme into the new social work departments whereby the client will be able to participate in planning, appeal against decisions and whereby his liberty may be protected and even promoted.

I will also adopt what may be a useful irritant and refer to the 'client' as the 'consumer'.

FOCUS ON SOCIAL WORKERS

Changes are taking place so swiftly in social work organization and practice that there is little opportunity for reflection or consolidation. Most social workers are excited by these developments but at the same time are understandably anxious about the adjustments they will be expected to make. It is partly this anxiety and partly the social worker's desire to be accorded professional status that has meant the focus of attention has been the social worker and the organization within which he works rather than the consumer for whom he provides a service.

It is, of course, true that the interests of the social worker and the consumer are to a considerable extent inter-related and indeed it is certainly to the consumer's advantage that enough resources are employed to ensure an efficient and an effective service. (Exactly what constitues an 'efficient and an effective service' is another subject for debate!)

Although it would be unfair to say that the consumer's interests are being neglected at present, it would I think be fair to say that social workers have taken it upon themselves to decide just what the consumer's interests really are. No 'market research' was undertaken by Seebohm and as far as I know, magistrates, police and social workers were responsible in the main for the Children and Young Persons Act, 1969. Not only was the consumer not consulted as to what services he required and how these should be provided, but there is no opportunity in the new legislation for him to have any say in subsequent developments and organization at a local level.

As another example, 'community care' is a concept embodied in much recent legislation. It may well be that as a method of caring for the dependent in society, be they the young, the sick or the old, it is generally approved of by the community. Do we really know whether this is so, however, and were the groups on whom community care imposes a burden ever consulted? (We still do not seem to have decided whether community care means care *in* the community or care *by* the community.)

Local authority councillors decide whether their capital spending will produce a new children's home, a new health centre, or a day hostel for the mentally sick. Is the result always a reflection of the wishes of that community? This is not to suggest that councillors do not attempt to gauge public feeling, but how do they do this, and are their impressions accurate?

Perhaps even more important, there is very little opportunity for the consumer to participate in decision-making regarding himself or his family or to question and appeal against these decisions.

This problem applies at present to all social work departments to a varying degree and is, of course, one of long standing. I will look at the services provided by local authority children's committees to develop my argument.

POWERS OF CHILDREN'S COMMITTEES

Existing legislation confers on children's committees wide powers and responsibilities and also affords wide discretion. A few examples of the range of decisions made on their behalf are as follows:

(1) The decision as to whether a child is received into care or not at the request of the parent. (There is considerable variation in the interpretation given to the relevant legislation by individual departments.)
(2) The decision as to whether financial or material aid is provided for a family. (How clearly have the criteria for these decisions been formulated and how much consistency is there even within departments?)
(3) The decision on how much to charge parents for the care of their children and whether in some instances to pursue the parent to prison for the debt. (It is probable that policy within departments is fairly consistent but my experience is that policy certainly varies from area to area.)
(4) The decision on how the needs of a child in care are to be best met and even whether a child is allowed home 'on trial'. (Discretion in this respect is widened by the Children and Young Persons Act, 1969.)
(5) The decision as to whether a person or a family is offered casework help. (Are there any real criteria for such decisions?

My experience is that policy on this varies from day to day even within departments!)

(6) The decision as to whether a couple are allowed to foster or adopt a child. (There seem to be virtually no recognized criteria for selection.)

Doubtless there are other areas of discretion in the child-care service and workers in other disciplines could add to this list from their own experience.

'Client self-determination' is taught to students as a sacred casework concept. In practice it is very often discarded. Social workers usually have fairly clear ideas as to the pattern of behaviour they feel the 'client' should adopt and self-determination is only permitted within this framework. Perhaps the concept is most often heard when a 'manipulative' or 'unco-operative' client is not prepared to accept help on the terms under which it is offered. The self-determination may be limited to the taking or leaving of a particular service.

The situation whereby a children's department considers whether or not to guarantee to the local authority the payment of rent for a particular tenant is illustrative.

First the housing department may refer the tenant to the children's department, without the tenant's knowledge or consent. The child-care officer then visits the family and attempts to make a tentative diagnosis as to the reasons the rent is in arrears. He then considers within his department whether this is an appropriate situation for a rent guarantee. The decision made, he returns to the family and may offer a particular service. The tenant has to decide whether to accept or reject this, although he may be unaware of its wider implications.

The tenant is not informed of the existence of a rent guarantee scheme; he is not informed that he is a candidate for the scheme; and he is not informed of the decision eventually taken.

This is, fortunately, an extreme example, but elements of it are common to other situations and the consumer is often excluded from the decision-making which concerns him and his problems.

INADEQUATE MACHINERY

At present, consumers who feel they are the victims of bad decisions do have some opportunity to seek redress. In some circumstances they may appeal to the courts. For local authority services they may appeal to their councillors. They may sometimes 'shop around' between different agencies and, more exceptionally, they may enlist the aid of the mass media.

This jumble of machinery is hardly adequate at present and it is likely to be much less so in the future.

The courts
   (1) Rely to a considerable extent on social workers to provide them with information and a professional judgement concerning the people who come before them. Such information is necessarily selected and such judgements debatable.
   (2) The consumer is at an obvious disadvantage in a setting familiar to all involved except himself, and he is often not legally represented.
   (3) Magistrates are not noted for their heterogeneity of social class or attitudes, and these are often far removed from those of the consumer.
   (4) The Children and Young Persons Act, 1969, limits the opportunity for juvenile courts to determine the particular treatment given to children under 14 years of age and will probably mean they are directly involved with far fewer children. This responsibility is being given to social workers and this could very well be the pattern for developments in other areas of court responsibility.

The councillor
   The councillor is continually being advised to concern himself less with individual decisions, 'interfere' less with his executive officers and concentrate more on overall planning and policy. Local government reorganization seems likely to endorse this view, and to accelerate this trend.

'Shopping around'
'Shopping around' is wasteful of resources in what may be described as a 'supplier's market'. Occasional benefit may accrue to a few individuals, but at the expense of an overall deterioration

in the service provided, as a few consume an inordinate share of the available resources.

The opportunities to 'shop around' are already decreasing.

(1) Voluntary agencies are seeking to co-ordinate their efforts more effectively, and often work in close liaison with each other and with the statutory services.

(2) Some societies, e.g. Barnardos, are concentrating their services into areas of high need. They will be able to offer a more effective service in these areas but the areas they evacuate will be left with less choice of agency.

(3) The Probation Service, short of resources and already stretched with their statutory responsibilities, will find it difficult to maintain, let alone extend, their service beyond court and prison work.

(4) The amalgamation of the local authority social work services will limit choice still further.

The extent to which a consumer has a choice of agency is likely to vary widely from one region to another.

The mass media

The mass media have a very important function to perform in encouraging debate, and in keeping the public aware of changing policy and practice. Particular cases will be used to illustrate general points or to raise particular issues, but these are usually only concerned with the controversial extremities of policy. Perhaps the main function of the mass media is the ever present threat of publicity which may keep chief officers and committee members aware that they are public servants, and publicly vulnerable.

The developments which have led to the run down of this machinery are, I believe, right in principle and should enable resources to be more efficiently utilized. I would like now to look at the decision-making process within children's departments and this will also apply to varying degrees in other social work agencies.

DECISION-MAKING

Ultimate responsibility for each decision rests with the children's committees, but quite obviously they can be aware of few of these in practice.

The management and administration of children's departments tend to be fairly hierarchical, but it is rarely possible to pinpoint exactly at which level particular decisions are made. In any organization there are formal and informal structures; formal and informal lines of communication. The formal structure is codified and written down, but beneath or alongside this recognized system exist other systems or structures which are in practice the operative ones, although the component members of these informal structures may not even recognize their existence. The informal structure is crucial in decision-making but is not easily identifiable, and is rarely static. In an organization with a rapid staff turnover these informal structures are of course even more likely to be continually shifting and taking new shapes.

Formal structures are more readily identifiable, and their prime function is the dissemination of information, usually in a downward direction. In a rapidly evolving organization even these formal structures often function inadequately.

These problems of management are considerable, but to add to the confusion and obscurity, in social work decisions are rarely objective or clear cut, and are not based on incontrovertible data. The information required for a decision usually involves an individual assessment of a wide range of variables. A social worker's skill should enable him to achieve some objectivity and consistency, but there is still wide scope for fundamental differences in individual assessments.

The social worker collects more information than he can, or needs, to pass on and consequently, at each stage of decision-making, information is *filtered*. In practice a child-care officer usually formulates how he intends to deal with a particular case, and then feeds selected information into the decision-making machinery which will produce the desired response. This is not to condemn him of fraud or deceit, as this process may be quite unconscious.

It can be seen, therefore, that the social worker's own skill in making assessments is crucial. Unfortunately, the social work theory with which he is equipped is very deficient in carefully evaluated criteria on which accurate predictive assessments could be made. The best a social worker can do is to graft his limited and unique experience on to his particular theoretical bias, and this is far from adequate in many situations where an assessment has to be made on which an important decision will be based. There can be little validity or consistency in this method. (Undoubtedly, advances in the behavioural sciences will assist social workers in the future, and there is an awareness of the urgent need for research to evaluate the effectiveness of different social work techniques. All this, however, is in the future.)

If this seems to present a bleak picture, how much bleaker it seems when it is realized that only 30 per cent of child-care officers have the minimum training recognized as adequate by the Home Office.

CONSUMER PARTICIPATION

I would now like to suggest a scheme whereby the consumer would have an opportunity to participate in the development of the services he will use and whereby he would be able to appeal against the arbitrary decisions of the social work departments.

For this purpose, I would like to see the establishment of a panel with a much more representative base than exists for example on the magistrates' bench at present. It would, I believe, be a mistake to establish a panel only representing one or two groups in society, even if these were the under-privileged groups from which many of our consumers come. (It is important to remember that we are all potential consumers of the personal social services – a point often overlooked by social workers themselves.) In my own experience, people from many professions are, or have been, consumers of these services and as the status of social work improves, we are increasingly going to be concerned with a wider cross section of society than has been the case in the past.

The effectiveness of the panel also depends on acceptance of it by the community, and on its ability to communicate its views. It is important that professional and middle-class people do not dominate the panel, but they can have a valuable part to play. Residents of old people's homes, unmarried or separated parents, ex-prisoners and other consumers would also have a great deal to contribute and I would hope that they could provide the main body of the panel. The expenses of panel members would need to be met in full to enable all income groups to participate.

To be effective such machinery must:

(1) Have its existence adequately publicized.

(2) Be readily accessible.

(3) Be independent and impartial.

(4) Have its hearings held in public where the consumer so requests.

(5) Have access to departmental files and confidential information.

Some of these proposals, particularly (5), concerned with confidential information, will be greeted with hostility by many social workers. Such information, however, is essential if a decision is to be carefully evaluated (perhaps such a move would encourage social workers to think and record more clearly and accurately, relying less on subjective judgements with little factual foundation).

Two points which would be particularly controversial are first whether the panel is given any executive power, i.e. whether it can actually reverse a decision made by the social work department, and secondly, who should be responsible for the appointment of panel members.

On the first point, I consider that if the panel has executive powers this would have the effect of placing it in the position of policy maker and I do not believe it should have sole responsibility for this. I feel that recommendations from the panel, supported by press coverage where desired by the appellant, would suffice in most cases. Social work committees of the local authority have to be sensitive to publicly expressed opinions.

Where a local authority and the panel are unable to agree on a course of action, it might be possible for an arbiter to be appointed and I would like to see this as an area of ministerial responsibility. Cases of dispute could be referred there for decision. In this way a body of 'case law' would be built up which would go some way to achieving more uniformity of policy nationally.

On the second point, the appointment of panel members could in the future be given to the local government Ombudsman we have been promised. His terms of reference would probably exclude responsibilities of the type being suggested for this panel but his office could very appropriately be used to appoint, establish and advise the panel.

The panel would quickly gain a great deal of detailed knowledge of the gaps in the social services and the areas of acute need. They would be able to identify confused or unhelpful policies and would be able to view the social services without the involvement for vested interests of the social worker.

They could act as a powerful pressure group in identifying such problems and in stimulating action to attempt to solve them. They could participate in the planning of such action and could always be consulted at an early stage on proposed plans for the allocation of resources and the development of policy.

TWO DANGERS

There is of course the danger that the panels could quickly become closely identified with the social work department and function less effectively as both a watchdog and a stimulant. A danger at the other extreme is that society's negative feelings about certain groups could be reflected in a harsher and more punitive attitude towards some of society's misfits. The 'voluntarily unemployed' are perhaps an obvious example of a group who might receive less help.

Of these two problems, the first is I think the more dangerous. But this could be counteracted by having a large enough group of panel members so that each member would only sit, for example, every third hearing. In addition, I feel a time limit on the period served, e.g. three years, would ensure that the panel did not become over-identified with the department and would ensure a continuing influx of new ideas. A useful by-product of the scheme could be an increasing number of people aware of social problems and prepared to participate in helping people with them.

Readers who were in agreement with me early on may well have found much to disagree with in the scheme I have outlined. I present it not as a blueprint but as an attempt to meet the problem of the bureaucratization of social work and to ensure that the liberty of the individual is not further undermined. I have suggested the scheme apply to those areas of responsibility covered by the proposed social work departments, but see no reason why it could not be extended to other areas also.

Although social work decisions are not invariably wrong, it is a mark of professional maturity to be able to admit that they are not invariably right.

Perspectives on Access to Social Services

A. Kahn

Reprinted with permission from 'Perspectives on Access to Social Services', *Social Work*, vol. 26, no. 3, July 1969

In 1966, in connection with a study of the need for information services in the United States, my colleagues and I considered the Citizens Advice Bureaux experience in some detail. The CABs are involved in the problem of social service access, one of several problems which I regard as residing at the core of modern social service planning concern.

ACCESS SERVICES AS REDISTRIBUTIONAL

Both in the United States and in the United Kingdom we have become increasingly aware in recent years of the degree to which expansion of social services – or, indeed, of the more extensive general policy measures of a Welfare State – does not necessarily and automatically increase either equality or equality of opportunity.

Professor Richard M. Titmuss of the London School of Economics has led the way for many scholars who have gradually disclosed the realities and explained the complexity of adequate solutions. For detail I refer you to the considerable literature about poverty, so-called multi-problem families, racial injustice, and inner-city crisis on my side of the Atlantic and some of the comparable materials on yours.

It is possible to multiply educational resources on a considerable scale, only to learn that members of the underprivileged population groups are in subtle ways discouraged from full participation, or are unable to utilize facilities for lack of essential home and other environmental supports. Nor do educators always successfully adapt method, materials and style to the context in which many of the children must learn. In fact, there are many cases throughout the world in which initial public investment in secondary education has had the major effect of relieving middle-class parents of the costs of tuition – and has done nothing for the lower classes.

Or a country may invest heavily in health programmes, only to find that what the very poor get is inferior to what is available, to the more fortunate, the more knowledgeable. The sophisticated and the mobile 'cream' the top, to use a figure of speech suggested by several investigators. Referring briefly to a field in which the problem is the policy *per se*, rather than the delivery system, we note that housing expenditures by government after the Second World War, in the United States at least, were heavily biased in favour of the middle-class purchaser of a detached suburban home. The investment in public housing for the very poor, by contrast, was very small. And this fact was not even widely understood – and certainly not reconsidered – until very recently. We have yet to redress the balance.

Similarly, by virtue of choice of modes of service, locational arrangements, staffing patterns or inherent value premises in the small details of how services are carried out, certain general programmes or social services may tend to a bias in favour of one class or group, to the disadvantage of another. Family services in the United States in the late 1950s and early 1960s were in this sense especially inaccessible to the most disadvantaged and disorganized citizens.

Even public child welfare was questionably selective: the many thousands of public assistance families in the Aid to Dependent Children programme were effectively deprived, by virtue of administrative arrangements, of the benefits of the best of child welfare services. Child guidance clinics operated with a distinct bias in favour of the middle-class or more stable components of the working-class and against the very poor and disadvantaged. The dual service system assigned mental hospital and public assistance services to the latter.

It is not my purpose fully to discuss the many ways in which the programmes of a 'communal', 'service', or Welfare State – the term does not matter – do not necessarily reach all who need such programmes, and are not necessarily distributed in accord with a rational priority system. Clearly, the acceptance of any given social objective, even if repeated in the rhetoric of contending political parties, does not automatically assure the attainment of difficult and costly goals. Yet because our societies are committed to redressing extreme inequality (or at least the severest of deprivation), and because the deprived are being heard and understood as never before, there is ever-increased awareness of the prerequisites of an acceptable social minimum. There is new understanding of the requirements for 'opening opportunity' to the disadvantaged. It has become apparent that effective social policy, to some degree, must seek consciously and planfully to be redistributional. The Welfare State considers a diversity of instruments with this end in view.

Many policies and programme devices have been identified as supporting redistributional goals and their relative efficacy has been assessed. A sales tax, being regressive, works to the disadvantage of the very poor while a truly progressive income tax is a major instrument for redistribution. Income maintenance programmes which are based on some criteria of need are effective in this sense. The minimum wage has a significant role – as do other aspects of labour policy and fringe benefits.

Some countries have undertaken to redistribute land and wealth. Education has major potential, often unrealized. The United States developed a host of special programmes in its anti-poverty 'war' which sought indirectly to hasten upward mobility through the redistribution of power, resources and opportunities. Concrete and practical social services, generally, may raise a standard of living, improve a nutritional level, enhance biophysiological capacity and thus have direct and indirect effects.

These are all familiar notions to students of the subject and are here mentioned only to introduce a new and, perhaps, underrated category. Those who work in the social services know that organization for access and for effective service delivery, too, is an important redistributional strategy. I believe that if this were better understood, functions discharged by the CABs in Britain and in other ways elsewhere would experience new and major support, expansion and adaptation.

My argument is that apart from passing new legislation, developing new policies and launching new programmes – and all of these are certainly needed in many fields – one also achieves redistribution by arrangements which facilitate access to the established rights, benefits, services, entitlements and which assure the actual delivery and use of intended services. The urgent and complex problem of organization for service delivery at the local level has far too many ramifications to permit coverage in the present context. The Seebohm Committee has offered a stimulating analysis, launched a valuable debate and influenced thinking on both sides of the Atlantic. In the narrower, yet by no means limited, field of access services alone, our concern in the remainder of this paper, attention must be directed to: (1) advice and information services, usually on a neighbourhood basis; (2) case advocacy services; (3) complaint machinery; (4) legal services. The emphasis is on the first of these.

It may be argued that information-advice-referral services are no more likely than are health, education, family welfare or mental health programmes to escape from class or ethnic bias or to reach the alienated and uneducated. If so, they are hardly instruments of redistribution. Of course this has been and is the case. Detail and illustration could be cited: the centralized service which is unreachable, the highly specialized service which does not bother to relate to the ramifications of an issue; the too passive service which rejects by its failure to build bridges; the diagnostically orientated service which ignores societal realities. The call then is for a *particular kind* of access service, one determined to cope with the problem of redistribution by its very goals and modes of operation.

On my side of the Atlantic the argument is heard that the creation of access services draws off pressure and resources necessary for the development of basic programmes of income and social service. The response has several facets. First, the provision of access is of itself a significant social service. Many people need to have information, application forms and advice – and can proceed on their own. Secondly, the more directly relevant, an access service system with adequate feedback and reporting machinery can contribute to identifying qualitative and quantitative lacks in the service system and can contribute significantly to the planning process. And finally, even given continuing service gaps, decent access services can end the conspiracy of silence or the organizational obfuscation which perpetuates inequality of usage of programmes. If there are to be shortages, why solve the problem by ignoring the needs of the most needy? The social services today can hardly justify adoption of a philosophy of 'the survival of the fittest'; yet this is what our present practice often offers in fact, if not in rhetoric.

ADVOCACY AS A COMPONENT OF ACCESS

In the 1950s, social workers began to talk about 'reaching out' to the most disadvantaged of problem families. If such people could not get to services, the services should and could find and engage them. The rationale came largely from public health: aggressive case-finding which uncovered and coped with pathology was a matter of enlightened self-interest for the total community.

But to a considerable degree, 'reaching out' was based on an inadequate premise. Deriving as it did from a long tradition, it placed much of the problem in the object of the service, the deprived individual and family. During the 1960s we in the United States have faced increasingly the need also to ask questions about agencies and institutions. Is it the client who is 'hard to reach', or is it the service? Are the non-participants truly 'drop outs', or are they 'push outs'? We were taught by hard and sad experience that to assume *a priori* that the case failure is always an instance of client pathology, incapacity and lack of motivation is to engage in modern-day 'poor law' social analysis, or in what we think of as 'social Darwinism'.

Thus, our anti-delinquency urban community development projects of the early 1960s, as they gradually evolved into or merged with the anti-poverty community action programmes of the mid-1960s, began to emphasize both community organization by clients and potential clients to create or to reform social welfare services (a subject in part beyond our scope here) as well as a considerable measure of what we would here underscore as *case advocacy*. Professional and indigenous staffs, committed to helping people in new ways and completely pragmatic in outlook, took on roles which they considered better described as 'social brokerage' or 'urban brokerage' than as psychotherapeutic counselling. Casework colleagues see this as part of a long tradition of service even though it was a depreciated role for some time. The important thing is that in local anti-poverty programmes, experimental community mental health outposts, new settlement programmes, pioneering welfare departments, practitioners began to work on the added premise (sometimes it was the sole premise) that the most important help to be given took the form of using one's contacts, know-how and sanctions to intercede on behalf of or with a client *vis à vis* an agency which was not giving him the full benefit of its resources.

One recognized that a person might need help with reference to bureaucratic structure, professional ritualism, unnecessarily restrictive guidelines, *de facto* discrimination, cultural chasms, problems in communication, practical obstacles which stood in the way of expression of one's needs or assertion of rights.

Many agencies and services staffed by the new 'social broker' kinds of workers moved from case advocacy to intercession on the general policy level. They often decided in fact that their major contribution was to facilitate client self-organization for social action. In general, I believe that such process has been useful and constructive. I also believe, however (and the view is far from unanimous), that it has buttressed the case for separating two functions: (1) community organization and client self-organization for social action and policy advocacy; (2) case advocacy activities by social service agencies focused on maximizing the entitlement, service access and help available to the individual or family unit.

Thus, while I cannot make any generalization in this regard with reference to the British context, I concluded when considering the applicability of the lessons of the CAB to the United States that our programmes would need a considerable measure of case advocacy. Obviously, assuming a national and universal system, with outlets in many kinds of areas and serving a diversity of populations, there are differentiations to be made. None the less, an information-referral-advice service which sees redistribution – or fair allocations – as a service goal must be prepared to work actively with people who often cannot manage alone even if given information. The advocacy component is essential.

One, then, faces the immediate need for the training, staffing and professional controls which will suit the advocacy to meet actual situations. The problem of privacy and its protection looms large. And the issue of how an agency may be so located and structured as to permit it to serve as clients' advocate *vis à vis* other agencies becomes critical.

ADVOCACY AND AUTONOMY

Following publication of our study of information and advice services in the United States we found ourselves involved in a series of debates. One of the most critical dealt with the question of whether the information-advice-referral machinery could not be a function of or relate to one or another of the agencies directly administering social services. Why not, we were asked, assign the function to the public welfare department, to the social security office, to the community mental health centre, to the settlement houses, to local health centres?

The answer is a bit complex because one obviously wants to encourage the availability of an 'open' doorway at the entry point of any social service. Citizens not too certain of the choice made should be able to enter anywhere and be well redirected.

This, however, is not the solution for the general access service. Let us assume that to the extent possible some social services do have open doorways and provide a measure of information-advice-referral. Let us even buttress them with specialized manuals, files, pamphlets, directories or information resources created for the CABs or their equivalents elsewhere. (Or let us connect them by console to the computerized information 'library' of the future.) One still requires a general, multipurpose doorway to the entire social service system, a place for information-advice-referral on a broad range of issues, an organization dedicated to case advocacy as needed. The protection of such function demands that the system be autonomous. Committed to rendering a specialized service, a given functional service agency can do little more than answer questions and refer. It can hardly take on continuous case advocacy, following a situation through with persistence and a measure of what might be considered 'constructive aggression'. Indeed such stance is seldom syntonic with the specialized intervention. Nor can an agency which would refer and be referred to, which would seek to integrate its direct services with the direct services of another, relate at the same time and for many cases as case advocate as well. Experience suggests the access service must not be a direct service agency for yet another reason: to avoid professional or organizational bias.

ACCESS SERVICES AND THE BOUNDARIES PROBLEM

For here is another vital notion: true access demands that a citizen be offered that advice, referral or information which comes closest to responding to his needs. The access service should not be shaped by the special perspectives of any given profession or by the distortions growing out of ties with any special functional field or specialized agency.

Initially, this may appear to be a peculiar concern. Are true professionals lacking in capacity for service? Do they not give highest priority to client interests? Why would agencies not guide inquirers to the services they most need?

The research data indicate that we are not here dealing only with problems of integrity or competence. Organizational factors and bureaucratic realities may supersede professional ethics. No one professional is a social service generalist. He is child welfare worker, psychiatrist, family service worker, child guidance staff member, school personnel officer – and so on. His specialization and competence demand of him that he have a special perspective. Yet professional and organizational perspectives do affect the ways in which a problem is perceived and structured, the values which are held supreme, the priorities given to components of and the sequences in a solution to a family's difficulties, the 'costs' to be tolerated for given outcomes or 'benefits'.

These normal realities, the realities which beset well-developed social services conducted by well-prepared personnel, demand that the social service network be provided with what might be thought of as an unbiased doorway – a professionally unbiased doorway. The rule of thumb might be as follows: an inquirer should have as great a probability of getting one type of information and advice as he is of getting any other kind until his story is heard. There should be no preference within the service for one kind of outcome. The major determinant should be client need as determined after it is expressed.

Now this is an ideal; hidden factors continue to operate. But it is an urgent goal for an access service. Its importance is such as to require that any comprehensive community service network place an access resource at its entrance. Thus an information-advice-referral service becomes an operationally autonomous, unbiased case-channelling device prepared for a case advocacy stance if needed and aware of its redistributional mission for the most disadvantaged.

However, all citizens in the modern industrialized State have rights and needs in domains as diverse as housing and vacation planning, consumer rights and recreation, educational planning and social security, health emergencies and long-range measures for retired parents, adolescent problems and investment opportunities, child-care and credit – and the list offers a mere sample. Thus, the unbiased service must also be universal and thus non-stigmatic. It is not for the very poor alone or solely for the poorly educated. When there are short-run choices to be made, pacing to be determined, the bulk of resources should go where the most deprived are to be found. In your vocabulary I believe this might be territorial or locational selectivity. However, the goal of true access and no professional bias actually demands a universal service – and this should be the target. A truly universal access system, protected against 'creaming' and bias against the disadvantage, yet good enough for every citizen, would have the redistribution potentials we have mentioned.

It may be noted parenthetically, for those concerned with local social services, that a generalized access service which is not the domain of one profession or speciality field allows the services to which one refers from the access service, be it a CAB or a neighbourhood information centre, to become true speciality outlets. This does not wipe out the need for a related local resource for those with problems of adjustment or inter-personal difficulties: a general or personal counselling office which has the same function in social work as does the general practitioner in medicine. The access service should be able to refer to, or citizens to take themselves to, a local service in this category. The general social workers in such office would provide direct help, refer to specialists, have continuing case accountability, and assure meshing of simultaneous and sequential services in many quarters. (I assume that the recent Seebohm Committee recommendations intend this and more.) The existence of such local resource, in turn, would permit the access service to avoid assuming a therapeutic or counselling stance.

During the past several years, there has been in the United States an encouraging – if thus far limited – development of information, advice, advocacy and referral resources under a variety of auspices and following several patterns. The emphasis has been on poverty areas. The notion of a universal service is not widespread despite its attractiveness in some quarters. In many places the service is a function of a multiservice centre, a relationship which I consider limiting since in our day-to-day practice our multiservice centres generally tend to focus on one or more specific fields and do not achieve the professional and organizational 'neutrality' which a good general access service requires. Too little has been done to assure the range of coverage and degree of expertise which are essential. Frequently, case advocacy is superseded by social action. We have, in short, islands of experiment, not a movement comparable to the CABs.

Yet it is also clear that this is only the beginning.

Recently, groups concerned at various levels with the revitalization of the city and with equity for Negro citizens also have been experimenting or outlining plans. City and State Governments have in several instances launched programmes. Large proposals have attracted interest in Washington, their fate of course awaiting the national election. Your next conference, I believe, will hear reports of a much expanded information-advice-referral-case advocacy development in the United States, perhaps even of the gradual emergence of a coherent movement. Such movement should offer technical assistance and basic standards from the centre while supporting what must obviously be great diversity at the actual operational level.

At such time we will need to achieve more agreement and clarity than now exists about the relationship between an information-advice-referral-advocacy service and the emerging interest in the Ombudsman. Britain has its Council on Tribunals and we recently established an Administrative Conference. Courts, legislators and departmental inspectors general or their equivalents also do much to respond to claims of administrative unfairness and abuse as it affects the individual case. Nonetheless, the citizen often continues to feel unprotected. Experimentation is developing with Ombudsman-type programmes at the local level and I expect it to continue. In our context, at least, there is interest in combining such development with the information-advice-referral-adovcacy programme. My own inclination is to urge separation: the Ombudsman is the neutral investigator reviewing acts of omission and commission. He issues recommendations, or in some contexts he makes decisions. The access service, on the other hand, must identify with the inquirer and his needs, help him find and reach what is possible and to advance his claim if the going is difficult. To join the two functions is to confuse the citizen-user and to entangle interagency relationships so that neither function can be discharged.

Similarly, we have welcomed what is now the considerable development of a neighbourhood legal services programme under our anti-poverty effort, and going well beyond the traditional legal aid, seeing this as yet another component of the total effect to assure access, open opportunity, end abuse and eliminate a dual system of law and policy which is traceable to 'poor law'. In short, the total effort requires components devoted to (1) access; (2) complaints about administrative abuse and failure; (3) legal assistance.

None of these is a substitute for the others. It is doubtful that the three – or any two – are readily 'packaged' together in most places. Nor are access services, complaint mechanisms or local legal aid programmes to be seen as substitutes for adequate legal entitlement and generally sound social policy. They do not solve the problem of service insufficiency or inadequacy. They do not represent the totality of what must be expected of a social service delivery system. They are hardly a substitute for the design of a network with appropriately decentralized components, while certain other components remain at the centre. And they do not resolve the issues of internal social service reorganization at the local level as formulated by the Seebohm Committee. In the United States, certainly, we would also hold that all of the much-needed provisions for social service consumer protection would be considerably enhanced – indeed are far more likely to be responsive and potent – if buttressed by (1) a considerable measure of local consumer monitoring or control (depending upon the service) and (2) by the participation of local citizens in the rendering of the services in both paid and volunteer capacities and on a variety of levels of responsibility.

In short, access services are difficult to do well. Nor are they everything. Yet they are very important; indeed they are indispensable. The Citizens Advice Bureaux have contributed much to the experience out of which can be developed what is appropriate for particular social welfare systems.

Further Reading
Purposes and Priorities

R. BRYANT, 'Professionals in the Firing Line', *British Journal of Social Work*, vol. 3, no. 2, Summer, 1973.

FABIAN TRACT NO. 382, *Social Services for All*, 1968.

E. GOFFMAN, *Stigma. Notes on the Management of a Spoiled Identity*, Penguin, 1970.

A. HOWLETT and J. ASHLEY, 'Selective Care', *New Society*, 2 November, 1972.

P. J. KEMENY and G. POPPLESTONE, 'Client Discrimination in Social Welfare Organizations', *Social Work*, vol. 27, no. 2, April, 1970.

B. MANDELL, *Where are the Children?*, Lexington Books, 1973.

R. MINNS, 'Homeless Families and Some Organizational Determinants of Deviancy', *Policy and Politics*, vol. 1, no. 1, September, 1972.

H. SPRECHT, 'The Deprofessionalization of Social Work', *Social Work* (USA), vol. 17, no. 2, March, 1972.

I. A. SPERGEL, *Community Problem Solving. The Delinquency Example*, University of Chicago Press, 1969.

P. TOWNSEND and N. BOSANQUET, *Labour and Inequality*, Fabian Society, 1972.

Chapter Five

The Reorganization of the Social Services

The years 1968-74 witnessed far-reaching changes in the framework of British Social Welfare. In England and Wales, the Local Authority Social Services Act (1970) and the Children and Young Persons Act (1969) along with the Social Work (Scotland) Act (1968) reorganized the structure of the juvenile courts and the personal social services. Further, the National Health Service Reorganization Act (1973), along with a companion act for Scotland, radically changed the administration of the National Health Service. During the same period, major legislation redrew the administrative boundaries of local authority units. In this chapter, attention will be focused on the personal social services, on the reasons for reform and on the issues and problems arising from it.

CRISIS IN WELFARE?

Prior to 1970 (1968 in Scotland) the local authority personal social services consisted of the Children's, Welfare, and Mental Health Departments. They were considered as departments whose main concern was social work but it was also recognized that the Health, Education and Housing Departments also had aspects of social work within their responsibilities. Outside of full local authority control (but closely associated with it), the Probation Department was also regarded as a social work service while many hospitals, through their medical social workers, provided some social work help. The fact that in one local authority eight social work settings – more if voluntary agencies are included – could be encountered gave rise to criticism concerning the fragmented and multiple nature of

social work organization. Indeed, some commentators believed
a crisis point had been reached.

Martin Rein, an American academic with experience in both
Britain and the USA, pointed out four main organizational
weaknesses stemming from the multiplicity of and history of
social work agencies. These are of continuing relevance to the
important concerns developed in this chapter.

Firstly, he observed that the large number of services
demanded effective co-ordination which was not always
forthcoming. Secondly, he described how – in a situation of
varying and co-ordinating agencies – the treatment awarded
clients depended not on their needs but on the particular
orientation of the agency concerned. For instance, agencies
developed ways of determining which kind of clients they
would take (or exclude) and how their problems would be
defined. If the agencies saw themselves as a form of supply to
meet a consumer demand then recipients were considered to be
customers. If they were seen as needing help from others to
understand themselves they were considered to be *clients* or
patients. Help was provided for those who were helpless and
these could be seen as *victims* of circumstances or of the
operation of the social system. Finally, agencies might promote
adjustment or conformity, and recipients could be viewed as
deviants which these agencies brought into line. 'Services may
therefore be "sold", offered, provided as rights, or imposed as
obligations. Customers and clients are supposed to have more
control over their fates than victims or deviants. Customers
are "sold", clients "treated", victims "cared for", and
deviants "controlled". "Sales and therapy" imply personal
responsibility; "care and control" mean community
responsibility.' It follows that one agency might treat the same
poverty stricken person as a client who required treatment,
another agency as a deviant who should be made to conform,
another as a victim whose circumstances counted against him.
Thus the factor taken into account for providing help was not
the actual nature of the person's problem but the orientation
of the agency he approached.

Thirdly, the different orientation would matter less – indeed
might be an advantage – if clients had a realistic choice of
which agencies to use. Kahn pointed out, in the last chapter,

that they frequently lacked access to agencies due to ignorance, misunderstandings or the complexity of the system. He said 'the servicing network is so recognized that many in extreme need cannot find their way to it'. On the other hand, even if finding their way, some agencies were reluctant to serve those clients whom they thought unlikely to improve. The result was that 'services originally designed to act as a doorway and a mirror for community needs often act instead as a barrier'.

Clearly, all these criticisms have implications for agency reform, yet, fourthly, the organizational framework had gone unchanged for so long that many agencies were not only set in their ways but would be resistant to any radical changes.

Given an unsatisfactory organizational situation combined with a reluctance to make final changes, innovations on two fronts become possible and new agencies would have to be created in order to remedy the defects of the old. At the same time, demonstration projects could show what could be done in the hope that existing agencies would learn from them. However, these proposals are themselves open to criticism. The creation of new agencies only increases the multiplicity and fragmentation of services. Further, demonstration projects are frequently seen as complementary to other services and, even if successful in themselves, do not necessarily create change elsewhere. Rein is thus forced to hope for 'more fundamental planning' on a large scale. He was rightly doubtful if large-scale organizational reform of welfare bodies would occur in the USA but such changes did happen in Britain.

THE SEEBOHM REORGANIZATION

The committee of Local Authority and Allied Personal Social Services was established in 1965 under the chairmanship of Sir Frederick Seebohm. Its brief was 'to review the organization and responsibilities of the local authority personal social services in England and Wales, and to consider what changes are desirable to secure an effective family service'. The completion of this task made it necessary also to consider how local authority services fitted in with the services provided

under other statutory powers, for example, with those offered
by general practitioners, other statutory departments such as
the old Ministry of Pensions and the National Assistance
Board, with hospitals, the probation service, and also with
voluntary bodies in general. The field of inquiry was thus a
wide one and included people of all ages who were the concern
of what were then the Welfare and Mental Welfare Services,
the Children's Service, and the relevant social work functions
in Health, Education and Housing departments.

The committee's findings were published in 1968 and
provoked a debate throughout (and beyond) social work circles
culminating in the Local Authority Social Service Act (1970).
The reading taken from the **Seebohm Report** succinctly states
some of the arguments which led it to propose radical
reorganization. Initially, the report outlined the weaknesses of
the previous fragmented system. In a similar vein to Martin
Rein, the committee reasoned that the multiplicity of
departments created severe disadvantages. In particular, it led
to difficulties of co-ordination with the result that the best use
was not made of resources. For instance, research by Dr Jean
Packman had indicated that the services to prevent children
going into public care – day nurseries, home helps, social
casework – were spread amongst a number of departments.
Frequently, these departments could not co-ordinate their
efforts in order to make all the services available to the
children's families at a time of need. Worse, evidence
suggested that some departments actually attempted to off-load
their responsibilities on to other departments. Such poor
co-ordination could thwart 'the growing desire to treat the
individual and the family as a whole and to see them in their
wider context'.

If a lack of co-ordination was one disadvantage, a
duplication of services was another. As the various needs of a
single family could fall within the scope of a number of
departments, opportunities existed for an overlapping of
services. Indeed, examples were found of families visited by a
large number of social workers who served both to bewilder
the clients as well as to minimize the use of scarce social work
skills. Yet even within the twin evils of a lack of co-ordination
and needless duplication, the organizational divisions still

allowed gaps. The responsibility for some client groups, such as unmarried mothers and so called problem families as well as the provision of facilities for pre-school children, were so ill-defined as not to fall squarely within any department's orbit.

The organizational solution proposed by the Seebohm Committee was to unite the personal social service departments into one family service – the Social Service Department. Other recommendations were also made. One of the most stimulating parts of their report was its encouragement to groups and individuals (outside of officials and councillors) to participate in the identification of need, the exposure of defects in the services, and the mobilization of new resources. In short, community involvement was regarded as an essential element in the new service. The image thus created by Seebohm was of a unified department, outgoing in character to the extent of encouraging people to use its services, and strengthened by community support and participation.

Despite the emphasis on participation and involvement, the core of the report remained as its proposal to concentrate social work functions into a single department. The reading from Seebohm outlines the rationale behind this proposal. Here it suffices to summarize five main parts of the case for unification.

Firstly, it would help to overcome the problem of co-ordination. Secondly, a family with multiple needs would be saved a multiplicity of workers and instead could be helped by one worker able to see the family as a whole unit. Thirdly, a single department would serve to lessen confusion as to which department clients should approach. By having to go through fewer doors access would be simplified. Fourthly, a single department would result in a larger staff and a better staff career structure. In turn, this would lead to a 'greater ability to increase the recruitment and training of appropriate staff and to deploy them better'. Fifthly, a larger, all embracing department would be better fitted to collect information, to fix objectives, to make plans to achieve them, and to evaluate progress.

In the eventuality, the government's legislation in the form of the Local Authority Social Services Act (1970), enacted only the recommendations in regard to reorganization. From

1 April 1971, in England and Wales, the previous Children's,
Mental Welfare and Welfare Departments, along with certain
social work functions of Health and Education departments,
were incorporated in the one Social Service Department.
Noticeably, the Probation Department was not taken into the
new service. The Children and Young Persons Act (1969) had
already strengthened the links between local authority social
workers and juvenile courts. The pattern was thus emerging
of local authorities being responsible for most young
offenders and those in need of residential care leaving
probation officers to cope with older offenders and adults who
were brought before the courts. In Scotland, the Social Work
(Scotland) Act of 1968 initiated a different system. Probation
was incorporated into the new Social Work Departments while
juvenule courts were replaced by children's hearings. Not least,
the Scottish local authorities were also given the overall
community responsibility 'to promote social welfare by making
available advice, guidance and assistance on such a scale as
may be appropriate for the area'.

The organization of the personal social services, then,
involved a trend towards the unification of previously separate
services. Interestingly, the same trend dominated the reform
of the National Health Service. Formerly a tripartite system
consisted of hospitals administered by Regional Hospital
Boards, general practitioners under local executive councils
(both largely financed by central Government); and local
authority health services. In the Government's White Paper,
National Health Service Reorganization, England (1972), the
Secretary of State for Social Services stated that he wanted a
service which ensured that people's 'needs for health and social
services are not divided into separate compartments' and that
would also counter the gaps within the health divisions.
Consequently, from 1974 the three divisions are united under
Health Authorities. For instance, in England all services will
be administered on a hierarchical structure consisting of
Regional Health Authorities, Area Health Authorities and
district teams. In addition, Community Health Councils will
represent the voice of the consumer although only with
advisory powers through members appointed by the Area
Health Authorities, the local authorities, and voluntary groups.

Simultaneously, central Government responsible for the National Health Service, Local Authority Personal Social Services and Social Security have all been placed under the Department of Health and Social Security. Thus unification has come at central and local levels.

PROBLEMS AND ISSUES

It is too early to comment on the problems encountered in setting up the new health authorities. However, the reorganization of the personal social services has been under way for over three years. Certainly, criticisms have been common and some were contained within the reading by Sinfield in Chapter 3. Two major criticisms, which can be mentioned here only in passing, concern the administrative structures of the new departments and their relationship with voluntary bodies. All the 174 Social Services Departments in England and Wales had to design an administrative structure for their staff. Most departments now show at least six distinct hierarchical grades of social workers with the resultant complaint that such a system is based too much on a mechanistic view of organizations. Indeed, a whole new literature has sprung up around the question of how to organize the new departments, one of the most notable publications being M. Kogan and J. Terry's *The Organization of a Social Service Department.* A further issue has concerned voluntary agencies. The Seebohm Report anticipated local authorities giving extensive financial and professional support to 'vigorous, outward-looking voluntary organizations'. Soon after, the Aves Report, *The Voluntary Worker in the Social Services,* underlined not only the unique contribution of voluntary bodies but also pointed to the role of volunteer workers within professional agencies. In practice, some Social Services Departments have experimented in using volunteers and nearly all have grant-aided some voluntary groups. But no uniform and comprehensive policies have emerged. Consequently, complaints are still made about untapped volunteer potential while a number of voluntary organizations feel that they receive less financial support than their value justifies.

Of the many issues with which the Social Services Departments have had to grapple, three of the most important have centred around the nature of the work undertaken by the social workers, the types of skills to be developed and the place of residential institutions within the welfare complex. The remaining readings will discuss these issues. But before commenting on them, it is right to record that the reorganization springing from the 1968 and 1970 Acts has won a place in social welfare history. It has replaced the old system which stressed special and separate social services to meet special and separate needs by one which emphasizes co-ordination, integration and unity. As Muriel Brown puts it, 'our whole concept of personal welfare has in fact radically altered over the last twenty years. It has altered from a concept of several minority oriented institution based casualty services towards a concept of unified preventive promotional community based service which must, logically, be as comprehensive in provision and universal in scope as, for example, the health service'.

GENERIC OR SPECIALIZED SOCIAL WORKERS?

The pre-Seebohm Children's, Mental Welfare and Welfare Departments did allow social workers to develop specialist skills in regard to particular client needs. A major argument behind the reorganization of the personal social services was that one social worker should work with one family in order that its needs should not be split into separate compartments. Following reorganization, many social workers then found themselves dealing with a wider variety of cases than they had previously encountered. In addition, legislation since the Seebohm Report gave social workers yet more duties in regard to young offenders and the sick and disabled. The demands were considerable. At the very least, they were expected to understand a vast amount of legislation. At most, the successful generalist social workers were expected to possess the emotional capacity to tolerate frequent changes of roles and the intellectual ability to grasp wide-ranging skills and knowledge. Not surprisingly, the initial years of the new system have given rise to concern about declining standards.

In particular, general practitioners and hospital staff have sometimes complained about the shortcomings of social workers lacking the expertise to deal with mental health cases. Simultaneously, some voices have suggested that the specialist casework-with-children skills are less in evidence. Calls have even been made for a return to the old system of specialist workers.

Few social administrators and social workers would support the idea of putting back the clock. Nonetheless, a pressing problem for the new Social Services Departments is how to allow social workers to function in a generic (or general) way without losing the specialized expertise which had been developed. It is to this question that **Olive Stevenson** addresses herself. Her paper was written in anticipation of the Seebohm recommendations but her perceptive analysis is as relevant now as it was then.

Firmly in favour of a generic approach, Miss Stevenson accepts that if there is a reduction in the formal specialization at field level then professional specialization is necessary at some point within the social service organization. She discusses whether specialisms might be retained if related to specific social problems, such as physical handicap or delinquency, or to methods such as casework or groupwork. In the end, she develops a model in which a field worker is initially given a wide breadth of experience

undertaking a broad range of tasks but with certain formal sub-divisions of task within the organization, and with the probability of informal specialization according to inclination; this could only be contemplated given the existence of senior specialists available for consultation.

Olive Stevenson's ideal is thus for specialism within generalism. Noticeably, both social work training and the social work profession has developed in this direction. Instead of separate training for child-care officers, mental welfare officers, etc., the prevailing mode of training is for a broad initial phase of understanding concepts and skills common to all social work practice followed by specialized (often optional) teaching and learning experiences on particular aspects of social work. Similarly, most of the former social work

associations – with the exception of the National Association
of Probation Officers – have now amalgamated into the British
Association of Social Workers. Yet within BASW there exist
special interest groups for social workers whose inclination is
towards problems of mental health, physical health, child-care
and delinquency.

The relevance of casework
Elizabeth Irvine, an authority on social work, has defined
casework as 'a way of helping people with personal and social
problems in a face-to-face relationship, and in a systematic
professional manner based on knowledge of personality
development and behaviour, and skill in human relations'.
Whether employed as generalists or specialists, most of the
trained staff available to the new Social Services Departments
were caseworkers. But casework, as Sinfield demonstrated in
Chapter 3, is increasingly under attack as the predominant
social work method. It follows that a vital question for the
new departments is how relevant is social casework and does
it achieve the successes some textbooks seem to claim? It is in
order to discuss this question that **Plowman,** in his reading,
assembles the results of research findings. He cannot fully
answer the question for, as he explains, the purposes of
casework are varied while the published studies are few and,
in many ways, unsatisfactory. Despite these limitations, two
conclusions can be reached. Firstly, casework can be effective
with certain types of cases. For instance, Plowman suggests
that it can be used to give greater self-understanding to certain
mentally ill clients. Again, other studies show that it can be
employed to enable foster children to understand and more
positively accept the reasons why they are separated from their
own parents. Secondly, casework alone is not sufficient for all
the problems facing the Social Services Departments.

As casework is not *the* answer, it is welcome that other forms
of social work are making their presence felt. Social group
work is at last finding a place within training courses. In
practice, group work amongst parents or parent substitutes is
increasingly common. A publication by the National
Children's Bureau, *Group Work With Parents in Special
Circumstances*, gives examples of groups of adoptive parents,

foster parents, parents of handicapped children, parents of
socially disadvantaged children and parents of deprived,
delinquent or disturbed children. Direct group work also involves
delinquent or near delinquent youths, foster children, drug
addicts and the mentally ill. The purpose of the groups varies
from information giving, to emotional support, to therapy.

Even more rapid has been the growth of community work.
The first Gulbenkian Report, *Community Work and Social
Change*, said that community work

> typically consists of work with groups of local people who
> have come into existence because they want to change
> something or do something that concerns them. Community
> work also embraces attempts to relate the activities of social
> agencies more closely to the needs of the people they serve.
> This may include inter-agency co-operation, study and
> planning.

The second Report, *Current Issues in Community Work*, served
to distinguish the various parts of community work and to
illustrate how it was developing both within and outside of
Social Services Departments.

In the field, the three social work methods cannot always be
so conveniently separated. For instance, all three were
employed in the Wincroft Youth Project in Manchester. Here
youth workers were released into a deprived area to relate to
boys already convicted before the courts. Their efforts
appeared successful in that their subsequent conviction rates
were less than a matched sample not so helped.

To some extent, then, the criticisms of Sinfield and the
analysis of Plowman are bearing fruit. No doubt casework will
remain a major social work skill. But, simultaneously, other
methods are coming to the fore and so provide Social Services
Departments with more means of meeting their objectives.

The place of institutional care
The erection of large institutions was a dominant theme of
Victorian social provision. The Poor Law workhouses, lunatic
asylums, orphanages and convict prisons were built so solidly
as to remain for over a century. Having inherited the buildings,
many Directors of Social Services Departments now face the

dual problems of how to maintain such expensive plant and how best to use the giant shells which seem to militate against individual concern. For the years immediately preceding the reorganization of the personal social services saw a strong reaction against residential care, especially care associated with large institutions. In the 1950s the popularized views of Dr John Bowlby sparked off a drive to take children out of children's homes and place them in foster homes. Attacks on the standards of certain residential units dealing with the elderly, the mentally ill and the mentally handicapped were followed by official encouragement and backing to policies aimed to keep people in the community if at all possible. During the 1960s and 70s, voices were also heard arguing for alternatives to prison.

The reading by Professor **Kathleen Jones** contributes an evaluation of the anti-institution movement. She identifies the two main grounds in the case. First, that institutions are expensive to run. Second, that institutions are destructive of the human personality. In particular, she refers to the work of Goffman and his strictures on 'total institutions'. Professor Jones counters that the case has been overstated. She contends that it is misconceived to treat the subject 'as though all institutional populations shared the same attitudes and motivation; as though all were confined, not only against their will, but for no useful purpose; as though all were equally capable at all times of full social functioning; and as though all shared indefinite or life-long confinement'. She explains that not all institutions are large, not all are restrictive, not all are total environments. In short, Professor Jones accepts the limitations of institutions but also shows that they can play a valuable role.

The arguments contained in the reading have been echoed in contemporary developments. Not all clients and patients are necessarily best helped by remaining permanently in the community. The positive contribution of institutions has been recognized in the emergence of therapeutic communities in the mental health field, in experiments in prison care, and in a re-kindling of enthusiasm in residential child-care. The revival of interest means that the Social Services Departments are not simply committed to a one sided anti-residential policy.

However, the departments must seek organizational developments in three directions if residential care is to be accepted by staff and community as having a valuable place in the social service field. The departments must build into their organization the skills to assess which clients do need institutional care and which particular type of care. They must acquire qualified residential staff in an occupation where training has had a low priority. Finally, they must decide how best to use buildings constructed at a time of different residential concepts.

The concerns of **Townsend,** in the final reading in this chapter, are with the establishment of the new Social Services Departments following the Seebohm Report. They bring together some of the themes involved in organization and reorganization and raise awkward questions about the definition of policy objectives through the traditional collection of subjective opinions or conventional definitions of needs. The social scientist can examine social or normative definitions of needs, in Townsend's view, in ways that bring them 'into the open, reveal contradictions and loose ends and show the different functions played by law, regulation, policy and custom. He can even show the degrees of efficiency with which different standards are being met and therefore suggest what might be gained with alternative emphases in policy.' In general the formulation of policy in many areas of the social services would seem to proceed with reference mainly to what exists already, and to objectives already defined, than to those which appear when judged from an external standpoint. Measures of inequality and of deprivation, and the varieties of these concepts, involving both objective and subjective criteria, would allow for comparisons and the planning of services.

The difficulties of equating or balancing objective and subjective factors are apparent but this model of policy formation, concluding with an attempt from outside the system to be objective, would be a great advance on planning and analysis of social policy at the moment. Townsend considers the ways in which the Seebohm Committee collected evidence and indicates its inadequacies in not undertaking research, in particular into what consumers thought about the services

provided, and therefore leading to a string of generalities about
services which are 'sadly inadequate', 'quite inadequate',
'seriously inadequate' and so on, which are not related clearly
to policy objectives or to any possibilities of measurement.
What emerges from Seebohm, in the view of the author, is an
impression 'of inchoate, multiple aims and loose reasoning', and
he suggests that the really important issues have been ducked.

The reading concludes with an outline of a possible policy
for what have become Social Services Departments. Although
written some years before the establishment of such departments
the context and the themes are even more relevant now than
they were. Some attention is given to the uses of Community
Development in equalizing resources and amenities and
supporting the family, and to the implications of aims such as
community integration which could involve not just
community care in a conventional sense but 'the promotion
of citizen rights and of certain kinds of group activity'. A
great range of relevant questions and issues are posed which
focus attention on many themes which have appeared in this
book and others which need to be considered about the
quality of family and community life and of the social services
which support them. The reform which has come about from
the Seebohm Report is that of administrative unification. It
has been carried out with little expectation at the present time
of a larger share of resources going to the social services. The
conflicts which are built into the departments, and the
bureaucratic problems which arise from larger aggregates of
often disparate professionals or officials, and questions of
access for consumers, require a continuing debate.

The readings in this chapter discuss the move towards the
reorganization of the personal social services, the actual shape
the new system took on, and some issues and problems arising
from it. Particular attention is given to the role of social
workers, to the skills they need and to the place of institutional
care. Issues springing from the reform of the local authority
services have tended to dominate social work thinking in the
last decade. But stimulating developments have also occurred
outside the context of local authority personal social
services as will be considered in the following chapter.

A Social Service Department

Reprinted with permission from the *Report of the Committee on Local Authority and Allied Personal Social Services* (Seebohm Report), H.M.S.O., 1968, pp. 44-51 (paras 139-66).

We are convinced that if local authorities are to provide an effective family service they must assume wider responsibilities than they have at present for the prevention, treatment and relief of social problems. The evidence we have received, the visits we have undertaken, and our own experience leave us in no doubt that the resources at present allocated to these tasks are quite inadequate. Much more ought to be done for example, for the very old and the under fives, for physically and mentally handicapped people in the community, for disturbed adolescents and for the neglected flotsam and jetsam of society. Moreover the ways in which existing resources are organized and deployed are inefficient. Much more ought to be done in the fields of prevention, community involvement, the guidance of voluntary workers and in making fuller use of voluntary organizations. We believe that the best way of achieving these ends is by setting up a unified social service department which will include the present children's and welfare services together with some of the social service functions of health, education and housing departments.

Such a unified department will provide better services for those in need because it will ensure a more co-ordinated and comprehensive approach to the problems of individuals and families and the community in which they live. It should be more effective in detecting need and encouraging people to seek help; it should attract more resources and use them more efficiently and it will be possible to plan more systematically for the future.

The unified approach

The need for a more unified provision of personal social services has been made plain by growing knowledge and experience. There is a realization that it is essential to look beyond the immediate symptoms of social distress to the underlying problems. These frequently prove to be complicated and the outcome of a variety of influences. In many cases people who need help cannot be treated effectively unless this is recognized. Their difficulties do not arise in a social vacuum; they are, have been, or need to be involved in a network of relationships, in social situations. The family and the community are seen as the contexts in which problems arise and in which most of them have to be resolved or contained. Similarly, residential establishments are no longer asylums, separated and insulated from the outside world. They are increasingly expected to maintain contacts with the families of those for whom they care and the communities in which they are located. To take another example, the local authority personal social services should accept the responsibility of concerning themselves with offenders and the families of offenders, co-operating for this purpose with the probation and aftercare service, the prison welfare service, and other statutory and voluntary organizations.

The present structure of the personal social services ignores the nature of much social distress. Since social need is complex it can rarely be divided so that each part is satisfactorily dealt with by a separate service. In the previous chapter we rejected a number of proposals for reform because they allocated the responsibilities of departments according to age or 'types' of problems. This, we believe, reflects an artificial and rigid view of human need. An integrated social service department will impose fewer boundaries and require less arbitrary classification of problems. Of course, important administrative boundaries will remain. Responsibilities for medical care, education and housing will continue to be separate, although the problems they deal with also have an obvious social component.

Because problems are complicated and interdependent, co-ordination in the work of social services of all kinds is crucial. In many cases effective help will continue to depend upon the assistance of more than one organization. But an integrated social service department will ease problems of collaboration as the number of separate units involved is reduced, and above all as issues of responsibility are clarified.

However, a social service department such as we propose will have its own problems of co-ordination. It will be larger and hence often require a greater degree of decentralization than exists in many areas at the moment. This is, in any case, likely to occur if services are to be made readily available at the point of need. All this will demand good internal co-ordination. This can be achieved in many ways: through the existence of a common authority; through commitment to a common purpose; and through mutual understanding, respect and sympathy for the work of colleagues which will be encouraged by the development of common basic training for staff in the new department.

Encouraging use

In the commercial world consumer demand is constantly encouraged through advertising and by granting credit. New 'needs' are created, old ones refashioned. Many of the skills of psychology and sociology are employed to entice people to adopt particular purchasing habits. Some of the social services, for example the maternity and child welfare service and the education service, also try to encourage the public to make use of them. In contrast, those who may require the help of the personal social services, for instance the welfare and children's services, encounter little encouragement to use them, nor is there a ready flow of simple information about their nature and how they can be obtained. Indeed historically the aim has often been to deter people from seeking such help and stigma has attached to those who did. It is not surprising therefore that many are prejudiced against seeking the help of services they may need and to which they are entitled; indeed some remain ignorant of the purpose or even the existence of certain services. Moreover, unlike the commercial situation, in order to receive appropriate help from the personal social services it is often necessary for the client to explain complicated problems or unusual circumstances. Some of those in greatest need do not have this facility: they find the task difficult and often harrowing.

We can and should encourage those who need help to seek it; and progress is being made. Information too must be simpler and more widely available, whilst research into need should become a permanent feature of the new service. But if the structure remains complicated, people will continue to be confused and hence often deterred. One single department concerned with most aspects of 'welfare' as the public generally understands the term, is an essential first step in making services more easily accessible. They must not be camouflaged by administrative complexity, or their precise responsibilities closely defined on the basis of twenty-year-old statutes. The organizational structure of these services should not deter those in need and they should be available to all. We believe that a unified comprehensive social service department will be an important step in the right direction. There need be no uncertainty about where to turn for help nor any ambiguity about where responsibility for providing assistance lies.

Attracting more resources

If improved services are to be provided, more resources are required. Although such items as accommodation and transport are needed, the principal resource of the personal social services is manpower. Hence, as we have already pointed out, a reformed organization should, in part, be justified by its greater ability to increase the recruitment and training of appropriate staff and to deploy them better. We believe a unified department has this advantage. Being larger it will provide a better career structure. A wider range of work and experience will be available without the present necessity of moving between departments. Movement in quest of promotion or extended experience may thus be reduced and a greater benefit derived from the accumulation of local knowledge, which we have come to consider an important factor in providing good services. It is unreasonable to expect staff to deal for the whole of their working lives with the same kinds of people with specified need. A unified department should enable such a change to be made without a major up-heaval for staff and their families. The Williams Committee on the *Staffing of Residential Homes* stressed this point in their report.

Training is as important as the recruitment and retention of staff. At the moment many departments concerned with the provision of personal social services are small. Staff sickness can create acute difficulties and release for training or refresher courses may be quite impracticable. A unified department will reduce the dimensions of this particular problem. In addition, the introduction of a variety of in-service training should become feasible in all areas. Part of such training is provided through the process of supervision in which a senior member of staff is responsible for assisting junior colleagues by discussion of cases and problems. Since work in the personal social services is frequently taxing and disheartening, such support and guidance is often essential. At the moment there are not enough well-trained and experienced staff to undertake this work. Some who could do so are over-burdened with their own responsibilities; others are concentrated in certain departments but absent in others. Unification, we believe, will facilitate the extension of supervision and the more effective use of those supervisory skills which are at present unevenly distributed.

Training for the personal social services also involves giving students practical experience of the work. At the moment these opportunities are limited but training programmes cannot be extended unless field placements become more numerous. The main obstacles are a lack of staff competent to undertake the necessary supervision; insufficient accommodation, and too little variety in the available work experience. We believe that a unified social service department could more easily overcome these difficulties and enable facilities for practical training to be increased.

We cannot be sure, of course, that a unified department will secure a relatively bigger budget, but for at least two reasons it seems justifiable to hope for this. First, within local councils a committee responsible for the whole range of the personal social services would rank as a major committee. Second, and more generally, the greater simplicity and accessibility of a unified department is likely to expose many needs which have hitherto gone unrecognized or unmet. Such a clear demonstration that a more extensive and better service is required on many fronts may in itself exert the necessary pressure for increased public expenditure. Even without a relatively larger budget the financial resources of a social service department ought to be more flexible. For instance, an organization with a total budget of £100,000 should be able to do more with it than the sum of the achievements of two separate organizations, each with £50,000.

However it is increasingly obvious that conventional resources alone are not enough to secure an effective family service. The goodwill and the direct assistance of the community are also needed. We still know comparatively little about how best these might be enlisted and encouraged; of what can or cannot be expected of mutual aid, 'community development', voluntary services, or neighbourliness particularly in urban areas undergoing rapid social change. What is more certain, however, is that the opportunities for involving the community will not always arise in a form which fits into the present fragmented structure of the personal social services. In this respect, a unified department should be able to adopt a more experimental and exploratory attitude to the stimulation and use of the community's potential contribution to social aid. In particular, it can and should exercise a general responsibility for community development.

Efficiency, intelligence and planning

The efficient use of existing resources basically demands two things. The first of these is a much greater clarity than exists at present about the aims of social action. Unless these are defined more precisely the relative priorities of competing or incompatible objectives cannot be settled. We feel that in broadening the responsibilities of a social service department this requirement will of necessity receive increasing attention. The second is to discover whether or not resources have been used efficiently. This is imperative and requires continuous evaluation. Only then can improvements be made. The organization which is best able to carry out regular assessment of its work in the light of the changing pattern of local social needs is likely to utilize its resources best. The new social service department will, we consider, be favourably placed to make a start in this respect.

Being larger and having a much broader range of responsibilities, the collection and analysis of comprehensive information about the services provided and local conditions should be easier. The overall present and future social needs of an area can be estimated and plans made to meet them. At the moment, where information is collected at all it tends to reflect the narrow responsibilities of particular departments and plans are, in consequence, not comprehensive. For example, the fragmentation of the present services inhibits the consideration of the inter-relationship of several existing services, domestic help (health) for old people can sometimes be an alternative service to part III residential accommodation (welfare), and day nurseries (health) can meet certain needs otherwise met by the admission of children to care (children). At present some complementary or alternative services are administered by different departments with different policies and different practices, and balanced comprehensive planning is therefore difficult. If one department is mainly responsible this should become easier and more common.

One of the long-term advantages of a unified local social service department is the opportunity it provides to adjust the service as more is learnt about social problems, as concepts of effectiveness change and as priorities are rearranged. The present structure tends to immobilize resources, whether they be administrators, field staff, residential staff, or residential establishments. It is difficult to use them differently should the need arise. As far as possible we must avoid incorporating our present beliefs and knowledge in an organizational structure that will outlive them. Unnecessary departmental boundaries, undue professional specializations and a too dogmatic, or orthodox vocational training are all, we consider, detrimental to securing future changes in the nature or pattern of service which a growing understanding, new problems or different resources may require.

ARGUMENTS AGAINST THE PROPOSED SOCIAL SERVICE DEPARTMENT

A monolithic department

It has been suggested in evidence that a unified social service department would be monolithic. As a result, 'difficult' people who needed its help might be neglected and it could prove unresponsive to the need for change. Though it would provide 'a door on which anyone could knock' it would be the only door and anyone who was turned away would have nowhere else to go; the present untidy pattern, it is argued, allows the public some measure of choice.

In fact, alternative public services hardly exist outside a few authorities; the 'shopping around' between departments within the present structure is accidental and wasteful and the advantages seem to us nebulous. We attach greater weight to the tendency of separate services to concentrate exclusively on the needs of particular groups, and to the temptation to steer 'difficult' people from one department to another. A service with a clear and comprehensive responsibility for meeting social need would provide a more secure base for helping those who are not the concern of any of the present departments; the responsibility for assisting any particular family would be clear and there would be less risk of people falling between departmental stools.

Any organization which combines professional power with public authority is bound to involve dangers, particularly where poor, vulnerable, inarticulate and sometimes difficult people are concerned. However, placing responsibility for social care on one committee and department would provide a clear and evident system of accountability. The need for safeguards against neglect and the abuse of power, and for the periodic critical review of the services provided, lies behind some of our recommendations.

With a unified social service department, elected members and the press would still be able to take up grievances; indeed its comprehensive nature should make this easier. Moreover, if the social service department comes to be used by a broader cross section of the population, that in itself will discourage inconsiderate treatment. Finally, risks such as these can be reduced by effective management within the department, including decentralization, and by the further development of professional responsibility among the staff.

The issue of size

It has been argued that a unified social service department would be too big for humanity or efficiency and lose the 'personal touch'. We do not believe there is any ground for fear on this score. Most of the present social service departments are, we consider, too small to be fully effective. Assuming the combination of welfare and children's departments with the social work parts of health departments, 7 per cent of local authorities would still have fewer than 10 social workers, 51 per cent would have fewer than 30, and only 8 per cent would have more than 100. Including the staffs of residential and day-care establishments, the home helps, administrative and clerical staff, the proposed department would not be large by local authority standards.

In their evidence to the Royal Commission on Local Government in England, the Home Office and the Ministry of Health both urged the need for the average local health, welfare and children's authorities to be bigger. Given the present range of sizes, we see great value in combining departments in the smaller authorities, and no harm in combining those in the largest, provided there is delegation of responsibility, especially through area offices. As we have noted, the small department is at serious risk of disruption because of absence through illness and leave; it is liable to serious difficulties when senior staff move; it is at a serious disadvantage in arranging in-service training and in seconding staff for full-time courses, and it is hard for it to contribute fieldwork placements for training students. It faces difficulties in maintaining a full range of specialist services and ensuring adequate administrative and clerical support.

Departmental specialization

One of the arguments advanced against the integration of the personal social services is that progress has come through specialization, which has enabled children's departments, for example, to concentrate on caring for deprived children, without the distractions of caring for other people in need, or a health department to develop a corps of workers who know a lot about the social problems of schizophrenia.

This argument rests to some extent on the historical development of the services through the break-up of the Poor Law where improvement in treatment for certain groups was secured by separate administrative arrangements. This was especially true of mentally disordered people and deprived children. In 1946, for instance, the Curtis Committee's report on *The Care of Children* recommended that a single committee and department should be responsible for all children who were in care so that their interests would be better safeguarded and better provision made to meet their needs.

Although significant progress has been made in the past as a result of introducing separate administrative arrangements for assisting particular groups in need, we do not regard this necessarily as a permanent blueprint for future development. In different periods of development other approaches may be more appropriate. At this point in time we consider that most progress in providing good personal social services will come through greater integration.

It has been suggested that a reduction in the standards of service may follow any reorganization. We could not support any proposals which carried a serious risk of such a decline, apart from minor and temporary dislocation. The suggestion that in a unified department skills might be diluted with a consequent fall in the standard of service rests on the assumption that skilled staff would be diverted from tasks they had been doing before re-organization to tasks which the new committee or chief officer thought were more important, or which they thought ought to be done within a mixed case load. As we indicate, we think it essential that the present barriers between departments and specialisms should be broken down, and that a prompt start should be made in this direction. This does not mean that everyone in a social service department would immediately drop what they had been doing and undertake entirely different work. There would naturally be a carry-over from the existing organiza-tion to ensure that clients' needs were not neglected. With careful preparation the transition should be followed by release of time and energy through a more rational approach to the work and, we hope, by essential additions to staff – apart from the responsi-bility of the new department to mobilize untapped resources in the community itself. We recognize that administrative compe-tence of a high order will be essential in the principal officers of the new department.

The development of particular services will naturally be affected by whether they are combined or left separate. We do not see this as an objection to unification, but rather an argument in favour of it. There is a great need in central and local government for more effective means of making choices between different kinds of service and assessing the priorities to be allotted to them. As we have indicated, the only way we can see this being achieved at local level is through the unification of the present personal social services in one department. Certainly we can see no reason why the formation of the new department should be any deterrent to the growth of services or their adaptation to meet new needs; on the contrary it will be better placed to anticipate changes and plan to meet them.

It was argued in evidence that the creation of a 'free standing' social service department would aggravate the separation between social work and medicine or teaching; that it would prevent medico-social or educational needs being met as a whole, and would create additional barriers to the growth of understanding between the professions. We recognize that these possibilities exist. However in our judgement the likely benefits of having a social service department outweigh these potential disadvantages. Indeed the clarification of social service functions which this reorganization will bring could well lead to a better understanding between these professions. Likewise easier co-operation between health, housing, and education departments and a social service department may be achieved partly because it will have a similar standing.

Specialization within a Unified Social Work Service

Olive Stevenson

Reprinted with permission from 'Specialization within a Unified Social Work Service', *Case Conference*, vol. 15, no. 5, September 1968, pp. 184-9

This is an attempt to clarify one of the issues involved in the consideration of a unified structure in local government personal social services. Reference has been made to the conflict between factors which lead to a demand for greater co-ordination and those which point to a need for continued specialization. The first question is, therefore, is there really such a conflict? At first glance this may be how it looks. A study of trends in organizations generally, however, leads to two conclusions. Firstly, that specialization is an inescapable aspect of progress in sophisticated organizations and, indeed, in all advanced societies. Secondly, the very fact of specialization increases the need for co-ordination by the organization. Wilbert Moore writes:

> Certain processes of change may be found to have a reliable and enduring direction. Most notable . . . is the presumably universal tendency to specialization or structure differentiation.

He adds:

Specialization is not of course an absolutely sovereign and irreversible dynamic process as its dangers to systematic cohesion may occasionally lead to renewed emphasis on unity . . . But the probability of continuing specialization in enduring social systems is high.

Thus it is reasonable to conclude that social work will prove no exception and that specializations of some kind will be found even if unified personal social services arise within local authorities. Furthermore, evidence from other organizations stresses that this specialization demands more of management, in order to ensure that communications run smoothly and that the various sections of the organization combine together effectively. In particular, it has been pointed out that 'specialization increases the relative importance of *lateral* relationships as distinct from hierarchical'. This implies that social workers in senior positions will have to become increasingly expert in what we are now coming to call management; for, as has often been pointed out, structural unification is no guarantee of organizational effectiveness.

The next general point is that there are said to be two kinds of specialization described as 'by task' and 'by people'. The first, 'by task' is usually illustrated by references to industrial organizations and factory workshops, where the job is broken down into its component parts and thus in fact made simpler for the operators. The second 'by people' applies in particular to the professions where it requires special expertise and a high level of training in a special field of activity. At first glance, it might seem that only the second kind of specialization is relevant to social work. On further consideration, however, it is clear that both kinds can be applied to social work; in fact it is the distinction between these two kinds of specialization which is so often blurred in our discussions and leads to confusion.

What then is the equivalent for our purposes of the factory workshop type of specializations? This would be the limitation of task at field work level, on the assumption that a 'ground floor' social worker cannot be expected to perform a range of duties across the board with equal skill and that efficiency will suffer if he is required to spread himself over too diverse a field of knowledge and practice. This has been called a 'sub-division of performance roles'. This I shall refer to as 'organizational specialization' and contrast it with 'professional specialization' which would arise at senior levels, as a product of acknowledged skill and expertise.

In the history of the organizational development of the social work services in this country we can detect three phases; first the undifferentiated care afforded by the workhouse to the destitute, whether young or old, mad or subnormal; secondly, the growth of services to cater for specific categories of human need; and now, thirdly, a trend to unification of these services arising from the belief that human need and in particular family problems cannot be administratively dichotomised. We can all point to absurdities which have arisen because of such administrative divisions but we can acknowledge at the same time that the impetus, which concentration on certain social problems gave to the relevant social work services, has not been without benefit. (The setting up of Children's Departments in 1948 is a good example of this.) Given a unified structure the problem which now arises is the extent to which specialization at field level is desirable and necessary.

It is very difficult to detach ourselves from our existing specializations and look at this objectively. Inevitably, when we know a good deal about one part of social work, there is a tendency to think that a 'general purpose' social worker could only be superficial by comparison. If we look to the medical model – the general practitioner – the problem is distanced a little and becomes clearer. Is the GP becoming a Jack of all trades and master of none in this age of rapidly expanding knowledge or has he a vital integrating role in medicine which society needs? Is the comparison between a general social worker and a GP a valid one, in terms of the amount of knowledge and skill to be acquired, and the attitudes and motivations to different types of patient or client?

Are we prepared to say that a general social worker needs to know more than a GP? Or that the underlying motivations enable him to work successfully with one group of clients rather than another – with the delinquent youth rather than the aged, for example, whereas the underlying motivation of the GP to heal the sick takes him across such boundaries? I do not pretend to know the answers to such questions. By raising them, I point to the possibility of comparisons with other professions which could be fruitfully studied at much greater depth. Equally fruitful would be comparative studies with other countries and their social work services. When I was in the USA I visited two voluntary agencies which ran, apparently successfully, on completely different lines. In one, a family agency in Washington, I learnt that there was no *formal* specialization at field level in relation to family problems – social workers had a varied caseload ranging from problems of illegitimacy to senility. However, in discussion, a certain degree of *informal* specialization became apparent; by virtue of certain workers' inclinations and gifts, they tended to draw a larger proportion of one or another type of problem. This necessitates case allocation by seniors who identify and allow for these inclinations. In another agency, however, field level specialization was much more formally defined, with workers dealing full time with problems of illegitimacy, for instance.

If it is decided that neither of these extremes is desirable – complete dependence on informal specialization or a rigid division by type of problem or person – but that nevertheless some kind of subdivision of task at field level is necessary, there then arises the difficulty of agreeing on subdivisions with the organization. Two such subdivisions which are conceivable are; firstly, services to families (interpreting the word widely to include married couples without children, fatherless families, etc.) in the community; secondly, services to individuals, to adults and children in long-term residential care (including hostels and foster homes) with or without family ties. There are cogent objections to such a division; the 'boundary' problems which arise when people move to and from the community and the institution; the danger of separating 'the community' from 'the institution' organizationally at a time when efforts are being made to bridge the gap. The difficulty is, however, to find any more viable alternative. It is clear that the arguments which have led to a wish for administrative unity in respect of the services to families in their own homes are overwhelming. These are too familiar to be restated. One factor, however, is worth restating – the growing body of theory about family interaction from many different sources, all of which tends to emphasize the subtle interdependence of family members in ways not fully recognized in the past. This has great relevance to the issue of specialization, whether by problem (delinquency, mental illness), or by family member (child, grandmother) because it suggests that almost any kind of specialization at general social worker level may reinforce identifications with problems or individuals which are unhelpful if the family is to be viewed as a dynamic system – anything that happens to one member having repercussions on the whole.

The analogy of the family with the human body is sometimes made to point up the argument. Just as physical injury or disease in one part of the body has far-reaching repercussions on the whole system, so the same may be said of the family members in terms of social and emotional factors. The analogy breaks down, however, in that human beings can and do exist separately from their family in a way that parts of the body do not. Adequate personal social work services must, therefore, also take account of the individual apart from his family. It may, therefore, be that this would be a possible basis for formal field level specialization: general social workers working with families, and general social workers specializing in alternative community provisions for those who cannot be within their families. This latter group would be particularly knowledgeable and skilled in the various forms of residential and foster home provision. I suspect that the problems of placement of mentally ill adults in hostels, children in foster homes or the aged in homes, for instance, would throw up many of the same problems of role relationships, for the social workers with residential staff or foster parents; many of the same problems in adjustment for clients in new situations and so on. Within such formal differentiations, there might still be room for informal specialization according to inclination and motivation. This is simply a suggestion in the hope it will provoke better alternatives. However, if we set up any model in which formal field level specialization is reduced to a minimum, this carries with it the absolute necessity of specialization at senior level so that the general social worker has access to skilled consultation when it is needed, in the same way as a GP. Thus we come to the second kind of specialization – professional specialization in which unique skill and expertise is acknowledged. The history of the professions shows that such specialisms are constantly evolving and changing as new knowledge and skill become available. One thing, in the midst of much uncertainty, is quite clear. Social work must have this kind of specialist. What is described as the 'information explosion' in the social sciences, the rapid increase of knowledge about social problems and social work provisions, makes it essential that certain people further the skill of the profession by concentrating their attentions on a certain aspect. Faced with the necessity of knowing about everything, the social worker retreats confounded: given the possibility of exploring with increasing thoroughness a facet of social work (adoption, mental illness, delinquency, perhaps) this can act as a stimulus and excitement. This does not contradict the earlier argument for general social workers and limiting specialization at field level. It is an argument for initial breadth of field experience followed by, either, the possibility of depth which specialization offers *or* movement into 'management' – a different kind of breadth, 'organizational' breadth. Either would offer an advanced career structure.

It is not fruitful at this stage to suggest any precise forms which such advanced specialization may take. It is helpful to put this in a general perspective. In an article by Bucher and Strauss 'Professional Association and Colleague Relations', the authors point out that sociologists, in writing about the professions, have tended to emphasize the 'shared identity, values, definitions of role and interests of members of a profession'. In short 'the sociology of the professions has largely been focused upon the mechanics of cohesiveness and upon detailing the social structure of the professions'. They suggest that in so doing, the conflict of interests within professions have tended to be overlooked. 'The assumption of relative homogeneity within the profession is not entirely useful; there are many identities, many values, many interests.' These 'tend to become patterned and shared; coalitions develop and flourish . . .' The authors call these groupings 'segments' and suggest that specialisms may be called major segments. One statement we can take to heart in our own deliberations at the present time – under the heading 'the sense of mission' the authors write:

It is characteristic of the growth of specialities that early in their development they carve out for themselves and proclaim unique missions. They issue a statement of the contribution that the speciality, and it alone, can make in a total scheme of values and, frequently, with it an argument to show why it is peculiarly fitted for the task. The statement of mission tends to take a rhetorical form, probably, therefore, it arises in the context of a battle for recognition and institutional status.

It seems that conflict between different segments or specialisms claiming particular knowledge and skills promotes growth; in social work these will arise as new social problems arise or are detected and appraised in different ways. (An example would be in relation to immigrants.)

Bucher and Strauss continue:

Segments are not fixed, perpetually defined parts of the body professional . . . they take form and develop, they are modified and they disappear . . . Each generation engages in spelling out, again, what it is about and where it is going . . . Out of this fluidity, new groupings may emerge.

The different types of professional specialism which could arise would be concerned with areas of knowledge. These areas of knowledge might be related to specific social problems (such as physical handicap or delinquency); to the phases of human existence (childhood or old age); to social provision (residential care) or to method (casework or groupwork).

There could be much argument about all these; perhaps least familiar to British social workers is the controversy over 'method' specialization, so heated in the States. It is clear that however the controversy is resolved at field level – can we have multi *method* social workers? – there will be room for specialists in the three methods we at present identify – casework, groupwork and community organization. Certainly one can be assured that the unified social work organization we envisage, combined with the likelihood of larger local government units generally, makes a career structure for a variety of senior specialists a real possibility.

So far I have been outlining a hypothetical model; it is one in which a general social worker undertakes a broad range of tasks but one with certain formal subdivisions of task within the organization, and with the probability of informal specialization according to inclination; this could only be contemplated given the existence of senior specialists available for consultation. One hopes that the medical parallel would not be exact; that the general social worker, unlike the average GP, would be free to move up the hierarchy towards specialization or management and that specialization would usually arise after a period of general social work.

I am bound to admit, however, that the ideas I have been putting forward may be quite unrealistic; for whatever structural alterations take place, the fact is that large numbers of people who will enter such a structure at field level will come with pretty strongly defined identifications with a certain field of practice. The question is – how far existing social workers themselves can make the role adjustment, apart from acquisition of further knowledge and skill, which will be required to function as 'general social workers'.

Change gets harder as we get older. It is likely that many young social workers could make such an adaptation; many of the *older* social workers would be equipped for specialist senior roles which would partly solve that problem. There would still be, however, large numbers of social workers for whom the strain of the adaptation would be considerable.

The saddest aspect of all this relates to developments in social work education in the past ten or twelve years. In 1955, the first 'generic' course at the London School of Economics burst upon the world and since that time there has been an increasing acceptance of generic principles; firstly, that there is a common base of knowledge, attitudes and skills which all social workers need; secondly, that these can be illustrated in different fields of practice – hence the customary practice of arranging field work placements in different settings. This is a pretty firmly held belief now amongst social work teachers. Yet in many ways the pull against such generic trends has been very strong. Firstly, the fragmentation of responsibility for social work education at Government level has led to very rapid expansion of courses outside the universities with clear associations to certain fields of practice. Even courses within universities are not free from this kind of conflict. Secondly, the fragmentation of the social work services in local government has meant that the identifications of students with fields of practice, which is implied from the outset by grants and labels, is strongly reinforced in their first posts. It is my opinion that the importance of unconscious motivation in determining choice of field or practice has been misunderstood.

People's unconscious motivation has to go somewhere – if, suddenly, all Child-Care or Probation Officers were abolished, applicants for such posts would not be lost to social work. They would find an alternative outlet for their unconscious needs. More important in terms of social work at the present time is the role image of the 'Child-Care Officer' or 'Probation Officer' fostered in training and reinforced in practice.

While recognizing the inevitability, given the present situation, of the emergency Child-Care Training scheme, which has just been launched, this affords a particularly vivid example of the dilemma we face. This rapid expansion, so greatly needed, so desirable, has taken place before structural unification at central or local level and before – just before – a National Association of Social Workers – comes into existence. This will make a task of reorientation a massive one and it may mean that the kind of general social work I have envisaged is simply not a practical possibility in the foreseeable future. I hope this is unduly pessimistic.

A further difficulty in relation to the 'general social work idea' is concerned, not only with emotional identification with the fields of practice, but also with the demands on intellectual capacity which a truly generic approach requires. The capacity to transfer knowledge from one field to another, to see general applications, is generally conceded to be related to intellectual capacity. How far can we assume that, at basic level, all social workers can be trained to grasp the general applicability of certain concepts rather than their specific application to certain situations? An example might be in connection with residential care – and raises a question about the recommendations of the Williams' Committee for generic training. This is a subject, however, on which we have no evidence and is purely speculative. It would be gratifying if this point could be disproved.

The implications of these ideas for social work education are threefold.

Firstly, we should attempt to establish a truly 'generic' social work education at basic level. Despite agreement in general terms that this is desirable, we are a long way from the reality. The implications of this must be recognized by practitioners. It means abandoning concentration on detail and attempting to paint on a wider canvas. Much that is now uneasily included in basic training under the heading of 'settings' – child-care law, detailed medical knowledge and so on – would be jettisoned.

This leads to the second implication – the extensive development of in-service training as an ongoing indispensable part of professional education. This would equip new social workers with the necessary detailed knowledge; and it would encourage mobility between whatever formal organizational specializations do arise.

Thirdly, universities and technical colleges should develop advanced trainings, of various lengths, in different specializations and in management.

Despite any efforts towards a unified policy and approach towards change – our British traditions will ensure that in fact there will be much diversity (or confusion, according to your point of view). There is, however, much to commend diversity on issues such as these, which can only be resolved by experience. Nevertheless, may I in conclusion press home two points.

Let us use whatever changes are proposed for some bold and adventurous reorganization – *not just a gathering together of existing fields of practice under one organizational umbrella.*

Let us build into any reorganization an ongoing system of inquiry so that we examine some of the questions which arise from consideration of this topic: questions such as the extent and type of division of task necessary at field level; the use of informal specialization; the differing capacities of social workers to transfer knowledge and skill from one field to another, and so on.

If ten local authorities involved ten universities or technical colleges in planned appraisal of their reorganization from the outset – not afterwards when the necessary data has not been recorded – we would have a fascinating study of the interaction between organizational processes and personal and professional identifications. This could be a real advance in the theory and practice of social work. It would be a tragedy if we missed the chance.

What are the Outcomes of Casework?

D. E. G. Plowman

Reprinted with permission from 'What are the Outcomes of
Casework?', *Social Work*, vol. 26, no. 1, Jan. 1969, pp. 10-19

Perhaps the most obvious question to ask about social casework,
or indeed about any form of social work, is 'Does it work?' The
question has been asked many times before. But any attempt to
answer the question encounters difficulties so massive that many
practitioners seem to assume that the question cannot be answered,
or even that it is improper to ask it. Halmos has recently suggested that, brought face to face with the 'mirage of results',
counsellors have tended to fall back on faith. The question can
be asked of all the 'helping professions', and the flight to faith may
have been launched both by the poverty of evidence about 'results'
and by recent critical assaults.

Apart perhaps from Barbara Wootton's broadside against the
social workers, the most famous attack is probably that of
Eysenck against verbal psychotherapy in general and psychoanalysis in particular, in which he claimed that there was no
evidence that these methods made any advance on 'spontaneous
remission', or the healing powers of nature, in the cure of
neurosis. This claim has itself been criticized, and all that is really
recorded is the verdict of not proven. But whatever one may say
in criticism, I believe that Eysenck did perform one valuable
service – he asked an awkward question, and one which has still
not been properly answered.

This is the question which I want to ask about social casework.
Unlike some of the critics, I start from a belief that the helping
professions can, and often do, succeed in helping the many
people who are obviously in need of help. But it is still important
to ask how, and how often. If casework works, we may not
always know why; and the reasons, if we can find them, may
sometimes be rather surprising. If the search for results is a
mirage, this may be not because they are unobtainable, but
because the question is being asked in too simple a form. Before
we can ask whether casework works, we must ask what it is trying

to do – in other words, what are its aims? Only if we know the aims can we go on to the second stage – to ask how effective it is. But in asking this, the question turns out to be so complex that we have to go on to a third stage, that of trying to examine the separate and individual processes which make up what we call casework. It may be more useful to talk about the outcomes of different forms or aspects of casework than about undifferentiated 'results'.

THE AIMS OF CASEWORK

The importance of defining the aims can be seen in the work on psychotherapy. Data on its effectiveness are vitiated by the different meanings given by different psychiatrists to terms like 'cure' and 'improve'. There can be many reasons for chalking up an 'improvement'. A patient may be able to go back to work; his marriage may no longer be on the rocks; a child may be more accepted by his mother; anxiety may be alleviated; specific symptoms, such as compulsive habits, tics, or delusions, may be removed; self-doubts may be resolved, insight gained, decisions be no longer an agony. Perhaps one could sum up the different kinds of improvement under three general headings: *social adjustment* of various kinds (which ought to, but often does not, include changes in the environment), *symptom-relief*, and increased *self-insight*. Possibly the total *personality reorganization* sometimes claimed by psychoanalysts is a fourth. What is more, all these categories are highly complex in themselves.

Particular examples illustrate this. The study of Rogers and Dymond suggested that Rogers's particular brand of non-directive counselling did lead to a movement of what was called the 'self-image' towards the 'ideal-image' of the sort of person one would like to be – a movement, perhaps, towards some kind of greater psychological consistency. But such a change is a far cry from some unidentified overall 'improvement'. The hypothesis was that many neurotics show unrealistic self-doubts, or an exceptionally low self-regard or 'self-image'. But this is a specific hypothesis about one kind of positive change in one aspect of personality, and Rogers chose his measuring devices in the light of this hypothesis.

The point about this example is not only that there are different possible criteria of improvement, but that the choice of criterion is dictated in part by the explanatory theory which one holds. Different theories, and different criteria, will in turn dictate the search for different kinds of evidence of success and different ways of measuring it. We cannot evaluate psychotherapy until we agree on the aims of treatment. But the aims are themselves not a matter of total agreement. They depend in part upon theories, and are to some extent controversial; and they presuppose different social values about what the desirable outcome is.

Similar problems arise over the aims of casework. These are illustrated by Kogan and Hunt's studies of the effectiveness of casework in America in the early fifties. The studies involved family casework with 38 families including 80 members, 73 of whom were interviewed in a follow-up some five to six years later. The results suggested a positive improvement during the casework, and a further slight improvement during the follow-up period. There are methodological flaws, such as the absence of a control group of comparable cases not given casework. But at the moment I am concerned with the criteria used. Kogan and Hunt define success in terms of what they call 'movement', which is in turn defined by four criteria. These criteria are, briefly: (1) changes in adaptive efficiency; (2) changes in disabling habits or conditions; (3) changes in attitudes or understanding revealed in what the client says; and (4) changes in environmental circumstances. Many people might not quarrel with any of these. But the four criteria mix up *outside* circumstances, *social adjustment* to circumstances including other people, *symptom removal* or improvement, and gains in *self-insight*. These may all be desirable, but they are very different things. Are they all equally important? Are they equally important for 73 different clients, or for 38 different families? Can they sensibly be combined, as Kogan and Hunt do, into *one single* measuring scale of so-called 'movement'? How much have we lost, in precision, clarity and understanding, by this hodge-podge of criteria? This study is an important and interesting one, but it begs a lot of questions.

If we consider the various aims which social work may have, even in the one field of probation, their diversity becomes obvious. The aims of marriage guidance alone are manifestly complex, and similar confusions arise with delinquency. We probably all agree that recidivism rates are a very crude measure of success, even if they are convenient. But are we seeking an improved capacity to establish relationships with others? Are we helping a young boy to come to terms with authority? (And why should authority not be challenged?) Are we satisfied with the social re-learning of majority values such as the Eighth Commandment? Are we acting merely as the agencies of social control? It seems to me that an identical criterion might properly mean either success or failure, according to the case. In the case of a casual misdemeanour by a 'high-spirited' youngster, then the lack of any reconviction probably *is* a good measure of success. But we would hardly say the same of the so-called affectionless or psychopathic boy, for we usually aspire to something much more.

Yet who are we to choose? But avoiding choosing, on the grounds that that is the client's prerogative, is just as much a value, and the social worker is just as much making a decision for the client to make his own decisions. The conclusion seems to me inescapable, in social work as much as in psychotherapy, that we have different criteria of success, that we do not fully agree on these, that different criteria might sensibly apply to different cases, and that these criteria imply social values, which are to some extent a matter of controversy.

Any attempt to measure the effectiveness of social work, therefore, would be doomed to failure *at least* until we had tried to come to some agreement about what we are trying to do. This brings me to my second stage – the effectiveness of casework.

THE EFFECTIVENESS OF CASEWORK

In trying to assess the effectiveness of casework, one is unfortunately handicapped both by the poverty of evidence and by the comparatively poor quality of what evidence there is. The famous Cambridge study of probation is an example. It certainly contains a mass of informative data, telling one about the *aftermath* of probation, in terms of whether the probation order was broken, whether it was revoked because of a subsequent offence, or whether there was any further conviction during the three years after the order. And it also tells us how the 'success' rates, so defined, varied for different categories of offender.

All this is valuable. But, in my view, the study is a misnomer, for it does not contain a word of evidence from start to finish about the *results* of probation, in the sense of the *effects* of probation upon further criminal or non-criminal behaviour. The authors suggest why this is when they note themselves that, although the so-called success rate is lower for the small minority on whom a residence requirement was placed, this does not prove the failure of residence requirements as such because such requirements may be imposed on tougher cases. They would only know by having a matched sample or control group of similar hard cases who were not given residence requirements – and this they have not got. But this criticism, which the authors apply to one of their findings, can be levelled against all of them. The lower success rates, or higher recidivism rates, of juveniles, such as the 8-11 group, might be due to special factors in children of this age; but it might just as well be the result of sentencing policy, in which probation tends to be given to this age group in preference to stiffer sentences which may be passed on similar offences in older people.

I do not wish to make *too* much of this sort of criticism. To begin with, proper control groups are extremely hard to find, especially when neither criminologists nor probation officers have any control over sentencing policy. My point is only that, even if we *do* agree on the criteria of success, we still have methodological problems in evaluating the outcomes. There are a few studies with proper control groups. Derek Miller's *Growth to Freedom* is a case in point. Small though his group is, and short the period of the follow-up, there is at any rate some evidence, backed by a comparable control group, that his kind of intensive and supportive residential care can lead to gains in maturity and independence in the very deprived group of Borstal after-care boys. We notice here, however, that although Miller necessarily used reconviction rates in order to quantity his data, he also uses other criteria, such as estimates of maturity as shown in relationships with girls. In addition, the whole project derives its rationale from the pervading theory, which concerns the ravages created in a boy's personality by early and continuous institutionalization, and the therapeutic means needed to try to repair the damage. Again, both the aims and the criteria of success are complex, and are dictated by theory.

I cannot attempt a systematic survey of the studies of the effects of casework. I am more concerned to illustrate the problems and principles involved. Apart from the lack of good studies using control groups, we also have difficulty in evaluating casework because we have bothered to find out far too little about such topics as the kinds of client who come, whether voluntarily or not; why they continue in casework or why they leave; how they perceive the situation; and what the barriers to communication may be. I should like to turn to just one aspect of this, the question of why people – given a free choice – do not continue with the help which is offered.

The problem of the 'drop-out' or the early terminator, of why people break off treatment, has never been adequately faced, and raises difficulties for any attempt to evaluate the success of casework. My attention was first drawn to this on reading of a study of psychoanalysis in which fewer than *one-quarter* of the *applicants* (45/190) were actually *accepted* for treatment. If these are at all representative cases, they make nonsense of attempts to calculate success rates for psychoanalysis. It may be that only 45 of the applicants *could* properly be treated by psychoanalysis, but do we know? If the analysts deliberately chose hard cases (and were right in their assessments) we should then expect a rather low 'success' rate. But if they chose easy cases (and were right again), we should have a higher success rate. This illustrates the urgency of asking just what we are trying to do.

Dennis Guest, of the University of British Columbia and at present at the LSE, has just looked at some of the literature on the early terminator from casework. It is worth bearing in mind that the literature is American, that it deals with cases coming to casework agencies, psychiatric clinics and child guidance clinics, that as is common in America the clients will mostly be voluntary, and that the kind of casework will have been much more psychiatrically orientated than is usual in Britain. Nevertheless, the results raise some disconcerting questions, which I shall deal with briefly. The following data have been drawn from Mr Guest's study.

In some ways the most disconcerting of all is the poverty of any real attempt to study the matter. George Levinger reviewed the literature on continuance in casework in America in 1960, but there are really only a handful of studies, before or since.

Secondly, and not surprisingly where the emphasis is psychiatric, most attention has been paid to the client and his alleged short-comings. Those who continue in treatment tend to be described as having more discomfort about the (usually psychological) problem which brings them to the agency, they tend to be more introspective, to show higher motivation to solve the problem, greater ability to respond to the caseworker and greater willingness to explore the problem. It may not surprise you to hear that these paragons also tend to be middle-class, and they do not sound typical of the British probation service's clients.

Thirdly, some other important problems have been relatively ignored. One such is the client's present environment. Another is the characteristics of the caseworker, although there is some slight evidence that degree of professional training is less important, for continuance in casework, than the caseworker's 'warmth' and social distance from the client (and I shall come back to what I mean by social distance). Equally the manifestly important area of the nature and quality of the relationship between the client and caseworker has also been neglected. One study suggests that continuance in casework is more likely where the client shares the worker's goals for treatment, has a positive attitude to the worker (and vice versa), and has a realistic conception of the worker's role. Again, how often do these conditions hold in probation?

Why, then, do people drop out of casework, when they are free to do so, against the advice of the worker? That this is a frequent occurrence is suggested by the figures. To take a psychiatric example, and an American one again, a report prepared by the US Veterans' Administration on mental health clinics showed that, in 1958, between 30 and 65 per cent of all patients accepted for psychotherapy terminated prematurely against the advice of the therapist. The reasons usually given for this sort of situation seem to have been in terms of the 'inadequacy' of the client, such as his deficiency of self-insight, intelligence or ability to communicate with the therapist or caseworker. And much of the work on drop-outs has been inspired by the search for screening devices to eliminate the 'bad risks' before they are ever accepted. Given that resources of trained manpower and money are limited, this is understandable – 'rationing devices' are needed. But eliminating the bad risks may not only have the effect of improving the apparent success rates. It may also eliminate those most in need of help.

This is indeed quite probable. Those who terminate prematurely have, for example, included those with more complex problems, or those who 'tended to report problems in family relationships, or as external to themselves, or who failed to recognize any problem at all'. How familiar this all sounds! It is often said, for example, that clients for verbal psychotherapy have the best prognosis when they are above average in intelligence, well educated and able to verbalize, when they already have some degree of self-insight, when they are acutely aware of a problem, when they see the problem *in themselves* (such as self-doubts about their own competence at work, or sexually), and when they are strongly motivated towards cure. Not surprisingly, such ideal clients tend to be middle-class once more. I am not aware of any adequate studies which do, in fact, demonstrate that working-class clients are less amenable to verbal psychotherapy. All too often they never get the chance, because of the assumptions of the psychiatrists. Studies of working-class culture tend to show on the whole (there are obviously many exceptions) that working-class people are more resistant to seeing problems as internal, or as a matter of relationships with others; they are more likely to see problems as material or concrete matters, which can be put right by manipulation of the environment. As a result they may resist psychotherapy or casework and not understand its objectives. Perhaps, after patiently waiting through the first session or two, they will plaintively ask 'But when does the treatment start?' or 'When are you going to *do* something?' This is what I meant earlier by *social distance*. It is not a simple or crude question of social class: but it does refer to quite fundamental differences in attitudes, expectations, and perceptions of the other, which are bound up with class-position.

What I am in general suggesting at the moment is several possibilities, which may not yet be proved, but which need examining. One is that, in the absence of studies of so basic a matter as voluntary terminators, we cannot even begin to assess how effective casework is. Secondly, the drop-out rate is, at any rate in some spheres, clearly rather high. Thirdly, at least where attendance is voluntary, those who drop out could be those who most need help. Fourthly, this drop-out of those most in need, to the extent that it occurs, may be unwittingly (or even deliberately) encouraged by some agencies, on the grounds of efficiency. Fifthly (and this is particularly relevant to large areas of work in probation), where the client cannot legally drop out in fact he can drop out in effect, by just not co-operating, and the reason may be tied up with all the kinds of failure to communicate at which I have briefly hinted. How far do social work agencies operate on some half-conscious theory of the '*good client*', where 'good' is defined more in terms of the convenience of the agency than of the needs of the client?

It is a variety of considerations such as these which make me cautious about talking of the effectiveness of casework at all. There are many technical and methodological problems involved in trying to assess effectiveness. But the chief difficulty is that of trying to decide what we mean by success in the first place. The very term 'success' in casework is both vague and loaded with values – values which are all too often not made clear. Perhaps we had better drop the term altogether, at least for the moment, and concentrate upon narrower and more clearly defined topics. This brings me to my third stage.

PROCESSES IN CASEWORK

It is the gist of my argument that, in order to understand casework, we need much more detailed inquiry than we have yet had. This will include questions such as how and why clients come to casework in the first place and why they do or do not continue. But it will also involve detailed analysis of the actual course of casework and the processes involved. What are the processes which go on between two people in casework? In what contexts should they be used? What are their effects, in the appropriate contexts, upon given kinds of client?

Such questions are not new. Casework methods, involving the nature and role of support, acceptance, permissiveness and interpretation, have been discussed extensively. But in my view we have far too little careful analysis of exactly what is involved in such ideas. I should like to concentrate on one or two aspects of process in casework.

Processes, on the level of techniques, have been studied in psychotherapy, for example by Carl Rogers and his colleagues.

Rogers has recorded many counselling sessions on tape, and analysed the effect on the client of specific non-directive 'techniques', such as the 'mirroring' or 'reflecting back' of the feeling-tone expressed by the client. There is some evidence that these techniques do lead to further exploration by the client of his problem, and later to increased self-insight and capacity to take decisions. On the other hand, techniques which Rogers called the use of 'directive questions' and 'interpretations' seemed to lead to resistance or retreat, rather than progress – at least as defined by Rogers.

Interesting though these results are, they need taking with caution. They are one-sided, in that they are produced by the exponent of the particular method which emerges favourably. They may depend upon the prevalence of special assumptions, such as the American 'democratic ethos', which is against solutions imposed by others. Most important of all, perhaps, is the fact that Rogers's clients were – yet again – typically middle-class, well-educated, voluntary and often with rather minor problems of adjustment and self-acceptance of the kind which may rarely reach either caseworkers or psychiatrists in this country. Perhaps we should also remember the personality of Carl Rogers himself, and it is less clear how well the techniques would work for others. Rogers himself seems more recently to have veered away from techniques towards an emphasis upon the 'warmth' of the relationship as such.

But if rigidly defined techniques, blindly applied, have obvious dangers, the concept of 'warmth' is itself too general and vague to be very illuminating. It leads one on to a consideration of the general nature of the 'relationship' between client and caseworker or therapist, which itself needs detailed study. First, let us look at those twin concepts of permissiveness and non-directiveness. Perhaps I am wrong in coupling them together, for they are clearly not identical. *Permissiveness*, I suppose, in so far as it does have a clear meaning, refers to something like the acceptance, without criticism, of the expression of feelings. No one, in either casework or psychotherapy, has, as far as I know, ever said that permissiveness can be absolute, especially as far as behaviour is concerned. Limits may have to be imposed; and in casework we have the awkward problem of allying permissiveness with the non-condonement of some kinds of behaviour. *Non-directiveness* refers more to the behaviour of the caseworker, in trying to avoid suggestions, directions, or any kind of interference with the client. Again, this is a major problem in casework in any statutory service, notably probation; and, once again, I wonder whether many caseworkers have ever seriously thought that they could be totally non-directive. But what I want to say is that the sort of approach implied in both permissiveness and non-directiveness may be useful as an ideal, but is actually impossible in principle.

Its usefulness as an ideal seems to rest on the following reasoning. Many clients have rarely or never experienced a close and accepting relationship with anyone, and have never acquired the capacity to trust someone or to establish close emotional ties. They have, on the contrary, often experienced only criticism and rejection; as part of this, they have never learned to accept themselves or even to see themselves as they are. The function of acceptance in the relationship is to allow the discovery of what sort of person one is and to encourage the capacity to develop. Permissiveness is justified on the grounds that it allows the client to develop and explore his problems without fear of rebuff. Whether or not this approach is effective, it seems to me that it makes certain presuppositions. It presupposes certain theories about the origin of clients' problems, and it presupposes values such as the worth of understanding oneself and making one's own decisions. These theories and values have dictated the methods or techniques adopted.

I should probably qualify my statement that this approach is impossible in principle, by saying that it is complete or total permissiveness and non-directiveness which are impossible in principle, even if we still accept them as useful ideals at which to aim. My reason for saying this is simply that casework, like any other relationship, occurs between two people, each of whom is thinking about the other as well as about himself, wondering what the other is about and trying to anticipate what he is thinking. Whatever the caseworker does – even if it is nothing – is going to be interpreted (correctly or incorrectly) by the client, who will respond accordingly. The casework relationship, after the mother/child and marital relationships, must be one of the most intense that there is. I do not see how the caseworker can fail to influence the client, whether he wants to or not.

Some of the evidence for this comes from recent experiments in social psychology, in which the whole course of group discussions – including both the actual topic and even such apparently arbitrary things as the use of singular or plural nouns – has been altered, unknown to the students taking part, by the systematic intervention of the group leader. All he needs to do is to say 'good' or 'uh-huh!' when the discussion gets near a prearranged topic, and nothing otherwise, for the students to take the subtle hint of approval and veer round. Any kind of vaguely encouraging grunting or nodding can be taken as a sign of approval (which it is often designed to be in ordinary conversation). In the formal language of learning theory, it becomes systematic reward or reinforcement.

Perhaps I should properly distinguish between permissiveness and non-directiveness on the one hand, and *influence* on the other. One may try to be permissive; one may try to be non-directive. But, according to this argument, it is impossible not to influence the client, one way or another. This is simply because the client is another person, watching you, wondering what it is all about. If we cannot fail to influence, for better or for worse, perhaps we should start asking what kind of influence, so that we can at least try to make rational choices.

This links up with the subject of authority, which is closely connected with concepts of influence. This also involves what seems to me to be a crucial aspect of social work which has, at least in terms of actual research, been surprisingly neglected – namely, the need to try to see things through the perceptions of the client.

The concept of authority seems to have at least three meanings which are relevant to probation or the prison service. It seems to mean, first, being a representative of others, such as the courts or the Prison Commissioners, who themselves have ultimate power which they can wield through sanctions. It can mean, second, being an actual wielder of power in the sense in which, for example, a probation order can be revoked or a boy recalled to Borstal. It can mean, third, being an influence or exemplar, where the authority is invested in one by the client because he sees and accepts one as an appropriate model. It seems to me that a probation officer can have authority in any or all of these three senses, at the same time.

But this may not be the way it is seen by the client, for example by a young lad from a rough working-class area put on probation. If I were to generalize rather wildly, I should guess that the courts tend to see the probation officer as authority in sense one, as a delegate of the courts. The officer will mostly want to see himself as authority in sense three, which is the most akin to casework. But the boy is likely to have at best a dim conception of authority in either of these senses, and will be more likely to think in terms of sense two, to see the officer as a wielder of power and retribution, perhaps even vindictively. The officer will most likely see his task as, in part, to get himself accepted as authority in sense three, as a willingly accepted model, for only thus, he will argue, can he begin to carry out effective casework. He will, of course, have to bear sense one in mind, for this is the agency function, and he may have to be prepared to use sense two; this is the process of 'working constructively through authority'.

I am not saying this is wrong. And if there is some incompatibility between the different senses of authority, if the boy's perception of the officer as a figure of power 'gets in the way' of his acceptance of the officer as a model or example, this may indeed be a challenge to the officer, and it may be capable of constructive use. But two aspects of this process intrigue me at the moment.

One aspect is the intrusion of values once again. For it seems to me that to be a representative of an agency, and of 'society' in general, and to try to act as a model, is to assume sets of values: values such as respect for property, for truth, for punctuality; respect for people, such as for girls as people in their own right instead of as objects of conquest or manipulation; and respect for and acceptance of oneself. But to generalize again about social class a little crudely, these are much more typically middle-class values. We may think of them as 'universal' or humanitarian values, but they are rather less commonly accepted in the sort of background from which many probationers come. Does 'working constructively through authority' mean that authority is right?

The probation officer has, in other words, in a rather more acute form the problem faced by all or most social workers. It is that of having to work in a framework of values, which he may indeed entirely accept himself, but which are to some extent imposed by the agency and the role it plays in society, and with which he may not fully agree. But, whether he agrees or not, the values are not as universal as all that, and tend not to be accepted by, or to be just unfamiliar to, many of our clients.

The other aspect which intrigues me is that the probation officer may wish to get the boy to *see* him as a model, or as authority in sense three. In other words, he wishes to alter the boy's perceptions. He may view this as merely helping to set up the casework situation. But he is implicitly trying to alter the boy's values in the process. This seems to me to be a process of re-education. It is education certainly in what casework involves. But, because of the ulterior ends of casework, especially in a statutory setting such as probation, it is also re-education in values.

What I am saying, in effect, is that casework as a process involves – at any rate in part, and amongst other things – the following aspects: it is impossible not to influence the client to some extent; this influence tends to be in the direction of certain values – we may say it should be, but the values are not universally held; and therefore casework involves what is really some degree of re-education of the client.

Let us look at what this suggests for the nature of the relationship.

The kind of *rapprochement* which has been taking place between psychoanalysis and learning theory in recent years has important implications for understanding what happens in a relationship between a client and a caseworker or a psychotherapist. I shall deal briefly with certain aspects.

The infant is born, both with needs which are usually met by the mother, but also with some degree of residual tension which seems to be the forerunner of anxiety and which can be soothed by handling, stroking and all the other techniques which we call 'mothering'. Gradually the infant learns to associate relief from pain, tension, anxiety and fear with the presence of some person – usually, in our society anyway, the mother. This can generalize, in the manner of all learning, to other associated things such as other people, whose mere presence can come to be relieving. Whether you call this a basic attitude of trust, with Erikson, or conditioned anxiety relief, with the learning theorists, seems to me a matter of choice as much as anything. We also know that fear and anxiety depend upon a part of the nervous system (the sympathetic division of the ANS) which is antagonistic to another part of the nervous system (the para-sympathetic division) which is concerned with digestion, respiration, sex, the endocrines, and, incidentally, all those processes associated with skin contact and the procedures of mothering. If anxiety is not too strong, the other side can be activated – by food, sex, reassurance, relaxation, comfort – sufficiently to, as it were, 'out-trump' the anxiety.

Applying this to the relationship, one sees that most people are already accustomed to obtaining relief from anxiety or doubt from others. The psychotherapist, for example, can first gain the patient's confidence and help him to relax. He can then evoke accounts of experiences which have caused distress. If the relationship is good enough, the mere presence of a trusted therapist, plus what support and reassurance he gives, may be enough to out-trump the anxiety. When the anxiety is less, the patient may be able to go on to explore more dangerous areas, having already learnt that *this* therapist is a rewarding person because he has already offered some relief.

Obviously this account is a very great oversimplification of a process which, if it works at all, can take a long time and suffer many setbacks. It is also in many ways speculative. But it suggests two points which are immediately relevant.

One is that the relationship will work differently according to whether the patient has or has not originally learnt the attitude of trust. If he has, fairly quick and so-called 'superficial' forms of therapy may work. If he has not, as with the deprived and affectionless person, he may have to learn it from the beginning, which may mean repeating experiences missed as a child. This could be expected to take much longer, and to involve the therapist's accepting, or even encouraging, regression and infantile dependence. Apart from relevant work such as Derek Miller's there is some supporting evidence to suggest that 'depth' therapy, which encourages dependence, can help very regressed schizophrenics, whereas a more superficial therapy which emphasizes social acceptance and independence works with less regressed schizophrenics.

The other point is that my description of the relationship has not mentioned the theoretical beliefs of the therapist at all. These may not be totally unimportant, and they may at least dictate the more specific techniques which are used. But there is some reason to think that the therapist's beliefs, whether he is Freudian, Jungian, Rogerian, a follower of behaviour therapy or just plain eclectic, may make rather less difference than we have tended to think.

There are several reasons for this. For example, amongst the few studies of the effectiveness of therapy, there is very little evidence to suggest that one school is any better than another. Again, expert therapists of different schools in fact agree more on what a good relationship is with each other than they do with beginners of their own school; and patients also perceive the relationship as much the same, especially for the experienced therapists, irrespective of the school of thought. This evidence suggests that a successful relationship in psychotherapy may depend more upon what happens in the here-and-now between the client and the therapist than it does upon the therapist's theoretical position about the origin and nature of mental disorders. Certainly this suggests an urgent need for much more careful investigation of the details of the relationship.

But there is yet another implication of this reinterpretation of the relationship in terms of learning. The situation of trust, and of relief of anxiety by the presence and support of some trusted person, is that situation in which attitudes and values are learnt initially by the child and in which they are most readily relearnt by adults. Work on attitude-change suggests that attitudes change most easily when the teacher (or propagandist) is liked and accepted and when the subject's attitudes are already somewhat near to the teacher's. In terms of psychotherapy there is now some evidence that when therapy is judged successful by both client and therapist the client's values have in fact moved towards the therapist's, and that this is most likely to happen, or the therapy be judged 'successful', when the client's values are already fairly near the therapist's.

I have said nothing about casework in the above account, and I know of no evidence from casework to compare with the still rather fragmentary work in psychotherapy. But I see no reason to doubt that the position is likely to be similar, and the implications seem important.

Earlier I was suggesting that caseworkers are bound to influ-

ence their clients to some extent, that this involves often controversial values, and that the process is in part one of re-education.
This view fits with an analysis of the relationship which suggests
that its very nature is supremely well-fitted for the relearning of
values. The more intensive the kind of casework, the more this
might happen. How could a caseworker be detached, Olympian
and hygienically disinfected from contaminating his client? It
just does not seem to me to be possible. The casework situation
seems to me to be one which has very high potential for learning –
and I mean more than the client's 'discovery of himself' in a
permissive climate.

In conclusion, I am suggesting that the search for 'results' is a
mirage only if one regards results in broad unanalysed terms.
The effectiveness of casework, or any form of social work, can be
discussed only in terms of its aims, on which we may not agree.
Even given agreement, it is necessary to ask a great many
questions about what goes on in the course of different kinds
and lengths of casework. On theoretical grounds it does not
seem to me possible that casework can go on without some
influence of the *caseworker upon the client* (and vice versa for that
matter). Very detailed analyses of the processes of change are
needed, however difficult technically they may be to obtain. In the
course of this many ideas, such as those of permissiveness,
acceptance, and the nature of the relationship, *may* have to be
revised. I do not know how far; nor do I think that forms of
direct influence in social work are necessarily wrong. But it is
time we began asking some searching questions.

The Development of Institutional Care

Kathleen Jones

Reprinted with permission from 'New Thinking about Institutional Care', published by the Education Sub-Committee, Association of Social Workers, 1967, pp. 7-16

The basic facts concerning the development of institutional care in this country are well known: small institutions for socially or physically handicapped groups have existed right through the history of Christendom. In the second half of the eighteenth century, the need for refuges from an increasingly harsh and competitive world was accentuated, and they increased both in number and in variety. In the nineteenth century, the technology of industry improved very rapidly, while the technology of institutions developed not at all. Social problems proliferated, and our capacity for dealing with them was quickly outstripped. The institutional system grew, because there seemed no alternative to it. Thousands of human beings lived out drab, less than human lives in obscurity.

Before the century ended, attempts were being made to break down or by-pass the monolithic structures – orphanages, asylums, prisons, workhouses – which had been created. In our own day, this policy has been sharpened and given shape by the community care movement and the extension of social work training.

The effect of these changes has been three-fold: some types of institution, such as the orphanage and the workhouse, have at least in theory disappeared altogether. Others, such as the general hospital and the mental hospital, now deal with a dynamic population instead of a static one. The average length of stay has dramatically decreased, and the function of intensive treatment has been stressed. At the same time, we have created new, smaller institutions – old people's homes, hostels, after-care centres – many of them under the care of the local authorities. There is a tendency to call these 'homes' or 'residential centres' rather than 'institutions'. When we talk of the 'rise and fall of the institution', we think in the main of those Victorian monoliths which substituted institutional values for personal ones, which dealt with problem groups in the mass rather than with people in need as individuals.

How this system grew and then declined is by now a familiar story. What we have to consider is the 'why' of history rather than the 'how': whether institutions served a useful social function in their day; why they went sour; and whether they ought now to be abolished entirely or somehow restored to their original purpose in a modern social context.

The system developed because of very complex economic and social forces which robbed the family and the small neighbourhood group of their former supportive functions. You may remember the story of Wordsworth's 'Michael', when the old man's son Luke 'to the city went'. There was a double social loss – to Luke, who

> . . . in the dissolute city gave himself
> To evil courses . . .

– and was driven to seek 'a hiding-place beyond the seas' and to his parents, who lived on into their nineties without a son to support them.

The double effects of urbanization and population growth were to create large, secondary, social groups, in which human relationships were tenuous or non-existent, in place of the small primary groups which could sustain the individual against social collapse. There was only one answer possible in the towns: to create protected primary groups for those who could not cope with this hostile and competitive society. Many of the eighteenth-century institutions were genuine centres of social care. The lack of techniques of management did not greatly matter as long as they were small – they could be managed by simple kindness and rule of thumb; but the numbers in care or in need of care grew until common sense alone could not provide the administrative answers needed.

One of the greatest differences between Victorian social thinking and our own is that, despite the great social and economic changes which were rending and re-shaping their society, the Victorians thought in static terms. We plan a hospital service for ten years, and then issue annual revisions to cope with a changing situation: they planned for all time. We build for changing circumstances – hospital and local authority architects talk in terms of movable partitions, alternative uses of space, growth potential and planned obsolescence. They built to last. We take population growth and movement into account. In the face of the greatest population explosion in the country's history, they continued to build for a static population, and to be both surprised and alarmed when their small institutions became inadequate and overcrowded.

Overcrowding meant lower standards of physical care – beds in the corridor, less straw in the pallets, more water and more barley in the meagre stew; and it inevitably meant lower standards of human relationships. Ten paupers were people. Fifty were just 'inmates' – a logical class whose social distance from their providers and betters was immense. It became easier to class them all together, harder to remember that they had individual needs and responses. Physical and emotional deprivation went together.

This process was reinforced from both sides of the political fence: by the Tory fear of revolution, and the Whig passion for efficiency.

The fear of revolution after the French pattern was to dominate Tory thinking well into the mid-nineteenth century. We look back now on the events of Peterloo, the rural riots of 1832, the Tolpuddle trial and the Chartist agitation as isolated events in the history book; we tend to forget that the Chartist movement was widely expected to end with a bang rather than a whimper; and that for more than half a century, the political and social thinking of the ruling classes in England was dominated by the fear of the mob. The Victorian emphasis on order and submissiveness in institutional inmates owed much to the belief that children, servants and the lower classes would soon get out of hand if given any degree of freedom of action.

Fear of another social group is partly a function of relative size. Race riots break out where there is a large coloured population, not where immigrants are few in number. Authoritarianism, which is largely an expression of fear, observes the same rules. It is difficult to be an authoritarian parent to one child – the generations live too closely together. It must be difficult not to be authoritarian to twelve children if parents are to have any life of their own. So the main trouble with the Victorian poor was that there were too many of them. The mob had to be kept down, and the institutionalized were, so to speak, a captive section of the mob. These at least could be taught obedience, docility, and a proper respect for their betters.

Whig reactions were more complicated. The country squires, among whom Whiggery was traditionally strong, must have shared many of the apprehensions of the right wing. Yet, in the days of the French Revolution, the party had supported the revolutionary leaders in France against king and nobles, and had broken its back in the process. From these contradictory attitudes, and the developing theory of the Utilitarians, came a curious new development: repression introduced in the New Poor Law of 1834 in the name of social enlightenment and good government. The whole scheme was conceived as a self-eliminating mechanism: a system which would eliminate poverty by dissuading men from becoming paupers. The harsh conditions of the Union workhouse were intended as a spur to self-maintenance rather than as a punishment for social failure; but the system became punitive in the hands of a bureaucratic class. The Radical element – who preserved the older Whig tradition of identification with the oppressed – were quick to compare the harshness of the new Poor Law system with that of the pre-revolutionary government in France. Wythen Baxter's book is perhaps the first example of the tendency to see Union workhouses (and by implication other kinds of institution to which the concept of less eligibility spread by reference) as Bastilles to be stormed:

> Had there been no lettre de cachet, the revolutionary Marseilleise would never have been tuned in retribution, and Louis XVI would have died in his bed and not on the block. Had there been no New Poor Law, the name of Chartist would never have been heard; nor would Birmingham have been heated with fire and fury, or Newport have run red with the gore of Britons from the hills.

Among the subscribers to this curious work were the editor of *The Times*, a number of leading Radicals and Mr B. d'Israeli.

I have dwelt on the attitudes of the major political parties to make one point clear: that in the setting of the 1830s, and indeed through much of the nineteenth century, both the main political parties were in favour of the institutional system, though for very different reasons: the Tories because it helped to maintain law and order (though it was admitted to be ruinously expensive) and the Whigs because it was thought to be an efficient way of tackling a grave social problem. Today, the two main political parties are both against the institutional system, again for very different reasons: the Right, because it involves heavy public expenditure, particularly if old buildings are to be brought up to modern standards of acceptability; the Left, because the institution is still seen as the Bastille, the symbol of intolerant and anti-democratic authority. I think we have to try to rid ourselves of the emotional overtones of these old arguments: to look squarely at the institution (or the residential setting) as a means of dealing with social problems, and to consider positive and realistic policies in the present-day situation.

We have seen how institutions became large, punitive and authoritarian; and of course many of them have also become old. That rash of 'low, brown, homely buildings' which the Poor Law Commission exulted to see spread across the face of England – the Union workhouses – proved easier to put up than to destroy. A corresponding rash of lunatic asylums, built in response to the Acts of 1828, 1845 and 1890, still forms the bulk of our mental hospital provision. Fifty-four convict prisons were built in the years 1842-8, and they still dominate the work of the Prison Department. As Mr Kenneth Robinson once commented, 'the Victorians could not build other than solidly'. These buildings have continued to be used because both the social services and the population at risk have continued to grow. There can be few politicians and administrators concerned with the social services who have not felt at some time a sheer despair at the sight of these buildings, so useful, even indispensable, so enduring, but so wholly inappropriate to our twentieth-century aspirations.

The movement towards community care in the last decade has been accompanied by a flood of literature about institutions which I am going to characterize as the Literature of Dysfunction. That is to say, it is concerned with what is wrong with institutions rather than with how they can be well run. I think it may be a sub-section of the Literature of Protest. This is a generation which is unusually intolerant of authority in any form, and it may be that those who manage and work in institutions have become popular targets in the same sense that the Government (any government), God, the Royal Family, and the Governors of the London School of Economics have become popular targets. I do not want to argue the merits of any of the controversies involved: simply to point out that protest is popular, anti-authoritarianism is an acceptable attitude (perhaps the only acceptable attitude for the young) and that it is sometimes blind and seldom analytical. It may for all that serve a purpose, and a very useful one.

In the past decade, to mention only some of the major works, we have had Dr Russell Barton's *Institutional Neurosis* on mental hospitals, Peter Townsend's *The Last Refuge* on old people's homes, Ann Cartwright's *Human Relations and Hospital Care* on general hospitals, Terence and Pauline Morris's *Pentonville* on the Prison Service. In the United States, the theme has been taken up by Belknap's *Human Problems of a State Mental Hospital*, Dunham and Weinberg's *The Culture of the State Mental Hospital*, Gresham Sykes's *The Society of Captives* (on prisons) and by Erving Goffman's *Asylums*. In the American sociological tradition, work from the States has tended to be less empirical and more theoretical than comparable English work; and more recent British writers have been profoundly influenced by American thinking, particularly by Goffman, who attempted (from a fairly limited experience – one year as an assistant remedial gymnast in a federal mental hospital in Washington) an eclectic analysis of what he calls 'total institutions'.

'Total institutions' comprise five categories of residential centres which are separated from society to a lesser or a greater degree: institutions for the 'incapable and harmless', such as those for the blind and the aged, and what he calls the 'orphaned' and the 'indigent'; institutions for those who are 'incapable and a threat to society' such as tuberculosis hospitals or centres, mental hospitals and leprosaria; institutions for those who are a danger to the community: prisoner-of-war camps, concentration camps, prisons; institutions 'purportedly established the better to pursue some worklike task' – army barracks, ships, boarding schools, work camps; and 'retreats from the world' – 'abbeys, monasteries, convents and other cloisters'. One's first reaction is that the terminology, and the thinking behind it, is pretty dated; and that this broad sweep may involve lumping together things which superficially look alike, but which are in reality very different; but the analysis is more cogent than the preliminary classification would suggest.

Goffman criticizes these 'total institutions' on three main grounds: the first is that they create 'batch living':

A basic arrangement in modern society is that the individual tends to sleep, play and work in different places, with different co-participants under different authorities, and without an overall rational plan.

In the institution, these three settings are merged. The domestic, work and leisure-time roles are all carried out in the same place and with the same group of people, integrated into a general plan which is related to the goals of the institution. There is no escape from the institutional life. Goffman talks of the 'assault on the self' which results from this situation, and of the individual trying to 'crawl down the cracks' in the institutional fabric.

Second, institutions have a binary character. They consist essentially of the managers and the managed. 'Staff tend to feel superior and righteous. Inmates tend, in some ways at least, to feel inferior, weak, blameworthy and guilty'. There is social distance between the two groups. One of the basic features of life of many large institutions is the identity anecdote, in which a master is mistaken for a sixth-former, a doctor is mistaken for a mental patient, an officer in mufti is mistaken for a ranker. Staff and inmates create 'antagonistic stereotypes' – the whole of the other class being seen as sharing undesirable and threatening attributes. There is consequently very limited communication between the two groups: the managers have the power to withhold information – doctors and nurses do not tell a patient about his condition, officers know a unit's destination when it is on the move, but rankers do not. The 'managed' group exists in a sort of blind dependency.

Third, this leads inevitably to an authoritarian structure, with the corollary of deprivation of personal rights for the managed. There may be 'indignities of speech and action' such as the ritual bath and the vesting of the inmate in institutional clothes. Institutional values will replace personal values. There will be a chronic anxiety about breaking the rules. To this situation, the inmate may make one of four types of adjustment: withdrawal, in which he cuts himself off from human contact; intransigence, in which he fights the system; 'colonization', in which he tries to show outward acceptance to the system and to get the most he can out of it for himself; and conversion, in which he genuinely acquires the 'institutional perspective'.

Goffman's main purpose is sociological analysis rather than social reform: and indeed he ends his essay on *Medical Model and Mental Hospitalisation* on a note of despair:

> Nor in citing the limitations of the service model do I mean to claim that I can suggest some better way of handling persons called mental patients. Mental hospitals are not found in our society because supervisors, psychiatrists and attendants want jobs; mental hospitals are found because there is a market for them. If all the mental hospitals in a given region were emptied and closed down today, tomorrow relatives, police and judges would raise a clamour for new ones.

His main intention is to delineate an ideal type for use as a sociological tool rather than to criticize existing institutions, or to suggest that they could be run in some other way; but his ideas have been taken up and developed by writers whose intentions are critical and reformist rather than analytical. For example, Gresham Sykes contributes in *The Society of Captives* an absorbing chapter on 'The Defects of Total Power'. Russell Barton contributes the idea of 'institutional neurosis' – the illness which, he contends, the mental hospital can give the patient in addition to the one which caused his entry. In the Prison Service, a number of writers, including Terence and Pauline Morris, have written of 'prisonization' – a rather different process which involves working the system rather than succumbing to it. Townsend has concentrated his attack on 'batch living'. In a chapter on 'The Effects of Institutions' he writes:

> People live communally with a minimum of privacy, and yet their relationships with each other are slender. Many subsist in a kind of defensive shell of isolation . . . they are subtly oriented towards a system in which they submit to orderly routine, lack creative occupation, and cannot exercise much self-determination . . . in some of the smaller and more humanely administered institutions, these various characteristics seem to be less frequently found, but they are still present.

Cartwright stresses the heritage of less eligibility:

The unhappy effects of parsimony are . . . evident in meagre accommodation and in understaffing as well as in the number of beds available . . . the lower standards of an earlier epoch continue today because of financial and administrative expedience (*sic*). But it is no longer appropriate to regard a pleasant atmosphere or the patient's privacy as extravagant luxuries.

But parsimony is not the only problem. She also stigmatizes the 'failure to recognize social and psychological requirements', and in particular the lack of communication with patients.

It is small wonder that people who work in or manage institutions have begun to buckle under the weight of this chorus of disapproval. The Literature of Dysfunction is compulsively readable and hits some fairly obvious targets. Most of us have at some time in our lives been classed among the 'managed' rather than the manager and the analysis strikes a genuine chord of protest. We may say that these things do not happen in our institution, but we know that they happen.

If the literature is to be used as a basis for reform, we need a more refined analysis. As Goffman notes, 'none of the elements . . . seems peculiar to total institutions, and none seems to be shared by every one of them'. What are the variables? I will suggest four which are worth further study: the motivation of residents in entering and remaining in residential accommodation; the purpose of the institution; the residents' degree of social functioning; and the duration of stay.

The critics draw heavily on American sources relating to prisons and mental hospitals. Prisoners are involuntarily institutionalized. In the United States, where voluntary admission policies and community care policies are less well developed than in this country, mental patients share this characteristic; but all residents in institutions are not confined against their will. A novice who enters the religious life is not in the same position as a prisoner under sentence. A patient who enters hospital for an urgent operation is not in the same position as a concentration camp victim. The hypothesis that the resident's degree of freedom to stay or to leave, and his motivation if he decides to stay, affect his attitude to institutional life, seems a reasonable one. In the case of old people's homes, the questions 'Do you think you did the right thing in entering this home?' 'Do you want to stay permanently?' 'Are you lonely?' are almost meaningless unless the research worker has objective data concerning the alternatives actually open to the respondent.

On the question of function: institutions exist for a specific purpose or a group of purposes: to heal, to shelter, to confine, to teach, to protect. Though the maintenance function can assume an undue importance, they were not created for the exploitation of one group by another, and we cannot do without them. We cannot run a health service without hospitals, or a penal service without prisons, at least in the present state of knowledge. All old people and mental patients cannot be sent home to their families: as Townsend demonstrates 'for both sexes, the proportion of unmarried persons admitted is much larger than the proportion of widowed and divorced persons, and many times larger than the proportion of married persons'. In other cases the patient has relatives, but the need for care or treatment is such that it cannot be met on a domiciliary basis. We have tended to stress the similarities between institutions, but in fact they are not homogeneous either in their basic purposes or in the populations with which they deal.

Residents' degree of social functioning clearly varies considerably. Some are so limited in capacity that care has to be of a fairly paternalistic character. Goffman's underlying assumption that people in institutions are fully capable of running their own lives and acting independently results from his own strong identification with the 'managed', but it is not as simple as that. There are admitted dangers in treating inmates as though they were incapable of independent action, and equal dangers in assuming total social functioning where it does not exist. As anyone who has worked in a mental hospital or an old people's home knows, the problem is to decide how much independence a particular patient can sensibly be given at a particular point in time. It may be possible to run a school, a convalescent ward of a hospital, a home for active old ladies in their sixties on *laissez-faire* lines; but it is difficult to imagine a *laissez-faire* prison, and few of us would want to be patients in a *laissez-faire* intensive care ward if we had a heart attack.

Some residents in institutions are likely to remain there for life; some have a definite date for discharge; some have an indeterminate period of care, treatment or confinement ahead of them. The total period of stay may be anywhere between the few days necessary for a tonsillectomy and most of a life-time. We can expect these factors to affect the attitude of the resident to the institution and of the institution to the resident; and the adaptation of the resident may vary at particular times during his stay, particularly where this is of a fixed duration. A Harvard sociologist, Stanton Wheeler, has recently contributed some interesting reflections on the dynamics of prisonization – the variation in the prisoner's attitude to the demands of prison life at the beginning, the middle and the end of his period of imprisonment.

We cannot treat the subject of institutions as though all institutional populations shared the same attitudes and motivation; as though all were confined, not only against their will, but for no useful purpose; as though all were equally capable at all times of full social functioning; and as though all shared indefinite or life-long confinement. The Literature of Dysfunction has tended to confuse the elements in criticism by treating the institutional situation as a whole. What exactly is being criticized? There is criticism of out-dated buildings; of low material standards; of large units; of authoritarian structure; of peer-group living – that is, of people living with others like themselves rather than in the more varied family setting; and of the unity of domestic, occupational and leisure-time roles.

Criticism of out-dated buildings and of low material standards seems to me to be wholly justified. This is our heritage from the Victorian age, and how quickly we can get rid of it depends on a straight question of economics: what priority we, as a nation, are prepared to accord to it in the allocation of national resources. The difficulty is that, as long as institutions as such are subject to public disapproval, it will be very difficult to get the money for up-grading and re-building.

Criticism of large units and authoritarian structures involves more difficult issues. We are all in favour of small units. So were some of the Victorians – Lord Shaftesbury campaigned over a period of fifty years or more for small mental hospitals, of not more than 500 beds, and yet they grew in size in spite of him. We are still in a period of expanding population. By the year 2000 we can expect a population of around 72 million, and it will be very surprising if small units do not still tend to get bigger, and the large old units do not disappear as fast as we would hope. Another factor is that our desire for small units conflicts with what is happening to the professions. In social work, medicine, nursing and allied professions, the tendency is for specialism to increase, and for career structures to develop more rungs on the ladder. Small units cannot support specialist staff, nor provide promotion opportunities. The answer must be some sort of federal structure, in which small units can have a life of their own within a larger unit; thus, in place of one large mental hospital of 3,000 beds, one might have ten small ones of 300 beds under group management; but this will call for complex techniques, and is again dependent on our power to re-build.

The question of authoritarian structure is not an easy one. In some kinds of institutions there must be authority, reasonably and wisely exercised; but what is reasonable authority and how do we induce staff to stop at what is reasonable? I think this is mainly a training question. As staff are better trained, they will become more aware of the social and psychological issues in institutional management. Perhaps many institutional staff could begin with a course in the Literature of Dysfunction; but social scientists will have to help to build up a Literature of Function by making positive proposals for good group interaction, rather than being content with largely negative criticism. It may be that help will come partly from psychiatry (where the 'therapeutic community' movement, despite some theoretical naïveté, offers clues to the humane and responsible conduct of institutional groups), and partly from the small but growing interest in social group-work in this country.

The last two factors – criticism of peer-group living and of the unity of domestic, occupational and leisure roles – involve sociological issues which have so far received little attention. Does Goffman's criticism of 'batch living' apply primarily to these factors, or to those of size and authoritarianism when he writes of 'large groups of managed people'? Is the criticism valid when it applies to comparatively small groups of people living in a democratic community, as in the Israeli kibbutzim? Or to large groups in the comparatively affluent circumstances of a residential university or a public school? Is the unit of domestic, occupational and leisure roles really undesirable in itself, or does it merely seem so to modern commuters? If town-planners are to be believed, the twentieth-century urban situation which creates a pattern of living in one area, working in another, and seeking recreation in a third has its undesirable features.

It may be that, where an institution has reasonably good material standards; where it is run with a reasonable sensitivity to the needs and human rights of its residents; where it is small, or where subgroups can be organized on a meaningful basis; above all where the institution has a useful purpose, and offers better facilities than any of the actual alternatives, the fact that it involves a pattern of living other than that of the life of the nuclear family may not in itself be harmful. In other words, much of the protest against institutions is rightly directed, not against institutions as such, but against bad ones.

To sum up, I have attempted to look at the reasons for three phenomena: why institutions developed at all; why they became large and punitive and depersonalized in the nineteenth century; and why there has recently been an outburst of protest against them. I have tried to analyse the bases of this protest, and to separate out those factors which result from historical accident (and so are remediable given time and money) from those which involve conceptual problems. The problems – of optimum size and the nature of authority, and above all of motivation and social interaction – are formidable; but in some form or other, institutions are likely to be a permanent part of the social scene; so perhaps it is time we made a start.

The Objectives of the New Local Social Service

Peter Townsend

Reprinted with permission from (Ed.) Peter Townsend, *The Fifth Social Service: A Critical Analysis of the Seebohm Report*, Fabian Society 1970, pp. 7-21

All planning must involve the formulation of objectives. The Seebohm Committee was appointed on 20 December 1965 to 'review the organization and responsibilities of the local authority personal social services in England and Wales, and to consider what changes are desirable to secure an effective family service.' The committee decided that these terms of reference allowed them to consider the needs of individuals and married couples as well as families and to inquire into the whole of the work of children's and welfare departments and those elements of the work of health, education and housing departments which were concerned with social work. The scope of the inquiry could therefore be widely drawn. Events in Scotland had moved more swiftly. The Kilbrandon Report in 1964 led to a working group being set up which reported on reorganization of services in 1966. This resulted quickly in legislation.

How should the Seebohm Committee have set about the job of defining policy objectives? There are a number of awkward alternatives. First, subjective opinions can be collected from both consumers and suppliers of services about the quality of existing services, how they might be improved in the future and what new services might be added. The comments of those with direct current experience of particular services can be illuminating but the comments of others may be largely meaningless. The opinions of individuals offer little guidance to the policy-maker unless they are founded on information and experience. Even then it is difficult to evaluate them without a knowledge of the social circumstances and situation of those expressing them. The same is true of subjective expressions of need. The individual may feel deprived even if others consider he has no cause to feel like this and even if there appear to be no objective criteria to justify his feeling. Equally, he may deny any need whatsoever and yet be destitute, ill or live in squalor. Subjective deprivation is subtle and hard to ascertain, because there are social rules and situations which govern whether or not and when it will be expressed, and yet this information is not superfluous. It is one bit of vital information in planning.

Second, there are conventional or social 'views' or definitions of needs and standards of service. These too can be identified and collected. There are social norms about the upbringing of children, the care of the ill and the handicapped and the help that should be given to families who are poor. These are often implicit in behaviour, organization and opinion rather than consciously formulated, and have to be analysed out. Sometimes they form the basis of law and regulation. For example, Government and local authority regulations embody social views about decent standards of housing and the point at which houses or flats are treated as overcrowded. Different societies (and indeed different sections of any single society) may define these standards differently but in principle the social scientist can measure the extent to which they are or are not met. He can help a society to understand how practice may differ from precept. How many in the population fall below the poverty line as defined socially by public assistance scales? How many are living in conditions treated by society as unsanitary or overcrowded? How many are in need of hospital care, residential care, sheltered housing, rehabilitation, special schooling, domiciliary service and so on, according to criteria implicit or explicit in laws and regulations and government policy statements? In examining social or normative definitions of need the social scientist can help to bring them into the open, reveal contradictions and loose ends and show the different functions played by law, regulation, policy and custom. He can even show the degrees of efficiency with which different standards are being met and therefore suggest what might be gained with alternative emphases in policy.

This gives a rough outline of a two-stage procedure or model that might be followed in planning. Certainly we would have a basis for comparing subjective with collectively acknowledged need, and policy aims with policy achievements. He could pursue the connections between the rise of subjective deprivation in particular groups and professions, change in society's definition of need and change in society's services and practices.

But this would be insufficient as a basis for planning. Social policy would be viewed too much from within, psychologically and institutionally. Services would be judged too much in terms of objectives already defined than of those which have yet to be defined, too much in terms of needs already recognized, subjectively and socially, than of those which have still to be recognized. Standards and needs have to be judged also from some external standpoint. While ultimately it may be difficult to substantiate a true objectivity, nonetheless this goal is worth striving for. Needs can be shown to exist, independent of the feelings engendered within a particular society and independent of those which are recognized by society's institutions. Just as there is subjective deprivation and socially acknowledged deprivation, so there is objective deprivation. A man may not feel deprived and he may not even meet society's rules defining someone who is deprived and yet he may be shown to be deprived. He lacks what his fellows can be demonstrated to have and suffers in some tangible and measurable way as a consequence.

This would complete a three part model for the analysis of social policy and the production of policy objectives. But how could need be defined objectively? How could standards be evolved, independent of those that have been developed historically and which society recognizes? The interconnections between the concepts of inequality and deprivation provide the best answer. Inequality has two aspects. There is inequality of resources: individuals and families fall into horizontal strata, according to their incomes, assets, fringe benefits received from employers, and benefits in kind received from the public social services. Through rigorous comparison between regions and communities as well as individuals and families the inequalities in the distribution of resources can be revealed in elaborate detail, including, for example, inequalities of space at home, working conditions and school facilities. There is also inequality of social integration: individuals, families and ethnic communities fail into vertical categories according to the degree of isolation or segregation from society. People vary in the density and range of their household, family, community and social networks: and some populations of hospitals and other institutions are extraordinarily isolated. There are inequalities of social support in illness, infirmity, disability and bereavement. While planning cannot make good private loss it can provide substitute and compensating services. Visiting services can be developed for the isolated elderly and home help services for the infirm and disabled. Services like teaching in English and information and legal aid services can also be developed as integrating mechanisms and protection against exploitation for immigrant communities.

Complementing these two measures of inequality would be measures of deprivation. In descending the scale of income or of other resources, such as assets, there is a point at which the individual's or the family's participation in the ordinary activities, customs and pleasures of the community is likely to fall off more sharply than the reduction of income. His opportunities to share in the pursuits and meet the needs enjoined by the culture become grossly restricted. As a consequence he may be malnourished, inadequately housed, disadvantaged in schooling, unable to use public services like buses and trains, and restricted to impoverished sectors of the social services. If he belongs to an ethnic group which feels itself to be cold-shouldered by external society and which responds by turning in upon its own improvised resources he runs the risk of being by-passed by new scientific and cultural developments, excluded from the ordinary range of information and communication media, ignorant of legal and welfare rights and left with the housing, the land and the commodities least desired by outsiders. If he is someone isolated from the community because he has not married, has been bereaved, has lost contemporaries during the ageing process, has become separated from family and friends because of work or migration, is disabled or lives in a sparsely populated area, or is affected by a number of these factors, he may not be put in touch with health and welfare services at necessary times, may remain unaware of social developments (for example, rent rebate schemes, decimal coinage, new advances in reading and hearing aids) and *become* deprived and perhaps liable to exploitation even if not deprived beforehand. The interaction of the two kinds of inequality – poverty of resources and isolation – can have devastating consequences for some sections of the population during periods of rapid technological and institutional change.

Such is a possible framework of thought and analysis. How

did the Seebohm Committee proceed? First, subjective opinion.
Through memoranda presented as evidence and through various
consultations the Committee learned the views of suppliers of
services. The opinions of 'all those concerned with the services'
were felt to be important but the opinions of those utilizing the
services were not collected. 'We were, regrettably, unable to
sound consumer reaction to the services in any systematic
fashion' (p. 21). This decision was taken, the Committee say,
because a research programme would have delayed publication
by a year or two. But the Committee took $2\frac{1}{2}$ years to report, and
the Government took a further 20 months to react to the report.
Much research of value could have been launched, even if some
of it could not have reached fruition until the months following
the publication of the report. The gross lack of information about
the nature and functions of the services covered by the Committee and about consumer opinion, could hardly have gone
unnoticed. The Younghusband Committee on local authority
social workers had toiled for $3\frac{1}{2}$ years in the late 1950s and had
dared to conclude 'We should like to have undertaken a complementary inquiry into the reactions of those using the services.
An investigation of this nature would, however, have prolonged
our own inquiries unduly.' And they went on, 'We were struck
. . . by the lack of any systematic study of the part played by
social workers in meeting needs within the framework of the
social services. Such information could have had an important
bearing on our own inquiry. We should like to draw attention to
the desirability of such study. We think much of the confusion in
regard to the functions of social workers in the health and welfare
services, as elsewhere, is due to lack of analyses of this kind.'

But the Seebohm Committee appear to have ignored this
recommendation and failed to clear up the confusion. Other
committees have instigated and brought to a successful culmina-
tion very large research inquiries within a similar time span.
The Robbins Committee on Higher Education, for example, had
launched a very ambitious research programme and yet had
reported within two and a half years.

The implications of failing to find out consumer opinion run
deep. Some far-reaching criticisms of professional activity may
be either undetected or underestimated. Some needs which are
felt by individuals or groups may be ignored. Most important,

some of the rights of the consumer to a voice in planning and administration may be unrecognized.

SOCIAL STANDARDS

The Seebohm Committee did in fact go some way towards fulfilling the second and third parts of our planning model. They attempted to present conventional views on needs and standards of service. They also attempted to collate statistics giving objective measures of need. However, such secondary analysis as was carried out was neither complete nor consistent.

For example, insufficient effort was made to define the criteria by which people are helped by the existing services and to subject these to searching examination. A rather haphazard collection of over a hundred pages of appendices attached to the Committee's report contain chiefly an account of administrative structure and statistics, and the data are not digested and integrated with the argument in the body of the text. What are existing standards of service? Which children are taken into care and why? How are homeless families defined in practice, and is it logical to exclude single persons and married couples from services? Which disabled persons are placed on registers and how does this vary among the different areas of the country? These are the kinds of question which have to be answered in detail if the standards of service which prevail at present are to be delineated.

Again, the attempts to measure objectively the extent of unmet need were very clumsy. Such attempts can determine the conclusions which may be reached not only about the *structure* but also the *scale* and *scope* of a future service. Thus it is vital to ask whether there are any important needs which are totally unmet at present and for which new social services might be developed. In terms of possible contribution to social integration there might be a public radio-telephone service and a transport service for certain disabled or elderly persons and their relatives and friends; an architect and design service for do-it-yourself enthusiasts; a mobile national housing repairs and improvement squad; neighbourhood and home tuition in speaking and writing English for immigrant families and handicapped pupils; and a shopping and sightseeing touring service for the hospitalized and infirm. Only by systematic study of social inequalities, comparing the circumstances of different families and individuals and comparing the real functions of the social services with implicit as well as explicit social objectives can these lacunae be revealed. The Seebohm Committee did not produce guidelines for fresh developments in social policy as a result of analysing social conditions and policies.

However, it did not measure possible developments in existing services either. Chapters on services for children, old people, the physically handicapped, the mentally ill and subnormal, other local health services and housing seem to have been allocated to different authors. This must partly explain their uneven quality. Some of these neglect valuable sources of information. For example, there is no analysis of trends in the development of services in relation to previous and prospective changes in population structure. Some chapters, like that on old people, mix the trivial with the crucial as if they were of equal importance. Present shortcomings are, however, emphasized. But they are emphasized without corresponding documentation and therefore lose thrust and power. A refrain runs through a number of the chapters. The services for children are 'sadly inadequate' (p. 53); for old people 'underdeveloped, limited and patchy' (p. 90); housing for old people 'quite inadequate' (p. 92); services for the physically handicapped 'in urgent need of development' (p. 101); for the chronic sick 'seriously inadequate' (p. 118); and community care for the mentally disordered 'still a sad illusion and judging by published plans will remain so for years ahead' (p. 107). Yet the Committee failed to bring these indictments together in a major challenge to the Government and public to find massive new resources for the creation of a major new service. Consider the weak advocacy in the introductory pages for a single department and in particular the incomprehensible surrender of judgements about social need to judgements about what is politically expedient in the statement that 'it would be naïve to think that any massive additional resources will be made available in the near future' (p. 15). Even if the Committee believed this to be true why did they have to say so and withhold an argument which might have won public imagination and induced a readiness to provide more resources?

By failing to document the extent to which services also fell short of needs the Committee made it difficult for priorities and the eventual structure of the service to be defined. The nearest it came in fact to specifying requirements on the basis of evidence was in the first few paragraphs of its discussion of services for children. The Committee accepted an estimate from appendix Q that '*at least* one child in ten in the population will need special educational, psychiatric or social help before it reaches the age of 18 but that at present *at most* one child in twenty-two is receiving such help' (p. 53). This is a deceptively exact statement. What does it mean? The estimate of need includes children who are in poverty, have a whole range of physical handicaps, including asthma and speech defects, are subnormal and have psychiatric disorders, are in homeless and fatherless families, as well as children who are taken into care and delinquent boys 'with at least three court appearances'. Quite a variety of trouble. And the reader who attempts to find which needs are least well met will emerge utterly baffled after studying appendix Q. One table includes statistics of the number of children experiencing a condition at a particular time (poverty) and a condition at any time during the first seventeen years of life (admitted to care). There is no discussion of the extent to which the local authority children's service fails to meet need. All that can safely be concluded is that the bulk of unmet needs are those – for special education and training, psychiatric supervision, health services, housing, home help, and financial help – which lie outside the scope of the children's service, as presently administered. But in discussing the new social service department the consequences for its structure and functions are not drawn by the Committee.

Yet this matter is crucial if we are to decide what should be the character and function of the future service. If material aid is to be dominant then casework may have to be minimal. If the children's part of the social work services is already reasonably well-developed then the fastest growing parts may be those for the elderly and disabled. This too will be crucial in determining the direction which the new service takes and the kind of staff required. In appendix L the Committee lists 90,000 staff working in 1966 in services proposed for inclusion in the new Seebohm department. Only 7,700 of them were child-care officers and other social workers. There may be a greater need for a small number of highly trained planners and managerial staff and for a large number of ancillary workers, like home helps and visitors, who receive short spells of training, than for a much larger middle tier of field-workers with a fairly lengthy training.

THE RESULTING AIMS OF THE NEW SERVICE

The relationship between research or the collection of evidence and the identification of need is therefore critical. And it is the identification of need on the basis of demonstrable inequality of resources and of degree of social integration that can justify the choice of objectives and the specification of those objectives. It was because the Seebohm Committee did not properly establish needs that it did not properly formulate the aims of the new service. If the reader combs the report he will not find a full and unamibiguous statement of the aims of the service. This criticism should not be misunderstood. There are numerous statements about the possible aims of the new service, but these are mostly 'second-order' aims. Thus, amalgamation is said to give the service more power to speak up for a rightful share of resources within local administration and help to make the service more adequate (pp. 30, 32-3 and 46-7). It is said to break down artificial boundaries between services, reduce divided responsibility and lead to better co-ordination and continuity (pp. 31, 34-5 and 44-5). It is said to allow the development of more emphasis on preventive as compared with casualty services for social distress (pp. 136-41). A number of specific aims are also expressed in the chapters on particular services.

But perhaps the best general statement about aims is the first paragraph of Chapter 7 of the report:

We are convinced that if local authorities are to provide an effective family service they must assume wider responsibilities than they have at present for the prevention, treatment and relief of social problems. The evidence we have received, the visits we have undertaken, and our own experience leave us in no doubt that the resources at present allocated to these tasks are quite inadequate. Much more ought to be done, for example, for the very old and the under fives, for physically and mentally handicapped people in the community, for disturbed adolescents and for the neglected flotsam and jetsam of society. Moreover, the ways in which existing resources are organized and deployed are inefficient. Much more ought to be done in the fields of prevention, community involvement, the guidance of voluntary workers and in making fuller use of voluntary organizations. We believe that the best way of achieving these ends is by setting up a unified social service department which will include the present children's and welfare services together with some of the social service functions of health, education and housing departments (p. 44).

An impression is given of inchoate, multiple aims and loose reasoning. Is the primary purpose to provide family services for those who lack a family or whose family resources are meagre? If so, there would be profound implications for the organization of residential homes and hostels for children, the elderly and the mentally and physically handicapped. Either the residential homes would all have to be run on a 'family' basis, which is an aim that would require detailed exposition or a policy of closing them down and integrating their occupants in different types of private households would have to be followed. There would be profound implications also for professional social work roles, staffing and training. The system would have to be recast to a very considerable extent.

In opening the debate on the second reading of the Bill in the House of Commons the Secretary of State for Social Services, Mr Crossman, plainly felt the need for a statement of aims. He said:

The primary objective of the personal social services we can best describe as strengthening the capacity of the family to care for its members and to supply, as it were, the family's place where necessary; that is, to provide as far as may be social support or if necessary a home for people who cannot look after themselves or be adequately looked after in their family. This is not the only objective of the personal social services. They have an important role to play in community development, for example. But it has been the idea of forming a 'family' service that has inspired the call for a review of the organization of the services with which the Bill is concerned.

He did not attempt to spell out what this view would imply for the reorganization of services. Had he attempted to do so; or had the Seebohm Committee done so beforehand, the recommendations would have taken a different form and there might not have been such a friendly welcome to the Bill from all political quarters in Parliament.

For the really important issues have been ducked in securing a precarious consensus. What kind of family relationships should the State support, and in what circumstances? How far must residential institutions be abandoned in favour of true community care? Is professional independence and the opportunity for the expression of public dissent threatened by monolithic bureaucratic conformity? Is the social worker an agent of social control or an articulate representative of minority interests and views? Should community development include a network of information and legal services, a policy of racial integration and an extension of democracy by means of local pressure-groups and protest groups?

A POLICY FOR SEEBOHM DEPARTMENTS

A radical statement of objectives would have to start by revealing the extent of inequality of resources and of social isolation and separation. Community development would be seen in terms of the equalization of resources, the reduction of isolation, family support and community integration. I will describe these briefly in turn.

Although national social services, such as social insurance, family allowances and taxation, would be primarily concerned with the redistribution of resources, local social services have a major part to play in equalizing amenities, providing special kinds of housing, supplementing transport services for the elderly and disabled, supplying aids in the home for the handicapped, delivering meals, undertaking housing repairs and improvement, and restocking houses which have become denuded because of debts, drug addiction, alcoholism or a husband's desertion. The identification and mobilization of resource needs would be a major part of the work of the social worker. The Seebohm department should take the initiative locally in equalizing facilities between different sub-areas of the authority and identifying and meeting the special needs of particular communities. For this there must be an area resource plan.

Second, the reduction of isolation. One important means of achieving this is by organizing routine visiting services. The Seebohm Committee lamentably failed to understand the importance of these, particularly as a means of prevention and developing comprehensive services. Once routine visiting and assessment is started many sceptics will finally become convinced of the need to expand services. A start could be made with services for people of advanced age, later extending to all the elderly and to the handicapped, including families with handicapped children. One valuable feature of such a service is that social workers would check systematically whether people were receiving the various local and national benefits for which they were eligible. Isolation can also be greatly reduced by means of day clubs and centres, group holidays and improved methods of communication (including telephones). By extension to ethnic groups the same principles can be applied.

Third, support for the family. We have to remind ourselves that any policy aimed at replacing the family is inconceivable in present or prospective conditions. The Seebohm Committee did not consider the evidence that exists of the functions played by the family, and its strengths and shortcomings as a means of obtaining insights into policy. Certainly the 'welfare' work of the family for children, the handicapped and the aged, dwarfs that of the officially established social services. And certainly family relationships help to keep people in touch with the feelings and problems of all age-groups, and also help them achieve a sense of individual identity and integrate them with a variety of social groups. Those with slender family resources are those who most commonly receive and need the help of welfare services. Home help services can include shopping, laundry, night attendance, evening relief and accompanied outings, as well as the preparation of meals and domestic cleaning. Several research reports have shown that they need to be expanded rapidly. A recent official survey found that the home help service could be doubled or tripled. Adoption and foster-care in approved conditions are extensions of the same principles.

The aim of supporting the family, however, merges into the fourth aim, that of community integration. Any logical development of a policy of family support must lead to a policy of community as against institutional care. The Seebohm Committee equivocated between the two and did not call attention to the fact, for example, that nearly three times as much is spent by local authorities on residential institutions as on home-help services for the elderly and disabled. It also failed to anticipate and resolve a possible conflict between the personnel from children's and welfare departments. The aim of the former has been broadly to keep children with their parents in their own homes and when that cannot be done to place them in foster homes or residential units similar in structure and operation to the family household. I believe that this policy should be applied consistently to handicapped adults and the elderly as well, and that the subjective and objective evidence so far collected supports it. Yet because in the past the local authority welfare department has lacked the means it has practised a rather different policy, of swelling the number of small residential institutions.

The Seebohm Committee recommended that the home-help service should be transferred to the new department but did not see the importance of placing the provision and management of sheltered housing under the same auspices. If at the time of admission to residential institutions the handicapped and the elderly (and their relatives) had a genuine choice of either sheltered housing in the community (with home services if necessary) or a residential institution the vast majority would opt for the former and be capable of living there up to the time of requiring admission to hospital.

Demand for residential institutions would decline. The new Seebohm departments could not of course start shutting down residential institutions overnight but they could adopt bold but feasible plans giving priority to sheltered housing and home services and gradually reduce residential accommodation. Residential institutions for the elderly and infirm could be transferred by stages to the new area health authorities and placed under the charge of geriatricians and others concerned with the nursing and medical care of those who are incapacitated. This would concentrate the attentions of the new Seebohm-type departments upon community care.

There are other arguments for reducing the emphasis on long-term institutional care, as shown in the anxious discussion going on recently about hospitals for the mentally handicapped. There is evidence in many cases of loss of contacts with relatives and friends without the substitution of social relations with fellow residents. There is the restriction of occupational activity and evidence of loneliness and apathy – by comparison with people of comparable age and physical condition outside. And quite apart from the deplorably low standards of amenities there is also the organizational rigidity of institutional life, which inevitably creates severe problems of adjustment and integration for residents from diverse backgrounds. Many old people are dismayed at the interruption of a life-time's routine, loss of contact with locality and family and reduction of privacy and identity. The closer a residential institution approximates to the scale, privacy and freedom of the private householder the greater the qualified expression of contentment. The promise in policy to protect people from admission to institutions except in extreme ill-health could attract public enthusiasm for the new service. In the 1950s and 1960s 'community care' has been interpreted variously and because of this is regarded with a measure of cynicism by some students, doctors and social workers. Even the term 'community' has no settled meaning in the social sciences. But if presented along the lines outlined here, of the equalization of resources, support of the family, and support for the individual to maintain a private household and an 'ordinary' pattern of local relations as opposed to entering a communal institution community care can become a meaningful objective.

Community integration means more, however, than community care. It means the promotion of citizen rights and of certain kinds of group activity. Tony Lynes puts the problem succinctly: 'The poor, as such, are in a weak bargaining position. The circumstances which make them poor also tend to make them powerless. Short of violent protest, just how are the homeless and the slum-dwellers, the disabled and the fatherless, to become a force on their own behalf?' The Seebohm department can foster this self-assertiveness but only if its relationship with local democracy is carefully worked out, its professional semi-independence of local bureaucracy emphasized and the nature of and training for social work restated. This is a tall order. Perhaps the best chapter in the Seebohm Report is on community development:

The term 'community development' is used primarily to denote work with neighbourhood groups. Community development in this country is seen as a process whereby local groups are assisted to clarify and express their needs and objectives and to take collective action to attempt to meet them. It emphasizes the involvement of the people themselves in determining and meeting their own needs. The role of the community worker is that of a source of information and expertise, a stimulator, a catalyst and an encourager (p. 148).

This view was cautiously presented, however, as adding to existing conceptions of social work rather than replacing them. Extra appointments and experiments were recommended. Certainly the conception of group work is beginning to be worked out in more detail. Much can be done in organizing tenants' associations, groups of mental hospital outpatients and of drug addicts, the homeless and so on. But group work can only be developed effectively if there are swift improvements in information services, legal services and political machinery.

Local political machinery has not been examined carefully in relation to community development and the evolution of the local social services. The Redcliffe-Maud Commission did not devote very much attention to this question and the opportunity was not taken up in the Government's White Paper on local government reform. There is a haphazard mushrooming of new procedures. The proposals of the Skeffington Report for a community forum and community development officers and of the Green Paper on the Health Service need to be linked with the work of the Community Relations Council and Race Relations Board, the Home Office experiments in community development, Ministry of Housing experiments in urban aid and the Seebohm proposals for the participation of the public in the local social services. Much more coherent systems of public involvement in the management of the social services (schools, residential homes, hospitals, day centres and so on), complaints procedures, and accountability of those administering services need to be worked out. At every level the traditional British assumption of the appropriateness of a hierarchical 'class' structure needs to be questioned. The consumer should have a much stronger voice in many different and even modest contexts. There is no reason, for

314 Social Welfare in Modern Britain

example, why old people in residential homes should not have a representative committee which could advise on a diary of events, the menu, the operating rules of management and other relevant matters.

The Seebohm departments should offer information shops in shopping centres. But the main national network of information services should be administered independently of local government.

From aiding and abetting the individual and the family by providing information in a digestible form, it is a logical next step to offer better legal services and to relate the two. In recent years there has been a growth of interest in the social responsibilities of the legal profession. Legal aid for poor families is grossly restricted and is mainly taken up with aid for matrimonial proceedings. There is a strong argument for a two-stage development in information and legal centres. Experimental schemes to increase the amount and quality of legal aid and advice should be financed by the Government and an incentive scheme introduced to encourage a better distribution of lawyers and persuade more of them to work in poor areas. At a second stage, a National Citizens' Rights Council should be established with members appointed by the Crown on the advice of the Lord Chancellor. The Government's record in reforming and extending legal services has been dismal and there is as yet little realization of what can be done to buttress and accelerate community development and the extension of democracy through an expansionist policy for legal and information services. In the meantime the Child Poverty Action Group established in April 1970 an experimental Citizens' Rights Office, including both legal and information services under its director, Mrs Audrey Harvey. Some other experiments are being tried elsewhere, for example in Notting Hill, London. Inevitably such experimental offices will need to have very close relations with the new Seebohm departments, and can do much to offer short courses of training in welfare rights to social workers.

The repercussions for the type of work undertaken by Seebohm-type departments would be considerable. There would be greater stress on the provision of information, the exploration and notification of need for financial, material and domestic aid, the initiation of contacts between families in need and appropriate pressure-groups as well as appropriate social and occupational groups, and, finally, representation of the needs and problems of families to authority – housing and education departments, supplementary benefit offices, the new lower tier local councils proposed by the Redcliffe-Maud Commission and the district committees proposed by the Green Paper on the Health Services, as well as the new main councils and the central departments of government. All this demands a large measure of professional autonomy on the part of senior staff. It also has ramifications for the training and ideology of social workers.

What is at stake is the quality of family and community life and the whole direction of community development. Is the new Seebohm service to be a poorly financed, meagre department which takes the edge off the distress and deprivation arising in modern society and which, in effect, reinforces the assumptions of an increasingly inegalitarian society? Or is it to be the fifth major social service, of a scale equivalent, eventually, in man-power and expenditure to the health, education, housing and social security services which has a deliberate commitment to the reduction of inequalities of resources and of social isolation, whether of individuals or groups?

A force for conformity to hierarchical society, or a force for non-conformity in an equal one?

Further Reading
The Reorganization of the Social Services

B. ABEL-SMITH and R. STEVENS, *In Search of Justice*, Allen Lane, 1968.

R. G. S. BROWN, *The Administrative Process in Britain*, Methuen, 1970.

U. CORMACK, 'The Seebohm Committee Report – A Great State Paper', *Social and Economic Administration*, vol. 3, no. 1, January, 1969.

HMSO, *People and Planning* (The Skeffington Report), 1969.

M. JEFFERYS, *An Anatomy of Social Welfare Services*, Michael Joseph, 1965.

M. KOGAN and J. TERRY, *The Organization of a Social Service Department*, Bookstall Publications, 1971.

R. MAIR, 'Reform of the Welfare Services', *Social Service Quarterly*, vol. 43, no. 2, October-December, 1969.

M. REIN, 'The Social Service Crisis', *Trans-Action*, 1970.

P. TOWNSEND, *The Last Refuge*, Routledge & Kegan Paul, 1962.

J. WARHAM, *An Introduction to Administration for Social Workers*, Routledge & Kegan Paul, 1967.

Chapter Six

New Developments in
Social Welfare

Few social scientists would now dispute that social deprivations – or unmet social needs – are still found extensively in our society. Readings in previous chapters have illustrated not just the varied attempts of the social services to meet these needs but also the comparative failure of established mechanisms, such as Supplementary Benefit, planning and social work, to achieve full success. However, the challenge of deprivation has not been ignored. The reorganization of the personal social services, described in Chapter 5, was an effort to maximize welfare efficiency. In addition, recent years have witnessed the emergence of major new approaches to meet social needs. This chapter, therefore, will focus on five modern developments. Two of these – the urban programme and the Family Income Supplement – were initiated by the central Government in order to direct more resources to those in greatest need. Two concern the attempts of social workers to utilize their skills more fully on behalf of the deprived; and the fifth concerns a major development outside the traditional social services – community action. The new features have not been without their detractors and in this introduction mention will be made of their points of view. The readings themselves serve both to describe and justify the new approaches.

THE URBAN PROGRAMME

During the 1960s, three factors contributed to the emergence of a novel Government initiative. They were the identification of concentrations of social deprivation in definable geographical areas, the realization that some local authorities lacked the resources to cope with their problems, and the knowledge that, abroad, the American Government had instituted a new agency to lead a war on poverty. The final spur to action came with the evidence that many black immigrants to Britain, unable to find alternative homes, were adding to the numbers in 'inner ring' zones. Consequently, in 1968 the Labour Government announced the creation of an urban programme that would direct extra resources to the areas of greatest need.

The urban programme is in two parts. The urban programme itself (sometimes called urban aid) allocates extra cash into needy areas. The community development project (CDP) allows the setting up of teams of workers in selected local authorities. The reading by **John Edwards** provides a useful outline of the structure and practice of the first. He shows that amongst the urban programme's achievements are the stimulation of new services for children and the winning of the interest of voluntary organizations (who can also apply for the extra resources providing their local authorities accept and forward their proposals). The urban programme is not the first Government effort to adopt a 'priority' approach, but it is noteworthy for offering aid for a vast range of projects not confined within the bounds of any one local authority department's responsibility; and as such, it is worthy of study. At the same time, the urban aid programme has been subjected to a number of criticisms which can now be mentioned.

A central feature of the urban programme's administration is that the responsible ministry, the Home Office, invites bids from local authorities and voluntary groups and *then* decides who should receive the money. This system has been criticized on the grounds that some councils, although having areas of high social need, have not submitted bids either because they lacked the technical skills to quickly make out a case, or because they did not wish to be publicly known as a 'deprived area'. The allocation decisions have similarly been challenged in that they do not always favour the areas in greatest need. For instance, it has been pointed out that phase six of the urban programme allocated half its funds for play schemes to the London boroughs although play resources are more extensively developed there than in any other part of the country. Further, some local authorities have protested that the 25 per cent of costs which they are asked to contribute is too high and claim that what they do receive is not really extra income in that the total is deducted from the Rate Support Grant which the Government already distributes between all local authorities. Some voluntary groups have also expressed dissatisfaction asserting that the local authorities' powers to veto voluntary bids means in general that voluntary bodies receive a small slice of the cake and in particular that 'radical' groups have little chance of gaining approval. These many criticisms no doubt arise because of differing expectations about the programme's objectives. On occasions the Home Office has stated that the purpose is to strengthen existing services, 'as a supplement and not an alternative to what local authorities may be expected to do'. At other times, it claims an innovating role declaring that the money is for 'those projects which lie outside the field in which local authorities are active in the ordinary way'. Such confusion is reflected in the different interpretations made about the urban programme.

Whatever the final opinion, any evaluation must be put against the diminutive nature of the urban programme's resources. The total allocation of some of its phases would not buy a first division football player! Yet it does constitute a new means of allocating resources and of stimulating activity within deprived areas. Providing its criteria for allocating funds and its objectives can be clarified, there will be much support for the statement by a leading politician, Roy Jenkins, that its resources should be expanded to £120 million a year.

The Government's community development project is also financed from urban programme money but is otherwise quite distinct. It consists of twelve deprived areas where the Home Office and local authorities have co-operated to set up a small team of workers and researchers. The CDP was based on the assumptions that residents of deprived areas possessed untapped capacities which could be used to free them from dependency on the social services and that existing social welfare agencies were not effectively reaching those in need. The manner in which practice was developed around these assumptions is well brought out in the reading by **John Benington,** the director of the Coventry CDP. It constitutes an

impressive account of efforts to intervene into social
deprivation at varied points.

Early radical criticisms of the CDP did not question the
need for direct intervention into areas of high social need.
However, three points were made about the nature and size of
the new initiative. First, it was pointed out that the method
of selecting areas excluded local authorities not willing to
co-operate with the Home Office, authorities often thought to
be the ones who did least for the socially deprived. Second, it
was considered that the insistence on running the projects
through the local authorities would both exclude deprived
residents from having any real control over the experiments
and inhibit the use of conflict strategies in order to achieve
change. Third, it was argued that small demonstration
projects, however successful, were rarely implemented at a
later stage by large-scale action. Indeed, some critics even
considered that small projects were merely a means of delaying
the chances of more fundamental changes. These three
criticisms were joined, at a later date, by those of Frank Field,
the director of the Child Poverty Action Group. He
challenged the CDP's assumptions by arguing, on the one
hand, that poverty was not contained within small geographical
locations and, on the other hand, by claiming that the level
of welfare benefits was so inadequate that a mere improvement
in the communication between social agencies and those in
need would not abolish deprivation.

Interestingly, Benington's reading reveals that the Coventry
CDP, after an initial period, reached conclusions not far
removed from some of the above criticisms. In particular, it
began to define social deprivation as inhering in the social
structures of society as a whole rather than in the attributes
of the deprived themselves. Accordingly, and with
commendable flexibility, its team has commenced to develop
alternative types of services and programmes. When the
Coventry and other CDPs have finished their time it will be of
great importance to discover both how the teams have
attempted to influence national issues from a local base and if
the Government is willing to act on a national scale as a result
of their experiences.

THE FAMILY INCOME SUPPLEMENT (FIS)

If the urban programme was the Labour Government's attempt to concentrate resources on geographical areas in most need, the Family Income Supplement was the Conservative Government's effort to direct money to families in most need.

One of the limitations of Supplementary Benefit is its failure to reach the working poor. Consequently, the Family Incomes Supplement Act (1970) was innovative in creating a significant source of income for families with a full-time worker. In brief, FIS prescribes certain minimum financial levels (related to family size) and allows families to receive half the difference between their income and the prescribed level. The structure of the scheme is explained fully in the reading by **John Stacpoole** although it is necessary to add that levels have been raised since he wrote the piece. From July 1974, the maximum amount that any family (with at least three children) could receive was £7.

In introducing FIS, the Government claimed it was preferable to an increase in family allowances which would have failed to help one-child families. The new benefit thus offered help to a group known to make up a large section of the poor – low wage earners – without limiting it to families of a certain size. FIS, as Stacpoole makes plain, has further advantages. Its receipt is not dependent upon previous insurance contributions: it applies to one-parent families: it can usually be obtained by postal application: and its receipt gives a 'passport' to other financial benefits such as free school meals and NHS prescriptions.

Despite its innovatory nature, FIS has met sustained opposition. In a sense, it subsidizes employers who pay low wages while employees do not fully gain from any wage increases because their income from FIS is thereby reduced. Further, the amounts received from FIS do not necessarily take recipients out of poverty. Not only have the prescribed amounts been criticized for their minimal levels but it must be stressed that only *half* the difference between these and actual incomes is awarded. As the average payment of FIS has been (up to 1973) just over £2, doubts about its effectiveness have been strong. David Barker in a penetrating critique (recommended at the end of this chapter) has also pointed out that employment entails expenditure – such as fares or in the case of single-parent families, the cost of day care – so that many recipients would actually continue to be financially better off by not working and drawing Supplementary Benefit. But the most pungent attack of all concerns the low take-up rate. Only 52 per cent of families considered eligible for FIS actually receive it, a finding attributed to the unpopularity and ineffectiveness of the means-tested aspects of this benefit.

The drawbacks just outlined appear to have received acknowledgement from the suggestion by the Government in 1972 for a new plan involving the abolition of FIS. The Green Paper, *Proposals for a Tax Credit System* (Cmnd 5116), put up for discussion the idea of a single assessment of income not only in order to calculate the income tax to be paid above a certain level but to give out financial benefits to incomes below it. It would replace FIS, the present child tax allowances and family allowances. The following year the *Select Committee on Tax Credit* added that within this scheme a tax credit of at least £2 should be payable to mothers for the first child. The Government has indicated broad approval although saying that a full scheme could not start until at least 1978. As a stop gap, it is considering paying family allowance to families with only one child. The Child Poverty Action Group has intervened to point out that the Tax Credit Scheme fails to include the lower paid and most people in receipt of Supplementary Benefit and would entail the retention of most means-tested benefits except FIS. Instead, it proposes that the same amount of money could be used to increase old age pensions, to pay higher and tax-free family allowances for all children, to provide universal free school dinners and to institute a special payment for single-parent families. Thus both the Government and the CPAG are agreed that FIS should go. Nonetheless it merits prominence as the first Government benefit in modern times to provide significant income maintenance for working families and for acting as the stepping stone to further proposals to modify poverty.

RECENT TRENDS IN SOCIAL WORK

Social work, as a previous chapter explained, has come under fire for having little impact on the material poverty of its clients. Social workers have responded in a number of ways, two of which are the subject of readings in the present chapter. Firstly, many more social workers have turned to welfare rights work as a means of improving the financial position of their clients. Secondly, others have attempted to side with or identify with clients through forms of direct action.

'Welfare rights' is usually taken to mean the entitlement of low income persons to statutory financial or material provisions. The reading by **Jane Streather** strongly advocates that social workers should assume the role of ensuring that those in need obtain all that is their due. Examples of such rights, which are often not taken up, are free health prescriptions and dental treatment, school meals, rent and rate rebates and allowances, educational maintenance grants, FIS and legal aid and advice. Best known is Supplementary Benefit and Jane Streather particularly urges social workers to check the amounts being received by claimants. She believes that welfare rights activity is an integral part of social work in that it can mitigate harsh conditions and enable some families to stay together whereas previously they would have split apart with their children being received into public care.

Any evaluation of welfare rights activity must consider its effects on other social work approaches, on inter-agency relationships and on social policy as a whole. In a book recommended for further reading, Ray Lees has pointed out that some social workers, particularly older ones, are not wholly in favour of the new trends. No doubt, they fear that a pre-occupation with welfare rights will replace the casework skills through which clients have been helped with problems rooted in their own personalities. Opposition from chief officers of social work agencies is also not unknown. On occasions, formal or informal disapproval has stemmed from the fear that welfare rights activity might lead to bad relationships with the agencies against whom it is directed – for instance, the Supplementary Benefits Commission, Housing

Departments or Education Departments. Perhaps the strongest case against a welfare rights strategy, however, has come from the late Professor Titmuss. He pointed out that social security officials have been given certain discretionary powers so that benefits can be partially adjusted according to individuals' needs. He feared that constant welfare rights badgering of officials would lead to a policy decision to protect them by removing discretion and so setting benefits at a completely inflexible level above which no one would receive more, whatever their circumstances.

Replies can be – and have been – made to the above points. It suffices here to record that the evidence suggests that welfare rights is increasingly accepted as legitimate social work activity. Already some Social Service Departments have designated certain officers as welfare rights specialists. Many training courses now incorporate teaching on the knowledge and skills necessary to win entitlements. Indeed, it may be possible to discern the emergence of what Bond calls 'radical casework' which rests on the belief that clients' depriving conditions must be changed before alterations in their individual behaviour can be expected. Welfare rights can be classified as one of the skills of radical casework along with various forms of collective action. However, it is important to note that welfare rights is not usually regarded as replacing traditional ways of social work intervention. Therapeutic treatment for the mentally disordered, emotional counselling for foster parents and children, casework with marital problems and so on are recognized as major social work contributions towards a more humane and happy society. Rather, emphasis on welfare rights is seen as an additional tool to improve, however slightly, the circumstances of persons whose problems spring from the grossly unequal distribution of resources in an affluent society.

Welfare rights is not enough to satisfy all social workers. Certainly, the adherents of *Case Con*, 'the revolutionary magazine for social workers', would seek more profound results than the take up of means-tested benefits. The emergence of *Case Con* is an indication of a radicalization of numbers of social workers and it is worth recording its basic belief that social deprivation can only be abolished when capitalism is replaced by a society 'based on common ownership and democratic control of all the community's resources'. To this end, it has urged its readers to support grass roots organizations of the deprived and to act jointly with trade unionists.

Articles in *Case Con* have stressed a point which is being increasingly perceived by social workers – that the practices of social service agencies and of social workers can, at times, actually perpetuate the deprivations of their clients. They may function to persuade clients to accept intolerable housing conditions, to make them satisfied with the low level of benefits, to define them as, and thereby have them treated as, inadequate. In reaction, a small but growing number of social workers have sought means of showing their dissatisfaction with certain agency practices and their support for those in great social need. The reading by **Carter** and **Barter** describes the steps taken by social workers in Islington. They believed that the policies of their local authority were exacerbating the plight of those needing adequate housing. Hence when squatters moved homeless families into empty property, the social workers made public their support of the deprived and their opposition to any attempts by the council to evict them.

Although by no means typical, the Islington experience does reflect an increasing reluctance by social workers to be used as a tool of social control. Yet it is fair to record that such behaviour has also provoked some condemnation. An organizational viewpoint is that administrative anarchy ensues unless employees accept that their ultimate loyalty is to their paymaster, the employers. The disregard of authority is further criticized for bringing higher social work management into disrepute and so lessening its prospects of winning a larger part of the local authority budget. From a professional angle, the militant tactics can be interpreted as besmirching the image of the British Association of Social Workers and so endangering its chances of achieving reforms by established lobbying and pressure group activities. Finally, there is the contention that identification with militancy will encourage behaviour so unacceptable to society as a whole that a backlash will follow so stopping any possibility of social improvements.

The response, no doubt, of radical social workers is that the prevailing practices of social agencies, social workers and professional associations are not sufficient to promote fundamental changes. The forthcoming years in social work may well be turbulent ones in which the radicals attempt to re-shape agency structures in order to give more voice to client opinion, to re-define the relationship between social workers and clients, and to persuade social workers to offer their primary commitment to societal change rather than to professional prestige.

COMMUNITY ACTION

The readings so far have illustrated developments within the social services and in the roles of social workers. A further marked feature in social welfare in the last decade has occurred outside of established agencies – community action.

The reading by **Richard Bryant** comprises a definitive statement of the nature and scope of community action. He explains that it involves local groups organized in definable geographical areas (or according to functional interests), problems defined in political terms, objectives ranging from immediate neighbourhood improvements to changes in the structure of society, strategies involving bargaining and confrontation, and membership and leadership weighted towards local residents rather than professionals employed by outside statutory bodies.

Tenants associations, claimants unions, local organizations protesting over planning decisions, groups of unsupported mothers, housing action groups, neighbourhood associations etc. have proliferated. Community action of this kind is not new but why has it multiplied in recent years? One interpretation involves the belief that in a period when the differences between the deprived and the privileged have become more apparent, traditional means of obtaining social redress have been found wanting. Social services have expanded but not with the result of abolishing poverty. Planning techniques have been established but, as Chapter 3 explained, redevelopment plans can still ignore the needs and

desires of the weakest members of society. The poor have
reason to doubt that elected local government representatives
adequately serve their interests and voting returns as low as
25 per cent or less are not uncommon in deprived wards. Both
major political parties have been accused of employing
selection procedures which overwhelmingly favour
parliamentary candidates from homogeneous public school or
Oxbridge backgrounds thereby discriminating against the bulk
of the population. The Labour Party is even held to have
deserted working-class interests and a recent important study
of it by Barry Hindess is significantly entitled *The Decline of
Working Class Politics*. With such democratic shortcomings
perceived in the once much vaunted British political system,
many persons concerned to combat poverty and deprivation
have sought in community action a means outside traditional
channels.

Whatever the reasons for the rise of community action,
there is no questioning that it has made an impact. The
positive side is discussed by Bryant in terms of its local
successes and qualitative changes. To provide a balance, it is
necessary here to mention some negative views. First
participants in community action have been called 'conflict
mongers' with the scarcely veiled innuendo that they are
interested only in causing trouble. Second, community action,
when directed against statutory departments, is said to reduce
public confidence in the integrity and efficiency of local and
central government. Third, some local authority councillors
have argued that community action is undemocratic in that it
enables small groups to obtain an influence which is not
available to the public at large. Fourth, Coates and Silburn,
although sympathetic to community action, contend that its
local orientation is not conducive to the national action
necessary for large-scale change.

Community activists are not silent in the face of these
accusations and Bryant meets many of them. It is sufficient
here to conclude that the significance of community action
according to its apologists is in constituting a voice for persons
in need who are not listened to as individuals. Through it,
some deprived persons have entered the political arena from
which they were previously excluded. Through it, they have

demonstrated that they are capable of action and are not to be dismissed as inadequates. However, the extent to which community action can alter Government policies, local authority practices and the distribution of resources remains an open question which will be answered in the coming years.

The Urban Programme

John Edwards

Reprinted with permission from 'The Urban Programme: Time to Take Stock', *West Midlands Grassroots*, Summer 1972, pp. 4-5

The urban programme will soon be four years old. Since its inception in 1968, it has authorized the spending of some £20·6m, this apart from expenditure on the twelve community development projects. The time is ripe therefore for some assessment of the programme in terms of its operation, effectiveness, and ability to meet such goals as have been expressed. A monitoring and evaluation exercise is at present getting underway by a team of researchers from Southampton University operating within and from the Home Office in London. These notes in no way represent an analysis or critique of the programme – it is too early in the life of the evaluation team to say anything along these lines – but merely present some factual background information on how the programme operates, what has been spent and where, and perhaps, most important, to say what the urban programme *is*. Information and explanation has to date been remarkably thin – so thin that there are still local authorities who apparently have not heard of the urban programme, and a good deal of confusion amongst many more (and many voluntary bodies), about what exactly it is and what use can be made of it.

Anyone working in the deprived areas of large cities and who has a notion of what the UP is, will have their own criticisms of it and ideas for its improvement. Maybe, the descriptive notes below will provide some information which will enable such criticisms to be more effectively articulated.

AIMS OF THE PROGRAMME

The UP initiative came in 1968 and the legislation which gave it effect (the Local Government Grants [Social Need] Act) in 1969. This act provides that 'The Secretary of State may, out of monies provided by Parliament, pay grants, of such amounts as he may with the consent of the Treasury determine, to local authorities who in his opinion are required in the exercise of any of their functions, to incur expenditure by reason of the existence in any urban area, of special social need.' It is, in effect, a means by which extra resources can be injected into 'deprived' urban areas.

Beyond general statements about the 'relief of multiple deprivation', the aims or goals of the UP have never been made clear and explicit. The most tangible statement of aims appears in the third Government circular to local authorities inviting submissions for the third phase of the programme. 'The purpose of the urban programme is to improve social services in areas of special social need, taking account of the contribution already made by major programmes like education, housing, and health and welfare.' In fact, this statement doesn't do justice to the scope and range of activities financed by UP and to some extent understates the innovatory role of UP. It needs to be added though, that what is meant by 'special social need' has never been made clear by the Home Office, apart from some broad guidelines for the selection of areas in the first circular.

HOW IT WORKS

The UP operates (leaving aside the CDPs which are funded from UP money, but operate separately) through ministerial circulars to local authorities, inviting submissions of projects which might be grant-aided. To date there have been six circulars (phases) to the UP, and the seventh and present phase has reached the stage at which authorities make submissions. Submissions cannot be made therefore on a continuous basis but only in response to 'invitation'. The financial arrangement is that central government will put up 75 per cent of the money for any approved project, the remaining 25 per cent to be found by the local authority.

Voluntary bodies can also benefit of course from the UP but any submissions they make must be processed through the local authority and then forwarded to the appropriate ministry. Voluntary bodies cannot make direct submissions, and the local authority itself must be prepared to put up the remaining 25 per cent of the money for any successful submission from a voluntary body. Because the local authority has a financial stake in any project initiated by a voluntary organization, it will also play a crucial role in 'vetting' of such projects. The shortcomings of such an arrangement are no doubt clear to all those working in voluntary bodies in deprived areas.

WHERE THE MONEY HAS GONE

The seven circulars inviting submissions for the seven phases of the programme have tended to lay emphasis on particular sorts of project. Thus, the first, in 1969 laid stress on provision for young children (nurseries, day schools, etc.), the fifth on capital costs, the sixth on holiday projects. The *range* of projects financed by the UP however, has been quite broad, but the largest slice of the cake has undoubtedly gone to provision for young children.

Part of the philosophy of the UP (implicit rather than explicit), is that the grants are not intended to finance standard social services (housing, health, education), but rather to provide for schemes which should have a rapid effect in alleviating multiple deprivation. Since the nature of 'multiple deprivation' let alone its root causes has not been examined nor articulated thus far in the UP, the efficacy with which this goal has been met is difficult, if not impossible to judge at the present stage. The (far from exhaustive) list of schemes thus far grant aided, given below, indicates that at least some good must have been done, but how much and how effective is another matter entirely. These are some examples of grant-aided schemes:

Holidays for deprived children, nursery provision for children, day centres for the mentally subnormal, temporary accommodation for the homeless, lunch and day clubs for the elderly, adventure playgrounds, playgroups, community associations, holiday homes for the handicapped, language schemes for immigrant children, play leadership schemes, hostel for adolescent 'drifters' in Soho, aid for alcoholics, housing centres, grants for GIAs, family planning organizations.

The range of schemes grant-aided, is then, impressive (given that the above is but a sample), and the gross number of schemes (1,600 in 118 local authorities at February 1972) not insignificant. Quite another matter is the total impact that all this has had on the phenomenon of multiple deprivation. No doubt those working in action groups at ground level will not have been impressed with the changes wrought in their areas and neither in fact would central Government deny that the level of expenditure in relation to the problem being faced is very modest. It is too early in the day though to write the whole initiative off as a failure though certainly not too early to begin assessing what impact, if any, has been made, or to search for more effective alternatives if such there be.

SOME PROBLEMS

A number of questions immediately spring to mind about the efficacy of the procedures of implementation of the UP, and these will be among the issues examined by the monitoring team. Thus, the procedure as it stands leans heavily on local authority initiative both in making submissions and deciding what areas within their boundaries are deprivation areas. The ability of some local authorities to do this effectively is in doubt. All too often, a knowledge of the sub areas within an authority rests on professional judgement (i.e. often the experience of the MOH) or on conventional wisdom. In many cases, more systematic and rigorous examination and identification of 'stress areas' is required.

Secondly, there are no formal mechanisms by which to ensure that monies are most justly distributed among local authorities. Since the onus lies on the authorities to make submissions and no procedures operate to prod the more dilatory ones, there is an inbuilt tendency for most submissions to come from those authorities that are anyway more go-ahead, more aware, and probably more active in combating deprivation. There is no guarantee therefore, that the cake is evenly divided as between indigent authorities.

Thirdly, is the difficult position of voluntary bodies which, though they certainly do not have a monopoly of knowledge about the problems of stress areas, are more likely to be better placed by virtue of their activities at ground level to know of pressing and urgent needs. That these can only be articulated through the intermediary of the local authority which may or may not be sympathetic, is an issue that may well cause frustration among community workers and create friction between them and elected representatives. Whether or not direct access to

UP funds by community groups is the answer to this problem is a question that demands immediate attention.

Fourthly, and more generally, we need to know a lot more about how decisions in relation to submissions are made at local level and how decisions at central Government level are made as to which should be successful. Until we know how and in what way, ideas about submissions are generated, and what criteria of deprivation are adopted by those who generate such ideas, we are in no position to judge whether we have our priorities right, nor whose priorities we are adopting.

The fact remains that the UP is a very important initiative and one that needs to be taken seriously. If it isn't right, the answer is not to write it off as irrelevant, but to make it better and more effective. This means making it more effective in alleviating those injustices which are perceived as being the most pressing by those who suffer them. If this means redefining the role of the UP then it should not be beyond our capabilities to do this.

The Community Development Project

John Benington

Reprinted with permission from 'Focus on Government', *Municipal Journal*, vol. 81, no. 4, 26 January 1973, pp. 114-18

Coventry is one of twelve local authorities collaborating with the Home Office in the national Community Development Project (CDP) launched in 1969 as 'a radical experiment in community development involving local and central Government, voluntary agencies and the universities in a concerted search for better solutions to the problem of deprivation than those we now possess . . . including the establishment of more valid and reliable criteria for allocating resources to the greatest social benefit'.

The budget for the overall experiment is about £500,000 in 1972-3, rising to around £750,000 in subsequent years. A total of between 70 and 100 staff will eventually be involved.

DIALOGUE APPROACH

The Coventry project began in January 1970 in the Hillfields district of the city, and for the first two years it followed the strategy envisaged in the Home Office source documents *Objectives and strategy* and *Research strategy*.

At this stage we defined the problems in terms of, on the one hand, the powerlessness of disadvantaged people to bargain for the protection of their interests; and, on the other hand, the unresponsiveness of the Governmental system to their needs and aspirations. This led us to work within the study neighbourhood to encourage groups in representing their views; and within the local authority to interpret the demands arising from the grass-roots, and to encourage more sensitive and relevant responses. The aim was to gain greater influence by disadvantaged groups on policy-making, and to develop towards structures which would guarantee them a constitutional right at important decision-taking tables.

The two principal achievements of this first phase of the project (which did not then include a research component) were first a slight easing of communications between some residents and the local authority, with an increase in the flow of information; and second, a small supplement to the provision of compensatory 'community facilities' (an information and opinion centre, adventure playground, seed money for community groups and so on) brought about through an increase in overt community participation. In other words, given the benefits of a progressive local authority and the absence of the grossest forms of deprivation CDP had been able to make at least some progress towards getting a response from relevant services via the 'dialogue' model.

RESEARCH FINDINGS

When the research team started work, however, it became clearer from their surveys and analysis that few of the problems in Hillfields were peculiar to that neighbourhood alone. Their determinants had to be looked for in city-wide and nation-wide processes. And secondly, it became apparent that the dialogue model of social changes was itself inadequate in that:

(1) it focused attention on symptoms rather than causes;
(2) such symptoms (e.g. lack of play provision) were relatively marginal to the forms of disadvantage (e.g. low incomes, poor housing) perceived by residents as the priorities for attention;
(3) the solutions possible through 'dialogue' between resource-holders and local people (e.g. grants to community groups) could only be palliatives, or at best short-term remedies;
(4) local people had come to feel that 'dialogue' with the decision-makers was frequently one-sided, and that their case received quicker and greater attention if they resorted to more direct confrontation and pressure.

Clearly a local CDP on its own is not in a position to tackle the ultimate causes of disadvantage which have their sources nationally in the economy and in Government policy; however, national policies are mediated through local institutions which often appear unconsciously to sustain and reinforce the inequalities of the wider economy. CDP with its simultaneous access to central Government, local government and the grassroots community, is in a unique position to examine such differential processes, and to propose forms of intervention and modification.

In the light of this analysis, and of the re-appraisal which followed the research group's arrival, the Coventry team resolved to include two further aims:

Services response increases the capacity of relevant services to respond to both needs and aspirations more effectively.

Social planning develops hypotheses about the causes of, and solutions to, social deprivation, and through further testing of these hypotheses to develop criteria for allocating resources to meet such needs.

This implied modifying the CDP operation by adopting:

(1) an approach to the study area not so much as a self-contained 'problem area', but as a laboratory for the study of problems which have their origins and implications beyond any one neighbourhood in processes which are city wide and nation wide;
(2) a preventive rather than a remedial strategy;
(3) a focus on organizational and operational change at the level of local and central Government rather than at the neighbourhood level alone;

(4) an operation which involves integration of action and research rather than independent action followed by research evaluation;
(5) a longer time-perspective deriving from planned action-research programmes with clear objectives rather than from short-term *ad hoc* action responses.

On the basis of these principles we highlighted six key areas for long-term action-research consideration: income maintenance; housing and environment; community education; the transition from school to work; the needs of the elderly; and social priority planning.

CURRENT PROGRAMME

Our current programme of work thus falls into seven main categories – neighbourhood work, plus the six key areas of institutional change highlighted above.

Neighbourhood work consists chiefly of grants, support and advice to various community organizations run by the residents themselves. But it also proposed to appoint a full-time solicitor to offer legal advice and aid to individuals and groups in the area.

Income programme involves an analysis of the Supplementary Benefits system and its interaction with its customers.

The housing and environment programme, it is hoped, will become a rolling programme of general area improvement (via districts of 2,000 houses); to develop a community planning approach (based on full participation of the residents) to re-development in one area at least; and to explore the feasibility of housing co-operatives and associations to provide a greater range of housing choice for disadvantaged groups.

Community education programme is a joint programme with the education department which has been worked out to develop school/community relationships and more relevant curricula, to extend pre-school provision through parent-run 'annexes' in schools, church halls and factories, to provide home tuition for immigrant women and others with literacy difficulties, and to develop an 'unattached' adult education programme based on pubs and clubs.

The needs of the elderly are being ascertained by a 100 per cent survey and transmitted to statutory bodies and residents' groups for action.

Within these broad areas of study we have come to a number of general propositions about the functioning of local and central Government in relation to the disadvantaged. We have called this field *social priority planning*. The propositions can be summarized under the following heads: delivery of services, planning processes and political representation.

DELIVERY OF SERVICES

At its most basic, the flow of routine factual information from departments to the public often fails to reach home. The enquiries at the information and opinion centre continue to reveal situations in which information through formal channels has been received and experienced by residents as a series of confusing, contradictory and unintelligible messages.

There is also widespread evidence of lack of knowledge about some of the basic welfare rights and services.

Knowledge of services, however, is not by itself sufficient to ensure their accessibility to the public.

There are sections of the population who are hesitant about approaching formal agencies direct. Thus as many as 22 per cent of households in a sample survey of the area said that some member of their family suffered a disability that prevented them leading a normal life; but when asked if they would like their names to be passed on to the social services department, nearly half these people declined the offer.

Various factors can account for this kind of reluctance. Some can be seen in personal terms, but others have to be understood organizationally.

Few of the statutory services key into the networks of informal relationships which link people on a day-to-day basis. And many people seem to prefer to approach agencies via go-betweens who can gain them access to the desired service. Particular local people seem to have become known as successful go-betweens and negotiators for particular services. This may mean that the people eventually seen by a department are a very arbitrary and unrepresentative sample of those in need. And this could lead to biases in planning and decision-making.

PLANNING PROCESSES

Coventry has pioneered the development of corporate management systems and these are clearly helping to rationalize and co-ordinate the authority's planning processes. However, our observations and reading have suggested areas of need which the management systems at present developed in this country cannot respond to adequately.

The concern with the wider context and the forward look means that corporate planning is normally a 'top-down' process which begins with the statement of broad general objectives and works down to particular concrete activities. This means that conflicts in objectives and diversities of needs between different sub-groups of the population can tend to be obscured under all-embracing formulas.

The data and the definitions of 'need' on which corporate planning is normally based will also have the unintended effect of giving greater weight to the interests of some sections of the population than others. The important attempt to put decision-making on a better informed footing tends to introduce a bias in favour of what can be measured.

Furthermore, these statistics about need tend to be based on the 'demand' for existing services and so tell us nothing, either about those in need who for one reason or another have not approached any agency, or about the potential need for altogether different services.

Capital and revenue programmes relate to priorities within broad city wide functions (e.g. education, housing, social services) rather than within geographical areas (e.g. Hillfields, Foleshill, Wood End), or in relation to client groups (e.g. one-parent families) or concrete social problems (e.g. vandalism). Many of the social problems experienced as priorities within the grassroots community do not fall neatly into the functional grid, and many of them cut across the departmental or programme area divisions. Thus the list of priorities generated by a 'top-down' planning process may be very different from the priorities felt within the grassroots community.

POLITICAL REPRESENTATION

The poll rates in local government are notoriously low, in most cases ranging from 20 per cent to below 50 per cent, thereby signifying a majority who have not voted at all. The response to public meetings, visual displays, exhibitions and other initiatives tried by local authorities has been similarly disappointing.

Such evidence is usually interpreted as an indication of widespread public apathy and lack of interest in community affairs. Our experience in Coventry, however, leads us to different conclusions.

The public meetings we have observed have been characterized by formal procedures – control of communication by the chairman, question and answer techniques and so on – all of which satisfy the decision makers' concern for logical debate, but which may not be the best way of helping the general public express its views and feelings. Indeed, people often leave such meetings feeling frustrated and impotent, only expressing their opinions fully in small splinter groups afterwards.

The inference we draw from all this is that 'the problem' of participation in Government is not primarily a problem of the attitudes or behaviour of sections of the public who do not want to participate; but of the structures, processes and values of the Governmental system.

CONCLUSIONS

(1) An exclusive focus on 'small neighbourhoods of concentrated multiple-deprivation' may prove to be misleading. Many of the critical problems identified in the project study area are not inherent in or specific to that neighbourhood, but are manifestations of wider processes in society.

(2) Because their causes do not operate at the local level alone, many of these problems are not susceptible to solution at the local level alone.

(3) Although the fundamental causes of inequality often lie ultimately within the national economy, they are sustained and reinforced by the operations of particular local social institutions,

many of which have a direct face-to-face contact with disadvantaged groups.

(4) Some of these institutions and services appear to have the unintended effect of confirming and reinforcing the social problems which they were originally set up to tackle.

(5) Government planning and policy-making takes place on a larger and larger geographical scale and a longer and longer time-scale; this means that decisions are increasingly based on a macro-view of the community which generalizes issues up to a level where conflicts and diversities are 'reconciled'.

(6) The concept of 'deprivation' is in some ways related to this assumption of a homogeneous community with a consensus about basic goals and values. The notion implies a common baseline of consumption to which all in society aspire and below which some unfortunately fall.

(7) The focus of study for CDP and the locus for change need to be shifted, therefore, from 'deprived people or areas' to the institutions and organizations of local and central Government. The project should be concerned with identifying and analysing the crucial points at which Government provision appears to be failing to meet relevantly the needs of the most disadvantaged. It should then help to devise strategies for modifying the structure and process of statutory provision to respond to the unmet areas of need.

Working with politicians

(8) To date CDP appears to have had only limited effectiveness as an instrument of social change. It has proved to be a labour-intensive operation, having greater success in introducing extra innovatory and entrepreneurial workers at the field level, than in achieving organizational or policy change at the centre.

(9) CDP needs to locate its strategies within a longer time-perspective and a historical view of change. This should lead to the identification of plastic areas within the movement of political ideas, and strategies for injecting our small-scale commentary into arteries of the wider debate.

(10) At the local level this is likely to imply working more directly to politicians than to professionals and feeding in information about the differential distribution of resources,

showing who gains and who loses from particular public programmes. Within this kind of analysis action resources could be
invested in a few key demonstration projects based on alternative
definitions of the problem.

Family Income Supplement

John Stacpoole

Reprinted with permission from 'Running FIS',
New Society, vol. 19, no. 485, 13 January 1972, pp. 64-5

The first point to emphasize is the novelty of the scheme. FIS is
not only a new benefit, but a new kind of benefit, and unique in
being payable only to people in full-time work. The 'full-time
work rule' – the rule that benefits cannot be paid to people who
are working full-time – is fundamental to the Supplementary
Benefit scheme and not much less important in National Insurance. In consequence, the border area, between those whose
earning power is more or less intact and those who clearly cannot
support themselves, is a very sensitive one. It includes, for
example, the treatment of part-time earnings, the 'earnings-rule'
for pensioners and the dependents of beneficiaries, and the rules
about registering for employment – some of the most complex
and controversial features of the social security scene.

It is true that some benefits – widows' pensions, for example –
have been paid unconditionally for some years, whether the
recipient was working or not. But FIS turns the rule upside down:
it can only be awarded when the claimant is in full-time work
(and so unable to claim Supplementary Benefit). In planning the
administration of the scheme, therefore, we were the other side
of the frontier, moving into unknown country.

The adjustment had to be made very quickly. An outline
proposal was put forward in July 1970, and before the first
payments could be made, in August 1971, a bill had to be
drafted, debated and passed into law; and organization planned
and manned; regulations prepared and staff instructions written,

forms, leaflets and payment orders designed and printed; and claims invited and assessed. Pressure of this kind can be an advantage. With more time we should have had to ponder each departure from precedent; as it was, the boot was on the other foot, and every step in the procedure had to be justified more than usually rigorously in terms of time and staff cost.

A brief outline of the act and regulations is unavoidable by way of introduction. For FIS purposes, a family consists either of a man and a woman and the children they provide for, or of a man or woman bringing up children on their own. At present, if there is one child in the family and the income is less than £18 a week, the benefit is half the difference (income for this purpose means gross income and includes family allowances). For a family with two children this 'prescribed amount' is £20, and it goes up by £2 for each additional child. The maximum benefit is £4 a week, and the minimum 20p. However, under proposals announced on 17 December 1971 these amounts will, if Parliament approves the regulations, rise to £20 for a one-child family, £22 for a two-child family, and so on. The maximum weekly benefit will rise to £5 but the minimum will remain at 20p.

To qualify for an award the claimant must be in full-time work, defined as 30 hours or more a week. Earnings are assessed on the basis of the five weeks preceding the claim, but if there is some reason to think that the claimant's earnings or his hours of work during that period were not normal for him we can ask for information about other periods. Once an award has been made it continues for six months (in all but a few exceptional cases) regardless of any changes in the composition of the family or any fluctuation of its income.

By National Insurance and Supplementary Benefit standards, there are some fairly remarkable omissions here. There is, for instance, no difference between the treatment of one-parent and two-parent families (the 'prescribed amounts' are the same for both); nothing about liable relatives, or the income of adult members of the household other than the parents; and although there is power to take account of the income of children, of capital assets and of income in kind, it has not, in fact, been invoked.

In working out the details of the scheme, our main objective was simplicity. It was not only the need for speed and administrative economy which dictated this. The simpler the structure of the benefit, the more easily it could be explained and understood; and the better it was understood, the less the risk of muddle and delay. We did our best to avoid unnecessary irritations for the customer, and unnecessary intrusions into his privacy. At another level was the hope, not yet shown to be illusory, that a simple scheme based on consistent principles could be as humane and efficient as a complex one that attempted to provide for all possible contingencies.

Running an income-related benefit by post from a single centre offered considerable advantages. Local social security offices were already heavily committed, and, since the maximum 'load' for FIS would be relatively small and widely diffused, a small central staff could handle it far more economically. Moreover, FIS needed a new approach, and it would be easier to get it if the staff were concentrated in one centre than if they were spread out over 800 local offices dealing mainly with other benefits. On the other hand there was the risk that there would be large numbers of cases too difficult to be dealt with by correspondence. The feasibility of postal administration turned mainly on whether we could design a claim form that would be easy for claimants to understand and complete, and would, nevertheless, elicit the information we needed.

The form now in use asks 13 questions. Besides identity details, the questions cover the composition of the family and members' ages; the hours worked by the adults in full-time work; their earnings and any other income they may have (there is a separate section for the self-employed). Combining the FIS and welfare milk claims in the one form made an extra question necessary. We made the job more difficult by standing out for a single form that could be used by claimants of all kinds– married or unmarried, couples or men or women on their own.

We did not at once commit ourselves irrevocably to the use of a single administrative centre. We invited claims from the beginning of May and arranged to deal with them at some 60 FIS units in selected local offices. This gave us a flexible organization to deal with the first batches of claims (bear in mind that we could not know how quickly they would come in, or how difficult they might be to deal with), enabling us to vary the numbers of staff involved as necessary. The local units processed the claims to the point of award or rejection and sent them to the central office at Blackpool, which sent out the payment orders. One of the units was also located at Blackpool and formed the nucleus for the national centre. Since August, the others have been gradually phased out, and new claims have been going direct to Blackpool.

If we now look at the procedure from the claimant's points of view, the sequence should go roughly as follows. He – or she – must first get a claim form from a post office or a local social security office, unless the Department of Health and Social Security or some other agency has supplied it unasked. With it he gets a franked envelope. He fills in the form, attaches – ideally – five weekly pay slips and posts it to Blackpool. (Couples are expected to fill in the form together and both are asked to sign.) If he has not claimed before and if the family is not drawing family allowances, he should also enclose his children's birth certificates. If he has no pay slips he need not wait to send in his claim. In such cases we will send him a form to pass on to his employer – all correspondence with employers is conducted via the claimant – and if the claim succeeds he will be paid benefit from the date of his claim.

We have now handled over 150,000 claims, and although we have had to ask for further information in some 60 per cent of them we seldom have to do so more than once. Fewer than 1 per cent have required interviews or home visits. The commonest reason for returning a claim form has been that both parents in a two-parent family have not signed. This is an unusual requirement, and one that we hope will become better known as time goes on. (We also hope to make it clearer on the form.) For a new benefit there have been rather few appeals – about 2,300 – and most of them have been concerned with assessment of income. Really difficult cases have been far fewer than we expected.

In straightforward cases, the claimant should get the award notice and his first payment within a couple of weeks. Those who are awarded more than 50p a week – seven successful claimants out of eight – receive books of cashable orders which look very much like family allowances order books. Those with smaller awards get a Giro order covering the first 13 weeks and a second order 13 weeks later. Both groups get a 'passport' to free prescriptions and optical and dental services which also enables them to claim free school meals without further income-testing – the passport is bound into the order book but sent separately to those who are paid by Giro.

The publicity methods we used may be of some interest. The FIS take-up campaign followed on an earlier campaign to improve the take-up of free welfare milk and exemptions from National Health Service charges. This put us in touch with large numbers of low income families with children; to them, and all other families known to us as likely claimants, we sent leaflets and claim forms. Leaflets were handed out to everyone who cashed a family allowance in one particular week. Sir Keith Joseph sent personal letters to nearly 200,000 social workers and others who would be in contact with potential claimants. Letters were also sent to local authorities and these approaches were followed up with a series of local briefing meetings.

Advertising in the press and later on television was timed to fit in with these efforts. We tried to ensure that all families who were qualified, or anywhere near qualified, to claim, received a leaflet – the ideal of course was to get a leaflet into the potential claimant's home just as, or just after, he saw an advertisement and to ensure that people to whom he might go for advice knew about the scheme and were able to help him.

By the end of the year, we had received over 153,000 claims and made nearly 75,000 awards; some 78,000 claims had been rejected or withdrawn. The diagram shows how the figures built up from week to week: the peaks follow the three advertising campaigns (the August peak – which is the broadest as well as the highest – also coincided with the first payments of benefit under the scheme). From May to October we seldom had less than 4,000 claims a week; the gradual reduction since then no doubt owes something to the effect of wage increases, though it is exaggerated by the effects of the Christmas holiday.

This steady intake of claims over a long period is an interesting feature. In addition to those who have claimed successfully when in work, the great majority of 'wage stopped' families benefit under the FIS act. Their Supplementary Benefit, which under the wage-stop rule is assessed so that it does not exceed their income when working, is now assessed as if when they were working they had been drawing a family income supplement.

Awards made to successful claimants during the 'take-on

346 Social Welfare in Modern Britain

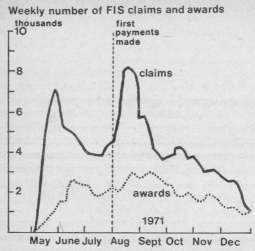

Weekly number of FIS claims and awards

following the sharp fall between 20 and 31 December 1971, 2,975 new claims were received in the week ending 7 January 1972

period' (4 May to 3 August) were made for periods of 13 to 38 weeks so as to run out evenly over the six months from November to April, thus spreading the work of dealing with renewal claims. Since November, they have been running out at the rate of about 1,200 a week; and although renewal claims have come in at an encouraging rate some awards have lapsed altogether. Even so, new claims have substantially exceeded the numbers lost in this way. The latest estimate is that about 93,000 families altogether were actually benefiting under the act at the turn of the year, roughly 70,000 of whom had claimed FIS as a separate benefit.

Welfare Rights and the Social Worker

Jane Streather

Reprinted with permission from 'Welfare Rights and the Social
Worker', *Social Work Today*, vol. 3, no. 13, 5 October 1972,
pp. 2-4

If anyone doubts that many low-income families are poorer than
they need be because they are unable to find (or unable to fight)
their way through our complex system of social services and
means-tested benefits, then read on. Moreover, if any social
worker doubts that among his colleagues are some who do not
define the mobilization of services to meet client needs as an
integral part of the social worker's professional role then he
should consider the story of Mrs Kirman and her ten children.

Mrs Kirman is a twice-divorced woman aged 37. Eight of her
children come from her two unsuccessful marriages and two
from a now terminated liaison. The children's ages range from
two years to 18 years, the youngest being mentally handicapped
and the oldest being the unmarried mother of three-month-old
twins. The family lives in a privately rented house in one of those
depressingly familiar inner rings of a provincial city, but is
fortunate nevertheless to have accommodation large enough for
there to be no statutory overcrowding. This house is the family's
most precious possession, since its acquisition in 1967 enabled
reunification after two years separation due to homelessness
following eviction. It was homelessness that brought this family
into contact with the then children's department, and Mrs Kirman speaks warmly of the support she received during the
traumatic period of separation from her children.

Since 1967, however, Mrs Kirman has received regular visits
from a succession of local authority social workers, which are
seemingly simply ritual occasions because no casework relationship has been established. Indeed, it appears that casework has
not been necessary for this close-knit family, which has generated
its own sources of mutual service and support, so necessary
given its isolation within the community. One might almost
wonder why 'the lady from the welfare' continued to visit at all,

given that her name was not known by the family and that she did not establish the kind of relationship which would have been so welcomed by Mrs Kirman, who told our interviewer that the worst thing about life as a divorced woman was 'being entirely alone and always feeling that you would like someone to talk to'.

This article is in no way intended as a personal attack on a particular social worker. It remains puzzling, however, that local authority workers visiting regularly either did not identify numerous material problems facing this family, or if they did identify them, did not consider it appropriate to intervene in order to facilitate improvements in Mrs Kirman's situation. Whatever the explanation the outcome was the persistence of material deprivation which left Mrs Kirman (according to our interview), 'doing all that she could to keep her family together in very difficult circumstances'. It is some of these difficult circumstances that I now wish to consider.

INCOME DEFICIENCY

On reading the interview schedule it was apparent that Mrs Kirman's income fell a long way short of her family needs. Her weekly income was £24.45, comprising family allowances of £5.90, contribution from oldest daughter and working son of £4, and Supplementary Benefit of £14.55. At a glance it was obvious that this was insufficient for the needs of an eleven-member household, and checking Mrs Kirman's requirements against the supplementary allowance scale rates suggested tentatively that she was short by approximately £7 per week. If the short fall were rectified, that is, her income would be increased by 30 per cent!

How could it be that this family in receipt of Supplementary Benefit was living so far below the poverty line? Talking to Mrs Kirman it soon became clear that she was receiving no financial benefit for her two youngest children. Because she was unwilling to apply for an affiliation order she had falsely told the Department of Health and Social Security that she was receiving weekly maintenance of £4, and thus received no allowance in her Supplementary Benefit. She was easily persuaded that in her children's best interests she should go to court, and consequently the Department of Health and Social Security increased her weekly allowance by £4.

Furthermore, the 15-year-old daughter had been out of work for two months, and although Mrs Kirman was entitled to claim £3 per week dependency allowance she did not know that this was the case. It was obvious from Susan's apparent lack of confidence in seeking work that she needed expert help. Contact was established with the youth employment service which also enabled her mother to claim benefit. Mrs Kirman received two weekly payments amounting to £6 and on Susan's sixteenth birthday she claimed in her own right.

Not surprisingly Mrs Kirman had been having difficulty in paying the rent of £4.50 as 'the children always need something', resulting in £10 of arrears which had been reduced from £23 by paying an extra 50p a week. This problem was also brought to the attention of the Department of Health and Social Security and the point made that it was absolutely crucial that the tenancy was not lost as such an event was likely to result in the family once again being split and the children being taken into care of the local authority which would be both tragic for it and costly for the community. The Department of Health and Social Security responded by granting £10 to pay the arrears.

One teenage child was without a bed or bedding and was sleeping on two chairs in the living room. An 'exceptional needs' grant was requested of the Department of Health and Social Security so that the child could be provided with proper sleeping facilities. The mattress, it seemed, had to be provided by the social services department and it would take three weeks to get it out of store. However, the Department of Health and Social Security did grant £10 which was promptly spent on buying blankets.

One letter and one telephone call did 'wonders' for Mrs Kirman in that within two weeks she received £34 and a substantial increase in her weekly supplementary allowance. Moreover, a letter to her new landlord pointing out that it is a criminal offence to attempt to evict a tenant without a court order demonstrated to Mrs Kirman despite threats of eviction (in order to turn the house over to multi-occupation) that she had security of tenure. A further letter pointed out that a landlord has legal obligations to maintain a house in good repair and it is hoped that he will take heed without further action being necessary.

This story represents but an extreme example of similar cases brought to my attention as a social researcher and which cause myself and other non-social workers to wonder how common is the view among the profession that 'surely the most important part of our work is the relationship we offer to our clients rather than the meeting of material needs'. And moreover, to wonder why it is that frequently social workers do not intervene when so much can be done with so little effort.

A ROLE FOR SOCIAL WORKERS

It may have been that the problems had not been identified. One is frequently told that this is not surprising given the lack of trained staff and that often local authority appointments are determined by the principle that 'the cheapest is the best'. But how much training is required to suspect that something is amiss when a 15-year-old school leaver is sitting at home all day, or to notice that school children are at home because they have no shoes to wear, or to query the sufficiency of £24.55 to keep a family of 11? Deciphering the cause of income deficiency is a little more difficult especially when relevant information is not forthcoming from the clients. However it is not great expertise in inter-personal relationships which is required but rather the asking of pertinent questions which the client sees as being related to the issues that concern her most – in this case security of tenure and weekly income. Focusing on such problems the social worker is likely to elicit the response: 'You have been straight with me so I had better tell you . . .' What better basis for establishing the 'relationship' that social workers wish to offer their clients?

It is possible that many social workers do see the glaring material needs but do not feel they have the skills to work out welfare entitlements or to engage in possible conflict with social security officers on behalf of their clients. Yet, the technical skills for well-educated people are simple given access to relevant information. The task, it is true, can be time consuming and irritating when the pressure of the caseload is great. But what about preventative social work? In the case of Mrs Kirman lack of income resulted in persistent rent arrears with the risk of rendering the family homeless with all that that implies in terms of human misery, financial cost to the community and use of scarce social work resources.

It is probable that many social workers do not conceive their function as being concerned with mitigation of the harsh realities of environmental factors such as inadequate housing and low income. To be concerned with material aspects of a client's problem does not for some social workers seem worthy in relation to their professional expertise and status. However, Barbara Wootton has made a strong case for the 'middle-man' role of social workers and what is more has described it as both 'skilled and honourable'. Writing about the 'Welfare State' more than a decade ago she made the point that

> . . . the complexity of relevant rules and regulations has become so great, that the social worker who has mastered these intricacies and is prepared to place knowledge at the disposal of the public, and when necessary to initiate appropriate action has no need to pose as a miniature psychoanalyst or psychiatrist: her professional standing is secured by the value of her own contribution.

With the growing complexity of income maintenance schemes and the known low 'take-up' of means-tested benefits her comments seem to have increasing relevance. While recognizing that professional opinion is divided concerning Wootton's conception of social work surely there must be agreement that an important aspect of such work is to help poor clients claim their Supplementary Benefits, free school meals, rent and rate rebates, attendance allowances and to see that they are protected by the landlord and tenant legislation.

In order to fulfil this role it may be that ideally, all social workers should be equipped with the necessary skills for such a task and therefore greater emphasis should be placed on welfare law and welfare rights issues in the syllabi of professional courses. However given the present deficiencies in training, the large number of untrained practising social workers, the sheer weight of caseloads and the conflict of professional opinion concerning the importance of meeting material need, Wootton's ideal seems a little remote. Even so, innovation by social service departments could improve on what is now an unsatisfactory situation.

WELFARE RIGHTS OFFICERS

The special appointment in social service departments of a person to deal solely with welfare rights issues is advocated. Primarily the officer's role would be an advisory one. At a general level social workers could be informed of the range of benefits and of conditions of eligibility by means of discussion and up-to-date handbooks. More specifically, in relation to individual families a standardized form might be produced which would elicit anonymously details of family size and structure, income, rent and other relevant circumstances. That is, sufficient information for the welfare rights officer to identify entitlement to benefits and for him to refer back to the social worker concerned details and instructions concerning procedures for claiming. Further, he could liaise with agencies and individuals such as the Department of Health and Social Security, the rent officer, the education welfare department and where necessary act generally as an advocate on behalf of clients and more specifically by representing them on social security tribunals.

Although rare, such appointments do exist already and the potential for ensuring that the rights poor clients have according to the law are rights they have in practice is very great indeed – at least for that minority section of poor families who come into contact with social service departments A number of independent groups are already engaged in welfare rights activities, and they would be the first to admit that their efforts are helping only a very small number of those in difficulty. Hence, short of a more universalistic framework of welfare provision, welfare rights officers operating on a regular basis could do much to improve the material circumstances of the poor clients of social workers.

Climbing off the Fence

Daphne Carter and John Barter

Reprinted with permission from 'Climbing off the Fence',
Social Work Today, vol. 3, no. 10, 10 August 1972, pp. 4-6

*Meanwhile Islington Council social workers have rebelled and
officially backed the squatters. Half the 110 social workers have
refused to 'carry out the council's dirty work over evictions' and
joined the squatters at the barricades. One said: 'We are sick of
being apologists for a policy we do not believe in'.*

Evening News, 28 June, 1972.

BACKGROUND

Action now being taken by social workers in Islington in conjunction with a group of residents living in abominable conditions
has far-reaching implications for the future development of
social work in this country.

The present confrontation between the council and its social
workers can be better understood by examining changes which
have been taking place within the borough. These internal
changes reflect national developments. Until ten years ago,
Islington was very much a densely populated, one-class, seedy
inner city area. A vigorous rehousing policy was started belatedly
in the mid-1960s. At the same time, parts of the borough became
fashionable. There was, and still is, an inflow of well-to-do
'colonists'. These movements, following on after the 1957 Rent
Act, put the heat on tenants of privately owned property. There
was big money to be made by any landlord able to sell with
vacant possession to either the council or property speculators.
Many districts in the borough were designated clearance areas.
Inevitably, the now familiar planning blight set in as those who
could afford to moved out or were rehoused by the authorities.
Housing which was already in poor condition deteriorated into
unhealthy demoralizing slums.

One of the worst hit areas lies just behind Pentonville Prison, the now notorious Westbourne Road and surrounding streets. How Westbourne Road has been turned into one of the most depressing parts of London has been well documented in recent weeks, so we shall not pursue the subject here.

Islington council has one of the most intractable problems of homelessness in the country. It still possesses furnished accommodation at rents that the poor can just afford, so attracts people newly arrived in London. The council's own development policy exacerbates the problem. By its doctrinaire reluctance to rehouse people from temporary accommodation into permanent council housing, the supply of temporary housing is inadequate to meet need.

THE SQUATTERS

In March, 1972, the Living Theatre group moved into a house in the Westbourne Road area. Three other families, two the responsibility of neighbouring Haringey, moved into houses in Lesly and Sonning Streets in May. These are the squatters. But there are also 140 residual families, tenants and licensees living in the clearance area. They do not know if and when they will be rehoused. Meanwhile the council's demolition teams are gutting the uninhabited houses. Rubbish and vermin abound. There is a very high risk of dangerous fires.

On 19 June the squatters came to the Market Road Area Team of social workers, in view of the council's decision to seek a High Court action to evict them. This proved to be the flashpoint as far as the team and their leader, John Connor, were concerned. Before taking up the story from this point, it is helpful to look at developments which have occurred within the social services department.

SOCIAL WORKER MILITANCY

Islington seems to be unique in that its form of reorganization of its social services was based upon careful research into the social structure and needs of the borough. Resulting from the research, ten small area teams were set up. Each was to be put into informal premises at strategic points throughout the district. The teams were given the task of discovering needs and mobilizing resources to meet those needs. They were to draw the recipients of services into the process of defining and solving problems. Consequently, social workers have grown closer to the people they hope to serve. It is essential to understand that this coming together of social workers and the deprived is still in its infancy, but the results already achieved are almost cataclysmic in their impact.

The small teams have generally proved cohesive. Through working with whole families, developing group methods of providing material and personal help, and by the employment of community workers, there has developed a heightened awareness of the misery caused by poverty and multiple disadvantages.

Militancy within the department has been increased by a series of inept decisions by top management and the committee. More and more work has been thrust on already overworked staff without concomitant increases in resources. Naturally the public have become dissatisfied when grandiose promises made by the council failed to be translated into better services. It is the social workers who bear the brunt of public anger. Matters have not been improved by what the social workers see as their Chairman's petulant scapegoating of staff. Changes in the senior management structure have resulted in leadership problems, a vacuum which has been more than adequately filled by the social workers themselves, as it happens. They feel that they have at last achieved direct communication with members and are thus able to influence policy. The departmental hierarchy has been short-circuited. Staff find this a liberating experience. The impact of poverty, bad housing and misery is not muffled by the formal structure but is now conveyed directly to councillors. It is interesting to note that in the mass of press reports on recent events, no mention is made of top management. We may perhaps reassess the opinions of the pundits who, at the time of reorganization, were laying such stress upon the importance of directors and principal officers. In the new synthesis appearing in Islington, management appears fairly irrelevant.

SYNTHESIS

Following the referral of the squatters, events have moved quickly. Thoroughly disillusioned with the 'formal channels' which had been used to try to resolve problems of poor housing, the social workers decided to throw in their lot with squatters publicly. There followed a series of meetings, protests and demonstrations. Connor and his colleagues received a message that they were in breach of their contracts by making statements to the press. Disregarding this veiled threat, they continued to use the media intelligently achieving local and nationwide coverage in the papers and on television. In the course of these events, the publicized focus of protest moved from the plight of the squatters to take in the equally horrifying plight of the 140 remaining families in Westbourne Road. Finally, the alliance of squatters, residents and social workers from Islington and other areas, has drawn public and official attention to the national failure to devise housing strategies designed to provide adequate accommodation for the poor, at prices they can afford.

The council has used various tactics to compel their social workers to retreat from their position of solidarity with the people in Westbourne Road. Supported by messages of sympathy from social workers in other London agencies and from as far afield as Oldham, Derry and Bristol, the Islington social workers have stood firm in their resolve to assist the residents and squatters to obtain a fair deal on housing. Significantly, their resolve has led to the dissolution of barriers of suspicion which had previously prevented social workers from achieving a working partnership with local people. This has prevented the council from driving a wedge between the squatters and the indigenous families, and from isolating the social workers from grassroots support. One of the least pleasant tactics employed by the council was the attempt to whip up anger among the indigenous population against the squatters.

The activities of the squatters, social workers and local people seem to have resulted in back-bench pressure being put upon the council to modify its hard-line policies. It is understood that the High Court eviction orders will not be implemented and that all the people in Westbourne Road area will be rehoused more quickly. A meeting was held by the residents, attended by councillors and housing representatives, the tone of which was bitter. It is reported that at this meeting, council representatives were asked to leave, having attempted to resolve people's housing problems by a prolonged recitation of their own. However, it resulted in demolition work in the area being halted, as demanded by the residents.

'TO BE OURSELVES'

An alliance of residents, back-benchers and social workers appears to be emerging. Whether this synthesis will prove sufficiently enduring to provide a political force for concern and humanity remains to be seen. The political maturity of the Market Road team and their Islington colleagues is remarkable. Doubtless, Connor's previous trade union and community work experience are invaluable assets. The events of recent weeks which have taken social workers off the fence and into the arena of grassroots politics should be a matter of urgent study by BASW, and by all those responsible for the selection and training of social workers. As one of the social workers concerned has said: 'We are sick and tired of being apologists for policies we don't believe in. From now on we are going to be ourselves and respond to people's needs in ways we believe can actually help to solve their problems.'

Community Action

Richard Bryant

Reprinted with permission from 'Community Action', *The British Journal of Social Work*, vol. 2, no. 2, Summer 1972, pp. 205-15

Much of the current debate about community or social action tends to confuse two different interpretations of the term, with the general effect of muddling discussion and analysis.

(1) Community action may be used as a general term to denote any planned attempt to involve local groups or welfare publics either in voluntary self-help schemes or as participants in the process of statutory policy-making and service implementation. In this broad and eclectic interpretation community action can

refer to a diverse range of initiatives, such as neighbourhood self-help groups, organizations representing consumer and client interests, protest or action groups focused around housing and income issues and statutory community programmes designed to improve the accessibility and take up of the social services. But whilst it may be useful, as a rudimentary and initial form of classification, to lump these various initiatives together, it is very deceptive to assume from this that they will share anything in common, other than a focus upon similar types of action settings, problems and groups.

Marris and Rein, in their study of American community action programmes, provide an illustration of the differences in approach which can exist.

> Community organization could be interpreted with a very different emphasis, according to the standpoint of the organizer. It could be used to encourage the residents of a neighbourhood to come to terms with the demands of a wider society, or conversely to force the institutions of that society to adapt more sympathetically to the special needs of a neighbourhood. Or it could be seen rather as a form of therapy, to treat apathy and social disorganization. And it might take an individual bias promoting the social mobility of potential leaders, championing causes of personal injustice – or a communal bias more concerned with the neighbourhood as a mutually supportive community.

The point being made here is a very simple one. To generalize indiscriminately about community action can obscure the differences, in terms of values, goals and strategies, which may exist between community groups.

(2) Community action may denote a particular approach to organizing local groups and welfare publics; an approach in which the political impotence or powerlessness of these groups is defined as a central problem and strategies are employed which seek to mobilize them for the representation and promotion of their collective interests. Some recent examples would include the claimants' and unemployed workers' unions, tenants' associations protesting about rent increases, the squatters' associations and the various neighbourhood-based groups which include representation as one of their goals. The central focus upon 'organizing

for power' and political definitions of problems predisposes community action to use conflict as a strategy for achieving change and, as Peter Hodge has indicated, this acceptance of conflict as a purposive organizing and tactical force clearly distinguishes community action from other approaches to community work, such as community development.

> Community development is a process which aims to achieve change through consensus. It is client-centred and based on the self-determined goals of the community groups with which the worker is involved . . . Community action is a parallel process but uses conflict to achieve change. The worker aims to verbalize discontent, articulate grievances, to form a pressure group with which to confront authority in a militant struggle for righting wrongs, gaining power, acquiring new resources and better services or amenities.

It is with reference to this specific interpretation that the term community action will be used in this article.

COMMUNITY ACTION–KEY FEATURES

When attempting to analyse the key features of community action it is necessary to distinguish between a range of related elements, each of which can contribute to the building up of a composite picture or model of community action. These elements include, at a minimum: settings, problem definitions, goals, strategies and the roles of local activists and professional change agents.

Action settings
The conventional setting for community action is a geographic locality, where issues relating to housing and the physical environment provide the initial stimulus for the growth of collective initiatives. For example, initiatives which develop around rent increases, lack of recreational amenities, slum clearance and urban renewal programmes. However, it would be misleading to assume from this that community action is exclusively based upon geographic settings or that the activities of locality based groups are narrowly restricted by the physical boundaries of a particular housing estate or neighbourhood.

Community action can develop on the basis of functional interests which unite people who have no direct geographic links – as is often the case with organizations representing welfare clients and claimants and the activities of local groups do at times transcend their immediate geographic boundaries. Thus a tenants' association protesting about rent increases may, if it is effectively organized, attempt to take action at a variety of political and administrative levels, including, on occasions, the level of national government. The very fact that formal political powers are normally located outside localities means that community groups will mobilize beyond their initial geographic base and operate in extra-territorial spheres.

Problem definitions

The assumptions which underlie community action invariably imply the existence of a conflict of interests between community groups and the public or private institutions which exercise a decision-making influence over their life situations.

This conflict definition of problems and issues can take a variety of forms, ranging from a 'them and us' frustration with the apparently entrenched and insensitive nature of public authorities, to a more politically sophisticated analysis in terms of the exploitation and powerlessness of local groups. Rather than being the product of a mindless form of 'conflict mongering', as some critics of community action have implied, these conflict definitions invariably represent rational expressions of the built-in tensions and inequalities which can exist between community groups, particularly those representing groups in poverty and ethnic minorities, and established private and public institutions. Just as in industrial relations it is naïve to speak of a harmony of interests between employers and employees, so it is equally simple-minded to assume, in the field of community relations, a natural consensus of interests between, for example, council tenants and housing authorities, privately rented tenants and their landlords, and welfare claimants and the various agencies which administer benefits and services. Community action merely makes explicit the tensions and inequalities which may exist in various situations, and, as previously noted, it is the recognition and purposive use of conflict which helps to distinguish community action from other approaches to community work.

Goals

The material or task goals of community action vary widely in scope and ambition, ranging from the relatively modest aim of winning new recreational facilities for an area to seeking basic changes in housing and welfare policies which, if they were completely realized, would entail fundamental changes at the level of national government. Underpinning these material objectives is a second set of organizational or process goals, which relate to the creation and maintenance of the organizational structures through which community action is mobilized. Included in these organizational goals are such tasks as fund raising, recruitment of members, publicity and information services, the forging of coalitional links with other community organizations and the devising of procedures through which members can participate in the planning of collective policies. The importance of these organizational goals should not be under-valued, for community action is rarely sustained over the long-term in a spontaneous manner. Even in crisis situations, where the force of circumstances can act as an immediate stimulus to collective action, organizational goals are needed to consolidate and sustain any spontaneous activism which may be generated.

Strategies

It is in relation to strategies and tactics that the conflict assumptions of community action are made particularly explicit. Two general sets of strategies may be distinguished, bargaining strategies and confrontation strategies.

Bargaining strategies are conventionally employed in situations where negotiation is possible between the various interests involved and the framework for action is defined by the institutionalized processes of formal and pressure group politics. The tactics adopted by community groups, operating in bargaining situations, may embrace the lobbying of councillors, MPs and prestigious public figures, petitions, and information and publicity campaigns directed at the mass media. In contrast, confrontation strategies are employed in situations where a polarization of interests exists and the conventional processes of political representation are viewed, by community groups, as being unproductive or dysfunctional for the pursuit of their ends.

The accommodated conflict of the bargaining situation is replaced by an open conflict or warfare situation and recourse is likely to be made to tactics of an extra-parliamentary and extra-legal nature; for example, street demonstrations, sit-ins, muck-raking campaigns, rent strikes, the takeover of private property and, on occasions, the threat and use of physical violence. Although the use of confrontation strategies can create divisions, on both tactical and ideological grounds, within community groups it would be too simple to equate directly bargaining and confrontation strategies with a theoretical choice between 'reformist' and 'revolutionary' models of social change. The local circumstances which prevail will tend to shape decision making about tactics and during the history of an initiative a mixture of strategies might be employed, which embrace both those of bargaining and confrontation. Thus a community group may be forced to adopt confrontation tactics after all the conventional political options have been unsuccessfully exhausted, while a group might only achieve a bargaining position after a period of open conflict has established its credibility as a force to be reckoned with.

The role of local leaders and professional change agents
The distinction between the roles of local leaders and professional change agents is one which has tended to become blurred in some of the recent community-work literature and an exclusive concentration upon 'professional approaches' can create the impression that all community work and community action is dependent upon the intervention of professional workers. A local leader is someone who has a natural claim, because of a particular life situation and status, to hold a position in a community organization or interest group. They may be residents on a council estate, claimants of welfare benefits, unmarried mothers or old age pensioners, who occupy a leadership position in organizations representing council tenants, welfare claimants, unmarried mothers, etc. In contrast, a professional change agent is someone who has no natural claim or status in relation to a local group but works with the group in order to provide certain specialist services and resources. He is invariably an 'outsider', in both status and class terms, who is either paid by a sponsoring body or has made a personal choice to associate with a community group. Confusion between local leaders and professional

change agents is unfortunate because it distorts the basic differences which should exist in terms of roles and functions. The local leader is essentially a spokesman, advocate and publicist for his organization. He represents a community organization to external institutions and provides a reference point for the communication of local views and grievances. On the other hand the professional change agent is a resource person and consultant, who provides services and information which would not normally be available or accessible to local groups. Although the professional may, on occasions, assume formal leadership roles, for instance in relation to local groups which have no tradition of self organization, his distinctive contribution is defined by the supportive aids and expertise he is able to command because of his outsider status. It does not rest, as is the case with the contribution of local leaders, upon the status he has as a natural member of a group of organization. When outsiders assume leadership roles, on a permanent basis, they invariably undermine the credibility of community groups.

WHAT DOES COMMUNITY ACTION ACHIEVE?

Any attempt to assess the effectiveness of community action is fraught with difficulties, primarily because we lack at the moment any systematic body of research into the activities, achievements and failure of community groups. Whereas British sociologists have devoted considerable attention to studying local social systems, comparatively little attention has been paid to documenting and examining the processes through which local groups engage in organized action. Thus any attempt at assessment must be very partial and impressionistic.

Material results
In terms of achieving material or concrete results the effectiveness of community action is likely to be dependent upon a variety of factors; especially the nature of the issue or set of issues at stake, the financial and organizational resources the local group can command, the degree of popular involvement in on-going initiatives, the influence and sanctions local groups can exercise and the coalitional links which exist between the local group and other community and political organizations. Of all these factors

the decisive one, in terms of deciding material effectiveness, tends to be the 'nature of the issue' which is the focus for action. Is the issue one which requires major policy and political changes for the achievement of a successful outcome, or is it one which merely requires a modification in local administrative procedures and practices? For example, we can compare a campaign which is concerned with protesting about increases in council house rents, with one which is focused upon improving the collection of dustbins and waste upon council estates. An initiative directed at rent levels will often raise policy questions which directly involve the policies of both local and national Governments, particularly when the local government is implementing national Government directives, as will be the case with the Conservatives' new Fair Rents policy. In such a situation the effectiveness of community action will ultimately depend upon the mobilization of broad-based political forces which are capable of having an impact in the national political arena. In contrast, a campaign about the dustbins, whilst it may arouse intense local passions and controversy, is not normally a 'big issue' which requires action at a variety of political levels and the reversal of major policy decisions for the achievement of a successful solution.

As a rule community groups lose the battles on the big issues but may win, as a result of their initiatives, secondary or 'spin-off' gains. Hampton provides an example of this in his study of politics in Sheffield. The 'big issue' which provided the stimulus for community action was the introduction of a rent rebate scheme for council house tenants, which provoked considerable opposition from the city's tenants' associations. The tenants' action did not prevent the implementation of the scheme, but did effect a number of secondary concessions.

The opposition to the rent rebate scheme did not succeed in forcing the withdrawal of the scheme, but the alterations made in response to the protests indicated that the tenants' campaign was effective. Both groups on the city council changed their policy during the course of the dispute. The Labour group made three major revisions to the scheme and these resulted in a rate contribution of over £600,000 to the housing revenue account. The Conservatives changed their mind about the 'lodger tax' and allowed for a rate contribution to the housing revenue account.

More generally we can note how community campaigns, representing the interests of groups in poverty, whether they be welfare claimants or homeless families, have succeeded, at times, in winning local reforms, without effecting any significant policy change at the level of central Government. The 'big issues' which are raised by community groups and which transcend local solutions require, for effective action, the mobilization of forces in the national political arena. As Coates and Silburn have observed:

> Direct action on the many grievances of the deprived members of the population is a crucial lever to the development of their self-respect and social understanding but it is not a sufficient remedy for their problems, which demand overall solutions such as can be only canvassed by nationally structured political and social organization. Unless a serious effort is made at this level, it is unlikely that basic change will take place.

Coates and Silburn also made the important point that the political impotence of community groups in the face of big issues, is a critical reflection on the existing policies and organization of the British Labour Movement. For, in theory, the Labour Party and the unions could provide the agency through which the demands of community groups might be given a national expression. In relation to this observation it is worth noting that, on the few occasions when community campaigns have made an impact upon central Government policy, these campaigns have invariably been fused with broader-based political and union action, as was the case with the Govan (Glasgow) rent strike, which contributed to the passing of the first Rent Control Act of 1915. The relationship between local and national action is obviously crucial in determining the effectiveness of community action, but questions relating to the means and ideologies of working for structural change are ones which tend to divide community activists. The positions taken on these questions vary widely. They range from the quasi-populist view that community groups themselves can provide a collective and independent agency for national action, to the more mainstream socialist view that coalitional links must be forged between community groups and the traditional organizations which represent working-class interest.

Qualitative change

An exclusive emphasis upon the material achievements and failures of community action can direct attention away from the qualitative changes, in terms of attitudes, self image and the acquisition of new skills, which can also result from an involvement in community action. A number of reports on community action initiatives have drawn attention, albeit on the basis of impressionistic evidence, to examples of qualitative change. For instance, Radford in a commentary upon the King Hill campaign pointed out:

> During 1965 not only the atmosphere but the attitudes and behaviour of the people in King Hill changed visibly. For the first time people were being encouraged to make decisions for themselves, and there was this tremendous feeling we were together, doing something important. Self-respect blossomed with the realization that they were capable of organization and that they could fight injustice . . .

Changes of this nature, which essentially express the unleashing of new human potentials, can prove as threatening to politicians, administrators and social workers as the material demands community groups make. Groups and individuals who previously have been defined as 'passive' or 'apathetic' may emerge through an involvement in community action as being active and organized, challenging conventional wisdoms and the competence of established institutions and official personnel. One of the central lessons which can be drawn from recent American experience is that community action does not, if it is a genuine expression of popular feeling, necessarily conform to the models of 'participation' embodied in statutory programmes. Fundamental conflicts, which often reflect contrasting sets of cultural and class values, can occur between official conceptions of 'participation' and actual expressions of 'participation in action'.

Beneath the rhetoric of the Johnson Administration's brief and romantic interlude with the poor was a deep-rooted distrust of the poor themselves, manifested when the poor – and particularly the Negro poor – choose to believe the rhetoric of participatory democracy and act on that belief. The poor as aggressors or as rude initiators of action, unresponsive to benevolent control, ungrateful and distrusting, and even violent, are less appealing to indulgent political leadership than the humble and apathetic poor.

However, as a precaution against over-simplified generalizations, it is relevant to note here that community action rarely involves, on a regular basis, the mass of a particular community or group. Except perhaps in times of crisis, the day-by-day involvement tends to be limited to a hard core of activists, whose work might be supplemented by a wider circle of occasional participants. The mass of a community or group are likely to have a relatively passive involvement; they may attend the occasional public meeting but will not usually be regular contributors to the on-going processes of organization and detailed policy decision making. The American community organizer Alinsky has remarked, with typical candour, that a 2 per cent involvement on a regular basis is the most any community organization can hope to achieve. This question of the different levels and intensity of participation is likely to have some implications for the qualitative changes which may result from community action. One may speculate that the changes which do occur may well be limited to those individuals who are members of the activist core of a community organization.

COMMUNITY ACTION AND STATUTORY AUTHORITIES

The revival of interest in community action, which has been particularly marked since the mid-1960s, is one strand in a broader trend which also embraces new developments in statutory welfare planning. Community work, which has been for so long the Cinderella of the social work services, is currently undergoing a period of unprecedented expansion. The growth points in this expansion include the newly reorganized social work departments, the Government's urban aid and community development programme, the local work of the Community Relations Commission, the linking of youth and community services and the growth of new training courses for professional community workers. One question, which naturally arises in relation to these developments, is whether community work in statutory agencies will embrace the conflict strategies of community action as well as the more traditional, and less contentious, consensus strategies of community development and community organization. From the evidence we currently have available it would appear that community action does not figure on the statutory agenda. Conflict, whether as a purposive strategy or as a natural consequence of promoting social change, has been carefully limited and circumscribed.

Holman has indicated the basic limitation which exists – statutory authorities will not, as a rule, sponsor projects which threaten to promote dissent against themselves:

> . . . there is no evidence that local authorities could tolerate, let alone promote any strategies which lead to direct conflict with themselves. On the contrary, Tower Hamlets got rid of an employee who stimulated clients to protest. Wandsworth withdrew financial support from a voluntary body which mildly criticized council policy; Brighton would not renew a lease for slightly unorthodox work with beatniks, and few councils will grant aid to community action groups. In other words, local authorities will run services for people, will finance voluntary community work which reflects their own methodology, but will encourage nothing that creates conflict even where it is the only hope of change.

Holman and others have strongly urged statutory authorities to adopt more flexible policies and to stretch their boundaries of conflict tolerance. But even if changes were to occur, it is still questionable whether the goal of client participation in the formal structure of the social services could be effectively realized. The American experience provides a sobering precedent for such proposals. As a number of studies have indicated, client participation in welfare organizations, to begin to be meaningful in decision-making terms, requires access to the informal processes of power and not merely membership of committees which exercise consultative and 'rubber stamping' functions. Almost by definition the life situation and status of the client pre-empts access to these informal processes and as a consequence there is always likely to be a credibility gap between the rhetoric and reality of client participation in policy-making. A 'we participate, they rule' situation could simply function to reinforce tensions rather than promote new collaborative relationships. While these observations do suggest that statutory community work is of limited potential when viewed within a strictly community action framework, they should not be interpreted as meaning that statutory community work developments will not yield results in other, less controversial directions – for example in extending the existing limited boundaries of preventative social work.

THE FUTURE OF COMMUNITY ACTION

The future of community action, like its past, is likely to be more directly determined by local circumstances, the existence of natural leadership and responses to national and local government policies, than by formal developments which occur within the field of social and welfare planning. The limitations of local groups and welfare publics in the face of 'big issues' and the lack of those supportive resources which middle-class pressure groups take for granted, will, one suspects, only be overcome in the long term through a radical realignment in the politics and organization of the British Labour Movement. Perhaps it is to the trade unions, rather than the social work departments, that community action theorists and activists should be directing their attention.

Further Reading
New Developments in Social Welfare

D. BARKER, 'The Family Income Supplement', in D. Bull (Ed.), *Family Poverty*, Duckworth, 1971.

J. BENINGTON, 'Are these the roots of social distress', *Municipal Review*, July 1973.

N. BOND, 'The Case for Radical Casework', *Social Work Today*, vol. 2, no. 9, 29 July, 1971.

GULBENKIAN FOUNDATION, *Current Issues in Community Work*, Routledge & Kegan Paul, 1973.

B. HINDNESS, *The Decline of Working Class Politics*, Mac-Gibbon & Kee, 1971.

R. HOLMAN, *Power for the Powerless, The role of community action*, British Council of Churches, 1972.

R. LEES, *Politics and Social Work*, Routledge & Kegan Paul, 1972.

R. SILBURN, 'The Potential and Limitations of Community Action', in D. Bull (Ed.), *Family Poverty*, Duckworth, 1971.

Chapter Seven

Social Welfare: Solutions and Future Strategies

Many aspects of social welfare have been covered by the readings in this volume. They have revealed that groups in need can be identified and have conveyed some indication of the extent of social deprivation. Space has been given to criticisms of certain approaches to meeting need and attention focused on new developments. The reorganization of the personal social services, the urban programme, FIS, community action, client organizations, are all modern responses to social need and thus worthy of close study. In addition, proposals have been put forward for and changes identified within the social security system, planning methods and social work. Underlying the readings are assumptions, theories, and interpretations which are not always made explicit. The final readings, therefore, will concentrate not on particular need groups or services but on explanations and analyses which can be applied to social welfare.

It is obvious that the kinds of services, programmes and policies employed should be based upon an understanding of and explanations of social need or deprivation. If poverty is the result of personality defects springing from defective psychological experiences in childhood, then changes could be sought through psychotherapeutic and casework services. If it stems from inadequate child socialization then compensatory and stimulation programmes are required. Yet frequently services appear to be introduced or expanded without serious consideration of the nature of the problems they are meant to counter. Thus the *Seebohm Report* was sharply criticized for promoting vast changes in the organization of social work without examining exactly how or if social work could alleviate social need. Similarly, the urban programme has come under fire for initiating many different projects without having any clear conception of what they could achieve. Interestingly, and perhaps because social deprivation persists on such a large scale, more attention is now paid to proposing solutions and explanations.

The readings in the present chapter illustrate four major explanations. They attribute continuing social deprivations to individual mal-behaviour, to a cycle of deprivation, to policy and service deficiencies, and to the very structure of society. A final reading reflects a multiplicity of analyses and proposals. Before commenting on the selections, two qualifications must be made. First, the explanations relate mainly to material and physical needs – poverty, overcrowding, ill-health – and not, for instance, to mental illness or handicap. Of course, the distinction is not a straightforward one for the stresses of poverty might precipitate mental breakdowns. Second, there are other explanations. None of the readings fully discuss child socialization theories or psychological interpretations of early family relationships.

In order to compare the various contributions, readers may find it useful to employ the following framework. Each writer directs attention to a basic cause or *explanation*. This leads them to propose certain *strategies* designed to effect change. A strategy is a pattern of action or, as Rein puts it, 'a settled course of action'. It is concerned with wide-ranging directions not specific tactics. A strategy, then, is a purposeful plan to reach defined *objectives*. The objectives contained in the readings can be examined in three ways: first by looking at the overall objectives, the fundamental changes it is hoped to create in society: second, the immediate objectives which may be necessary prerequisites to the more fundamental ones: third by identifying who or what is the object of change, the deprived person, the social services, the Government or society as a whole. The objectives, it is hoped, will be reached and the strategies channelled through appropriate *forms* or mechanisms. These may be, for instance, universal social services, selective benefits, priority area approaches or local political action. Related to the forms will be the differing sponsors or *auspices*, national Government, local authorities, voluntary societies or profit-making enterprises. Lastly, and implied in all the foregoing are the *values* of the contributors. Their values will determine the kind of relationships they believe should exist between people, the manner in which resources should be distributed and the type of political structure they want for society. In short, values will determine the choices of objectives, strategies, forms and auspices.

INDIVIDUAL MALFUNCTIONING

Most readings have assumed that expanding statutory welfare provision is an acceptable part of contemporary society. Yet an important school of thought has consistently attacked state welfare not only for doing too much for people but for actually being the means of creating or perpetuating unmet social need. Its leading academic exponents include Hayek, Seldon, Clark, Lees and Wiseman but the most pungent is **Dr Rhodes Boyson** MP whose contribution makes up the first reading.

Boyson argues that state social services compare unfavourably with private ones on the grounds of offering less choice, of attracting less financial investment and of lacking the competition which promotes efficiency. Above all, he believes that state social services encourage the worst tendencies in individuals who can become content to live on state handouts. He thus cites the case of low-paid workers who find it more profitable to draw Supplementary Benefit than wages. Consequently, taxation for the social services means that money is taken 'from the energetic, successful and thrifty to give to the idle, the failures and the feckless'. The result is that not only are numbers in poverty increased but so is 'disorder, crime and lack of civic duty' while the weakening of the nation's 'moral fibre' reduces its economic strength. It can be seen that the focus of Boyson's explanation is directed at the poor themselves who react in inappropriate ways to statutory social services.

The solution put forward is to return to Victorian standards when individual hard work and effort were at a premium. The overall strategy entails introducing moral and physical pressures which condemn poverty as moral failure and so encourage self-help, individualistic achievement and competitiveness. The main mechanisms to achieve such ends appear to rest in moral leadership by national figures. Their example would be reinforced by highly selective state social services available only to the minority unable to afford private insurance coverage. It follows that social services would not disappear but that their sponsorship would be largely through private enterprise and voluntary organizations. In short, there would be a free market in welfare which, through competition and the price mechanism, would ensure greater efficiency and services more responsive to consumers' requirements. Such a market would reflect the values which are stressed in Boyson's reading – freedom of choice, individualism, conformity, nationalism and material achievement.

Counter-arguments to the above analysis are not hard to find. The late Professor Richard Titmuss led another school of thought which disagreed with it at almost every point. The charges of inefficient statutory services are contested and Titmuss was at pains to compare the National Health Service with private health schemes in the USA. Research reveals that the numbers who choose to draw state benefits rather than work are exceedingly small. The meaning of 'freedom' is challenged with the accusation that the moral and statutory pressures proposed by Boyson and his colleagues are more constraining of freedom than any Welfare State. The virtues of the Victorian free market are contested by pointing out that it co-existed with terrible poverty, disease and unemployment. In short, freedom and choice existed only for those able to afford it. All the pros and cons of this debate cannot be repeated here and the reader is referred to the recommended books. In the meantime, Rhodes Boyson's reading is timely in that it comes from a man who is concerned about poverty and whose views have much in common with those of many citizens.

THE CYCLE OF DEPRIVATION

That social deprivation continues and even increases is acknowledged in the reading by **Sir Keith Joseph**. As Secretary of State for Health and Security, he was prepared to make public his analysis of the problem and to propose solutions accordingly.

Sir Keith accepts that many factors contribute to unmet social needs but believes one is of particular importance – the cycle of social deprivation. His explanation is that deprived parents pass on to their children the very habits and behaviour which cause their own condition. Not given the skills or motivation to improve, the next generation reproduces the failings of the former.

Whereas the reading of Rhodes Boyson sought an explanation in the behaviour of individuals, that by Sir Keith Joseph focuses on families. However, the families are not held morally responsible for their poverty for it is recognized that the cycle of deprivation does not provide them with motivation or capacities to achieve anything better. His belief in the values of the family as an institution which should provide opportunities for individual self-improvement and happiness means that he is committed to finding ways of breaking into the cycle.

The record of Sir Keith Joseph in initiating FIS showed him to be aware of the need for the immediate amelioration of poverty. But his major strategy is that of prevention. In the short-term, he sees family planning services as a means of reducing the actual numbers joining the cycle. In the long-term, he envisages services and projects that will enable present participants to move out of it. Playgroups to develop children's social and intellectual skills, casework to change the habits of parents, education to teach children and adults the role of 'good' parents. Through such devices he believes the cycle can be run down.

In order to reach the deprived in the above ways, Sir Keith favours the mechanisms of selective services and priority area approaches. These would operate under the auspices of central Government, local authority and voluntary bodies. Although of the same political persuasion as Boyson, it is hard to see how his plans can result in anything but an extension of statutory involvement in social welfare. The combined efforts of the increased State and voluntary involvement are aimed to effect changes in the families so as to enable them to benefit from the educational and job opportunities in society at large.

Criticisms of the cycle of deprivation thesis are found in the reading by Holman. Here it suffices to say that Sir Keith's explanation has had an undoubted political and public impact. The British Association of Social Workers has given it qualified approval. The National Children's Bureau is to undertake research on the subject. Not least, it has facilitated the planning of future services according to defined objectives instead of relying on *ad hoc* improvisations.

INADEQUATE SOCIAL SERVICES AND SOCIAL POLICIES

The reading by **Roy Jenkins** contains a comprehensive analysis of the outcomes of contemporary Government policies and statutory services. More than the other contributors, Jenkins seeks the major explanation for continuing social deprivation at a policy level. He thus criticizes the direction of Conservative policy towards selectivist benefits, outlines the weaknesses of FIS, and points to certain anomalies in the taxation system. At the same time, he concedes that many Governments have been responsible for long-term policy failures in the areas of employment, education and social security which have also contributed to the plight of the poor. Similarly, he argues that local government policies, or the lack of them, have resulted in services of such varying quality and quantity that social needs are met in some parts of the country but not others. Roy Jenkins by no means excludes the cycle of deprivation thesis but the thrust of his explanation is towards policies and services so inadequate that they do not offer the poor a reasonable chance of removing themselves from that cycle. It follows that his major objectives are policy reforms to enable social agencies to reach the deprived more effectively.

Although aware of the importance of long-term preventive measures through re-training, education and social work, the emphasis of Jenkins's proposals is on immediate ameliorative steps. He believes that quick, albeit partial, relief could be afforded through the raising of the rates of social security benefits, a reform of the tax system and the introduction of a child endowment payment. Consequently, the mechanisms of change would be through universal services, for instance to administer the child endowment scheme, along with priority approaches in order to strengthen areas of greatest need. This stress on both universal benefits combined with direct Government intervention via an expanded urban programme would entail an increased role for central Government although local authorities would simultaneously be expected to improve the personal social services. Noticeably, voluntary organizations receive less attention from Jenkins than is given in the other readings.

The strategy envisaged thus consists of short-term and long-term steps which, Jenkins believes, could be achieved by the various sections of society agreeing on common ends and means. Roy Jenkins is frequently called a 'liberal' and the importance he places on the values of rationality and consensus and his desire for a society where the poorest would be lifted above the present poverty line would seem to justify the title. Certainly, his liberal and humane objectives and strategies earn the respect and support of many people both within and without his own political party. Equally, they arouse the opposition of those who see liberalism as going too far or not far enough.

A STRUCTURAL EXPLANATION

If the readings discussed so far have sought explanations of unmet social need in the individual, in families, and in deficient social policies and services, the fourth completes the widening of the circle by focusing attention on the social and economic structures of society.

The study of society in terms of social stratification is as old as sociology itself. In recent years, the publications of Peter Townsend and of Coates and Silburn have revived the study in relation to poverty. The reading by **Robert Holman** argues that the stratified nature of society determines the distribution of resources and power so giving certain sections of the population little choice but to remain in poverty. Such a global explanation does not mean that individuals or groupings are ignored. Indeed, poverty is interpreted as functional in that it 'justifies' some persons having extensive wealth and income while other groups have very little.

Not surprisingly, an explanation which concerns the very shape of society requires a strategy which is long-term and concerned to alter the relationship between the deprived and the rest of society. A major objective thus becomes to enable the poor to influence the distribution of resources in their

favour and hence to the loss of those at present holding
disproportionate amounts. The implications are undoubtedly
political but this does not mean that changes are not sought
in the social services. Holman wants them to operate to
abolish rather than to maintain deprivation. Whether their
form is universal or selectivist, he argues that a major priority
is to improve the material and political position of the most
deprived members of society. However, recognizing the
strength of existing institutional practices, he believes that the
driving force for radical reform must come from outside
traditional Government, local authority and voluntary bodies
and rather must spring from community action and the poor
themselves.

The values made explicit in Holman's contribution are
egalitarian in desiring resources to be shared more equally and
for involvement in decision making to be spread amongst
more people. Criticisms can be made at precisely these points.
It is sometimes argued that the deprived lack the motivation to
such ends and the capacities to make decisions. Others, taking
a contrary view, believe that opportunities already exist for the
hard-working individual to reach the top whatever his
background. Another view is that the Welfare State has gone
far enough and that changes on the scale called for would lead
to anarchy. Perhaps most strong amongst those wishing for
further reform is the belief that change is only possible through
existing party political machineries. They conclude that it is
best to work within the limitations of these mechanisms for
immediate marginal achievements rather than seeking more
radical but less probable change outside.

MULTIPLE SOLUTIONS

In practice, strategies to meet social needs are rarely based on
any single or over-riding explanation. Instead, concern to take
immediate action either pre-empts any discussion of causes or
various opinions find some compromise in agreed plans of
action. The official reading is included as an example of policy
recommendations emerging from differing viewpoints. In 1970,
the Secretary of State for Health and Social Security, perturbed
that the needs of residents in socially deprived areas were not

being met, requested a conference. The participants represented a wide range of opinion and under the chairmanship of **Professor David Donnison** were able to issue a report the bulk of which makes up the reading.

The report notes that a number of factors may explain the condition of socially deprived areas. Economic factors such as the loss of employment or the routing of a motorway are particularly mentioned. However, the report is not prepared to argue for any one causal explanation and, after acknowledging that further research is necessary to understand deprivation, it then specifies steps towards three major strategies – the development of comprehensive planning, the involvement of residents, and improvements to statutory services. Within these, some provocative proposals are made including the setting up of geographical (as well as functional) committees within local government and, if necessary, the institution of 'old town corporations' with the far reaching powers and resources of new town corporations. It is reasoned that the proposals, by involving residents, would lead to a more complete understanding of social need, by improving agency management would lead to more efficient services, and by setting up new structures would enable more resources to be channelled to the socially deprived. Services would be expected to develop under the auspices of central Government, local government and local voluntary community organizations and little attention is given to private profit-making welfare services. The result, hopefully, would be to improve the material and psychological functioning of deprived persons. The implicit values of the report – namely that all persons have the right to influence the decisions affecting their lives and to receive incomes which strengthen their self respect – would then be upheld.

The comprehensive nature of the report's recommendations opens it to a number of critical questions. Is it inconsistent to propose major changes *before* involving the residents whose participation the report also supports? If extra resources are to be deployed from where are they to come? And if the gains of the deprived mean losses for the privileged how is the opposition of the latter to be overcome? In short, who is to put the recommendations into practice? Finally, it can be argued that the suggestions are too diverse and that implementation would have been more likely had they concentrated on one major issue. The retort, no doubt, is that a single, unpopular proposal can be more easily ignored. The putting up of a large number of possible reforms may actually increase the likelihood that the Government will act on some of them. Certainly, the report's suggestions for old town corporations, urban parishes, direct funding to deprived areas and area committees have since been examined and studied within central and local Government.

To conclude, it can be observed that the report has two elements in common with a number of other readings in this volume. First, that unmet social need can be so destructive of individual personalities that it should not be tolerated in a humane society. Second, that attempts to abolish deprivation without the participation of the deprived themselves may only lead to a reinforcement of their present position. Acceptable social welfare now means not only the provision of certain benefits and services but also the direct involvement of the recipients.

Down with the Poor

Rhodes Boyson

Reprinted with permission from *Down with the Poor*,
Churchill Press, 1971, pp. 1-9

I recently read about the breeding in America of the first bald
chickens. Apparently it seemed obvious to detached observers
and researchers, if not to the chickens, that farmers could save
much time and money if chickens ceased to have feathers.
Valuable food is wasted on the production of feathers and an
appalling amount of effort is required to pluck them before the
chicken is oven ready. The interests of the chicken would further
be served by the elimination of the superfluous feathers since
these provide a home for dirty little parasites which make the
chicken itch and scratch to ease its discomfort. Compassion as
well as economy required the disappearance of the feathers!

Alas the result was completely different from what was intended.
Economically the first 200 bald chickens suffered so severely from
the cold that they actually required much more food and warmth
than did their feathered brethren. In addition to these economic
disincentives the chickens suffered from such a lack of physical
and moral fibre that they laid fewer eggs and tended to develop
ulcers.

THE BROILER SOCIETY

The present Welfare State, with its costly universal benefits and
heavy taxation, is rapidly producing a similar economic and
spiritual malaise among our people. Planned, introduced and
encouraged by good men who believed that State intervention
would bring both economic and spiritual returns, the end-product
is completely different.

The National Health Service was introduced by men of
compassion who wished to improve the health of the poor and to
remove the worry of medical bills. The end-result has been a
decline in medical standards below the level of other advanced
countries because people are not prepared to pay as much

through taxation on other people's health as they would pay directly on their own and their families'. Long queues in surgeries, an endless waiting-list for hospital beds, and the emigration of many newly trained doctors are among the unexpected results. Small wonder that more and more people are looking to some form of private insurance to give them wider choice in medicine and surgery.

Unemployment schemes and other social security benefits have been universalized and increased to their present level because people remembered the millions of unemployed and the poverty and deprivation of the 1930s. The 'means test' is still a dirty word despite the fact that all of us in paying (or not paying) income tax regularly face a means test, as do others in seeking legal aid or applying for any of dozens of allowances or rebates which give preference to poorer people. Those of us with children at university face regular means tests.

There is also encouragement for the lower paid with large families to become unemployed or to go sick. Similarly, millions of workers are encouraged to break the monotony of factory routine by strikes when meagre strike pay can be augmented by supplementary benefits to their families and tax rebates for themselves. The reliable and industrious worker looks with irritation and animosity at his idle fellows whom he helps to maintain, and the general sense of responsibility and personal pride declines. National economic strength and personal moral fibre are both reduced. Officers administering Supplementary Benefit and unemployment insurance are so afraid of complaints being made to newspapers and MPs about harsh treatment that rules are bent, and scores of teachers even in London are paid unemployment pay whilst there are vacancies in the schools. Thus teachers trained at considerable national expense and now desiring more exotic careers in professions, rarely if ever recruited from employment exchanges, are encouraged to waste their teacher training.

THE WASTES OF 'WELFARE'

State education, introduced 100 years ago by men and women concerned first to provide the benefits of universal literacy and later to develop leisure and cultural pursuits, is more and more coming under control of the trendy 'expert', who seeks to make his name at the children's expense while he gathers his money from the state. There is little choice of school either by type, discipline or area and the neighbourhood comprehensive school with a complete egalitarian ethic could have disastrous effects upon educational standards. So long as choice is confined to parents who can afford expensive school fees, the lower- and middle-income groups will have less freedom of choice than they had in 1870. Similarly at university level student grants have increased demand beyond the genuine scholar while the hunt for other economies threatens the excellence of our higher studies and research.

Housing subsidies and rent controls, also introduced by good if short-sighted and muddled men, have produced the appalling slums and homelessness of the present day. Many working-class families are virtually prisoners of their council houses since they would lose the subsidy – and perhaps a roof – if they moved elsewhere. The large tower blocks with their tragic effect upon young and old inmates would never have multiplied in a free market where the producer has to take careful account of the preferences of the sovereign consumer. The tower blocks are like the bald chickens produced by outside and detached experts and researchers who would not deign to consult their victims. Larger local government units have removed officials and councillors from contact with the ratepayers as people, and every increase in size of local authorities transfers more power to officials concerned more about their professional advancement than with satisfying the ratepayer. Hence the fashions which run through professions are immediately perpetrated upon the innocent citizen.

Meanwhile the landlord penalized by restricted rents allows his property to deteriorate and the stock of houses to rent continues to diminish. The prices of large and modern houses are increased because, on high incomes, tax relief obtained against building society mortgages is one of the shrewdest forms of capital gain in an age of inflation.

We can all recall that Mr Crossman's grandiose scheme for national superannuation would have drastically widened the breach in National Insurance by requiring that present 'contributors' (for which read 'taxpayers') should pay for present pensions in the hope that 'future contributors' (for which read 'future taxpayers') would pay for future pensions. This would have been a further confidence trick on the contributors made possible only by the bemused state of the electorate after five years of continually increasing Governmental imposts. The chicken was not only bald, it was about to be popped in the oven, yet it had almost ceased to protest against its own destruction as a free and individual creature.

'RAMPANT STAGFLATION'

The result of all this extra State interference financed by taking over 50 per cent of the gross national product in taxation has been not the production of an economically viable society but what might be called rampant stagflation, that is to say stagnation in production and raging inflation which further destroys belief in the future. The moral fibre of our people has been weakened. A State which does for its citizens what they can do for themselves is an evil State; and a State which removes all choice and responsibility from its people and makes them like broiler hens will create the irresponsible society. In such an irresponsible society no one cares, no one saves, no one bothers – why should they when the State spends all its energies taking money from the energetic, successful and thrifty to give to the idle, the failures and the feckless?

Religious philosophy holds that man is moral only when he can freely exercise his choice between good and evil. This requirement is the basis of free will. The same applies equally to economic, social and family life. A man will grow to full moral maturity only when he is allowed to take risks, with subsequent rewards and penalties and full responsibility for his decisions. Yet in Britain the State now decides how half or more of a man's income shall be spent, how his family should be educated, how their health care should be organized, how they shall save for misfortunes and retirement, what library and in many cases what cultural provision they should receive, and where and at what cost they should be housed.

In recent years the State and the local authority have also decided what charities a man should support. Missionary societies dependent upon private charity decay while overseas aid has dissipated hundreds of millions of pounds levied on the public through the tax system. State youth clubs flourish on the enforced largesse of the rates while church clubs and societies dependent upon hard-pressed voluntary contributions decline. We are witnessing not only an attack on the right of the individual to decide his own charities and grow in moral stature by his free gift, but also the expenditure by Government and local authorities of large sums on causes and items often repugnant to the involuntary contributors. Tower blocks, foreign aid. subsidies to decaying firms and student grants to individuals aiming at the overthrow of our society are all illustrations of such expenditure.

Not only is the present Welfare State inefficient and destructive of personal liberty, individual responsibility and moral growth, but it saps the collective moral fibre of our people as a nation. John Stuart Mill wrote 'The worth of a state, in the long run, is the worth of the individuals composing it'. Disraeli in another context declared, 'We put too much faith in systems and look too little to men'. The truth is that a strong, free country can be built only on strong, free men and the weakness of our foreign policy and defence provision over the last few years is not only a reflection of weak Government but is symptomatic of an enfeebled people. Samuel Smiles wrote 'The solid foundations of liberty must rest upon individual character; which is also the only sure guarantee for social security and national progress'.

STRENGTH THROUGH SELF-HELP

In *Down with the Poor* we are concerned to point towards a society which will be more efficient on the one hand in abolishing poverty and want because it will give equal priority on the other hand to building up the strength of the individual and the family as good in themselves and essential to a strong country. Some people look with amusement or even horror at the self-help of the Victorian age, but its virtues of duty, order and efficiency have been replaced in the muddled thinking of our age by a belief in individual irresponsibility: a neglect of our responsibilities to the past, to our fellow citizens and to the future. The predictable outcome is seen in disorder, crime and lack of civic duty, and in the palsied inefficiency so often visible throughout the public service, nationalized boards and even private industry. We have been heading for economic and moral bankruptcy.

The Victorians also had another watchword – economy – which meant that if one was careful how much was spent on a particular cause not only would inefficiency be avoided but money or resources would be husbanded for other causes. Self-help to Samuel Smiles was not a eulogy of selfishness. Indeed to Smiles the duty of helping oneself in the highest sense involved not only helping one's family but helping one's neighbours and the unfortunate in all classes. Religious responsibility and individual conscience ensured that profits and wealth were seen as a trust to be spent aright.

The massive increase in taxation since Victorian days has crippled voluntary welfare, while permitting poverty to linger unnecessarily. Where poverty remains it is the fault of politicians whose double sin has been to spread benefits too widely and raise taxes on a scale that hinders the increase in the national income. It is significant that during the six years of the last Labour Government there was an increase in the number of families living below the 'poverty line' despite an unprecedented increase in taxation, public expenditure and the bureaucratic machine.

Since we are concerned to restore a strong independent society based upon free men, we have provided an exciting outline of a better future in which all could be free and none need want. Legislation and State interference could be cut back and limited to a requirement that all should insure against ill-health, misfortune and old age, and that the minority whose resources are insufficient to pay the premiums because of mental or physical handicap would be helped by some form of reverse income tax with the cash or vouchers necessary to pay their way in the free market. State schemes would need to be continued as a safety net only so long as some of the newly enfranchised failed to join a private or company scheme. Educational vouchers would widen educational choice and make schools responsive to parental demands, and housing would be completely freed. Voluntary welfare would take on a new lease of life in caring for family and personal needs that should be kept beyond the clumsy, costly reach of bureaucrats.

General Moshe Dayan recently recalled the ancient fertility of some of the Israeli lands which had over hundreds of years of foreign rule lost their fertility because of poor husbandry. He described how such fertility was being restored so that the soil now produced crops again. *Down with the Poor* shows how resurgence of the past pride and responsibility of our people, bringing a rapid increase in the gross national product linked with the concentration of aid on the deprived and handicapped, will eliminate poverty and the poor.

On many occasions the freedom of the world has depended upon our courage, efficiency and love of liberty. We must build these virtues anew in our people so that we shall not be found wanting in any future crisis. As in higher self-help we owe this not only to ourselves – it is part of our duty to all men.

The Cycle of Deprivation

Sir Keith Joseph

Reprinted with permission from a speech given by Sir Keith Joseph, at a conference organized by the Pre-School Playgroups Association on 29 June 1972. The reading covers paragraphs 14-20, 33-43 and 47-53 of the speech.

Yet the family is under attack. It has enormous potentialities for good: but, as is inherent in the human condition, if it does not function properly it can do harm. If the family is to do the good of which it is capable, the parents need to show a consistent combination of love and guidance, understanding and firmness. But an understanding of this by parents cannot be taken for granted. There are many forces at work to discourage and distort priorities and attitudes. Many parents had no chance when they were children to learn what a happy home can be. Surely then we need to consider how family life can be strengthened. There are some positive steps that we may be able to take, and I shall say more about these in a minute. But first I suggest that there is a profound issue here to which we should perhaps give more sustained and ordered thought than we have done in the past.

THE PARADOX

Why is it that, in spite of long periods of full employment and relative prosperity and the improvement in community services since the Second World War, deprivation and problems of maladjustment so conspicuously persist? Indeed, some would say that they have actually increased. This is a paradox to those who hoped that they would dwindle as standards of consumption and health and education rose.

Deprivation is, I know, an imprecise term. What I am talking about are those circumstances which prevent people developing to nearer their potential – physically, emotionally and intellectually – than many do now. Deprivation takes many forms, and they interact. It shows itself, for example, in poverty, in emotional impoverishment, in personality disorder, in poor educational attainment, in depression and despair. It can be found at all levels of society – not only among the poor – but the most vulnerable are those already at the bottom end of the economic and social ladder. The causes are many and complex. There are economic factors – persistent unemployment and low income: living conditions play a part – bad housing and over-crowding and few opportunities for recreation. There are personal factors arising from illness or accident or genetic endowment. And there are many factors which affect patterns of child rearing. When a child is deprived of consistent love and guidance he is deprived of that background most likely to lead to stability and maturity. All these factors are interactive, and a combination of them produces the greatest hazards. In short, deprivation embraces many disadvantages, which can occur singly or in different combinations throughout society, and which we see persisting despite all our advances.

'THE CYCLE OF DEPRIVATION'

Perhaps there is at work here a process, apparent in many situations but imperfectly understood, by which problems reproduce themselves from generation to generation. If I refer to this as a 'cycle of deprivation' I do not want to be misunderstood. On the one hand the use of such a term may suggest rather more certainty about the phenomenon I am trying to describe than the state of our understanding warrants; on the other, I may be accused of talking about the blindingly obvious. But I am not suggesting that there is some single process by which social problems reproduce themselves – it is far more complex than this. I am saying that, in a proportion of cases, occurring at all levels of society, the problems of one generation appear to reproduce themselves in the next. Social workers, teachers and others know only too well the sort of situation I am referring to, where they can be reasonably sure that a child, because of his background, is operating under disadvantage and prone to run into the same difficulties in his turn as his parents have experienced.

Do we not know only too certainly that among the children of this generation there are some doomed to an uphill struggle against the disadvantages of a deprived family background? Do we not know that many of them will not be able to overcome the disadvantages, and will become in their turn the parents of deprived families?

Of course there are services struggling to prevent this. They work with the most difficult casualties of society – the problem families, the vagrants, the alcoholics, the drug addicts, the disturbed, the delinquent, and the criminal. Behind many of these conditions lies a deprived childhood.

In my view we need to study the phenomenon of transmitted deprivation – what I have called the cycle of deprivation. It is not something new: it has become more apparent for the very reason that developments over the past 20-30 years have had the effect of raising standards and have revealed more clearly situations where standards have failed to rise. The cycle is not a process that we fully understand, but a number of objective studies do tend to bear out the subjective belief of many practitioners that cyclical processes are at work.

On all these questions of research I am hopeful that it will be possible to mount studies that will give us a better understanding of the nature of the cycle of deprivation and of the dynamics of poverty and help us to decide the directions in which further research can most usefully be undertaken. But much more than this I hope it will point the way to possible means of developing preventive strategies and of influencing change for the better.

WHAT CAN WE DO BEFORE THE RESULTS OF RESEARCH ARE KNOWN

What can be done in the meantime? We must, I believe, do all we can to reinforce those activities which already help parents while they are bringing up their children. There are a number of ways of doing this. I have already talked about one: the further development of playgroups and other services for children under five. And I want to talk about three others. The first of these is family planning.

Family planning

There is no doubt that, if effective family planning were more widely practised and if those most in need of advice could be reached, the size of the problem – that is, the numbers caught up in the cycle of deprivation – could over the years be kept below what it would otherwise be.

Studies have also found a positive association throughout the social classes between, on the one hand, large family size and, on the other, delinquency, low intelligence and poor reading skills – factors likely to propel people into the cycle. These are not necessarily signs of low innate ability: they tend rather to reflect family circumstances. It may be that there is less time for conversation between parents and children, for reasoned explanation and for individual support for each child.

Of course, I am not suggesting for one moment that large families as such are undesirable: on the contrary, large families can have great strengths and value, and some parents no doubt can cope with more children than other parents. But where parents with large families are immature and in danger themselves of marital breakdown, the more so when they are also poor and badly housed, the children are virtually sure to be deprived.

Clearly, then, an understanding use of family planning could reduce the numbers afflicted by deprivation. I am currently reviewing family planning policies with this and many other factors in mind, and I hope to announce later in the year the results of this review.

Support for parenthood

Another area for study and perhaps action is, I suggest, the promotion in our society of greater awareness and understanding of the processes of child development and the importance of the parental role.

Is there not a profound contrast between on the one hand the scrupulous attention which our society, through the health services, gives to women in pregnancy and childbirth and, on the other hand, the limited extent to which our society seeks to help the mother and the father, where this is necessary, to understand the child's emotional and intellectual needs? Yet where these needs are left unmet – and this can be in homes that are not poor and in housing that is not bad – the children will find school unrewarding – because they are ill-prepared for it; will carry into adolescence and adult life an inability to form trusting and stable relationships – because they have never experienced them; and will become in their turn the parents of the next generation of children who are deprived emotionally and intellectually.

It is easy to say that this is obvious: that inadequate people tend to be inadequate parents and that inadequate parents tend to rear inadequate children. But surely we have to carry this argument through and recognize that the process will continue into the future – unless we can do something to help. This is the reason why I am looking for means of helping parents who either out of ignorance or for some other reason do not give their children the consistent context of love and guidance, understanding and firmness. I am thinking here of what some have called preparation for parenthood.

The needs of children

Over the past 20 or 30 years there has been a great advance in knowledge about child development and the effects of childhood deprivation on later behaviour – knowledge about the manner in which a child's personality and character develop in the first years of life when he is dependent on adult care.

These first years are crucial: the roots of much deprivation go back to infancy. A child's growth is rapid, and the capacity to develop intellectually and to form and to maintain emotional and social relationships is established so early that it soon becomes increasingly difficult to put things right. The basis of future behaviour patterns is laid when an infant experiences a rewarding relationship with his mother and, through consistent guidance and love, gains control over impulse. The process, it seems clear, is extended through a relationship with the father and with others who form the intimate family circle. And during pre-school years – as you in this audience have led the way in understanding so long and so passionately – intellectual curiosity needs stimulation, and verbal and manual facilities need exercise and encouragement. Child rearing practices that do not take account of these known factors about early development are storing up trouble for the future; and stressful, inadequate or deprived family situations, which hinder good parental practice, damage the development of the child.

The special needs of emotionally deprived parents
For some parents it is not simply a matter of help to better understanding of their children's needs. They have great emotional needs on their own account, and until these are met they are unable to meet the needs of their children. It is in such families that the children are most at risk. Social workers and health visitors have long been aware of this. That is why, in preventive social work with families, much effort has been put into casework with parents, to help to meet *their* personal and emotional needs. Only as this is done can they begin to value themselves and form healthy relationships. Only then is there hope that they will be able to be effective parents, to tolerate their child's dependency, and accept his primitive urges as being an expression of normal needs rather than an attack on them as parents. For these families, the imparting of knowledge about child development is inextricably woven into the social help and support the parents themselves need.

Further action on preparation for parenthood
So there is this need for knowledge and understanding which is in part unmet. What should be done about it? To what extent should social agencies become consciously involved in filling the gap? And to what extent should central Government concern itself with encouraging social agencies to do this more effectively and more widely? If, as I believe, we should all be concerning

ourselves with these matters, what are the most effective ways by which the social agencies directly in touch with children, young people and adults can set about their task?

In some places much is being done already – by health visitors and social workers, by teachers, by general practitioners and psychiatrists. And this is a field in which the Churches and voluntary social service agencies such as the Marriage Guidance Council are deeply interested. Their efforts are many and diverse, and it would be useful to collect information about them to see what lessons of wider application we can learn.

Preparation for parenthood with children
The schools can, and do, play a large part. Children of school age are intensely interested in themselves, in their relationships with other people and with the outside world.

Much work relevant to all this has long been going on in schools, and there is already, I understand, a trend towards extending this to education about marriage and about parental roles and children's needs. On wider social as well as educational grounds I should welcome any further developments in these directions which the schools and the local education authorities, the teaching profession and bodies such as the Schools Council and the Health Education Council, can bring about.

Preparation for parenthood with adults
For those who have left school something different is wanted. There is need to build on and extend what has been learned at school. There is surely an extended role here, or a new role, for many parts of the medical, social, educational and other services, statutory and voluntary, and the Churches.

The greatest difficulty will be to influence those who are already deprived. We know we shall not succeed in reaching all those who most need help. But we can, if we try, reach some of those who need help. Certainly it is worth trying. Is there scope for developing the role which the health visitor and the social worker already have in this field?

Poverty is Preventable

Roy Jenkins

Reprinted with permission from *What Matters Now,* Fontana 1972, pp. 47-57

There is not one single simple remedy for poverty. But it could be massively attacked if we carry through certain policies. It is to these that I now turn. *Substantial spending will be required.* Finance will probably limit the speed at which the programme can be carried out. But sensible and realistic commitments will only follow from a view of longer-term objectives. It is vital to sort out these objectives. The first priority is that of short-term changes in social security benefits to help the two million people who are living below Supplementary Benefit level. But we also need changes in our tax and social security systems to improve the economic security of all that fifth of the population who are near the poverty level. Such changes in social security and taxation need to be accompanied by measures to help the less skilled to earn a living. But increased retraining would also be useful. The measures proposed, so far, would both raise the current incomes of those of the poor who cannot work, and raise the earning power of those who can. But we should also increase investment in the next generation. We must break the cycle by which the children of the poor become poor themselves. This will mean changes in our policies for the social services. Finally we need new efforts to provide alternatives to institutional care.

The aim of any scheme is to provide a reasonable minimum income for all. This was the Beveridge goal – but in practice no Government has yet achieved it. The State retirement pension has been below the Supplementary Benefit level. The National Insurance Pension for a married couple is now £10.90. Supplementary Benefit for a married couple, taking into account the rent allowance and the long-term addition, is about £13.90. Nor has the level of family allowances reflected the subsistence costs of children. Currently the allowances are 90p or £1. The Supplementary Benefit scale allows £2.25 for a child aged five to eleven and more for an older child. The effect of the child tax allowances is to give more support to children from richer homes to those from poorer.

Various schemes have been proposed to provide a minimum income for all. The boldest, simplest and quickest of these is the 'new Beveridge plan' combined with tax clawback. The increases in retirement pensions, family allowances and other National Insurance benefits needed to bring them to minimum subsistence levels would be very substantial.

The present Government has tried to deal with the problem by introducing the Family Income Supplement. Its disadvantages are great. The rate of take-up is low and is likely to remain so. It gives help only to those in the most dire need – and admittedly not even to all of them. Finally it adds one more to the great confusion of means-tested benefits which face people on low incomes.

In the interests of incentives to hard work and initiative, the Government has reduced the maximum income tax and surtax liability, even on the highest incomes, to 75 per cent. The top-paid will now therefore keep 25p on each further pound. Today the £21 a week man, however, will certainly take home less of each further pound *he* earns and may well actually take home *nothing* of an extra pound he has won by harder work or longer hours.

This absurdity arises simply because the Government, in order to make cuts in social expenditure – quite unnecessary in the present economic circumstances – have introduced a massive proliferation of means tests. Their housing and welfare measures will subject fully a third of the entire population to means tests. Altogether six or seven times more *working* families, that is with the man in full-time employment, will be liable to means tests than were subject previously to all other means tests put together – and there are 3,000 of them in Britain today.

Now all these means tests have a ceiling for eligibility within the same broad range of income. To the extent therefore that more and more means-tested benefits are concentrated on low wage earners, they will stand to lose more and more as they push up their earnings to, and beyond, this ceiling band. Consider the man on £21 a week with two children in July 1972. If he were able to push up his gross earnings, he would lose out on an extra pound:

	£
Income tax	0·30
Loss of FIS	0·10
Graduated contribution	0·04
School meals charges	1·20
Rent allowance	0·17
	£1·81

He is thus 81p *worse off* as a result of his harder work, higher productivity or whatever. And there is nothing whatsoever exceptional about such a man.

If the family were also getting school uniform grants, education maintenance allowances, students' grants, family planning facilities and exemption from charges for prescriptions, spectacles and dental care, and for local authority services like home help and the care of the children (or any combination of these), the position would be still worse. Indeed recent research surveys have come across wage-earners subject to a disincentive of more than 200 per cent; that is they would be more than twice as worse off for each extra £1 they earned.

This ridiculous situation, symbolized by the nonsense that a low wage-earner family may well be receiving FIS while at the same time paying income tax, is full of ironies. Labour has always feared the disincentive effects of accumulated means tests. Previously however when means tests were few and unco-ordinated, such fears may have been insubstantial.

The Tories on the other hand have traditionally been suspicious about scrounging and evasion by the poor. Their fears have been grossly exaggerated, but now a Conservative Government have produced a situation in which incentive has been completely destroyed – and indeed reversed for a very large segment of the population.

The other possible approaches are those of negative income tax or of tax credit schemes. In principle, these schemes have strong intellectual appeal and certainly deserve more careful and detailed consideration than they have received so far. Some versions of the schemes are open to the objection that they give help only to the few; all of them pose very considerable administrative problems, although over a period these should not be insurmountable.

In any case the tax and social security systems have to be brought closer together. In 1968 I took the first step in this direction when I raised family allowances substantially by combining the increase with a tax clawback provision. We must now move towards a complete integration of child tax allowances and family allowances. Instead of these two forms of payment, families would receive a child endowment payment which would be partly taxable – and they would receive this payment for all children including the first.

Changes in social benefits are clearly necessary in the attack on poverty. These involve considerable financing problems, which are far more easily solved within a generally buoyant economy climate. Such changes are not imperative if we are to help the two million in poverty. Where they are needed is to help the other nine million who are near the poverty line. The current faults in our social security and tax systems are felt most severely at these levels of income. The first fault is that we lack an adequate pension scheme. It was a major tragedy that we just failed to leave one on the Statute Book at the end of the last Labour Government. Occupational pensions schemes have grown rapidly because the State has not provided a decent alternative. The old pension scheme has even failed in its relatively limited objective of providing minimum for all. The better off have occupational pensions. It is the poor who have suffered.

It must be accepted that the tax system is very hard on poorer families because the tax threshold is so low. I raised it several times but not as much as I would have liked or as was necessary. It is now relatively much lower than 20 years ago. In 1950 a married man with one child started paying tax when his earnings reached 75 per cent of the national average. Now he starts paying tax when his earnings are a little over half the average. This means that a family can both pay tax and receive benefit under the Family Income Supplement. A family with one child and an income of £19·50 a week gross will get a payment of 30p under FIS – but will pay almost the same amount in tax. We have moved away from the old principle that we should not tax the income required for subsistence.

We must also recognize that our social services are no longer

on a par with the best. Our system of family support is less generous or equitable than in most European countries. Our post-war
pension scheme has also worn less well than the American social
security system. The view is taking hold that the social services
should act as a safety net to private provision. Yet only the State –
as the American experience shows – can run an adequate pension
service. The firm – in a time of rapid change in labour markets and
in the structure of industry – is the wrong unit on which to base
provision for old age. Who can predict the structure of industry
in thirty years' time? Nor can pension arrangements based on
firms do much for those who work outside the more prosperous
and capital intensive sectors of industry. Equally only Government can bring about redistribution in favour of families.

Changes in social security are the first part of any programme
for poverty. The second is help to the less skilled in the job market.
Job prospects matter to all the high risk groups which make up
the poor. They matter to the elderly, to single parent families, to
large families and to unskilled workers. Some pensioners are in
full- or part-time employment, as are some single women supporting families. Job prospects affect every group among the
poor · not simply the adult male wage earning poor.

Unemployment at its 1966-70 level – let alone today's far worse
level – is damaging to the vulnerable groups in the labour force. A
return to full employment would substantially brighten the job
prospects of the unskilled. It would also reduce the numbers of
disabled drawing Supplementary Benefit. Some of them would be
able to find jobs in a more buoyant labour market. Fuller employment would help not only the very poor but that fifth of the
population whose standard of living is constantly under threat.
We have to create economic conditions such that the chance of a
job and of self-respect is open to older workers and the less
skilled – not just to the young and the highly trained.

We must also change our policies for the other social services,
such as education. The standard of schools in poor areas is too
low. Hence special help has been given to Plowden priority areas.
But the problem may not just be that schools in a few areas are
inadequate. There may have been a wider shift of emphasis within
our social services.

Originally the purpose of the social services was to relieve
poverty. So great was the need that almost any increase in public

spending in whatever form helped to reduce poverty. This is no longer the case. The social services have come to serve many accepted social purposes other than the relief of poverty. They provide opportunities in higher education. They attempt to achieve a reasonable pattern of urban development, through the new towns policies. They provide care in sickness for all. This is in itself very desirable. It is essential for a civilized life. But it also means an increase in the general level of public spending may not in itself reduce poverty. It all depends on who gets the increase.

Some of the fastest growth in spending recently has been for services from which the poor benefit little. Few children from an unskilled manual background go to university. Few of the poor move into new housing in new towns.

We must be careful that services which are used by the less affluent get their full share of extra resources. We must be concerned with the distribution of the services as well as their scale. We must, within the framework of a high standard of universal services, direct more help to poorer areas and groups. There may be a case for priority areas in the NHS as well as in education and in housing. We have greatly underestimated the human and financial resources required to improve standards in deprived areas.

There is one further change in our policies for the social services which would be of great help to the poor. This would be an increased commitment to the personal social services, for children needing help and guidance in the schools, for the disabled and for the old. The extension and development of community care has a particular importance for groups at risk of poverty. This is so for children in deprived families. In the schools there is a grave shortage of psychologists, psychiatrists and trained staff concerned with child guidance. The Seebohm Report calculated that at least one child in ten will need special educational, social or mental help before the age of 18 and that at most one child in twenty-two was getting such help. In parts of the country children in distress may have to wait many months for an appointment. Children with educational handicaps suffer as well as those with physical and emotional difficulties. Disturbed adolescents also get little help. Troubles in school contribute to employment problems later. A child whose school career is interrupted or hampered will often leave without qualifications and will find it difficult to get and keep a job. Help earlier might make the difference between poverty and the ability to earn an adequate living later.

The elderly also need personal services. They use meals on wheels, home nursing, the home help and chiropody services. Better services are needed as well as improved pensions if we are to eliminate poverty in old age. In most local authority areas these services are quite inadequate. We need much more sheltered housing and more help so that the elderly can continue to lead a normal life in the community. Even at present the great majority of the bed-bound and the house-bound live at home and not in institutions. We need to develop both services which help the infirm among the elderly and those which help the elderly to maintain their independence.

Finally a policy for poverty must involve help to those in institutions. The poor are much more likely than the population as a whole to find themselves at some stage in life in institutions, whether these are homes for the elderly, psychiatric hospitals or even prisons. The elderly poor are often in local authority residential accommodation. People from unskilled occupations are more frequently admitted to mental hospitals. Hospitals for the handicapped have a number of patients who could lead a fairly normal life in the community if they were helped to do so.

The institutional populations are growing rather than shrinking. At present about 320,000 people are in institutions – counting only local authority old people's homes, and hospitals for the mentally ill and handicapped. For one group – children in care, there have been significant advances away from institutional care. But we have not moved nearly as rapidly to provide a more normal life for other groups.

These institutions have common effects on the personality. They lead to the destruction of identity and the reduction of independence. In spite of the efforts of staff, most of our institutions in their present form make people worse not better. Progress here will be slow, but we can and must do better than we have done in the last decade. In the past we have adopted the slogans of community care, without always making the practical commitments. We have had plans for community care – for instance that for the mentally ill. But we have not in practice carried them nearly far enough.

Social, health and education services tend to be provided at a lower level relative to need in the areas where the need is greatest. This is not usually the fault of the local authorities. At root, it is the fault of the system within which they have to operate.

Local authority expenditure is paid for partly out of rates and partly – 58 per cent – out of Rate Support Grant from the Government. Poor areas suffer a multiple handicap; the yield of a 1p rate per head of the population is low, poor people can ill afford high rates, yet the formula which redistributes Rate Support Grant does not take fully into account the effects of variations in resources and the costs of providing services. I have already stressed the need for additional sources of revenue for local authorities; but we must reform the existing rating system as well. At present the ordinary householder's rate bill is determined less by conscious political decisions of his elected representatives than by the quirks of the Rate Support formula and by the accident of whether his home is within the same local authority boundaries as a reasonable spread of factories, shops and offices. If central Government is to cede to local authorities control over a substantial source of revenue – be it local income tax or one of the major indirect taxes – then I believe rates from industry and commerce should be redistributed directly by the Government to local authorities on a basis of need.

This would end the present situation, where the authorities which can afford the highest level of expenditure per person are simply those with a substantial rate yield from commercial and industrial property. The wealth of Westminster, Croydon and even Port Talbot would go to improve facilities in less fortunate areas. This would be an important change, for the demands on local authority expenditure created by industry and commerce are in no way proportional to the income which they provide to the local authority under today's system. We often find that the authority where industry and commerce are situated is not the authority where the people who work in the factories and shops and offices are living. And it is people, particularly the young and the old, on whose behalf most local authority expenditure is incurred. However, if a local authority did not derive any immediate financial benefit from additional commerce and industry, there would be less pressure to build offices and shops where it should be building homes and health centres and libraries.

Redistribution of the Rate Support Grant goes a long way to

help the poor authority, but it does not overcome the whole of its handicap. If an authority wishes to improve or extend its services, it can do so by raising its rates. This is a straightforward choice for the richer areas which are the least likely to have a great need to compensate by unusually high standards of public provision for unusually low standards of amenity for the people who live there. It is the poor authority which most needs a generous supply of school books and equipment, or of social workers, or a well-staffed and equipped children's service. But the people who live in these areas are least able to pay higher rates. They can best be helped by a continuing positive redirection of resources, over and above the redistribution of grant according to needs.

To do this we need an expanded urban programme not only for the renewal and redevelopment of outmoded or unsuitable buildings or other capital stock, but also to give continuing support to welfare and community development projects, some of which are voluntary as well as to improve the standard of the ongoing services which the local authority provides. The present scale of the urban programme is very small. Local authority current expenditure totals some £4,000 million a year; local authority capital expenditure is another £2,000 million. Yet expenditure on the urban programme, to direct additional resources where they are most needed, is estimated to rise to a grand total of little over £14 million in 1972-3. There is no shortage of worthy projects. In 1971, for example, the London Borough of Lambeth submitted projects to cost £103,500. Only £13,650 of this was approved for inclusion in the urban programme. An eightfold expansion of the whole programme would cost only about £120 million per year. This is not too heavy a price to pay to attack the manifold squalor in areas where poverty abounds.

It is for Government to ensure that public standards of provision are *higher* in relation to needs in areas where there is poverty than they are elsewhere. To make them equally high would be a good start, but it is only by positive discrimination that we can hope to break into the vicious circle of poverty and deprivation that we see about us.

I have endeavoured to outline the problem and suggest some but not complete remedies. We will achieve little until we make the reduction of poverty a goal of our general social and economic policies. Poverty can be eliminated only if we improve the standards of our social services generally, and change our priorities for them. Poverty can only be eliminated if we make it a goal of our general economic policies and make a success of those policies.

The main danger is that our society will become increasingly divided between the affluent and the less well off. On one side will be the world of youth and opportunities – on the other the poor, with an increasing sense of deprivation and shut-offness from the affluent world about them. The old are still far too much in a deprived world on their own. Let us make sure that we do not allow to persist still longer another private world of continuing hopelessness for at least a fifth of our citizens. That would be the road to a dangerously split, morally unjust and damagingly insecure society of which none of us could be proud.

Poverty: Consensus and Alternatives

Robert Holman

Reprinted with permission from 'Poverty: Consensus and Alternatives. The British Journal of Social Work, vol. 3, no. 4, Winter 1973

The purpose of this article is to examine the published views of two leading politicians who can claim to speak for their parties. From their discussion of poverty and social deprivation (and the terms will be used inter-changeably) an attempt will be made to demonstrate that their policies or proposals rest on similar assumptions about society and a similar model of poverty. Their consensus of approach will mean that no alternative policies are being seriously mooted within the party political system. Their assumptions will be examined critically and the suggestion made that an approach deriving from an alternative model is required to counter poverty.

Sir Keith Joseph has been a notable Secretary of State for Social

Services. His keenness to 'see for himself', his grasp of detail and his humanity have been impressive. He has given much thought to poverty and in June 1972 he put his ideas together in a speech to the Pre-school Playgroups Association. Obviously, the minister placed some importance on his now well-known 'social deprivation' address, for he caused it to be circulated widely.

The speech contains a graphic description of features associated with poverty, low income, poor educational attainment, inadequate housing, depression and despair. This prompts the minister to ask why social deprivation can persist in a period of relative prosperity. The answer, he suggests, can be found in the concept of a cycle of deprivation 'by which problems reproduce themselves from generation to generation'.

Sir Keith then outlines a theory of 'the phenomenon of transmitted deprivation' in which the carriers of poverty are the families themselves. He accepts that the early years are the most vital ones in shaping the social and emotional development of children. They are the years in which the way they will function as adults is established. Certain inadequate parents do not provide the love, firmness, guidance and stimulus which most normal children receive. Being poorly socialized, their children do not acquire the motivation, skills and capacities necessary to avail themselves of educational and job opportunities. In turn, they will grow up only to transmit the same behaviour patterns to their offspring who, therefore, will also remain in poverty. A cycle is in existence which condemns any joiners to poverty as the following quotations will show:

> Do we not know only too certainly that among the children of this generation there are some doomed to an uphill struggle against the disadvantages of a deprived family background? Do we not know that many of them will not be able to overcome the disadvantages and will become in turn the parents of deprived families?
>
> . . . large numbers of children [are] doomed to lives stunted physically, emotionally and intellectually because of their early years.
>
> Parents who were themselves deprived in one or more ways in childhood become in turn the parents of another generation of deprived children.

So serious, antisocial and unresponsive are the behaviour patterns of these families that they actually militate against the steps taken by the social services and prevent efforts to help the new generation of children.

> . . . I must revert, finally, to problems of family background, which lie behind so many of our other ills – mainly because of their effects on children here and now, but also because they prejudice everything we are trying to do for children in the next generation.

As an example of 'transmitting' families, Sir Keith instances 'problem' families who not only pass on deprivation but because of their breeding habits, do so to a very large number of children.

The cycle of deprivation theory is not new. Indeed, Sir Keith's exposition is similar to that published by Jamieson Hurry over 50 years ago. It is new to find a minister embracing a theory so fully and being prepared to shape public action accordingly. For beyond the basic social security system, which acts as a minimum level safety net, he is calling for forms of social intervention which will change the behaviour pattern of poor persons. In particular, he believes the cycle of deprivation can best be broken into by improving and supplementing the families' child rearing practices which shape the later behaviour of their children. Thus the minister advocates measures which reach children in their most formative years – playgroups, compensatory education and 'preparation for parenthood' schemes – and measures which have a direct influence on the immediate behaviour of adults, for instance, therapeutic relationships with an increasing number of social workers. He hopes that by the shaping and changing of their behaviour, families will learn how to function adequately in society. Further, the numbers joining the cycle can be reduced by teaching families to use one of the minister's favourite projects – family planning schemes for the poor.

The concept of the cycle of transmitted deprivation is related to certain assumptions about society. At the risk of over-simplification, certain of these assumptions, upon which Sir Keith appears to base his poverty policies, can be identified. On the whole, the economic and social machinery of society is regarded as working well, providing a tolerable standard of living for most people.

Unfortunately a minority of certain families are the grit in the machine, being unable to use it themselves and causing trouble for other people. The deprivation of this minority is due mainly to their inadequate child-rearing practices which fail to instil in their children the skill and will to perform like the rest of the population. If these family habits and practices can be improved, however, the minority will be enabled to achieve better education and jobs and so move out of poverty. The other sections of society wish to abolish poverty and will willingly provide the necessary resources and be prepared to incorporate the poor into their ranks.

Roy Jenkins, Home Secretary, and former Chancellor of the Exchequer and Deputy Leader of the Labour Party, is a political heavyweight who commands much support in his party. His wide-ranging interests, in particular his views on poverty, are presented in his latest publication, *What Matters Now*. Here Jenkins eloquently, even passionately, describes the many faces of poverty, stressing that it involves not just a lack of money but also deprivation in terms of health, education, housing and employment. Moreover, he makes it clear that these factors are multiple and interrelated, with one deprivation leading to another.

> Housing standards affect attitudes and the ability of children to learn. It is difficult to perform effectively outside if the home circumstances are those of over-crowding or damp.

Further, he perceives that poverty characterizes certain localities as well as individuals, and he details the vast differences in resources and standards of living between regions, especially between the south-east and the rest of Britain. He strongly states his belief that such discrepancies are socially unjust and should be rectified.

In *What Matters Now*, Roy Jenkins devotes more space to describing poverty and suggesting solutions than to making explicit the reasons for its existence. However, from the whole of the book it is possible to discern the conceptions of society and poverty on which are based his policy proposals. First, he views society mainly within an economic framework. It is a market and being an uncontrolled market it 'strengthens rich regions at the expense of poor regions, successful firms at the expense of small men, the well-organized at the expense of the badly organized'. Those unfortunate enough to live in depressed regions are likely to be poor for 'poverty is a matter of employment prospects'. Second, his economic orientation does not mean that he underestimates the role of family socialization experiences in perpetuating poverty. He refers to the 'cycle of deprivation' less often than Sir Keith Joseph, but clearly accepts that deprivation is transmitted when parents are unable to pass on the skills which give access to higher education and well-paid jobs. Third, he believes that basically the different sections of society will act together to remove poverty. Acknowledging that strong groups 'load the dice in favour of their members' he yet believes that a call to idealism can persuade them to favour policies to combat deprivation. He regrets class politics and confrontations and puts his faith in the 'generosity of all men and women of goodwill, irrespective of their economic interests or class positions'.

The solutions proposed by Jenkins, following his analysis, require an improvement of the social services within the context of a better economic climate. He uses the term 'social services' broadly (as it is held in this article) to cover those services with a social work orientation (usually called the personal social services) those which operate on a selectivist basis to provide financial support to people in need, and those of universal application such as the National Health Service and educational services. Jenkins advocates an expansion of the personal social services in order to provide individualized guidance; higher social security benefits, a new child endowment payment and tax reforms to aid those with low incomes; increased retraining schemes to equip the unemployed and low wage earners with better earning skills; an extension of the priority area approach to include the National Health Service as well as education; and an enlarged urban programme to stimulate voluntary and local authority projects. These and other improvements, he believes, would 'break the cycle by which the children of the poor become poor themselves'. However, the advances in the social services, he warns, would be dependent upon a revitalized economy and decreasing unemployment. His faith in solutions through a combination of more social services and an expanding economy is revealed in his conclusion:

Poverty can be eliminated only if we improve the standards of our social services . . . [only] if we make it a goal of our general economic policies.

CONSENSUS OF APPROACH

At first sight Jenkins's analysis may appear to differ from Sir Keith's. He gives more prominence to economic factors, concedes that different social groups may have differing interests, and desires a greater degree of social equality. But these differences may serve to hide the fundamental similarities in analysis and the consequent similarity in policy proposals. Both politicians accept that poverty is an unfortunate occurrence, with no specific function to perform in society, with the result that they focus on the inadequacies or inabilities of poor families rather than on the structures of a society which tolerates or even requires poverty. Not surprisingly, Sir Keith and Jenkins conclude that poverty can be overcome simply by directing social services towards deprived families or by creating an economic climate through which the families can reach higher benefits. The families are not quite blamed for their plight but their lack of skills or abilities are seen as the cause. Thus the families – not the rest of society – are expected to change. Moreover, both politicians accept that the social services are effective instruments through which the changes can be wrought, so that if the services are expanded poverty will be correspondingly decreased. Further, both implicitly assume that 'experts' can devise solutions which will be both effective and acceptable to the major political parties. The emphasis is on policies made from above, transmitted downwards via social and economic services, with the expectation that those in poverty will respond and change.

The basic homogeneity of the two approaches – which reflects that of the two major political parties – is further revealed in three omissions or defects in both analyses. First, neither concedes or even discusses the point that to concentrate services on changing the deprived will be of limited value if the causes of deprivation rest mainly in the social structures of society rather than in the personalities of the poor or in their immediate environment. The emphasis on better socializing experiences for children will avail little if schools are required to maintain present hierarchies by ensuring that some children fail. The counselling or training of parents into different forms of behaviour will have little outcome if the public and private housing market is such that some people must be 'selected' for, or 'rationed' into, private slums or local authority sub-standard property. Increased job training will mean little in a situation where institutionalized occupational prejudice operates against the poor. In other words, why change people if the opportunity structures of society remain unchanged? Indeed, if poverty inheres in factors outside the control of the poor their reaction in terms of despising school, lacking motivation to work, and refusal to conform to middle-class behavioural standards, may be regarded as a rational adaptation to intolerable circumstances rather than as the direct result of inadequate childhood socialization experiences.

The questioning in the above paragraph of the politicians' assumptions about the causes of poverty should not be interpreted as an argument against the expansion of the social services. But the social services may not be the only weapon needed to attack poverty. The second omission made by both politicians is that their assessment fails to lead to proposals that require changes in those who are not poor. An effective attack on poverty needs not just a break into the familial cycle of deprivation but radical changes in the opportunity structure, in the methods of allocating resources and in the power structure of society at large. Neither makes much reference to it. Sir Keith gives no indication that a reduction in poverty may be dependent upon a reduction in wealth and privilege. Jenkins discusses economic factors and makes nodding mention of the unequal distribution of economic power, but his proposals concentrate on traditional social services for the poor. Both politicians apparently assume that poverty can be tackled by more of the present social services operating within the existing pattern of society.

Third, in their eagerness to make a case for the expansion of the social services in their present form, they give little if any attention to their negative effects. They mention that the services may be ineffective in reaching certain clients, but they do not appreciate how the same services may actually reinforce and perpetuate poverty. For instance, they do not discuss how services can act as social regulators containing the discontents of the poor within social agencies, and so preventing the build-up of pressure for reform. Nothing is said of the conveyance of official judgements of inadequacy or fecklessness which clients may eventually accept and to which they then conform.

ANOTHER MODEL OF POVERTY

It is not claimed that certain differences do not occur between the two major political parties. The parliamentary scene does witness forceful arguments over superannuation plans, immigration bills, means tests and so on. However, this paper has aimed at demonstrating that two leading spokesmen for these parties hold a similar understanding of poverty and hence propose similar kinds of solutions within an agreed framework. Obviously, the criticisms made of them spring from an alternative analysis of society in general and poverty in particular. This analysis will be briefly outlined but first of all a number of qualifications must be made. Theories of poverty cannot be discussed with any finality. As yet it is hardly possible to compose hypotheses about the causes of social deprivation and then to prove or disprove them in a scientific manner. The following is an interpretation which makes sense to the writer in terms of his experience, limited as it is, in highly urbanized areas of great social need. In addition, all theories of poverty would appear to be value-based and the explanation put forward here is no doubt influenced by the writer's own egalitarian values. Thus the model is presented with some hesitation, but done so because the party political consensus makes it necessary that alternatives should be articulated.

The functions of poverty

The basic assumption of the alternative model is that society consists of identifiable groups whose interests are in conflict. Power – the potential ability of one group to influence another – is unevenly distributed. Indeed it rests mainly with a minority grouping. As Rex baldly puts it: 'This is the model of a society in which a ruling class, possessed of private property in the industrial means of production, capitalizes on its power base to engineer the consent of the ruled.' This minority (be it called an *élite*, overlapping *élites* or ruling class) uses its power to maintain its interests and will not willingly make substantial concessions to other sections of the population in terms of resources, position or power.

These 'structural principles on which a capitalist society is built' are used by Rex to discuss the means by which this minority controls the resources awarded to workers. They have equal relevance to that section of the population considered poor, for in such a society poverty is to be regarded not as an unfortunate mishap but as functional in helping to preserve the existing divisions of society and thereby the disproportionate distribution of resources. The existence, even the creation, of a group identifiable as the poor serves to set them apart from the rest of the population. The result is not just, as Jordan says, that the working class is divided and thereby weakened. Rather, the use of the poor as a reference group persuades those sections of society (which are neither wealthy nor poor) that their lot in terms of status, resources and power is acceptable. Consequently, the possibility that they will strive to change the position of the *élite* is reduced. Further, the poor act as a warning. They demonstrate the fate of those who do not conform to prevailing work and social standards. Their plight is needed to reinforce the will of others to work for low returns in unpleasant and even degrading conditions from which the economic output gives a disproportionate financial reward to a minority of existing resource holders. Not least, those in poverty act as scapegoats, a vulnerable group on whom the blame for social problems can be placed, so diverting attention away from that minority which has some control over social affairs.

Mechanisms to preserve poverty

Poverty, then, is to be regarded as an enforced condition. It contributes to the stratified divisions in society which are the channels for an unequal distribution of resources. Hence the continuation of poverty is essential to the continuation of wealth. In turn, certain social mechanisms operate to preserve poverty or social deprivation. Here only three of the mechanisms can be mentioned. First, there are the institutions which select and train recruits for the *élite* positions, those posts which control the economy, run the apparatus of Government and so on. Most obvious are the public schools and Oxbridge which serve to socialize a very small section of society who are then channelled into positions of influence. Rex has commented: 'So far as the administrative apparatus is concerned, the astonishing thing in Britain is the resilience of the system of recruitment and socialization through Oxbridge.' He could have made the same observation about higher posts in university administration, the armed forces, the city, and both political parties. There is no evidence that ability is confined to this minority yet their insularity and homogeneity mean that groups with different attitudes, assumptions and views have little prospect of gaining ground. In other words, the possibility of alternatives is minimized. The institutions thus function to restrict recruitment from below (although, of course, some individuals are allowed in on condition of conforming to the institution's values) and to confirm in society the principle and practice that the means to position, power, and resources should be grossly unequally distributed throughout the population. Clearly, the mechanisms which promote power or wealth and preserve poverty are closely related so that policies which aim merely to change the latter are unlikely to be effective.

Secondly, persons from this same minority tend to dominate another mechanism – the means of mass communication. It is sadly amusing to examine the names which dominate the newspaper and television discussions about poverty. A balance is maintained between Conservative and Labour, right and left, yet both sides frequently are drawn from the homogeneous minority to which reference has been made. Discussions, therefore, have all the trimmings of a debate between two houses at the same public school. Points are made about the minutia of poverty policies but the speakers share the same assumptions and interests. Rarely, if ever, will they question their own privileged position or suggest that poverty is dependent upon the hierarchical structure of society. Hence no radical challenge to the existing distribution of resources can be communicated. Simultaneously, the very fact that the poverty case is put by those from an *élitist* background reinforces the belief that the poor are inadequate – they cannot speak for themselves.

Thirdly, the social services themselves are partially used to maintain poverty and deprivation. Obviously, the low levels of social security benefits and cash transfer schemes limit any major redistribution of income and so preserve the financial distance between different groupings. Noticeably, the recent Green Paper on the proposed tax credit system gives examples showing high-income families gaining more than low-income ones. Similarly, the Government's new dual pension scheme will increase the gap between those dependent upon the State reserve pension and those able to use private occupational schemes (not to mention the windfall for those with investments in insurance companies). At the same time, by making small but periodic increases in levels of benefits, the impression can be given of helping the poor and so diverting attention away from the need for radical structural reforms.

The social services may further perpetuate poverty by being the means by which the poor are sharply distinguished from the rest of society and thence treated in ways which reinforce the gap between them and others. Recently, Jordan has pointed out that not only does the receipt of Supplementary Benefit mark out the non-working poor but the introduction of Family Incomes Supplement makes clear who are the working poor. Once identified as the poor, the title bearers can expect inferior treatment from society's institutions. For instance, Kay has explained how those forced to accept means-tested welfare benefits also accept a stigma. The stigma conveys a message to others and so lowers the school's expectation of their children's performance, reduces the chances that employers will offer them well-paid jobs and even makes the police more suspicious of them. In general, the recipients of state assistance are regarded with caution, given help only after careful scrutiny and expected to behave in antisocial ways. Once the label of 'poor' is imposed, it is extremely difficult to remove it.

At worst, the officials of some social services can make subjective, moralistic and stereotyped judgements about clients which serve to condemn them to inferior treatment from the social services themselves. Those assessed as 'inadequate', 'feckless', 'deadlegs', 'spongers' and 'irresponsible' receive services and attitudes considered apt for the dregs of society. Applicants for council houses with children who swear, whose house smells, whose decorations are not in good order, who are simply not 'suitable' may receive a low grading which qualifies them only for sub-standard council housing. Thereafter, no matter how hard the tenants try, it is impossible to keep such property in good order and so impossible to change their grading. They will be shunted from one condemned property to another until, at last, they refuse to pay rent and so confirm, in the eyes of officials, that they are not worthy of decent accommodation. This mechanism of using moralistic judgements to identify those who should receive the worst resources is even found in the Government's White Paper on pensions which stated that 'personal enterprise and foresight' would be rewarded by higher pensions. Conversely, those lacking such qualities, that is, people with low incomes, would be awarded only the lowest pension. Whether in regard to welfare benefits, housing or income, the consequences are the same. Whatever the individuals' needs and capacities, once defined as 'undeserving' or 'unworthy' they are awarded service inferior to those of others. Other social agencies accept the classification and continue the process so that the possibility of any alternative way of life is minimized. As Minns summed up his careful study of the treatment of the homeless,

> a borough which based its policies on assumptions of repre-
> hensible behaviour on the part of homeless families established
> a control mechanism which narrowed the options the homeless
> could take in dealing with complicated problems and com-
> pelled them to act in accordance with the assumptions on which
> help was based.

In these ways the social services can ascribe the poor with certain stereotyped characteristics and, by so doing, prevent them from ever throwing off their poverty. Social deprivation is maintained.

Finally, the condemnatory fashion with which some clients are treated will affect the latter's own image of themselves. Hagg-strom has explained how extreme dependency is destructive of personal self-respect and draws particular attention to the condi-tion of those fully dependent upon state sources for their income. When the dependency is linked with the impossibility of change and condemnation from others then the recipients may react by withdrawal, by apathy or even by an acceptance of their lot and treatment as deserved and justified. Such responses explain why some deprived persons refuse to take up their welfare entitle-ments or even shape their behaviour to meet the expectations of outsiders. No doubt their children will be placed in similar situations and will respond like their parents, being set aside and setting themselves aside from the rest of society. In this sense poverty is transmitted, but less by the families concerned and more by outside structural and organizational influences.

So far little reference has been made to professional social workers. Probably most would regret the use of such terms as 'feckless', 'spongers', etc., and are only too aware how often the social services fail to provide sufficient resources for clients. Yet consideration must also be given as to whether the casework relationship, so central to professional social work practice, when applied to people in poverty, only serves to maintain their depriving situation. The casework relationship, like all professional relationships, is an unequal one. The social worker is cast as an expert possessing skills and knowledge which the client lacks but needs. The client is cast as a deviant whose difference from other people marks him out as in need of the professional's treatment in order to restore him. He is seen as a person who receives help not as one who can give it. Relevant as this approach is to individuals with problems of a psychological or emotional origin, it is of doubtful validity to those whose poverty arises from structural factors in society. On the contrary, the client is marked out as being in need of treatment yet put in a relationship which fails to remove his problem and which conveys the implication that therefore something is wrong with his character, motivation, child-rearing practices, or whatever. In effect, the client finds himself in a structured relationship which only emphasizes his inadequacy and powerlessness. Thus attention is directed at the client's internal deficiencies with the result that attention is turned away from the external causes of poverty. The social workers find themselves, unwittingly, in a double-bind situation. They want to relieve poverty but the powers of their departments and their present skills are not sufficient to help in any significant way. The limited role they can perform may bring some comfort to the poor, but at the same time they function to humanize poverty, making it more acceptable to the deprived and to the rest of society.

Some qualifications must be added to the above interpretation of the role of the social services and social workers. It refers to the function of poverty and it is not implied that the forces of society are unwilling to use the social services to tackle the problems of, say, the mentally handicapped and the physically ill.

Moreover, the officials and social workers concerned are not regarded as consciously plotting to create poverty. They, too, must be placed within a context of social and economic structures which shape and constrain their practices. Further, this article should not be used to support any outright attack on casework. In the writer's opinion, the development of casework has been a major humanizing influence and is a valid method of social work help. It is a valuable means of therapy and emotional support to children in care, foster parents, the mentally disordered and so on. Instead, the argument is that when applied to persons in poverty this particular method may worsen rather than improve the over-all situation. One of the great unanswered, even unposed, questions of social work is how to distinguish when the therapeutic case-work relationship should or should not be used. Within these limitations, it has been argued that the social services can function to uphold poverty and thereby the existing divisions within our society.

PROPOSALS FOR CHANGE

Poverty, then, remains not because the poor are the grit in the social machine, not because of self-perpetuating 'problem families', but because certain social mechanisms require poverty to fulfil the function of maintaining inequalities. If this analysis has any validity, then it follows that policies based on the Joseph–Jenkins model are unlikely to promote radical changes in the poverty situation. Their proposed packages aim to improve the socialization of the poor without altering the societal structures which require them to be poor. They want to increase the skills of the poor without transforming the mechanisms which promote inequality. They want to expand the social services without questioning their part in maintaining deprivation.

Given that poverty should be abolished, what can be done? It can be hoped that a spread of idealism and altruism will persuade powerful groupings to make radical concessions. The writer's own position as a Christian and a socialist makes him believe that this *should* happen. Unfortunately, there is little evidence of even the beginnings of such action. Some would advocate profound structural changes via physical revolution. But this cannot be accepted by those who reject physical violence on grounds of principle. An alternative is to attempt to deduce how change is possible given the structural nature of poverty as described in this article. Only a brief outline can be offered in a short space but the analysis does lead to three major points. First, as wealth and poverty are closely related then the latter cannot be changed unless the powers of the resource-holding minority are reduced. Secondly, profound institutional changes are required in the social mechanisms which at present uphold poverty. Thirdly, the major impetus for reform is unlikely to come from those who benefit from the present system but rather from its victims – the poor. Indeed, any action which excludes the poor will serve to bolster their inadequacy and ensure that they remain powerless in regard to the distribution of resources.

If power resides in a minority who use it unjustly to maintain extremes of wealth and deprivation then clearly it is not enough to centre anti-poverty policies on poor families. Instead a direct reduction in the power and resources of the privileged minority is required which, in turn, would entail an attack on the mechanisms by which power is maintained, in particular educational institutions and the vehicles of communication. No doubt the familiar argument that a redistribution of wealth amongst the population would mean comparatively little gain *per capita* will be raised. But the point is that structural changes in the mechanisms would enlarge access to resources and positions of influence to other groupings in society. The breaking of the social hold of a small homogeneous minority would have important implications for poverty: the cycle of deprivation could be broken because changes in the opportunity structure would give it something to break into while the entry of groupings with different assumptions and values would lead to a different distribution of resources; the focus of attack on to the minority *élite* would serve to counter the reinforcing process by which the poor are blamed for their poverty; and the need for poverty to function as a means of preserving rigid social divisions would be reduced.

The social services, as one of the societal mechanisms of control, must also be subjected to change. As will be mentioned, pressure from the poor themselves can be anticipated but Government policies should also be directed towards institutional reform. In particular, the agency processes by which clients are evaluated in moral terms and subsequently condemned to inferior treatment must be eradicated. Only when such persons are protected against poverty discrimination (just as black people need protection against racial discrimination) can the tendency of social services to promote social deprivation be said to be in check.

As the social services need to serve the poor rather than the powerful, so too the role of social work in relation to social deprivation requires rethinking. It must suffice briefly to suggest three objectives for social workers. First, to promote institutional reform within their own agencies. Social workers are well placed to identify the selection, delivery and rationing systems which can operate against the poor. Secondly, to enable the poor to maximize their use of the social services and to become as adept at handling bureaucracy as are members of higher income groups. Thirdly, to politicize clients in the sense of encouraging them to perceive their condition as the result of societal forces rather than individual inadequacies.

It may well be objected that the very strength and sophistication of the present structural system will operate to prevent any radical changes being made. Precisely for this reason the major drive will need to originate outside of that system. Just as in the nineteenth century skilled workers had to organize a new collective grouping – the trade unions – in order to have weight in society's conflict of interests, so too will the poor have to develop collective action. Already there is a noticeable growth of community action amongst residents of deprived areas and of organizations of client groupings. Amongst the latter, some Claimants' Unions have a prepared plan for collective action through which it is envisaged that they can bring about changes in the nature of the social security system, in the attitudes with which the poor are regarded and a total reorganization of the wages structure.

Despite the growth in collective action, it is generally conceded that at some stage the groupings of the poor will need alignments with other power forces such as a major political party or trade unions. Further, it is argued that community groups need the stimulus of Government funds. Here then is a major dilemma, for the two major parties can also be regarded as part of the mechanisms by which poverty is maintained. Even the Labour Party's composition at a parliamentary level is drawn heavily from the *élite* minority and powerful arguments can declare that it no longer represents the interests of the working class, let alone the poor. So why should Government be expected to take steps which would reduce the power of that minority? Radical concessions will be made only if considered politically expedient or unavoidable. Jordan believes that the polarization between rich and poor in our society is leading to increasing violence and the disruption of a stable political system. Possibly radical reforms will be made in favour of the organized poor in order to forestall such trends. Moreover, there is some suggestion that community action and the social involvement of the poor lead to a decrease in delinquency, a lessening of the possibility of racial violence and the promotion of a stable community. Interestingly, Midwinter in his study of urban education concludes that 'the threat of urban breakdown is that much nearer and more apparent, and yet there is no doubt that the potential for community education and community development exists even in the most disadvantaged districts'. Following his historical and contemporary analysis, Midwinter argues that only the full and meaningful involvement of the poor can prevent that breakdown. Thus the desire to avoid social dislocation may persuade a Government to financially support local movements of poor residents and clients although such steps may also lead to greater political strength for the latter. Not least, mention must be made that the rapid growth of the new and well-organized claiming class could carry political weight simply through the number of votes it would control. But regardless of Government support, the developing grassroots movements are already involving some of the very people written off as the casualties of society and are so providing for them an alternative which neither political party offers. The question is whether they can win the resources, support and organization which will lead to significant changes; to a society without extremes of wealth and poverty; to a society where poverty does not have to function in order to maintain social divisions; to a society where balancing interests allow the development of qualities of caring and attitudes of mutual respect.

Policies for Social Deprivation

David Donnison

The reading consists of a *Report of Conference on Areas of Social Deprivation* 1970. It is reprinted with the permission of the Chairman of the conference, Professor David Donnison, and of the Department of Health and Social Security under whose auspices it was held.

The conference was arranged at the request of the Secretary of State for Health and Social Security, to discuss the problems of areas of social deprivation with a view to finding solutions to some of them. Professor Donnison, Director of the Centre for Environmental Studies, accepted an invitation to chair the conference and to report its views to the Secretary of Sate. Whilst this report may not fully represent the views of any one person attending the conference, all have had the chance to comment on it and to suggest amendments.

The representatives of the Government departments have confined their comments to matters of fact and presentation and are not to be taken as associated with the recommendations, since their part at the conference was to act as observers only.

AREAS OF SOCIAL DEPRIVATION: A DESCRIPTION

The areas of social deprivation discussed at the conference are characterized by many of the following features: a high concentration of poor people in insecure or ill-paid jobs more heavily dependent on social security payments and other social services than the rest of the population; old, ill-managed, overcrowded and often over-priced housing; lower than average educational attainment; higher-than-average mortality and morbidity rates; a lack of open space and recreational resources; poor physical amenities, and a general air of squalor.

Some of these areas never had the facilities to make an acceptable physical environment: they were born deprived. Others became deprived as a result of gradual physical decay or social change. Yet others had deprivation thrust upon them, sometimes by a single decision, such as the closure of a major local source of employment or the routing of an urban motorway.

Such deprivations are not only found in large towns. Smaller towns and villages may be just as severely deprived. But the conference decided to concentrate on more intensively populated urban areas, believing that these contain the bulk of the problem and that such deprivations are a greater scandal when they are found in great and wealthy cities.

THE NEED FOR DETAILED STATISTICAL ANALYSIS OF CHARACTERISTICS OF SOCIALLY DEPRIVED AREAS

Some areas are readily identified as deprived, but the needs and problems of other areas could be more quickly and clearly understood if we made better use of the statistical data already available to central and local government. If this data was better organized and analysed in more revealing ways it would show the areas of most acute deprivation, and might help to explain the reasons for their poverty and suggest how to set about giving their residents new and wider opportunities. These results could help to formulate future decisions about priorities. They should at least help central and local authorities to identify deprived areas more objectively. It is therefore suggested that research be sponsored to see how existing information could be used to achieve these ends.

THE DIRECTIONS OF FUTURE POLICY

The conference considered a number of ways in which existing institutions and services might be brought to bear on deprived areas, once they have been identified. Three general principles emerged.

The need for comprehensive planning

The needs of deprived areas are wide ranging. Low or inter-mittent wages, poor skills and lack of education, inaccessibility of employment (for wives and young people as well as the chief earner) – all of these lie at the root of their problems. Thus those responsible for physical planning, the location of industry, and the development of transport services must all figure in the search for solutions. In many places, responsibility for these aspects of urban structure is divided between different local authorities, and everywhere central Government bears much of it: hence the need for better co-ordination of the central and local Government departments concerned.

At the local level the focus for action must clearly be at a scale smaller than most local authorities. Local authorities may have to set up committees concerning themselves with areas rather than functions. Thus Birmingham Council might have committees for Sparkbrook, Handsworth, etc. as well as for education, housing and welfare. Local government committees for neighbourhoods may have to be paralleled – and sometimes criticized – by auto-nomous groups and elected representatives speaking for the same areas. In deprived areas, such committees would be concerned with the whole range of local government activities. They could be a focus for comprehensively planned renewal efforts, and a channel for the deployment of grants from the central Government.

If it proves impossible to achieve effective co-ordination of interests through the development of existing machinery, 'old towns corporations', organized on the lines of new towns corporations, might be an alternative to local authority area committees capable of providing a similar focus for redevelop-ment.

The need to involve those facing the problems of socially
deprived areas
Central Government and local government tend to be attuned to the 'normal' problems of Government and to be out of touch with the complex and interacting problems of areas of social deprivation. Central Government departments deciding priorities for deprived areas could benefit from contact with those who live or work in these areas, through the establishment of an Advisory Committee on the Problems of Socially Deprived Areas, similar to the Home Secretary's Advisory Committee on Research into Race Relations.

Local authorities should be encouraged to involve local people in decision-making. If people are given the chance to play a part in decisions about their areas – if necessary with the help of community workers – they acquire self-confidence and the capacity to gain control of their own fate; and the authorities benefit from the views and information they put forward. Anything that enables deprived areas to escape from the apathy and defeatism which so often overwhelm them can be enormously valuable.

There are many ways in which people can be brought into the decision-making process at the local level; involvement in political parties and co-option to council committees, statutory local advisory committees, school governors, hospital management and other bodies are possibilities too often neglected. A suggestion which might prove more effective, however, is the establishment of 'urban parishes' dealing with selected areas within local authorities. These would be based on small units, for example single wards, and would elect councils to act as intermediaries between the local authority and the people. Such a council is being promoted by community workers in Notting Hill; it is an experiment worth study, and possibly emulation.

Improvements to central and local Government services
Existing services in areas of social deprivation must be raised to a higher standard. The turnover of teachers at schools in some of these areas is well above average, for example, and clinics, schools and other public services often occupy old and unsatisfactory buildings. These deficiencies are dispiriting enough. In addition, playgrounds, nursery schools, community centres, youth clubs and new facilities which should be particularly plentiful in such areas are often scarcer there than in more affluent neighbourhoods.

There is a tendency among local and central Government officers in day-to-day contact with people living in areas of social deprivation to impose bureaucratic and sometimes punitive views of human problems and their solutions. Socially deprived areas have special difficulties: those living in them may need more help than most people, and help with a wider range of problems. They must be given sympathetic and more flexible services. That will not happen unless social services staff are better trained, and local people are brought into discussions of the services provided. The Community Development Projects should help to resolve some of these problems if pursued with sufficient resources and determination.

Little can be achieved by better co-ordination of planning, or by bringing local residents with direct experience of the problems of social deprivation into decision-making processes, or by improving existing services, unless resources are concentrated more heavily on such areas. Socially deprived areas cannot solve their own problems unaided. In some cases local authority resources, even if concentrated, will be insufficient. The urban aid programme acknowledges this, through grant aid to selected authorities, and any more intensive effort to meet the problems of the socially deprived areas must start from the same assumptions.

The present urban aid system has begun to make an impact and should be continued. But it is open to two criticisms. Some authorities treat aid as a substitute for locally financed action. The Government must ensure that aid is an addition to local finance, not a replacement for it. Secondly, aid has to be accepted by the local authority, which has to meet 25 per cent of the cost of aided projects. Sometimes this means that aid which is needed and available is not used.

Even when they have much wider powers, some local authorities confine their activities to the traditional tasks of local government. Whilst these are tremendously important they are not in themselves sufficient to revitalize socially deprived areas. There is a need for community based projects, not competing with local authority services, but of a distinctly different nature. These would include the development of centres for community action, and projects (such as adventure playgrounds for example) which are outside the normal scope of local authority provision but which may be very important in deprived areas.

The central Government may have to consider direct funding of community projects put forward by community organizations in areas of accepted need. Such projects would be chosen by central Government because they were worth backing, did not compete with local authority services, and were outside the normal provision made by local authorities. Community effort should raise some of the funds needed, but central Government funding should not depend on the local authority's willingness to contribute to the project. A policy of direct funding would pose problems of administration and accountability, but precedents elsewhere show they should not be insuperable.

Further Reading
Social Welfare: Solutions and Future Strategies

R. BOYSON (Ed.), *Down With The Poor*, Churchill Press, 1971.

A. CHRISTOPHER *et al.*, *Policy for Poverty*, Institute of Economic Affairs, 1970.

K. COATES and R. SILBURN, *Poverty, The Forgotten Englishmen*, Penguin, 1970.

V. GEORGE, *Social Security and Society*, Routledge & Kegan Paul, 1973.

R. JENKINS, *What Matters Now*, Fontana, 1972.

M. REIN, *Social Policy*, Random House, 1970.

R. TITMUSS, *Commitment to Welfare*, Allen & Unwin, 1968.

P. TOWNSEND (Ed.), *The Concept of Poverty*, Heinemann, 1971.

Bibliography and Reader Reference

A book of readings is not intended as a substitute for a study of the original sources. Hopefully, the readings in this book – not all of which are easily available – will stimulate readers to pursue the topics in more depth. To facilitate such a study, a bibliography is now added. Ideally, it should be able to point to major textbooks which cover nearly all the topics, as well as placing them in a context of social welfare. Unfortunately, as yet, there are few comprehensive textbooks of this kind. Where appropriate, attention will be focused on the few textbooks but generally references will be made to publications which deal specifically with the various topics raised in the chapters.

1 BACKGROUND TO SOCIAL WELFARE

Development of the Welfare State

M. BRUCE, *The Coming of the Welfare State*, Batsford, 1971. PB

D. FRASER, *The Evolution of the British Welfare State*, Macmillan, 1973.

P. GREGG, *The Welfare State*, Harrap, 1967.

B. RODGERS, *The Battle Against Poverty*, vols I & II, Routledge & Kegan Paul, 1968.   PB

Features of Social Welfare

W. FRIEDLANDER, *An Introduction to Social Welfare*, 3rd ed., Prentice-Hall, 1968.

D. HOWARD, *Social Welfare, Values, Means, Ends*, Random House, 1969.

D. MARSH (Ed.), *An Introduction to the Study of Social Administration*, Routledge & Kegan Paul, 1965.

J. ROMANYSHYN, *Social Welfare*, Random House, 1971.

PB = Available in paperback.

Major Issues in Social Welfare

D. DONNISON *et al.*, *Social Policy and Administration*, Allen & Unwin, 1965.

D. MARSH, *The Welfare State*, Longman, 1970.   PB

T. H. MARSHALL, *Social Policy in the Twentieth Century*, Hutchinson, 1971.   PB

R. PINKER, *Social Theory and Social Policy*, Heinemann, 1971.
          PB

R. TITMUSS, *Essays on 'The Welfare State'*, Allen & Unwin, 1968.   PB

P. WEINBERGER (Ed.), *Perspectives on Social Welfare*, Macmillan, 1969.

The Framework of the Welfare State

M. BROWN, *Introduction to Social Administration in Britain*, Hutchinson, 1969.   PB

A. FORDER (Ed.), *Penelope Hall's Social Services of England & Wales*, Routledge & Kegan Paul, 1969.

J. SLEEMAN, *The Welfare State*, Allen & Unwin, 1973.   PB

P. WILLMOTT (Ed.), *Public Social Services*, Bedford Square Press, Rvd., 1973.   PB

2 THE DEPRIVED: GROUPS IN NEED

The Meaning of Need

K. SLACK, *Social Administration and the Citizen*, Michael Joseph, 2nd ed., 1969, chapter 6.   PB

C. TOWLE, *Common Human Needs*, Allen & Unwin, 1973. PB

J. WARHAM, *Social Policy in Context*, Batsford, 1970, chapter 5.

The Poor

E. BUTTERWORTH and D. WEIR (Eds.), *Social Problems of Modern Britain*, Fontana, 1973, chapter 4.   PB

P. TOWNSEND, *The Social Minority*, Allen Lane, 1973, chapters 2-4.

M. YOUNG (Ed.), *Poverty Report 1974*, Temple Smith, 1974. PB

The Homeless

B. GLASTONBURY, *Homeless Near a Thousand Homes*, Allen & Unwin, 1971.   PB

J. GREVE *et al.*, *Homelessness in London*, Scottish Academic Press, 1971.

K. SPENCER in R. Holman (Ed.), *Socially Deprived Families in Britain*, Bedford Square Press, Rvd. 1973, chapter 2.   PB

Single Parent Families

V. GEORGE and P. WILDING, *Motherless Families*, Routledge & Kegan Paul, 1972.

R. HOLMAN, *Trading in Children*, Routledge & Kegan Paul, 1973, chapter 8.

D. MARSDEN, *Mothers Alone*, Pelican, 1973.   PB

Immigrants

J. CULLINGWORTH, *Problems of an Urban Society*, vol. II, Allen & Unwin, 1973, chapter 4.   PB

D. HUMPHREY and A. JOHN, *Because They're Black*, Penguin, 1971.   PB

J. REX and R. MOORE, *Race, Community and Conflict*, Oxford University Press, 1967.   PB

Areas of Need

Central Advisory Council for Education, *Children and their Primary Schools*, vol. I, HMSO, 1967, chapter 5.

K. COATES and R. SILBURN, *Poverty: the Forgotten Englishmen*, Penguin, 1970, chapter 3-7.   PB

3 MEETING NEEDS

Supplementary Benefit

V. GEORGE, *Social Security: Beveridge and After*, Routledge & Kegan Paul, 1968.

J. KINCAID, *Poverty and Equality in Britain*, Pelican, 1973. PB

T. LYNES, *The Penguin Guide to Supplementary Benefits*, Penguin, 2nd ed., 1974. PB

O. STEVENSON, *Claimant or Client?*, Allen & Unwin, 1973. PB

Planning

Committee on Public Participation in Planning, *People and Planning*, (Skeffington Report), HMSO, 1969.

N. DENNIS, *People and Planning*, Faber, 1970.

D. EVERSLEY, *The Planner in Society*, Faber, 1973.

H. GANS, *People and Plans*, Pelican, 1972. PB

North West Economic Planning Council, *The Social Planning of Urban Renewal*, 1972. PB

Social Work

R. BESSELL, *Introduction to Social Work*, Batsford, 1970. PB

P. HALMOS, *The Faith of the Counsellors*, Constable, 1965.

N. TIMMS, *Social Work*, Routledge & Kegan Paul, 1973. PB

K. WOODROOFE, *From Charity to Social Work*, Routledge & Kegan Paul, 1962.

B. WOOTTON, *Social Science and Social Pathology*, Allen & Unwin, 1959, chapter 9.

E. YOUNGHUSBAND, (Ed.), *Social Work with Families*, Allen & Unwin, 1971. PB

4 PURPOSES AND PRIORITIES

The Purposes of Social Welfare

E. BUTTERWORTH and D. WEIR (Eds.), *The Sociology of Modern Britain*, Fontana, 1970, chapter 7. PB

W. RUNCIMAN, *Relative Deprivation and Social Justice*, Penguin, 1972, chapters 12-14. PB

R. TITMUSS, *The Gift Relationship*, Allen & Unwin, 1970. PB

E. YOUNGHUSBAND (Ed.), *Social Work and Social Values*, Allen & Unwin, 1967. PB

Priorities

J. EYDEN, *Social Policy in Action*, Routledge & Kegan Paul, 1969, chapter 3.   PB

R. PARKER, *Planning for Deprived Children*, National Children's Home, 1970.   PB

M. REIN, *Social Policy: Issues of Choice and Change*, Random House, 1970, chapters 12-13.

Who Are The Services For?

T. GOULD and J. KENYON, *Stories from the Dole Queue*, Temple Smith, 1972.   PB

B. MANDELL, *Where are the Children?*, Lexington Books, 1973.   PB

R. TITMUSS, *Essays on the 'Welfare State'*, Allen & Unwin, 1958.   PB

Professionalism

B. HERAUD, *Sociology and Social Work*, Pergamon Press, 1970, chapter 10.   PB

SOCIOLOGICAL REVIEW MONOGRAPH, *Professions and Social Change*, University of Keele, 1973.   PB

H. WILENSKY and C. LEBEAUX, *Industrial Society and Social Welfare*, The Free Press, 1965, chapter 11.   PB

Access to Services

R. BROOKE, *Information and Advice Centres*, Bell, 1972.   PB

B. JORDAN, *Paupers*, Routledge & Kegan Paul, 1973.   PB

B. LAPPING and G. RADICE, *More Power to the People*, Longmans, 1968.   PB

J. MAYER and N. TIMMS, *The Client Speaks*, Routledge & Kegan Paul, 1970.   PB

5 THE REORGANIZATION OF THE SOCIAL SERVICES

The Arguments For Change

D. DONNISON, *The Neglected Child and the Social Services*, Manchester University Press, 1954, chapters 5 and 6.

J. PACKMAN, *Child Care: Needs and Numbers*, Allen & Unwin, 1968, chapters 11-14.   PB

E. YOUNGHUSBAND, *Social Work and Social Change*, Allen & Unwin, 1964, chapters 1-8.   PB

The Seebohm Report and Resulting Issues

HOME OFICE, *Report of the Committee on Local Authority and Allied Personal Social Services*, (Seebohm Report), HMSO, 1968.

W. ROBSON and B. CRICK (Eds.), *The Future of the Social Services*, Penguin, 1970.   PB

B. RODGERS and J. STEVENSON, *A New Portrait of Social Work*, Heinemann, 1973, part 3.

Organizing the New Departments

R. FOREN and M. BROWN, *Planning for Service*, Knight, 1971.

P. LEONARD, *Sociology and Social Work*, Routledge & Kegan Paul, 1966, chapter 4.   PB

J. WARHAM, *An Introduction to Administration for Social Workers*, Routledge & Kegan Paul, 1967, chapters 4-6.   PB

Casework and Other Social Work Methods

GULBENKIAN FOUNDATION, *Community Work and Social Change*, Longmans, 1968.   PB

R. KLENK and R. RYAN (Eds.), *The Practice of Social Work*, Wadsworth, 1970.   PB

R. LEAPER, *Community Work*, National Council of Social Service, 1968.   PB

H. MEYER *et al.*, *Girls at Vocational High*, Russell Sage, 1958.

J. PARFITT, *Group Work with Children in Special Circumstances*, National Children's Bureau, 1971.   PB

C. SMITH *et al.*, *The Wincroft Youth Project*, Tavistock, 1972

The Place of Institutional Care

C. BEEDELL, *Residential Life with Children*, Routledge & Kegan
Paul, 1970.   PB
J. BOWLBY, *Child Care and the Growth of Love*, Penguin, 1953.
                                                        PB
R. DINNAGE and M. KELLMER PRINGLE, *Residential Child
Care: Facts and Fallacies*, Longmans, 1969.   PB
P. MORRIS, *Put Away*, Routledge & Kegan Paul, 1969.
T. and P. MORRIS, *Pentonville*, Routledge & Kegan Paul, 1963.

6 NEW DEVELOPMENTS IN SOCIAL WELFARE

The Urban Programme

J. BENINGTON (Ed.), *Coventry Development Project: Background and Progress* (pamphlet) Coventry CDP, 1972.
COMMUNITY DEVELOPMENT PROJECT, *The National Community Development Project*, CDP Information and Intelligence Unit, 1974.
H. GLENNERSTER and S. HATCH (Eds.), *Positive Discrimination and Inequality*, (pamphlet), Fabian Society, 1974.
R. HOLMAN (Ed.), *Socially Deprived Families in Britain*,
Bedford Square Press, revised 1973, pp. 175-86.   PB
J. MCCONAGHY, *Another Chance for Cities*, Shelter Neighbourhood Action Project, 1973, chapter 9.   PB

Family Income Supplement

D. BARKER in D. BULL (Ed.), *Family Poverty*, Duckworth,
1971, chapter 6.   PB
HMSO, *Proposals for a Tax Credit System*, Cmnd. 5116, 1972.

Social Workers, Welfare Rights and Radical Action

D. BULL, *Action for Welfare Rights*, (pamphlet), Fabian Society,
1970.

R. LEES, *Politics and Social Work*, Routledge & Kegan Paul, 1972.   PB

T. LYNES, *Welfare Rights*, (pamphlet), Fabian Society, 1969.

M. REIN, *Social Policy: Issues of Choice and Change*, Random House, 1970, chapter 15.

H. ROSE, *Rights, Participation and Conflict*, (pamphlet) Child Poverty Action Group, 1971.

Community Action

S. ALINSKY, *Rules for Radicals*, Random House, 1971.   PB

GULBENKIAN FOUNDATION, *Current Issues in Community Work*, Routledge & Kegan Paul, 1973, chapter 4.   PB

R. HOLMAN, *Power for the Powerless: The Role of Community Action*, (pamphlet), British Council of Churches, 1971.

A. LAPPING, *Community Action*, (pamphlet), Fabian Society, 1968.

R. SILBURN in D. BULL (Ed.), *Family Poverty*, Duckworth, 1971, chapter 11.   PB

7 SOCIAL WELFARE: SOLUTIONS AND FUTURE STRATEGIES

Individual Malfunctioning

A. CHRISTOPHER *et al.*, *Policy for Poverty*, Institute of Economic Affairs, 1970.   PB

P. GOLDRING, *Friend of the Family*, David & Charles, 1973.

R. PAGE, *The Benefits Racket*, Stacey, 1971.

A. PHILP, *Family Failure*, Faber, 1962.

W. RYAN, *Blaming the Victim*, Orbach & Chambers, 1971.

Cultural Explanations

N. GEDDIE (Ed.), *Tinker, Tailor, The Myth of Cultural Deprivation*, Penguin, 1973.   PB

A. HALSEY (Ed.), *Educational Priority*, vol. 1, HMSO, 1972. PB

O. LEWIS in D. MOYNIHAN (Ed.), *On Understanding Poverty*, Basic Books, 1968, chapter 7.

C. VALENTINE, *Culture and Poverty*, University of Chicago Press, 1968.

Inadequate Social Services

T. ATKINSON, *Poverty in Britain and the Reform of Social Security*, Cambridge University Press, 1970. PB

P. TOWNSEND and N. BOSANQUET (Eds.), *Labour and Inequality*, Fabian Society, 1972. PB

M. ZALD (Ed.), *Social Welfare Institutions*, Wiley, 1965.

Structural Explanations

V. GEORGE, *Social Security and Society*, Routledge & Kegan Paul, 1973. PB

F. PIVEN and R. CLOWARD, *Regulating the Poor*, Tavistock, 1972. PB

P. TOWNSEND (Ed.), *The Concept of Poverty*, Heinemann, 1973, chapter 1. PB

J. URRY and J. WAKEFORD (Eds.), *Power in Britain*, Heinemann, 1973.

D. WEDDERBURN (Ed.), *Poverty, Inequality and Class Structure*, Cambridge University Press, 1974. PB

Index

Index

Fontana Social Science

Books available include:

African Genesis Robert Ardrey

The Territorial Imperative Robert Ardrey

The Social Contract Robert Ardrey

Racial Minorities Michael Banton

Ideology in Social Science
Edited by Robin Blackburn

The Sociology of Modern Britain
Edited by Eric Butterworth and David Weir

Social Problems of Modern Britain
Edited by Eric Butterworth and David Weir

Men and Work in Modern Britain
Edited by David Weir

Strikes Richard Hyman

The Dominant Man H. Knipe and G. Maclay

Strike at Pilkingtons Tony Lane and Kenneth Roberts

Figuring Out Society Ronald Meek

Drugs, Science and Society Alan Norton

Dockers David Wilson

Ronald Meek

Figuring Out Society

This book is the first comprehensive non-technical
introduction to the use of quantitative methods
in the social sciences. It is written with the needs
of the non-mathematical student and general
reader very much in mind, and in fact the book
grew out of a series of highly successful voluntary
lectures in the University of Leicester.

Figuring Out Society provides a highly
individual approach to social and economic
models, regression analysis, sampling, the theory
of games, cost benefit analysis, and much more.

Not only is the mathematical content kept to a
minimum, but a special mathematical appendix is
added. There are numerous diagrams and all
points are made clear, interesting, and often
amusing, by means of brilliantly chosen examples.

Dockers

David F. Wilson

The central conflict in the docks is how to reconcile a conservative industry to the technological advances necessary for the economic running of the ports. Containers, sealed boxes of cargo which do not require detailed handling by dockers, speed the movement of freight. But they also threaten the traditional job of the docker. The result is a crisis which has frustrated a decade of intense pressure to modernise the docks.

'It is just the sort of book which is needed to look behind the myths and instant opinions which build up around labour relationships and to try to explain the significant social, technological and political developments of the docks. David Wilson's story is backed up with detailed facts which make the book a worthwhile source of reference as well as a good narrative.' *The Financial Times*

'This study should be read and pondered for its wider lessons by everyone concerned with the human issues of industry but, above all, by the next generation of directors, managers, union leaders, politicians and sociologists now enjoying further education.' *The Times Educational Supplement*

Fontana Politics

Battle for the Environment   Tony Aldous

The English Constitution   Walter Bagehot
Edited by R. H. S. Crossman

Tocqueville   Hugh Brogan

The Backroom Boys   Noam Chomsky

For Reasons of State   Noam Chomsky

Problems of Knowledge and Freedom   Noam Chomsky

Selected Writings of Mahatma Gandhi
Edited by Ronald Duncan

Marx and Engels: Basic Writings
Edited by Lewis S. Feuer

Governing Britain   A. H. Hanson and Malcolm Walles

The Commons in Transition   *Edited by* A. H. Hanson and
Bernard Crick

Europe Tomorrow   *Edited by* Richard Mayne

Machiavelli: Selections   *Edited by* John Plamenatz

The Cabinet   Patrick Gordon Walker

The Downfall of the Liberal Party 1914-1935
Trevor Wilson

The Conservative Party from Peel to Churchill
Robert Blake

Chomsky in Fontana

Noam Chomsky has become world famous in recent years in two very different roles. He has revolutionised our understanding of the meaning of language, while his writings on political questions have made him one of the most influential spokesmen of the Left today.

Problems of Knowledge and Freedom

This book contains the revised text of the Bertrand Russell Memorial Lectures which Chomsky delivered at Cambridge in June, 1971. The lectures reflect his concern with some of the problems that Russell investigated and the causes to which he devoted himself. The first discusses how, through the study of language, Russell's thinking can be taken further. The second develops Russell's ideas on freedom and human nature and on social and political issues, into an outline of Chomsky's own views on these matters.

The Backroom Boys

In this dispassionate examination of official indifference and duplicity, Chomsky focuses on the image of the United States as reflected in Vietnam, and provides a devastating indictment of the way American power operates today. Both the Pentagon papers and the implications of the Paris Peace Agreements receive detailed examination.

For Reasons of State

Here Chomsky debates the issues raised by the relationship of government to society, and suggests some ways in which the individual can respond to growing State power. Opening with an analysis of the social, moral and legal issues raised by Vietnam and a discussion of the future of Indochina, he then goes on to an examination of civil disobedience, the role of the university, and the philosophy of anarchism. In addition this book includes the complete text of Chomsky's famous critique of B. F. Skinner, and a very important essay on language and freedom.